# Fodor's

# PUERTO VALLARTA

# Welcome to Puerto Vallarta

Sunbathing and sipping margaritas is just one of many ways to spend a vacation in Puerto Vallarta. Mexico's prettiest resort town is also one of its most diverse. Old Vallarta—El Centro and the Zona Romántica—is a goldmine of quirky boutiques and winding cobblestone streets. In Marina Vallarta, shopping centers and deluxe hotels spread around the city's yacht marina. And from Costalegre to the Riviera Nayarit, miles of sandy beaches and scores of stellar restaurants and lively nightclubs, surrounded by historic mountain towns, keep visitors returning again and again.

## TOP REASONS TO GO

★ **Resorts:** Everything from luxurious beachfront high-rises to quaint boutique hideaways.

★ **Nightlife:** Vallarta after dark is one of Mexico's best party scenes.

★ **Beaches:** From lively town beaches to secluded natural havens, each beach is unique.

★ **Golf:** A top golf destination with exclusive links and accessible courses for all players.

★ **Water Sports:** Windsurfing, snorkeling, and scuba diving are just a few top options.

★ **El Malecón:** PV's seaside boardwalk is always a lovely stroll, especially at sunset.

# Contents

**Fodor's** Features

## Chapter 1

# EXPERIENCE PUERTO VALLARTA

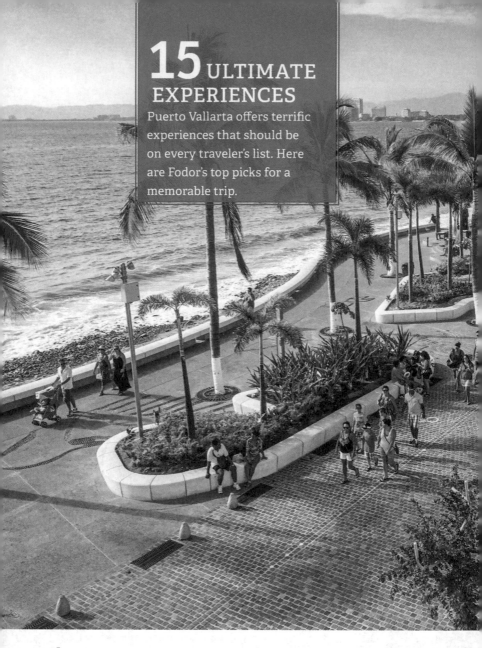

# 15 ULTIMATE EXPERIENCES

Puerto Vallarta offers terrific experiences that should be on every traveler's list. Here are Fodor's top picks for a memorable trip.

## 1 The Malecón

On the mile-long Malecón you'll find statues, street performers, and people-watching. When the sun goes down, live music can be heard the length of the boardwalk. *(Ch. 3)*

## 2 Whale-Watching

Puerto Vallarta Bay is a very popular vacation spot for humpback whales. Visitors can spot them flipping and splashing around. *(Ch. 3)*

## 3 Church of Our Lady of Guadalupe

Dominating the skyline is Our Lady of Guadalupe Parish. Every year, thousands of tourists head down the streets of downtown PV to stop at the landmark church. *(Ch. 3)*

## 4 Shopping

Puerto Vallarta shops sell crafts created by famous Mexican and international artists. You'll also find excellent pieces by lesser-known artists at flea markets and the seafront promenade. *(Ch. 3)*

## 5 Marina Vallarta

Marina Vallarta is an exclusive zone for shopping and luxury hotels and condos, with a high-class marina filled with yachts, sailboats, charters, and a variety of watercraft. *(Ch. 3)*

## 6 Las Islas Marietas

These uninhabited islands were formed by underwater volcano eruptions, off the north coast of Banderas Bay. The Hidden Beach here is accessed by swimming or kayaking through a tunnel. *(Ch. 4)*

## 7 Take a Cooking Class

Puerto Vallarta is known for its world-class gourmet dining and humble but tasty street food and tacos. Plenty of cooks will welcome you into their homes and restaurants and share their recipes. *(Ch. 3)*

# 8 Mirador de La Cruz

To catch Puerto Vallarta's best sunset angle, you'll have to do a little bit of hiking. At the top of the city, Mirador de La Cruz is a lookout point adored by locals. *(Ch. 3)*

# 9 National Marine Park of Los Arcos

Kayak, paddleboard, or snorkel to the city's famous granite islands, just south of Banderas Bay. This National Marine Park has been protected since 1984. *(Ch. 5)*

## 10 Scuba Diving

Puerto Vallarta is the main diving destination in the Pacific Coast of Mexico, with several PADI sites available for enthusiasts. Expect to see turtles, sharks, rays, eels, and much more.

## 11 Tequila

At a tequila distillery you can witness the production process, taste the results, and sample traditional Mexican food. There's more to tequila than shots with lemon and salt. *(Ch. 7)*

## 12 Vallarta Botanical Gardens

This 64-acre area features an assortment of wildflowers and insect life that provides a relaxing getaway from the day-to-day hustle of Vallarta's downtown. *(Ch. 5)*

## 13 Eat Fresh Oysters

In Puerto Vallarta you can get fresh oysters on the beach; vendors are abundant in places like Playa Los Muertos and just under the bridge that crosses the River Cuale. *(Ch. 3)*

# 14 Mismaloya

On the southern part of Banderas Bay is the fishing village of Mismaloya, where The Night of the Iguana was filmed in the 1960s. *(Ch. 5)*

# 15 The Zona Romántica (Old Town)

Zona Romántica, aka "Old Town," has small-town charm, friendly people, and hip restaurants, bars, clubs, and galleries. *(Ch. 3)*

# WHAT'S WHERE

**1 Puerto Vallarta.** This resort town in Jalisco encompasses Zona Romántica, El Centro, Zona Hotelera, Marina Vallarta, and Olas Altas. South of the Cuale River, the Zona Romántica (Romantic Zone, including Col. E. Zapata) has PV's highest density of restaurants and tourist-oriented shops; Zona Hotelera (Hotel Zone) has malls, businesses, and high-rise hotels; El Centro (Downtown) is lined with white-washed homes and shops; the shopping centers and deluxe hotels of Marina Vallarta are sandwiched between a golf course and the city's main yacht marina; and Olas Altas is comprised of two upscale residential neighborhoods on the southern edge of PV: Amapas and Conchas Chinas.

**2 Riviera Nayarit.** Just north of Nuevo Vallarta, Riviera Nayarit has pristine beaches, luxurious resorts, and dozens of laid-back towns loved by artists, hippies, surfers, and celebrities. Nuevo Vallarta, also in the state of Nayarit, is composed mainly of golf courses, exclusive condos, and luxurious restaurants, and has the second-highest number of hotels in the country.

**3 South of Puerto Vallarta.** This area stretches all the way to Mismaloya. South of El Tuito, Cabo Corrientes has tiny towns and gorgeous beaches.

**4 Guadalajara.** The capital of the state of Jalisco and often called "The Mexican's Mexico," Guadalajara is a vibrant, culturally rich city teeming with activity, and has great shopping and museums.

**5 Costalegre.** This region is a series of secluded bays and white-sand beaches located south of Puerto Vallarta in Jalisco, with a few luxury resorts and hotels in Barra de Navidad.

**6 San Blas and the Mountain Towns.** A region North of Riviera Nayarit, this rustic area has a few basic attractions but lots of "Old Mexico" culture and striking natural beauty. In addition to San Blas, the towns here include San Sebastián, Mascota, and Talpa de Allende.

PACIFIC OCEAN

TO MAZATLÁN

San Blas

Bahía de San Blas

Las Varas
Chacala
Bahía de Jaltemba
Rincón de Guayabitos    La Peñita
Lo de Marcos
San Francisco
Sayulita
Las Palmas
Punta Mita    Bucerías    Dirt
Las Islas Marietas    Nuevo Vallarta
La Cruz de    Ixtapa
Huanacaxtle    **Puerto Vallarta**
Bahía de Banderas
Mismaloya
Boca de Tomatlán
El Chimo

Aquiles Serdan    Dirt
Dirt    El Tuito
Bahía Tehualmixtle

El Tequesquite

La Cruz de Loreto
Presa Cajón de Peña

La Cumbre

José María Morelos

Perula
Bahía Chamela
Chamela

0    20 mi
0    20 km

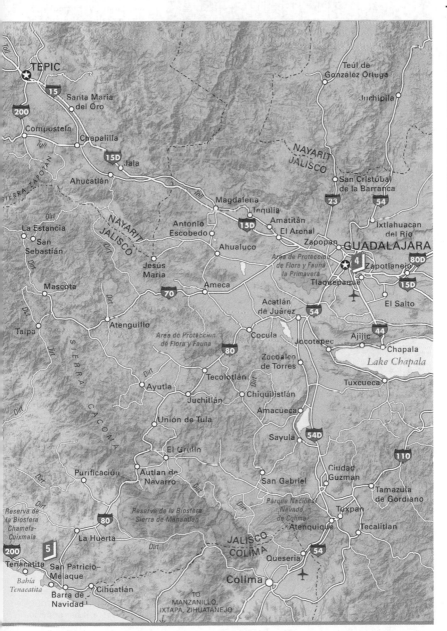

# Puerto Vallarta's Best Resorts

### THE ST. REGIS PUNTA MITA RESORT

Two Jack Nicklaus Signature Golf courses are accessible through the resort. Add to that three different outdoor pools and signature award-winning signature restaurants and you won't be able to resist a stay here.

### W PUNTA MITA

W Punta Mita is the best hotel for wealthy millennials. It combines impressive, funky design heavily inspired by local Huichol aesthetics with weekly DJ sets and high-end amenities.

### SHERATON BUGANVILIAS RESORT & CONVENTION CENTER

According to the locals, this resort serves the best Sunday brunch. Completely renovated, this 1978 hotel has cabins right next to the ocean, a luxury spa, scenic gardens, and jovial staff.

### SECRETS VALLARTA BAY PUERTO VALLARTA

A 30-minute walk from the Malecón, this adults-only resort will guarantee quiet mornings by the pool after a long night in the clubs of Vallarta. It boasts unlimited luxury: gourmet food and drinks and free Wi-Fi and international calling to some countries. They also host fun theme parties.

### HARD ROCK HOTEL VALLARTA

This all-inclusive resort gained status among the local community by hosting concerts and other popular events open to the public. The resort is also known for its extensive spa services, in-room audio experiences (you can even reserve your own Fender), and the Flamingos golf club. It is not within walking distance from downtown, but waters in this part of town are calmer.

### GARZA BLANCA PRESERVE RESORT & SPA

This resort is well hidden from most of Puerto Vallarta tourists; you will need to travel a bit south of the city, along the curvy, narrow road to get to the hotel. Surrounded by the jungle and towering over a hidden bay, it offers unique and unforgettable views in addition to all-inclusive amenities.

### HOTEL MOUSAI

Hotel Mousai is one of the newest additions to the landscape of Puerto Vallarta and a trend-setter in the resort world. Made for guests with discerning design taste, it has superior

Four Seasons Punta Mita

bay views from its lavish infinity pool. It's also the first and only AAA Five Diamond rated resort in Puerto Vallarta, and in all of Jalisco.

### MAYAN PALACE PUERTO VALLARTA

If you are looking for a real escape from your everyday routine, the resort with its facilities and staff will go above and beyond to make it possible.

### FOUR SEASONS RESORT PUNTA MITA

Mixing the spirit of Mexican hospitality with the highest luxury, this resort is a favorite with celebrities for its guaranteed privacy and proximity to the best beaches of the region.

### HACIENDA ALEMANA FRANKFURT

Hacienda Alemana is not truly a resort, but it is one of the best boutique hotels in the Puerto Vallarta area. Visit the biergarten for a quaint outdoor experience in a charming setting. Rooms will make you right feel at home with rustic-chic decor.

### HOTEL PLAYA LOS ARCOS

Located right on Playa de los Muertos and surrounded by the shops, restaurants, and entertainment of Zona Romántica, Hotel Playa Los Arcos is captivating both inside and out. The decor has more character than some of the bigger chain resorts, and the pool is exceptionally scenic.

### HILTON PUERTO VALLARTA RESORT

This all-inclusive beachfront hotel caters to both families and single travelers as it just opened its new adults-only section, La Hacienda. Located at the best beach in the downtown area, it is surprisingly cozy for a big chain hotel and its cuisine will satisfy the most discerning diners.

# What to Eat and Drink in Puerto Vallarta

### FISH TACOS
These light, crunchy, fried fish tacos are made with a batter that resembles tempura in texture. You can find some of the best ones at Marisma in Zona Romántica (Old Town) and Marina Vallarta.

### CEVICHE
Ceviche consists of fresh seafood (anything from shrimp to tuna or mackerel), mixed with veggies and then bathed in citrus juice. Here and along the Riviera Nayarit, they chop up the fish into very small pieces and add lots of cucumber, onion, tomato, and sometimes carrots.

### CHILES EN NOGADA
While originally from Puebla in central Mexico, there couldn't be anything more authentic to this coastal town than chiles en nogada—it tastes unbeliev-able and is a favorite of Puerto Vallarta. It consists of rice and poblano peppers stuffed with ground meat, bathed with a nutty sauce and pomegranate seeds.

### BIRRIA
Birria is a spicy, meaty stew usually made with goat or lamb, but sometimes beef or pork. What makes this slow-braised stew so special is each restaurant's signature spice blend. Like most Mexican soups, it can be topped with onions, cilantro, and lime juice. There are lots of places in Puerto Vallarta where you can get a big bowl of birria, but if you want to try it in taco form, Robles Birria Tacos is the place to go. They serve this regional specialty in tacos dorados, or golden tacos, which are crispy fried tortillas instead of the usual soft ones. Birria tacos tend to be a breakfast or lunch thing, so go out early to find them.

### AGUACHILE
You won't find a better place to eat aguachile than Puerto Vallarta. Here you can taste the wide range of flavors and presenta-tions: green, black, red, with coconut, and more. Traditionally, aguachile consists of a fresh, raw shrimp tossed in a sauce of lime juice and chile, then mixed with red onions and cucumbers.

### TACOS AL PASTOR
Lebanese immigrants brought the idea for al pastor to Mexico—which is why you'll see the spits of meat typically used to make kebabs and shawarma. With al pastor tacos, you get thinly sliced, moist pork on a tortilla, topped with raw onions, cilantro, and a selection of sauces—usually a spicy red and a green avocado-based sauce. There's one place you must

Aguachile

go to try the best al pastor tacos in Puerto Vallarta: El Carboncito. It's always busy and everybody recommends the food.

### TORTAS AHOGADAS
You've not been to Mexico unless you've eaten *tortas a hogada*. This very typical regional dish starts with a white bread called *birote* or *salado*, which is stuffed with pork in pieces (some variations include shrimp and other fillings) and then covered, or "drowned," with a generous amount of spicy chili and tomato sauce.

### POZOLE
Another local favorite is pozole soup; in the Jalisco and Vallarta areas it consists of a tasty broth that includes pork or chicken meat, seasoned with chili and corn kernels. Enjoy it with lettuce, radishes, and tostadas. You can also find the seafood version with shrimp at The Blue Shrimp, one of the most popular restaurants in town, located in Playa Los Muertos.

### TEQUILA, RAICILLA, AND MEZCAL
Don't forget to enjoy all these delicious dishes with the local drinks. You'll find craft beer, wine, tequila, and mezcal. Be sure to request at least a shot of the local liquor, Raicilla, which is similar to mezcal but distilled and made in Puerto Vallarta. To know the difference between these three beverages, join a tequila tasting tour at Cava Antigua.

### PESCADO EMBARAZADO
One of the most typical dishes of Puerto Vallarta is *pescado embarazado*, literally "pregnant fish." The name doesn't have anything to do with the fish itself; it is a linguistic deformation of *pescado en vara asado*, which is fish roasted on a stick.

# Puerto Vallarta's Best Beaches

## LA LANCHA

Many consider this to be one of the nicest beaches in all of Bahia de Banderas. It happens to be one the most consistent surf breaks in the bay (boards can be rented nearby, or you can join a private surf tour from Puerto Vallarta), ideal for beginners and fun for intermediate surfers when the swells are big. During the winter months the odds of seeing turtles and whales are very high, and in summer the water does not become murky brown like it does in Puerto Vallarta. Grab a bus or rent a car to get here from Puerto Vallarta, get off at the PEMEX station, cross the road, and walk along the well-marked trail.

## COLOMITOS

Well-known but hardly visited, this tiny beach is south of Puerto Vallarta and can only be reached by boat or by walking the long trail from PV. It is surrounded by dense vegetation that projects a shade of emerald green making it appear far away from civilization.

## DESTILADERAS

Open to the public and accessible by car or bus, this beach has what is probably the whitest sand in all Bahia de Banderas. Though it's beloved by locals and there are three hotels here, it's more than 1½ km (.9 miles) long, so there is plenty of space for you to stretch out. Note that the shorebreak can get quite dangerous as soon as there's somewhat of a swell and it gets very windy between March and June (kite surfers who know about it have a blast during this time of the year).

## PLAYA DE LOS MUERTOS

While the name of this beach is anything but comforting (nobody seems to know where it really comes from), it's a favorite among Puerto Vallarta locals, expats, and visitors. Expect it to be crowded, loud, not particularly clean, and close to the action. Playa de los Muertos is at the south end of Puerto Vallarta in Zona Romántica, home to the better part of the large LGBTQ+ community and also very family-friendly.

## NUEVO VALLARTA

The beach in Nuevo Vallarta is spacious, with clean water and picture-perfect sunsets. You're likely to see whales breaching or turtles crawling up the beach to lay eggs in winter, or even see baby turtles hatching and trying to reach the ocean. Ask the concierge at your hotel if it has a turtle protection program through which you can participate in the release of baby turtles. The beach offers wave runner rentals, banana boats, and parasailing opportunities. There is no snorkeling here, and the shorebreak can get dangerous when a large swell hits the bay.

Yelapa

### EL ANCLOTE
Anclote is a small town on the very north end of Bahia de Banderas, right before the very luxurious Punta Mita Estates. While the town itself doesn't have much going on, it does have a few great beaches, especially the eponymous El Anclote. You'll find numerous restaurants that range from very expensive to dirt cheap, a fun wave paddle surfers love, hotels, and plenty of condos for all budgets. From here you can rent pangas that can take you whale-watching or to the Marietas Islands.

### YELAPA
Both the name of the town and its beach, Yelapa is only accessible by boat and is located in a small bay 20 minutes south of Puerto Vallarta. Mountains wrap around both the beach and the bay. Visitors don't come here looking for wild parties and all-inclusive resorts; instead you'll find small inconspicuous restaurants and hotels. Grab a good book and a towel and catch a water taxi from the *muelle* in Puerto Vallarta, or from the beach at La Jolla de Mismaloya.

### MISMALOYA
Also on the south side of Puerto Vallarta, this is the last beach that can be reached by car. It's in a small bay surrounded by hills. The town of Mismaloya is also right there, so the beach is never empty. Grab a bite from the beach joints, stay at the only all-inclusive resort there, join a tour to Los Arcos, or come here for a day and visit nearby attractions including the location where *Predator* was filmed three decades ago—the remains of the helicopter are still there.

# Under-the-Radar Things to Do

## JOIN A FOOD TOUR

Mexican food is so much more than tacos, chiles, and quesadillas, and the best way to learn more about the local gastronomy is to join one of the Vallarta Food Tours. This reliable company offers a mix of culture, walking, biking, and food tours, making it a great way to learn about the city while simultaneously feasting and stretching your legs.

## VISIT LAS CALETAS

Located on the south of Puerto Vallarta, Las Caletas is a beautiful 3/4-mile-long beach that can be reached only by boat. The land is leased by the tour company Vallarta Adventures, and visitors are only granted access to the beach as part of one of the company's tours. At this exclusive beach guests can peacefully enjoy nature trails, spas, and dining facilities. Two different tour options are available: one is a full-day excursion, while the other begins with a sunset cruise, then dinner on the beach, and a theatrical performance by the Rhythms of the Night, which features live music, dancing, contortionists, fire-twirlers, and more.

## JOIN A CHOCOLATE-MAKING CLASS AT THE CHOCO MUSEUM

Learn about the history behind cocoa and find out how Mexican chocolate is made (from harvest to production) by visiting Puerto Vallarta's ChocoMuseo. For a fun, interactive afternoon that will let you try delicious chocolate, sign up for a 2–3 hour workshop in either chocolate-making, truffle-making or mole-making—the latter also takes you to a local market to shop for fresh ingredients before cooking. The Choco Museum also offers a mini-workshop (45 minutes) for those visitors with children in tow or with a limited time frame.

## RELEASE BABY TURTLES IN NUEVO VALLARTA

In Nuevo Vallarta, you can take part in a conservation project to release baby sea turtles. There are several companies offering these types of activities, but one of the best (if not the best) is Puerto Vallarta Tours. They offer year-round visits allowing you to participate in this wonderful and not widely available preservation mission. For about $40 per person, transportation, snacks, and English-speaking guides are included.

## VISIT PLAYA LAS GEMELAS

PV's beaches improve the farther from downtown you venture. Avoid the popular and most crowded points in favor of more peaceful, authentic, and beautiful sandy spaces. Playa Las Gemelas is located just outside Vallarta and has white sand and turquoise waters, and is much less populated on weekdays. As you would with any other beach, stay vigilant for strong tides, jellyfish, and submerged rocks, but most of all, enjoy the calm atmosphere and stunning surroundings. There's no dedicated parking for the beach, so you'll need to find some on the street. Alternatively, you can take a local bus here.

## HORSEBACK RIDING AT RANCHO EL CHARRO

Rancho El Charro is located in a rural area only 15 minutes away from downtown PV, and it provides guests with lovely horseback rides into the Sierra Madre Mountains. The horses are well-cared for and bred right on the ranch, and every effort is made to match riders with the most appropriate horses. They offer a variety of day trips, ranging in length from three to eight hours. There are several multiday options to choose from as well, and some are even suitable for children.

## STROLL AROUND AND SHOP AT CUALE RIVER ISLAND

Cuale River Island is a small isle just south of downtown. Check out the colorful market to get a glimpse into the city's culture of years past, before the all-inclusive resorts came to town. Make sure not to miss the old staircase. There's also a museum housing an excellent collection of pre-Hispanic ceramics dating back to 5000 and 2000 BC. It isn't necessarily undiscovered, but you'll definitely find fewer tourists here than on the Malecón boardwalk.

## GO FISHING AT CAJÓN DE PEÑAS

The Cajón de Peñas development is a lakefront residential and golf course community located in Costalegre, about 130 km (80 miles) from PV. It's a paradise for anglers, and a unique destination for visitors looking to get away from the heat and the city's hustle and bustle. Bird lovers will also have the chance to see a variety of native species, and there are some modest accommodations. With its wonderfully scenic routes, ecological attractions, and relaxed atmosphere, Cajon de Peñas becomes a great destination for both locals and visitors.

## RELAX IN TEHUAMIXTLE AND MAYTO

Found on the Costalegre corridor, the beaches of Tehuamixtle and Mayto are under two hours from PV and are ideal for a day trip. The small cove of Tehuamixtle ("La Playita de Amor" or the little beach of love) is a must-visit if you love fresh seafood and immersing yourself in the local atmosphere. A few minutes further north you'll find the beach of Mayto where there's open ocean, coral sands, and a few small hotels. You'll also find some places to eat and a few panga owners that can take you fishing or sightseeing.

## WANDER THE "PUEBLO MÁGICO" OF SAN SEBASTIÁN

San Sebastián del Oeste is one of Mexico's "Pueblo Mágico" (magical town) and is a 90-minute drive from Puerto Vallarta, deep in the Sierra Madre. The town was granted this status by the Mexican Tourism Board for many reasons, but there's no doubt that the rich history and natural beauty of this place and surrounding area have much to do with it.

# LGBTQ+ Hot Spots

## MARCO REINAS BAR

Marco Reinas ("reinas" meaning "queens") Bar is not filled with typical Mexican decor, but instead wall art depicting royalty like Lady Di and Queen Elizabeth. It is a very popular place to talk over a few beers, and they host many drag shows throughout the week.

## THE PALM CABARET AND BAR

The Palm Cabaret has been on Puerto Vallarta gay scene for more than 20 years, and went through a complete renovation in 2013. The Cabaret brings artists from both Americas for well-produced shows during the high season. The drag acts there are one of a kind but music shows are also dazzling.

## SAPPHIRE OCEAN BEACH CLUB

The LGBTQ+-friendly Sapphire Ocean has the best food of any beach club at Los Muertos. Enjoy brunch and then spend the rest of the day sunbathing in their lounge chairs or swimming in the pool. If you are not staying at the hotel you can still purchase a day pass and enjoy all of the amenities.

## EL MOLE DE JOVITA

El Mole de Jovita is a favorite of the local LGBTQ+ community. Located on Basilio Badillo street, it rivals the best restaurants in Puerto Vallarta with its mole sauces based on secret family recipes passed down to the owner by his mother.

## MANTAMAR BEACH CLUB

Mantamar Beach Club is a relative newcomer in town. It's part of the Almar adults-only gay hotel and an essential stop on the pool party circuit. This chic oasis offers one of the most spectacular infinity beachfront pools in town, a flying pool, and lots of private event spaces. The club has gained notoriety for its DJs and its gourmet cuisine.

## CASA CUPULA

Casa Cupula is a beautiful boutique gay hotel with a restaurant famous for its Sunday brunch. All the rooms are luxurious and some suites have a private hot tub with breathtaking ocean views. The staff is known for going above and beyond to meet guests' wishes. There are two pools, one of them is clothing-optional.

## ACT II ENTERTAINMENT STAGES

The growing LGBTQ+ community in Puerto Vallarta was in need of more sophisticated entertainment, and Act II Entertainment rose to the occasion with the top productions and visiting acts in the area. The Theater has two stages and the Encore Piano Bar, and hosts live music, cabaret, drama, and comedy.

## BOANA TORRE MALIBU

It's all about location, and Boana Torre Malibu is situated in the ideal area, close to lively Los Muertos Beach. Homey suites in this condo-hotel come with a sofa bed and a kitchen. They have one of the largest LGBTQ+-friendly swimming pools in Puerto Vallarta.

## LOS MUERTOS BEACH

Los Muertos is where the Puerto Vallarta gay scene congregates, and is unofficially considered the main LGBTQ+ beach. The beach is popular with locals, visitors, and expats. It starts south of the Malecón at the Cuale river and finishes at the original Seahorse statue at Las Pilitas. It's not a beach where you can relax and read your book in silence but a place with nonstop action and the most well-known gay beach clubs in town.

## BLUE CHAIRS BEACH CLUB AND RESORT

The legendary Blue Chairs Beach Club is famous for being a LGBTQ+ fun spot. The club has a daily sunset happy hour and all-day, nonstop parties.

# Snapshot of Puerto Vallarta

## GEOGRAPHY

Puerto Vallarta sits at the center point of C-shape Banderas Bay. Spurs from the Sierra Cacoma run down to the sea, forming a landscape of numerous valleys. This highly fractured mountain range is just one of many within the Sierra Madre—which runs from the Rockies to South America. Sierra Cacoma sits at the juncture of several major systems that head south toward Oaxaca State. Forming a distinct but related system is the volcanic or transversal volcanic axis that runs east to west across the country—and the globe. Comprising part of the so-called Ring of Fire, this transverse chain includes some of the world's most active volcanoes. Volcán de Fuego, southeast of Puerto Vallarta in Colima State, and the giant Popocateptl, near the Gulf of Mexico, are active. Visible from PV are the more intimate Sierra Vallejo and the Sierra Cuale ranges, to the north and south, respectively.

Heading down to the sea from these highlands are a number of important rivers, including the Ameca and the Mascota, which join forces not far from the coast at a place called Las Juntas (The Joining). Now mostly dry, the Ameca forms the boundary between Jalisco and Nayarit states. The Cuale River empties into the ocean at Puerto Vallarta, dividing the city center in two. In addition to boasting many rivers, the area is blessed with seasonal and permanent streams and springs.

Banderas Bay, or Bahía de Banderas, is Mexico's largest bay, at 42 km (26 miles) tip to tip. The northern point, Punta Mita, is in Nayarit State. Towns at the southern extreme of the bay, at Cabo Corrientes (Cape Currents)—named for the frequently strong currents off its shore—are accessible only by boat or dirt roads. The mountains backing the Costalegre

are part of the Sierra Madre Occidental range. The hilly region of eroded plains has two main river systems. the San Nicolás and Cuitzmala

Several hundred miles east of Banderas Bay, Guadalajara—capital of Jalisco State—occupies the west end of 5,400-foot Atemajac Valley, which is surrounded by mountains. Just south of Guadalajara, Lake Chapala is Mexico's largest natural lake.

## FLORA

The western flanks of the Sierra Madre and foothills leading down to the sea have tropical deciduous forest. At the higher levels are expanses of pine-oak forest. Many species of pines thrive in these woods, mixed in with *encinos* and *robles*, two different categories of oak. Walnut trees and *oyamel*, a type of fir, are the mainstays of the lower *arroyos*, or river basins.

Along the coast magnificent *huanacaxtle*, also called *parota* (in English, monkey pod or elephant ear tree), mingle with equally huge and impressive mango as well as kapok, cedar, tropical almond, tamarind, flamboyant, and willow. The brazilwood tree is resistant to insects and, therefore, ideal for making furniture. *Matapalo*, or strangler fig, are common in this landscape. As its name hints, these fast-growing trees embrace others in a death grip; once the matapalo is established, the host tree eventually dies.

Colima palms, known locally as *guaycoyul*, produce small round nuts smashed for oil or sometimes fed to domestic animals. Mango, avocado, citrus, and guava are found in the wild. Imported trees and bushes often seen surrounding homes and small farms include Indian laurel, bamboo, and bougainvillea.

The coastal fringe north of San Blas is surprisingly characterized by savannas. Guinea grass makes fine animal fodder for horses and cows. Lanky coconut trees line roads and beaches. Watery coconut "milk" is a refreshing drink, and the meat of the coconut, although high in saturated fat, can be eaten or used in many types of candy. Another drink, *agua de tuba,* is made from the heart of the palm; the trunk is used in certain types of construction. Mangroves in saltwater estuaries provide an ecosystem for crabs, crustaceans, and birds.

South of Banderas Bay, thorn forest predominates along the coastal strip, backed by tropical deciduous forest. Leguminous trees like the *tabachin,* with its bright orange flowers, have long, dangling seedpods used by indigenous people as rattles. Other prominent area residents are the acacias, hardy trees with fluffy puffballs of light yellow blooms. The dry forest is home to more than 1,100 species of cacti. The *nopal,* or prickly pear cactus, abounds; local people remove the spines and grill the cactus pads or use them in healthful salads. The fruit of the prickly pear, called *tuna,* is used to make a refreshing drink, *agua de tuna.*

## FAUNA

Hunting, deforestation, and the encroachment of humans have diminished many once-abundant species. In the mountains far from humankind, endangered margay, jaguar, and ocelot hunt their prey, which includes spider monkeys, deer, and peccaries. More commonly seen are skunks, raccoons, rabbits, and coyote. The coatimundi is an endearing little animal that lives in family groups, often near streambeds. Inquisitive and alert, they resemble tall, slender prairie dogs. Along with the tanklike, slow-moving armadillo, the sandy-brown coatimundi is among the animals you're most likely to spot

without venturing too deep within the forest. Local people call the coatimundi both *tejón* and *pisote* and often keep them as pets.

Poisonous snakes include the Mexican rattlesnake and the fer-de-lance. Locals call the latter *cuatro narices* (four noses) because it appears to have four nostrils. It's also called *nauyaca;* the bite of this viper can be deadly. There are more than a dozen species of coral snakes with bands of black, yellow, and red in different patterns. False corals imitate this color scheme to fool their predators, but unless you're an expert, it's best to err on the side of caution.

The most famous of the migratory marine species is the humpback whale, here called *ballena jorobada,* or "hunchback" whale. These leviathans grow to 51 feet and weigh 40 to 50 tons; they travel in pods, feeding on krill and tiny fish. In a given year the females in area waters may be either mating or giving birth. During their annual migration of thousands of miles from the Bering Sea, the hardy creatures may lose some 10,000 pounds, or approximately 10% of their body weight. Hunted nearly to extinction in the 1900s, humpbacks remain an endangered species.

A few Bryde whales make their way to Banderas Bay and other protected waters near the end of the humpback season, as do some killer whales (orca) and false killer whales. Bottlenose, spinner, and pantropic spotted dolphins are present pretty much year-round. These acrobats love to bow surf just under the water's surface and to leap into the air. Another spectacular leaper is the velvety-black manta ray, which can grow to 30 feet wide. Shy but lovely spotted eagle rays hover close to the ocean floor, where they feed on crustaceans and mollusks. Nutrient-rich Pacific waters provide sustenance for a wide range of other sea creatures. Among the most eye catching are the graceful king angelfish, iridescent bumphead parrotfish, striped Indo-Pacific sergeants and Moorish idols, and the funny-looking guinea fowl puffer and its close relative, the equally unusual black-blotched porcupine fish.

The varied landscape of Nayarit and Jalisco states provides a tapestry of habitats for some 350 species of birds. In the mangroves, standouts are the great blue heron, mangrove cuckoo, and vireo. Ocean and shorebirds include red-billed tropic birds as well as various species of heron, egret, gulls, brown and blue-footed boobies, and frigate birds. Military macaws patrol the thorn forests, and songbirds of all stripes live in the pine-oak forests. About 40% of the birds in the Costalegre region are migratory. Among the residents are the yellow headed parrot and the Mexican wood nymph, both threatened species.

## ENVIRONMENTAL ISSUES
The biggest threat to the region is deforestation of the tropical dry forest. Slash-and-burn techniques are used to prepare virgin forest for agriculture and pasturing of animals. This practice is counterproductive, as the thin soil fails to produce after the mulch-producing trees and shrubs have been stripped.

The tropical dry forests (also called tropical thorn forest) are now being deforested due to the increasing tourism and human population. Controlled ecotourism offers a potential solution, although failed projects in the area have significantly altered or drained salt marshes and mangrove swamps.

The dry forest is an extremely important ecosystem. It represents one of the richest in Mexico and also one with the highest level of endemism (plant and

animal species found nowhere else). Several species of hardwood trees, including the Pacific coast mahogany and Mexican kingwood, are being over-harvested for use in the building trade. The former is endangered and the latter, threatened.

South of Puerto Vallarta in the Costalegre are two adjacent forest reserves that together form the 32,617-acre Chamela–Cuixmala Biosphere Reserve. Co-owned and managed by nonprofit agencies, private companies, and Mexico's National University, UNAM, the reserve protects nine major vegetation types, including the tropical dry forest, tropical deciduous forest, and semi-deciduous forest. A riparian environment is associated with the north bank of the Cuixmala River. Within the reserve there are approximately 72 species considered at risk for extinction, including the American crocodile and several species of sea turtle.

Hojonay Biosphere Reserve was established by the Hojonay nonprofit organization to preserve the jaguar of the Sierra de Vallejo range and its habitat. The 157,060-acre reserve is in the foothills and mountains behind La Cruz de Huanacaxtle and San Francisco, in Nayarit State.

There are no tours or casual access to either of the reserves, which serve as buffers against development and a refuge for wildlife.

## THE PEOPLE
The population of Puerto Vallarta is overwhelmingly of mestizo (mixed Native American and white/European) descent. According to the 2010 census, fewer than 1% of Jalisco residents speak an indigenous language. Compare that to nearby states: Michoacán with 3.6%; Guerrero with about 14%; and Oaxaca, where more than 33% of the inhabitants converse in a native language.

Those indigenous people who do live in Jalisco State are small groups of Purépecha (also called Tarascans), in the south. The Purépecha were among the very few groups not conquered by the Aztec nation that controlled much of Mesoamerica at the time of the Spanish conquest.

Although not large in number, the indigenous groups most associated with Nayarit and Jalisco states are the Cora and their relatives, the Huichol. Isolated in mountain and valley hamlets and individual *rancherías* (tiny farms) deep in the Sierra Madre, both have, to a large extent, maintained their own customs and culture. According to the CDI (Comisión Nacional Para el Desarrollo de los Pueblos Indígenas, or National Commission for the Development of Native Peoples), there are about 24,390 Cora in Durango, Zacatecas, and Nayarit states, and some 43,929 Huichol, mainly in Nayarit, Jalisco, and Durango. Nearly 70% of the culturally related groups speak their native language.

No matter their background, you'll notice nearly all locals have a contagiously cheery outlook on life. There's an explanation for that: In 1947 a group of prominent vallartenses was returning along twisty mountain roads from an excursion to Mexico City. When the driver lost control and the open-sided bus plunged toward the abyss, death seemed certain. But a large rock halted the bus's progress, and Los Favorecidos (The Lucky Ones), as they came to be known, returned to Puerto Vallarta virtually unharmed. Their untrammeled gestures of thanks to the town's patron saint, the Virgin of Guadalupe, set the precedent for this animated religious procession. Today, all Puerto Vallartans consider themselves to be Los Favorecidos, and thus universally blessed—hence, the

story goes, their optimism. For those of us fortunate enough to visit, taking home a bit of that spiritual magnetism can be the best souvenir.

## THE MAGIC OF MEXICO

To say that Mexico is a magical place means more than saying it's a place of great natural beauty and fabulous experiences. Cities like Catemaco, in Veracruz, have a reputation for their *brujos* and *brujas* (male and female witches, respectively) and herbal healers (*curanderos/curanderas*). But Mexicans use these services even in modern Mexico City and Guadalajara and in tourist towns like Puerto Vallarta. Some might resort to using a curandera to reverse *mal de ojo,* the evil eye, thought to be responsible for a range of unpleasant symptoms, circumstances, disease, or even death.

A *limpia,* or cleansing, is the traditional cure for the evil eye. The healer usually passes a raw chicken or turkey egg over the sufferer to draw out the bad spirit. Green plants, like basil, or branches from certain trees can also be used, drawing the greenery over the head, front, and back to decontaminate the victim. Prayer is an essential ingredient.

Some cures are of a more practical nature. Mexican herbalists, like their colleagues around the world, use tree bark, nuts, berries, roots, and leaves to treat everything from dandruff to cancer. *Epazote,* or wormseed, is a distinctly flavored plant whose leaves are used in cooking. As its English name implies, its medicinal task is to treat parasites.

Most folk wisdom seems to draw from both fact and, if not fiction, at least superstition. Breezes and winds are thought to produce a host of negative reactions: from colds and cramps to far more drastic ailments like paralysis. Some people prefer sweating in a car or bus to rolling down the window and being hit by the wind, especially since mixing hot and cold is something else to be avoided. Even worldly athletes may refuse a cold drink after a hot run. Sudden shock is thought by some to cause lasting problems.

Although it doesn't take a leap of faith to believe that herbal remedies cure disease and Grandma's advice was right on, some of the stuff sold in shops is a bit "harder to swallow." It's difficult to imagine, for example, that the sky-blue potion in a pint-size bottle will bring you good luck, or the lilac-color one can stop people from gossiping about you. Those that double as floor polish seem especially suspect.

Whether magic and prophecy are real or imagined, they sometimes have concrete results. Conquistador Hernán Cortés arrived on the east coast of Mexico in 1519, which correlated to the year "One Reed" on the Aztec calendar. A few centuries prior to Cortés's arrival, the benevolent god king Quetzalcoatl had, according to legend, departed the same coast on a raft of snakes, vowing to return in the year One Reed to reclaim his throne.

News of Cortés—a metal-wearing godman accompanied by strange creatures (horses and dogs) and carrying lightning (cannons and firearms)—traveled quickly to the Aztec capital. Emperor Moctezuma was nervous about Quetzalcoatl's return and his reaction to the culture of war and sacrifice the Aztecs had created. In his desire to placate the returning god, Moctezuma ignored the advice of trusted counselors and opened the door for the destruction of the Aztec empire.

## LA VIDA LOCA

Living the good life in Mexico—specifically in and around Banderas Bay—seems to get easier year by year. Americans and Canadians are by far the biggest groups of expats. In addition to those who have relocated to make Mexico their home, many more foreigners have part-time retirement or vacation homes here. A two-bedroom property in a gated community by the sea begins at around $230,000. You could get more modest digs for less; at the upper end of the spectrum, the sky's the limit.

The sheer number of foreigners living in Puerto Vallarta facilitates adventures that were much more taxing a decade or two ago, like building a home or finding an English-speaking real estate agent or lawyer. Contractors and shopkeepers are used to dealing with gringos; most speak good to excellent English. The town is rich with English-language publications and opportunities for foreigners to meet up for events or volunteer work.

# Weddings and Honeymoons

Mexico is a popular wedding and honeymoon destination for Canadians and Americans. Many area hotels—from boutiques to internationally known brands—offer honeymoon packages and professional wedding planners. Although there's an obligatory civil ceremony that must accompany the Big Event, you can get married in a house of worship, on a beach, at a hotel chapel, or on a yacht or sailboat.

## THE BIG DAY

**Choosing the Perfect Place.** Puerto Vallarta—including resorts to the north along the Riviera Nayarit and south along the Costalegre—is one of Mexico's most popular wedding and honeymoon destinations. Many couples choose to marry on the beach, often at sunset because it's cooler and more comfortable for everyone; others chuck the whole weather conundrum and marry in an air-conditioned resort ballroom.

The luxury of enjoying your wedding and honeymoon in one place has a cost: You may find it hard to have some alone time with your partner with all your family and friends nearby. Consider booking an all-inclusive, which has plenty of meal options and activities to keep your guests busy. This will make it easier for them to respect your privacy and stick to mingling with you and your spouse at planned times. Among PV's best options for on-site, catered weddings are the Marriott Puerto Vallarta Resort & Spa, the Westin, the Villa Premiere, and Casa Velas. El Dorado restaurant offers stunning views from their wedding-reception area; Las Caletas offers unique beachfront weddings accessed by boat through Vallarta Adventures.

**Time of Year.** Planning according to the weather can be critical for a successful PV wedding. If you're getting married in your bathing suit, you might not mind some heat and humidity, but will your venue hold up under a summer deluge? We recommend substituting the traditional June wedding that's so suitable for New England and Nova Scotia with one held between late November and February or March. April through mid-June is usually dry but extremely hot and humid. Summer rains begin to fall in mid-June. Sometimes this means a light sprinkle that reduces heat and humidity and freshens the trees; other times it means a torrential downpour that immediately floods the streets. Although hurricanes are rarer along the Pacific than the Caribbean, they can threaten September through early November. For an outdoor wedding, establish a detailed backup plan in case the weather lets you down.

**Requirements.** A wedding planner will facilitate completing the required paperwork and negotiating the legal requirements for marrying in Mexico. Blood work must be done upon your arrival, but not more than 14 days before the ceremony. All documents must be translated by an authorized translator from the destination, and it's important to send these documents certified mail to your wedding coordinator at least a month ahead of the wedding. You'll also need to submit an application for a marriage license as well as certified birth certificates (bring the original with you to PV, and send certified copies ahead of time). If either party is divorced or widowed, an official divorce decree or death certificate must be supplied. The bride, groom, and four witnesses will also need to present passports and tourist cards.

Jalisco State has additional requirements; for this reason some couples choose to have the civil ceremony in Nayarit State (Nuevo Vallarta or anywhere north of there) and then the "spiritual" ceremony in the location of their choice. Since church weddings aren't officially recognized in Mexico, even for citizens, a civil ceremony is required in any case, thus making your marriage valid in your home country as well. Another option is to be married in a civil ceremony in your own country and then hold the wedding event without worrying about all the red tape.

## THE HONEYMOON

If you've chosen a resort wedding, you and many of the guests may be content to relax on-site after the bustle and stress of the wedding itself. Puerto Vallarta has a huge variety of accommodations, from name-brand hotels with spas and multiple swimming pools to three-bedroom B&Bs in the moderate price range. Many properties have special honeymoon packages that include champagne and strawberries on the wedding night, flowers in the room, spa treatments, or other sorts of pampering and earthly pleasures.

# Kids and Families

What better way to bond with your kids than splashing in the pool or the sea, riding a horse into the hills, or zipping through the trees on a canopy tour? Puerto Vallarta may be short on sights, but it's long on outdoor activities like these. It also has a huge range of accommodation options: everything from B&Bs that leave lunch and dinner wide open for a family on the go to all-inclusive resorts where picky eaters can be easily indulged and kids of all ages can be kept engaged by activities or kids' clubs.

## PLACES TO STAY

**Resorts:** Except those that exclude children entirely, most of Vallarta's beach resorts cater to families and have children's programs. Meliá is great for little kids, as it offers lots of games and activities geared toward them; there's not so much of interest to teens here. The Marriott is kid-friendly, offering children's menus at most of its restaurants and kids' clubs for the 4-to-13 set. In addition to things like Ping-Pong, tennis, and volleyball, kids absolutely love liberating tiny turtle hatchlings into the sea during the summer/early fall turtle season.

At the high end of the price spectrum, Four Seasons has plenty for the kids to do, as well as golf and spa appointments for parents. The protected, almost private beach here is great for the children, who also love floating on inner tubes in the ring-shape swift-water swimming pool. The children's center, with loads of cool games and computer programs, keeps kids of all ages entertained.

Old Vallarta (El Centro and Colonia E. Zapata, aka Zona Romántica) consists mainly of moderate to budget hotels. Independent families are often drawn to such properties on or near Los Muertos Beach. Playa Los Arcos, for instance, is right on the sand; Eloisa, with its

inexpensive studios (with kitchenettes) and suites, is a block from the bay.

**Vacation Rentals:** Apartments, condos, and villas are an excellent option for families. You can cook your own food (a big money saver), spread out, and set up a home away from home, which can make everyone feel more comfortable. If you decide to go the apartment- or condo-rental route, be sure to ask about the number and size of the swimming pools and whether outdoor spaces and barbecue areas are available.

## BEACHES

Los Muertos Beach is a good bet for families who want access to snacks and water-sports rentals, and there are (usually) lifeguards here, too. Families favor the north end near Playas Olas Altas, but there's plenty of sand and sun for all. The all-inclusive resorts of Nuevo Vallarta rent water-sports equipment for use at a long, wide beach that continues all the way to Bucerías. The scene here is very laid-back, involving more lounging than anything else.

## WATER ACTIVITIES

If you surf, or want to learn, Sayulita is a good option. There are also many good surfing beaches off the point at Punta Mita as well as around San Blas and Barra de Navidad.

Year-round you can catch glimpses of manta rays leaping from the water and dolphins riding the wakes of bay cruises. Winter sees whale-watching expeditions on which you can spot humpbacks and, occasionally, orcas.

Turtle season is summer through late fall; children love to take part in liberating the tiny hatchlings. Larger resort hotels on turtle-nesting beaches often encourage guests to participate in this, and wildlife operators offer turtle tours.

There's snorkeling (though sometimes lots of little jellyfish join you in the hot summer months) around Los Arcos just south of PV, at the Marietas Islands off Punta Mita, and at other beaches north and south. Divers haunt these spots, too, in addition to farther-away destinations.

PV's yachts and *pangas* (skiffs) are available for shore- or deep-water fishing excursions. Nuevo Vallarta has a much smaller fleet based at Paradise Village marina. In small towns like Mismaloya, Boca de Tomatlán, Rincón de Guayabitos, Sayulita, Tenacatita, and Barra de Navidad, you contract with local fishermen on or near the beach for angling expeditions.

## LAND ACTIVITIES

Puerto Vallarta proper has a lovely botanical garden with a river in which kids can splash. In the hills behind town, you can go on horseback, mountain-bike, ATV, dune-buggy, or canopy-tour adventures. Golf courses range from private links at Punta Mita to fun and accessible courses in Nuevo Vallarta and Marina Vallarta. There are excellent courses to the south at El Tamarindo and Barra de Navidad.

## AFTER DARK

Nightly in high season musicians, clowns, and mimes perform at PV's Los Arcos amphitheater. Walk along the malecón en route, stopping to enjoy an ice cream, admire the sunset, or pose for pictures beside a sculpture.

Dinner shows often offer Mexican-theme buffets, mariachi music, and, sometimes, cowboys doing rope tricks. The pirate-theme vessel *Marigalante* has both day and evening cruises that kids love. PV has three modern movie theaters with English-language movies; note, though, that animated films or those rated "G" are usually dubbed in Spanish, as kids aren't fond of subtitles.

# What to Watch and Read

### THE NIGHT OF THE IGUANA, BY JOHN HUSTON (1964)

This is the movie that made Puerto Vallarta famous. Any locals could show you some of the spots where it was filmed, and you might even meet someone who remembers the time when Richard Burton, Ava Gardner, and Elizabeth Taylor were frequent visitors to the region. The film gives you a sense of downtown Puerto Vallarta in the early 1960s, the Malecón, the Lighthouse, and last but not least, Mismaloya.

### PREDATOR, BY JOHN MCTIERNAN (1987)

*Predator* is the second most famous movie that was filmed in Puerto Vallarta. Most of it was shot in El Edén; the jungle south of PV and Boca de Tomatlán was immortalized in the initial scenes. In this sci-fi action movie, an elite group of soldiers on a rescue mission in Central America find that they've become the prey for an extraterrestrial predator.

### LE MAGNIFIQUE, BY PHILIPPE DE BROCA (1973)

In this slapstick comedy that shows Puerto Vallarta in the '70s, Jean-Paul Belmondo is an espionage novel writer with a great imagination. You'll see beaches, the old Malecón, and the Main Plaza of PV, plus the Hotel Posada Vallarta (then known as the Krystal Hotel).

### LIMITLESS, BY NEIL BURGER (2011)

Bradley Cooper stars as Eddie Morra, driving his Maserati on the Malecón toward Las Islas Marietas. An observant viewer might also spot some luxurious villas and a resort in Punta Mita. Eddie is a writer who takes an experimental drug to enhance his brain capacity. Unfortunately side effects and some powerful enemies make his new perfect life less than perfect.

### I BRAKE FOR GRINGOS / SUNDOWN, BY FERNANDO LEBRIJA (2016)

*I Brake for Gringos*, known as *Sundown* on the American market, is a comedy about two high school students on spring break in Puerto Vallarta. Beautiful beaches, memorable parties, plus DJs Steve Aoki and Paul Oakenfold (as themselves) make an appearance.

### PUERTO VALLARTA SQUEEZE, BY ROBERT JAMES WALLER AND PUERTO VALLARTA SQUEEZE, DIRECTED BY ARTHUR ALLAN SEIDEMAN

Robert James Waller, the author of *Puerto Vallarta Squeeze*, also penned *The Bridges of Madison County*. The film adaptation stars Harvey Keitel. Both tell the story of an American journalist who lives in Puerto Vallarta with his young Mexican lover, who together help a former Marine travel north of the Rio Grande. Much of it was filmed in downtown PV.

### PUERTO VALLARTA ON 49 BRAIN CELLS A DAY, REFRIED BRAINS, AND PUERTO VALLARTA ON A DONKEY A DAY, ALL BY GIL GEVINS

These three books are collections of funny—and mostly true—stories set in Puerto Vallarta that portray the surreal early years of an American expat in Mexico.

### BOOMERS IN PARADISE: LIVING IN PUERTO VALLARTA, BY ROBERT NELSON

This book has interviews with and stories from 14 different baby boomers living in Puerto Vallarta as expats, and shows different perspectives of moving here for retirement. If you're considering moving your whole life to this paradise, this is the book for you.

# Chapter 2

# TRAVEL SMART

Updated by
Federico Arrizabalaga

★ **CAPITAL:**
PV is in the state of
Jalisco, whose capital is
Guadalajara.

♔ **POPULATION:**
275,640

💬 **LANGUAGE:**
Spanish

$ **CURRENCY:**
Mexican Peso (MXN)

☎ **AREA CODE:**
322

⚠ **EMERGENCIES:**
066 or 060

🚗 **DRIVING:**
On the right

⚡ **ELECTRICITY:**
127v/60 hz; plugs have two or
three rectangular prongs

🕙 **TIME:**
1 hour behind New York

🌐 **WEB RESOURCES:**
www.visitpuertovallarta.com

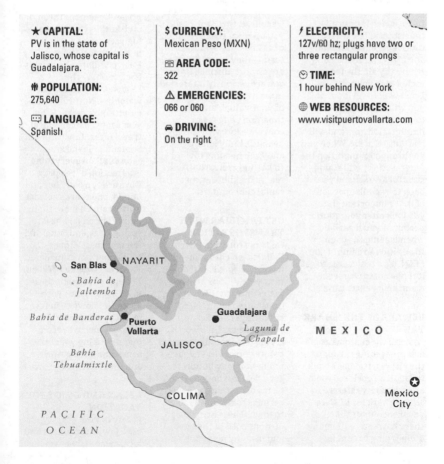

# Know Before You Go

Not sure what to pack or how to best get around Puerto Vallarta? Follow these tips to help you make the most of your visit.

hotspots, and the fares are a fraction of taxi tariffs. The destinations are written on the windshield of each bus, but before you step onto the bus be sure to verbally verify with the driver that his route includes your destination as it is confusing. Renting a car is also an option but expect to pay hefty fees for the privilege, and there is Uber, which can be the best option.

### DON'T MISPLACE YOUR TRAVEL VISA

When traveling to Puerto Vallarta, you'll be asked to fill out an immigration form, which is basically a tourist visa. The fee for the tourist permit is around 500 MXN, but if you enter Mexico by air, the fee is included in your airfare. Don't wait to fill it out or you will not be allowed to move forward to the immigration area and will be shuttled aside. When you go through immigration the federal officer will stamp your form and hand you back the smaller portion of it. It's important that you look after your tourist permit as you'll need it when leaving the country. In addition to a fine of 500 MXN, it's a real hassle to get it replaced, so we recommend being extra careful.

### BEWARE OF THE "SHARK TANK"

Leaving the customs area and proceeding through the airport, travelers walk through an enclosed room, affectionately referred to as the "shark tank." Here you'll encounter time-share hawkers, with many often trying to convince arriving passengers that they must stop and disclose their final hotel destination so they can be offered discounted transportation. Of course, they won't tell you up front they are part of a time-share-selling team—they'll act like they are airport officials. Unless you are seriously interested in wasting several hours of your valuable vacation time, don't engage in conversation with these people. Kindly ignore them and keep heading toward the actual arrival hall with real taxis, shuttles, and rental car counters.

### GET FAMILIAR WITH TRANSPORTATION

Getting around in Puerto Vallarta isn't difficult, but it can be expensive if done incorrectly. Cabs are the fastest way to reach your destination, but they're not always the cheapest. If you take a taxi, it's worth trying to negotiate the price before you get in. If you're polite, you may be able to get a deal on the rate. In terms of cost, riding a bus is perhaps the best way to get to town. There are plenty of stops both in the city and in many neighboring

### KNOW WHEN TO VISIT

Finding the perfect travel time requires weighing several factors, including weather, crowd sizes, and prices. December through mid-April is considered high season and the busiest travel time in Puerto Vallarta, as crowds flock to enjoy the city's best weather and whale-watching. Naturally, these months also feature the year's most astronomical travel fares. July through September is the low season, when everything is a fraction of the price. Days are typically hot and humid, and there's at least a little rain on more than half of the days. The late spring (May and June) and fall months (October – November) are considered Vallarta's shoulder season. Though affordable, these months can come with sporadic showers. In terms of both price and agreeable weather, we recommend booking your stay sometime during April–June, and October.

### RELAX AND ENJOY YOUR VACATION

Safety is a top priority for both law enforcement and locals who strive to make the city safe for visitors. Whether booking your first trip to the coastal town or returning for your annual visit, you'll be able to relax and enjoy yourself on vacation. Just bear in mind, much like you would in any crowded area, that you should keep track of your belongings, not flaunt your money, and always be aware of your surroundings. While safety shouldn't be the first thing on your mind when visiting PV, it also shouldn't be the last.

## CHECK EXCHANGE RATES

Exchange rates are another important thing you should check before traveling. Like the rest of Mexico, Puerto Vallarta uses the peso as its standard currency. However, US dollars are also widely accepted in the region. A good rule of thumb is to hold on to your U.S. dollars if the exchange rate is 18.5 pesos or more to the dollar. However, if the exchange rate is less than 18.5 pesos to the dollar, you'll want to withdraw pesos from an ATM and use them instead. This is because vendors tend to use the 18.5 MXN to 1 USD exchange rate when giving quotes. Credit cards are accepted at most places, but cash is still king so you'll definitely want to have cash ready.

## PACK FOR THE OUTDOORS

Located near the equator, Puerto Vallarta stays mild year-round. As such, some of its most popular activities and attractions are outdoors. In order to enjoy all the things Puerto Vallarta has to offer, pack outdoor clothes and gear suitable for warm weather. Swimsuits and sunscreen are essential. An umbrella is also a necessity—it can double as a sun shield on clear days and rain guard should sporadic showers show up. Be sure to pack a good pair of shoes for hikes and other outdoor excursions, and always check the local forecast before traveling.

## BOOK EARLY AND BUILD A SMART ITINERARY

Puerto Vallarta is one of the premier oceanside destinations in the entire Western Hemisphere. At this coastal hotspot, reservations for hotels, resorts, and tour activities tend to fill up fast. So when you're making plans for travel to PV and have your heart set on experiencing specific tours and adventure activities during your trip, you'll want to book as early as possible and build an itinerary. This will aid you in putting together a desired schedule of excursions for your upcoming vacation, and you can make reservations accordingly.

## LOCALS ARE EASY TO INTERACT WITH, BUT BE POLITE

Locals start every conversation with a "Buenos Dias" (good morning), "Buenas Tardes" (good afternoon), or "Buenas Noches" (good evening). You may be used to just replying with whatever request you have for them, but you should respect their culture and return their greeting first. Similarly, "Mucho gusto" (a great pleasure) is a polite thing to say when you're introduced to someone, accompanied by a handshake. An invitation to a Mexican home is an honor for an outsider; you'll be treated very hospitably. Take a small gift, such as flowers or something for the children, and be at least 30 minutes late; being on time is considered rude. The locals are a friendly group and generally love to hear that you're enjoying their country. Don't be afraid to let loose and make new friends.

## BE AWARE OF ALL THE ENTRY AND EXIT FORMALITIES

U.S. citizens traveling by land or sea can enter Mexico and return to the United States with a pass card, but if traveling by air will need a passport. Citizens of other countries need their passports and some nationalities also require a visa. All tourists must have a Mexican-government tourist permit, easily obtained on arrival. The length of your permitted stay in Mexico is written on the card by the immigration officer. To get a permit extended, apply to the INM—the procedure costs the same as the tourist permit and should only take half an hour or so. In order to protect yourself against this area's common diseases (zika, dengue, and malaria), there are some recommended or required vaccinations: hepatitis A and B, typhoid, cholera, rabies, meningitis, polio, measles, mumps, and rubella, Tdap (tetanus, diphtheria, and pertussis), chickenpox, shingles, pneumonia, and influenza.

# Getting Here and Around

##  Air

Flights with stopovers in Mexico City tend to take the entire day. There are nonstop flights from a few U.S. cities, including Atlanta (Delta), Los Angeles (Alaska Air, American Airlines via Mexicana de Aviación), San Francisco (Alaska Air, United), Seattle (Alaska Air), Dallas (American), Denver (Frontier Air, United), Chicago ORD (American Airlines), Kansas City, and Newark (United).

Air Canada has nonstop flights from Toronto and connecting flights (via Toronto) from all major cities. Web-based Volaris is a Tijuana-based airline with reasonable fares. It flies direct to Puerto Vallarta from Tijuana and between Guadalajara and San Francisco, Los Angeles, and Cancun. You can fly to Manzanillo, just south of the Costalegre, via many airlines with a stop in Mexico City.

If you plan to include Guadalajara in your itinerary, consider an open-jaw flight to Puerto Vallarta with a return from Guadalajara (or vice versa). There's almost no difference in price when you fly a Mexican airline like Aeroméxico, even when factoring in bus fare; sometimes the open jaw is even cheaper.

Flying times are about 2¾ hours from Houston, 3 hours from Los Angeles, 3½ hours from Denver, 4 hours from Chicago, and 8 hours from New York.

### AIRPORTS

The main gateway, and where many PV-bound travelers change planes, is Mexico City's large, modern Aeropuerto Internacional de la Ciudad de México (Benito Juárez; airport code: MEX). It's infamous for pickpocketing and taxi scams, so watch your stuff.

Puerto Vallarta's small international Aeropuerto Internacional Gustavo Díaz Ordáz (PVR) is 7½ km (4½ miles) north of downtown.

### GROUND TRANSPORTATION

Vans provide transportation from the airport to PV hotels; there's a zone system with different prices for the Zona Hotelera (Hotel Zone), downtown PV, and so on. Outside the luggage collection area, vendors shout for your attention but you can prebook your hotel transportation online with some companies. It's a confusing scene. Purchase the taxi vouchers sold at the stands inside the terminal, and be sure to avoid the time-share vendors who trap you in their vans for a high-pressure sales pitch en route to your hotel. Avoid drivers who approach you, and head for an official taxi kiosk, which will have zone information clearly posted. As in any busy airport, don't leave your luggage unattended for any reason.

Before you purchase your ticket, look for a taxi-zone map (it should be posted on or by the ticket stand), and make sure your taxi ticket is properly zoned; if you need a ticket only to Zone 3, don't pay for a ticket to Zone 4 or 5. Taxis or vans to the Costalegre resorts between PV and Manzanillo are generally arranged through the resort. If not, taxis charge about 200 to 250 MXN ($15–$19) an hour—more if you're traveling beyond Jalisco State lines.

##  Bus

### LONG-DISTANCE SERVICE

PV's Central Camionera, or Central Bus Station, is 1 km (½ mile) north of the airport, halfway between Nuevo Vallarta and downtown.

First-class Mexican buses (known as *primera clase*) are generally timely and comfortable, air-conditioned coaches with bathrooms, movies, and reclining seats—sometimes with seat belts. Deluxe (de lujo or ejecutivo) buses offer the same —sometimes with fewer, roomier seats—and usually have refreshments. Second-class (segunda clase)buses are used mainly for travel to smaller, secondary destinations.

A lower-class bus ride can be interesting if you're not in a hurry and want to experience local culture; these buses make frequent stops and keep less strictly to their timetables. Often they will wait until they fill up to leave, regardless of the scheduled time of departure. Fares are up to 15%–30% cheaper than those for first-class buses. The days of pigs and chickens among your bus mates are largely in the past. ■TIP➔ Unless you're writing a novel or your memoir, there's no reason to ride a second-class bus if a first-class or better is available. Daytime trips are safer.

Bring snacks, socks, and a sweater—the air-conditioning on first-class buses is often set on high—and toilet paper, as restrooms might not have any. Smoking is prohibited on all buses.

Estrella Blanca goes from Mexico City to Manzanillo, Mazatlán, Monterrey, Nuevo Laredo, and other central, Pacific coast, and northern-border points. ETN has the most luxurious service—with exclusively first-class buses that have roomy, totally reclining seats—to Guadalajara, Mexico City, Barra de Navidad, Chamela, and Manzanillo. Primera Plus connects Mexico City with Manzanillo and Puerto Vallarta along with other central and western cities.

TAP serves Mexico City, Guadalajara, Puerto Vallarta, Tepic, and Mazatlán. Basic service, including some buses with marginal or no air-conditioning, is the norm on Transportes Cihuatlán, which connects the Bahía de Banderas and PV with southern Jalisco towns such as Barra de Navidad.

You can buy tickets for first-class or better in advance; this is advisable during peak periods, although the most popular routes have buses on the hour. You can make reservations for many, though not all, of the first-class bus lines, through the Ticketbus central reservations agency. Rates average 70–120 MXN ($2.70–$5.70) per hour of travel, depending on the level of luxury. Plan to pay in pesos, although most of the deluxe bus services accept Visa and MasterCard.

## CITY BUSES

City buses (8 b MXN) serve downtown, the Zona Hotelera Norte, and Marina Vallarta. Bus stops—marked by blue-and-white signs—are every two or three long blocks along the highway (Carretera al Aeropuerto) and in downtown Puerto Vallarta. Green buses to Playa Mismaloya and Boca de Tomatlán (7 MXN) run about every 15 minutes from the corner of Avenida Insurgentes and Basilio Badillo downtown.

Gray ATM buses serving Nuevo Vallarta and Bucerías (20 MXN), Punta Mita (30 MXN), and Sayulita (50 MXN) depart from Plaza las Glorias, in front of the HSBC bank and Wal-Mart, both of which are along Carretera Aeropuerto between downtown and the Zona Hotelera.

■TIP➔ It's rare for inspectors to check tickets, but just when you've let yours flutter to the floor, a figure of authority is bound to appear. So hang on to your ticket and hat: PV bus drivers race from one stoplight to the next in jerky bursts of speed.

There's no problem with theft on city buses aside from perhaps an occasional pickpocket, which could be said of anywhere in the world.

# Getting Here and Around

##  Car

From December through April—peak season—traffic clogs the narrow downtown streets, and negotiating the steep hills in Old Vallarta (sometimes you have to drive in reverse to let another car pass) can be unnerving. Avoid rush hour (7–9 am and 6–8 pm) and when schools let out (2–3 pm). Always lock your car, and never leave valuable items visible in the body of the car. The trunk is generally safe, although any thief can crack one open if he chooses.

■ TIP→ It's absolutely essential that you carry Mexican auto insurance for liability, even if you have full coverage for collision, damages, and theft. If you injure anyone in an accident, you could well be jailed until culpability is established—whether it was your fault or not—unless you have insurance.

### GASOLINE
Pemex (the government petroleum monopoly) used to franchise all of Mexico's gas stations but some competitors have stepped up after the energy reform of 2013, which you can find at most intersections and in cities and towns. Gas is measured in liters. Stations in and around the larger towns may accept U.S. or Canadian credit cards (or dollars).

Premium unleaded gas (called *premium,* the red pump) and regular unleaded gas (*magna,* the green pump) are available nationwide, but it's still best to fill up whenever you can and not let your tank get below half full. Fuel quality is generally lower than that in the United States, but it has improved enough so that your car will run acceptably. At this writing gas was about 21.5 MXN per liter (about $3.78 per gallon) for the cheap stuff and 22 MXN per liter ($4.12 per gallon) for super.

Attendants pump the gas for you and may also wash your windshield and check your oil and tire air pressure. A small tip is customary (from just a few pesos for pumping the gas only to 5 or 10 for the whole enchilada of services). Keep an eye on the gas meter to make sure the attendant is starting it at "0" and that you're charged the correct price.

### PARKING
A circle with a diagonal line superimposed on the letter *E* (for *estacionamiento*) means "no parking." Illegally parked cars may have the license plate removed, requiring a trip to the traffic-police headquarters for payment of a fine. When in doubt, park in a lot rather than on the street; your car will probably be safer there anyway. There are parking lots in PV at Parque Hidalgo (Av. México at Venezuela, Col. 5 de Diciembre), just north of the Cuale River at the malecón between Calle A. Rodríguez and Calle Encino, and in the Zona Romántica at Parque Lázaro Cárdenas. Fees vary depending on time of day, ranging from 12 MXN (just under $1) per hour to 20 MXN (about $1.50) per hour.

### ROAD CONDITIONS
Several well-kept toll roads head into and out of major cities like Guadalajara—most of them four lanes wide. However, these *carreteras* (major highways) don't go too far into the countryside, and even the toll-roads have *topes* (speed bumps) and toll booths to slow you down. *Cuota* means toll road; *libre* means no toll, and such roads are often two lanes and not as well-maintained. A new 33½-km (21-mile) highway between Tepic and San Blas will shorten driving time to about 20 minutes.

Roads leading to, or in, Nayarit and Jalisco include highways connecting Nogales and Mazatlán; Guadalajara and Tepic; and Mexico City, Morelia, and Guadalajara. Tolls between Guadalajara and Puerto

Vallarta (334 km [207 miles]) total about $25.

In rural areas roads are sometimes poor; other times the two-lane, blacktop roads are perfectly fine. Be extra cautious during the rainy season, when rock slides and potholes are a problem.

Watch out for animals, especially untethered horses, cattle, and dogs, and for dangerous, unrailed curves. *Topes* (speed bumps) are ubiquitous; slow down when approaching any town or village and look for signs saying "Topes" or "Vibradores." Police officers often issue tickets to those speeding through populated areas.

Generally, driving times are longer than for comparable distances in the United States and Canada. Allow extra time for unforeseen occurrences as well as for traffic, particularly truck traffic.

### ROADSIDE EMERGENCIES
To help motorists on major highways, the Mexican Tourism Ministry operates a fleet of more than 250 pickup trucks, known as the Angeles Verdes, or Green Angels, reachable by phone throughout Mexico by dialing 078 or, in some areas near Puerto Vallarta, 066. In either case, ask the person who answers to transfer the call to the Green Angels hotline. The bilingual drivers provide mechanical help, first aid, radio-telephone communication, basic supplies and small parts, towing, tourist information, and protection.

Services are free, and spare parts, fuel, and lubricants are provided at cost. Tips are always appreciated (around 65–130 pesos [$5–$10] for big jobs and 40–65 pesos [$3–$5] for minor stuff; a souvenir from your country can sometimes be a well-received alternative). The Green Angels patrol the major highways twice daily 8–8 (usually later on holiday weekends). If you break down, pull off the road as far as possible, and lift the hood of your car. If you don't have a cell phone, hail a passing vehicle and ask the driver to notify the patrol. Most drivers will be quite helpful.

### RULES OF THE ROAD
When you sign up for Mexican car insurance, you may receive a booklet on Mexican rules of the road. It really is a good idea to read it to familiarize yourself not only with laws but also customs that differ from those of your home country. For instance: if an oncoming vehicle flicks its lights at you in daytime, slow down: it could mean trouble ahead; when approaching a narrow bridge, the first vehicle to flash its lights has right of way; right on red is not allowed; one-way traffic is indicated by an arrow; two-way, by a double-pointed arrow. (Other road signs follow the widespread system of international symbols.)

■TIP➜ On the highway, using your left turn signal to turn left is dangerous. Mexican drivers—especially truck drivers—use their left turn signal on the highway to signal the vehicle behind that it's safe to pass. Conversely they rarely use their signal to actually make a turn. Foreigners signaling a left turn off the highway into a driveway or onto a side road have been killed by cars or trucks behind that mistook their turn signal for a signal to pass. To turn left from a highway when cars are behind you, it's best to pull over to the right and make the left turn when no cars are approaching, to avoid disaster.

Mileage and speed limits are given in kilometers: 110 kph and 80 kph (66 mph and 50 mph, respectively) are the most common maximums on the highway. However, speed limits can change from curve to curve, so watch the signs carefully. In cities and small towns, observe the posted speed limits, which can be as low as 20 kph (12 mph).

# Getting Here and Around

Seat belts are required by law throughout Mexico. Drunk driving laws are fairly harsh in Mexico, and if you're caught you may go to jail immediately. It's difficult to say what the blood-alcohol limit is since everyone you ask gives a different answer, which means each case is probably handled in a discretionary manner. The best way to avoid any problems is simply to not drink and drive.

If you're stopped for speeding, the officer is supposed to take your license and hold it until you pay the fine at the local police station. But the officer will usually prefer a *mordida* (small bribe). Just take out a couple hundred pesos, hold it out discreetly while asking politely if the officer can "pay the fine for you." Conversely, a few cops might resent the offer of a bribe, but it's still common practice.

If you decide to dispute a charge that seems preposterous, do so courteously and with a smile, and tell the officer that you would like to talk to the police captain when you get to the station. The officer usually will let you go rather than go to the station.

## SAFETY ON THE ROAD

Never drive at night in remote and rural areas. *Bandidos* are one concern, but so are potholes, free-roaming animals, cars with no working lights, road-hogging trucks, drunk drivers, and difficulty in getting assistance. It's best to use toll roads whenever possible; although costly, they're safer, too.

Off the highway, driving in Mexico can be nerve-wracking for novices, with people sometimes paying little attention to marked lanes. Most drivers pay attention to safety rules, but be vigilant. Drunk driving skyrockets on holiday weekends.

A police officer may pull you over for something you didn't do, unfortunately a common scam. If you're pulled over for any reason, be polite—displays of anger will only make matters worse. Although efforts are being made to fight corruption, it's still a fact of life in Mexico, and for many people, it's worth the $10 to $100 it costs to get their license back to be on their way quickly. (The amount requested varies depending on what the officer assumes you can pay—the year, make, and model of the car you drive being one determining factor.) Others persevere long enough to be let off with a warning only. The key to success, in this case, is a combination of calm and patience.

## RENTAL CARS

Mexico manufactures Chrysler, Ford, General Motors, Honda, Nissan, and Volkswagen vehicles. With the exception of Volkswagen, you can get the same kind of midsize and luxury cars in Mexico that you can rent in the United States and Canada. Economy usually refers to a Dodge i10 or similar, which may or may not come with air-conditioning or automatic transmission.

It can really pay to shop around: in Puerto Vallarta, rates for a compact car (Chevrolet Aveo or similar) with air-conditioning, manual transmission, and unlimited mileage range from $19 a day and $120 a week to $50 a day and $300–$400 a week, excluding insurance. Full-coverage insurance varies greatly depending on the deductible, but averages $25–$40 a day. As a rule, stick with the major companies because they tend to be more reliable.

You can also hire a taxi with a driver (who generally doubles as a tour guide) through your hotel. The going rate is about $22 an hour without crossing state lines. Limousine service runs about $65 an hour and up, with a three- to five-hour minimum.

In Mexico the minimum driving age is 18, but most rental-car agencies have a surcharge for drivers under 25. Your own country's driver's license is perfectly acceptable.

Surcharges for additional drivers are around $5 per day plus tax. Children's car seats run about the same, but not all companies have them.

## CAR-RENTAL INSURANCE

You must carry Mexican auto insurance, at the very least liability as well as coverage against physical damage to the vehicle and theft at your discretion, depending on what, if anything, your own auto insurance (or credit card, if you use it to rent a car) includes. For rental cars, all insurance will all be dealt with through the rental company.

Bucerías. From downtown south to Mismaloya it's about $5 to Conchas Chinas, $10–$12 to the hotels of the Zona Hotelera, $12 to Mismaloya, and $15 to Boca de Tomatlán. You can easily hail a cab on the street. Taxi Tel Flamingos and others provide 24-hour service.

## 🚕 Taxi

PV taxis aren't metered and instead charge by zones. Most of the larger hotels have rate sheets, and taxi drivers should produce them upon request. Tipping isn't necessary unless the driver helps you with your bags, in which case a few pesos are appropriate.

The minimum fare is 40 pesos (about $3), but if you don't ask, you'll probably be overcharged. Negotiate a price in advance for out-of-town and hourly services as well; many drivers will start by asking how much you want to pay or how much others have charged you to get a sense of your street-smarts. The usual hourly rate at this writing was 300 pesos per hour. In all cases, if you are unsure of what a fare should be, ask your hotel's front-desk personnel.

The ride from downtown to the airport or to Marina Vallarta costs about $10; it's $20 to Nuevo Vallarta and $25 to

# Essentials

## ⊕ Customs and Duties

Upon entering Mexico, you'll be given a baggage declaration form and asked to itemize what you're bringing into the country. You are allowed to bring in 3 liters of spirits or wine for personal use; 400 cigarettes, 25 cigars, or 200 grams of tobacco; a reasonable amount of perfume for personal use, and gift items not to exceed a total of $500. If driving across the U.S. border, gift items shouldn't exceed $75, although foreigners aren't usually hassled about this. ■TIP➜ **Although the much-publicized border violence doesn't affect travelers, it is real. To be safe don't linger long at the border.**

You aren't allowed to bring firearms, ammunition, meat, vegetables, plants, fruit, or flowers into the country. You can bring in one of each of the following items without paying taxes: a cell phone, a camera, a musical instrument, a laptop computer, and a portable copier or printer.

Mexico also allows you to bring a cat or dog, if you have two things: (1) a pet health certificate signed by a registered veterinarian in the United States and issued not more than 72 hours before the animal enters Mexico; and (2) a pet vaccination certificate showing that the animal has been treated (as applicable) for rabies, hepatitis, distemper, and leptospirosis.

For more information or information on bringing other animals, contact the Mexican consulate, which has branches in many major American cities as well as border towns. To find the consulate nearest you, check the Ministry of Foreign Affairs website (go to the "Servicios Consulares" option).

## ⊕ Dining

There are many good hotel-based restaurants in PV, but most of the city's top spots are independent and can be found in El Centro or Zona Romántica. There are also several good spots in Marina Vallarta and north along the Riviera Nayarit.

**Beach Dining:** For those who prefer dining alfresco (and wearing flip-flops), almost every popular beach has a *palapa* shanty or two selling fish fillets and snacks, sodas, and beer.

**Cuisine:** Everything from haute cuisine to casual fare is available. Some of the best food is found outside of fancy restaurants and familiar chain eateries at the streetside tacos stalls and neighborhood *fondas*, unassuming spots serving Mexican comfort food.

**Prices:** Most restaurants offer lunch deals with special menus at great prices, though at more traditional spots, the lunch menu may not be available before 1 or 1:30 pm. If you're dining at a small restaurant or beachside bar, make sure to have some bills in your wallet; these casual places tend to be cash-only.

**Restaurant-lounges:** Many PV restaurants combine dining and dancing, with a ground-floor eatery and a dance club above.

## ⚠ Emergencies

If you get into a scrape with the law, you can call your nearest consulate; U.S. citizens can also call the Overseas Citizens Services Center in the United States.

#  Health

## FOOD AND DRINK

In Mexico the biggest health risk is *turista* (traveler's diarrhea), caused by consuming contaminated fruit, vegetables, or water. To minimize risks, avoid questionable-looking street stands and bad-smelling food even in the toniest establishments; and if you're not sure of a restaurant's standards, pass up *ceviche* (raw fish cured in lemon juice) and raw vegetables that haven't been peeled (or that *can't* be peeled, like lettuce and tomatoes).

Drink only bottled water or water that has been boiled for at least 20 minutes, even when you're brushing your teeth. *Agua mineral* or *agua con gas* means mineral or carbonated water, and *agua purificada* means purified water. Hotels with water-purification systems will post signs to that effect in the rooms.

Despite these warnings, keep in mind that Puerto Vallarta, Nuevo Vallarta, and the Costalegre have virtually no industry beyond tourism and are unlikely to kill (or seriously distress) the geese that lay their golden eggs. Some people choose to bend the rules about eating at street stands and consuming fresh fruits and chopped lettuce or cabbage, as there's no guarantee that you won't get sick at a five-star resort and have a delicious, healthful meal at a shack by the sea. If fish or seafood smells or tastes bad, send it back and ask for something different.

Don't fret about ice: Tourist-oriented hotels and restaurants, and even most of those geared toward the locals, use purified water for ice, drinks, and washing vegetables. Many alleged cases of food poisoning are due instead to hangovers or excessive drinking in the strong sun. But whenever you're in doubt, ask questions about the origins of food and water and, if you feel unsure, err on the side of safety.

Mild cases of *turista* may respond to Imodium (known generically as loperamide), Lomotil, or Pepto-Bismol (not as strong), all of which you can buy over the counter; keep in mind, though, that these drugs can complicate more serious illnesses. You'll need to replace fluids, so drink plenty of purified water or tea; chamomile tea (*te de manzanilla*) is a good folk remedy, and it's readily available in restaurants throughout Mexico.

In severe cases, rehydrate yourself with Gatorade or a salt-sugar solution (½ teaspoon salt and 4 tablespoons sugar per quart of water). If your fever and diarrhea last longer than a day or two, see a doctor—you may have picked up a parasite or disease that requires prescription medication.

## MEDICAL CARE

All modern hospitals accept various types of foreign health insurance and traveler's insurance. Some of the recommended, privately owned hospitals are Hospital San Javier Marina and CMQ. Although most small towns have at least a clinic, travelers are usually more comfortable traveling to the major hospitals than using these clinics.

*Farmacias* (pharmacies) are the most convenient place for such common medicines as *aspirina* (aspirin) or *jarabe para la tos* (cough syrup). You'll be able to find many U.S. brands (e.g., Tylenol, Pepto-Bismol), but don't plan on buying your favorite prescription or nonprescription sleep aid, for example. The same brands and even drugs aren't always available. Prescriptions must be issued by a Mexican doctor to be legal; you can often get prescriptions inexpensively from local doctors located near the pharmacy. You

2

Travel Smart ESSENTIALS

# Essentials

can bring your own medications into the country (as long as you are not into heavy doses of morphine or something like that), but if you need to get more during your stay, you will have to explain to a local doctor your situation and the specific drugs you need, so he can provide you with a new Mexican prescription, which will be valid in any pharmacy in the country.

Pharmacies are usually open daily 9 am to 10 pm; on Sunday and in some small towns they may close several hours earlier. In neighborhoods or smaller towns where there are no 24-hour drug stores, local pharmacies take turns staying open 24 hours so that there's usually at least one open on any given night—it's called the *farmacia de turno*. The Farmacias Guadalajara chain is found throughout the Riviera Nayarit and Puerto Vallarta, and most are open 24 hours; the website provides a full list of all branches.

## MEDICAL INSURANCE AND ASSISTANCE

Consider buying trip insurance with medical-only coverage. Neither Medicare nor some private insurers cover medical expenses anywhere outside of the United States. Medical-only policies typically reimburse you for medical care (excluding that related to preexisting conditions) and hospitalization abroad, and provide for evacuation. You still have to pay the bills and await reimbursement from the insurer, though.

Another option is to sign up with a medical-evacuation assistance company. Membership gets you doctor referrals, emergency evacuation or repatriation, 24-hour hotlines for medical consultation, and other assistance. International SOS Assistance Emergency and AirMed International provide evacuation services and medical referrals. MedjetAssist offers medical evacuation.

## OTHER ISSUES

According to the CDC, there's a limited risk of malaria and other insect-carried or parasite-caused illnesses in certain areas of Mexico (largely but not exclusively rural and tropical coastal areas). In most urban or easily accessible areas you need not worry about malaria, but dengue fever is found with increasing frequency. If you're traveling to remote areas or simply prefer to err on the side of caution, check with the CDC's International Travelers' Hotline. Malaria and dengue are both carried by mosquitoes; in areas where these illnesses are prevalent, use insect-repellent coiling, clothing, and sprays/lotion. Also consider taking antimalarial pills if you're doing serious adventure activities in tropical and subtropical areas.

Make sure your polio and diphtheria–tetanus shots are up-to-date well before your trip. Hepatitis A and typhoid are transmitted through unclean food or water. Gamma-globulin shots prevent hepatitis; an inoculation is available for typhoid, although it's not 100% effective.

Caution is advised when venturing out in the Mexican sun. Sunbathers lulled by a slightly overcast sky or the sea breezes can be burned badly in just 20 minutes. To avoid overexposure, use strong sunscreens, sit under a shade umbrella, and avoid the peak sun hours of noon to 3. Sunscreen, including many American brands, can be found in pharmacies, supermarkets, and resort gift shops.

## PESTS

Mosquitoes are most prevalent during the rainy season, when it's best to use mosquito repellent daily, even in the city; if you're in the jungle or wet places and lack strong repellent, consider covering up well or going indoors at dusk (called the "mosquito hour" by locals).

An excellent brand of *repelente de insectos* (insect repellent) called OFF is readily available; do not use it on children under age 2. Repellents that are not at least 10% DEET or picaridin are not effective here. If you're hiking in the jungle or boggy areas, wear repellent and long pants and sleeves; if you're camping in the jungle, use a mosquito net and invest in a package of *espirales contra mosquitos,* mosquito coils, which are sold in *farmacias* and *tlalpalerías* (hardware stores).

## ⊙ Hours of Operation

Banks are generally open weekdays 9 am to 4 pm. In Puerto Vallarta most are open until 4, and some of the larger banks keep a few branches open Saturday from 9 or 10 to 1 or 2:30; however, the extended hours are often for deposits or check cashing only. HSBC is the one chain that stays open for longer hours; on weekdays it is open 8 to 7 and on Saturday from 8 to 3. Government offices are usually open to the public weekdays 9 to 3; along with banks and most private offices, they're closed on national holidays.

Some gas stations, like those near major thoroughfares, are open 24 hours a day. Those that are not are normally open 6 am–10 pm daily.

Stores are generally open weekdays and Saturday from 9 or 10 to 5 or 7; in resort areas, those stores geared to tourists may stay open until 9 or 10 at night and all day on Saturday; some are open on Sunday as well, but it's good to call ahead before making a special trip. Some more traditional shops close for a two-hour lunch break, roughly 2–4. Airport shops are open seven days a week.

## HOLIDAYS

Banks and government offices close on January 1, February 5 (Constitution Day), March 21 (Benito Juárez's birthday), May 1 (Labor Day), September 16 (Independence Day), November 20 (Revolution Day), and December 25 (Christmas). They may also close on unofficial holidays, such as Day of the Dead (November 1–2), Virgin of Guadalupe Day (December 12), and during Holy Week (the days leading to Easter Sunday). Government offices usually have reduced hours and staff from Christmas through New Year's Day.

## LODGING

Puerto Vallarta is the center for area beach hotels. Look for smaller budget hotels downtown, and oceanfront high-rise hotels to the north in the Hotel Zone, Marina Vallarta, and Nuevo Vallarta. Even farther north, Riviera Nayarit is where to go for unique B&Bs, boutique hotels, and some truly luxurious villas.

**Boutique Hotels:** Small boutique hotels are another option in PV, especially in the Zona Romántica and El Centro.

**Chain Hotels:** In PV these have excellent rates and can be good last-minute options. Chains include the Holiday Inn/InterContinental Group, Marriott, Sheraton, and various Starwood chains, like Westin and St. Regis.

**Apartments/Villas:** When shared by a few couples, a spacious villa can save you a lot on upscale lodging and on meals. Villas often come with great amenities like stereo systems, pools, maid service, and air-conditioning.

# Essentials

##  Mail

The Mexican postal system is notoriously slow and unreliable; letters usually arrive in one piece (albeit late), but never send packages through the postal service or expect to receive them, as they may be stolen. Instead, use a courier service or MexPost, the more reliable branch of the Mexican Postal Service.

Post offices (*oficinas de correos*) are found in even the smallest villages. International postal service is all airmail, but even so, your letter will take anywhere from 10 days to eight weeks to arrive. Service within Mexico can be equally slow. It costs 10.5 MXN (about 80¢) to send a postcard or letter weighing less than 20 grams to the United States or Canada; it's 13 MXN (97¢) to Europe and 14.5 MXN ($1.08) to Australia and New Zealand.

### SHIPPING PACKAGES

FedEx, DHL, Estafeta, and United Parcel Service (UPS) are available in major cities and many resort areas. It's best to send all packages using one of these services. These companies offer office or hotel pickup with 24-hour advance notice (sometimes less, depending on when you call) and are very reliable. From Puerto Vallarta to large U.S. cities, for example, the minimum charge is around $30 for an envelope weighing 227 grams (½ pound) or less.

## ⓢ Money

Prices in this book are quoted most often in U.S. dollars. Some services in Mexico quote prices in dollars, others in pesos. Because of the current fluctuation in the dollar/peso market, prices may be different from those listed here, but we've done our best to give accurate rates.

| Item | Average Cost |
| --- | --- |
| Cup of Coffee | 80¢–$2.50 |
| Glass of Wine | $3.50–$8 |
| Bottle of Beer | $1–$3 |
| Sandwich | $2.50–$5 |
| One-Mile Taxi Ride | $3 |
| Museum Admission | $1 |

A stay in one of Puerto Vallarta's top hotels can cost more than $350, but if you aren't wedded to standard creature comforts, you can spend as little as $40 a day on room, board, and local transportation. Lodgings are less expensive in the charming but unsophisticated mountain towns like San Sebastián del Oeste.

You can get away with a tab of $50 for two at a wonderful restaurant (although it's also easy to pay more). The good news is that there are hotels and eateries for every budget, and inexpensive doesn't necessarily mean bargain basement. This guide recommends some excellent places to stay, eat, and play for extremely reasonable prices.

Prices throughout this guide are given for adults. Substantially reduced fees are almost always available for children, students, and senior citizens.

### ATMS AND BANKS

ATMs (*cajeros automáticos*) are widely available, with Star, Cirrus, and Plus the most frequently found networks. Your own bank will probably charge a fee for using ATMs abroad; the foreign bank you use may also charge a fee. You'll usually get a better rate of exchange at an ATM, however, than you will at a currency-exchange office or at a teller window. And extracting funds as you need them is a safer option than carrying around a large amount of cash.

Many Mexican ATMs cannot accept PINs with more than four digits. If yours is longer, change your PIN to four digits before you leave home. If your PIN is fine yet your transaction still can't be completed, chances are that the computer lines are busy or that the machine has run out of money or is being serviced. Don't give up.

For cash advances, plan to use Visa or MasterCard, as many Mexican ATMs don't accept American Express. Cash advances are allowed at most local ATMs, however it's the most expensive way to get your money. It may be better to leave cash advances just for emergencies. Large banks with reliable ATMs include Banamex, HSBC, BBVA Bancomer, Santander, Banorte, and Scotiabank Inverlat. Some banks no longer exchange traveler's checks; if you carry these, make sure they are in smaller denominations ($20s or $50s) to make it more likely that hotels or shops will accept them if need be. Travelers must have their passport or other official identification in order to change traveler's checks.

## CREDIT CARDS

Credit cards are accepted in Puerto Vallarta and at major hotels and restaurants in outlying areas. Smaller, less expensive restaurants and shops tend to take only cash. Note that many doctors, including many in modern facilities, only accept cash. In general, credit cards aren't accepted in small towns and villages, except in some hotels. The most widely accepted cards are MasterCard and Visa.

When shopping, you can often get better prices if you pay with cash, particularly in small shops. But you'll receive wholesale exchange rates when you make purchases with credit cards. These exchange rates are usually better than those that banks give you for changing money. U.S. banks charge their customers a foreign

transaction fee for using their credit card abroad. The decision to pay cash or to use a credit card might depend on whether the establishment in which you are making a purchase finds bargaining for prices acceptable, and whether you want the safety net of your card's purchase protection. To avoid fraud or errors, it's wise to make sure that "pesos" is clearly marked on all credit-card receipts.

Before you leave for Mexico, contact your credit-card company to alert them to your travel plans and to get lost-card phone numbers that work in Mexico; the standard toll-free numbers often don't work abroad. Carry these numbers separately from your wallet so you'll have them if you need to call to report lost or stolen cards. American Express, MasterCard, and Visa note the international number for card-replacement calls on the back of their cards.

## CURRENCY AND EXCHANGE

Mexican currency comes in denominations of 20-, 50-, 100-, 200-, and 500-peso bills. Coins come in denominations of 1, 2, 5, 10, and 20 pesos and 20 and 50 centavos. (Twenty-centavo coins are only rarely seen.) Many of the coins are very similar, so check carefully; bills, however, are different colors and easily distinguished.

U.S. dollar bills (but not coins) are widely accepted in tourist-oriented shops and restaurants in Puerto Vallarta. Pay in pesos where possible, however, for better prices. Although in larger hotels U.S. dollars are welcome as tips, it's generally better to tip in pesos so that service personnel don't have to go to the bank to exchange currency.

At this writing, the exchange rate was 18.95 pesos to the U.S. dollar. ATM transaction fees may be higher abroad than at home, but ATM exchange rates are the

# Essentials

best because they're based on wholesale rates offered only by major banks. Most ATMs allow a maximum withdrawal of $300 to $400 per transaction. Banks and *casas de cambio* (money-exchange bureaus) have the second-best exchange rates. The difference from one place to another is usually only a few pesos.

Some banks change money on weekdays only until 1 or 3 pm (though they stay open until 4 or 5, or later). Casas de cambio generally stay open until 6 or later and often operate on weekends; they usually have competitive rates and much shorter lines. By law, no more than $300 can be exchanged per person per day, so plan in advance. Some hotels exchange money, but they give a poor exchange rate.

You can do well at most airport exchange booths, though not as well as at the ATMs. You'll do even worse at bus stations, in hotels, in restaurants, or in stores.

When changing money, count your bills before leaving the window of the bank or casa de cambio, and don't accept any partially torn or taped-together notes: You won't be able to use them anywhere. Also, many shop and restaurant owners are unable to make change for large bills. Enough of these encounters may compel you to request *billetes chicos* (small bills) when you exchange money. It's wise to have a cache of smaller bills and coins to use at these more humble establishments to avoid having to wait around while the merchant runs off to seek change.

## 🗂 Packing

High-style sportswear, cotton slacks and walking shorts, and plenty of colorful sundresses are the palette of clothing you'll see in PV. Bring lightweight sportswear, bathing suits, and cover-ups for the beach. In addition to shorts, pack at least a pair or two of lightweight long pants.

Men may want to bring a lightweight suit or slacks and blazers for fancier restaurants (although very few have dress codes). For women, dresses of cotton, linen, or other lightweight, breathable fabrics are recommended. Puerto Vallarta restaurants are extremely tolerant of casual dress, but it never hurts to exceed expectations.

The sun can be fierce; bring a sun hat and sunscreen for the beach and for sightseeing. You'll need a sweater or jacket to cope with hotel and restaurant air-conditioning, which can be glacial, and for occasional cool spells. A lightweight jacket is a necessity in winter, and pack an umbrella, even in summer, for unexpected rainstorms.

Bring along tissue packs in case you hit a place where the toilet paper has run out. You'll find familiar toiletries and hygiene products, as well as condoms, in shops in PV and in most rural areas.

## 🌐 Passports and Visas

U.S. citizens reentering the United States by land or sea are required to have documents that comply with WHTI (Western Hemisphere Travel Initiative), most commonly a U.S. passport, a passport card, a trusted traveler card (such as NEXUS, SENTRI, or FAST), or an enhanced driver's license. The U.S. passport card is smaller than a traditional passport (think wallet size), cheaper, and valid for just as long, but you can't use it for travel by air.

Upon entering Mexico, all visitors must get a tourist card. If you're arriving by plane from the United States or Canada, the standard tourist card will be given to you on the plane. They're also available through travel agents and Mexican consulates and at the border if you're entering by land.

■ TIP→ **You're given a portion of the tourist card form upon entering Mexico. Keep track of this documentation throughout your trip; you will need it when you depart. You'll be asked to hand it, your ticket, and your passport to airline representatives at the gate when boarding for departure.**

If you lose your tourist card, plan to spend some time (and about $15) sorting it out with Mexican officials at the airport on departure.

A tourist card costs about $20. The fee is generally tacked on to the price of your airline ticket; if you enter by land or boat you'll have to pay the fee separately. You're exempt from the fee if you enter by sea and stay less than 72 hours, or by land and do not stray past the 26- to 30-km (16- to 18-mile) checkpoint into the country's interior.

Tourist cards and visas are valid from 15 to 180 days, at the discretion of the immigration officer at your point of entry (90 days for Australians). Americans, Canadians, New Zealanders, and the British may request up to 180 days for a tourist card or visa extension. The extension fee is about $20, and the process can be time-consuming. There's no guarantee that you'll get the extension you're requesting. If you're planning an extended stay, plead with the immigration official for the maximum allowed days at the time of entry. It will save you time and money later.

■ TIP→ **Mexico has some of the strictest policies about children entering the country. Minors traveling with one parent need notarized permission from the absent parent. And all children, including infants,**

**must have proof of citizenship (the same as adults;** *above* ■ TIP→ **) for travel to Mexico.**

If you're a single parent traveling with children up to age 18, you must have a notarized letter from the other parent stating that the child has his or her permission to leave the country. The child must be carrying the original letter—not a facsimile or scanned copy—as well as proof of the parent/child relationship (usually a birth certificate or court document), and an original custody decree, if applicable. If the other parent is deceased or the child has only one legal parent, a notarized statement saying so must be obtained as proof. In addition, you must fill out a tourist card for each child over the age of 10 traveling with you.

## ✚ Safety

Horror stories about drug-cartel killings and border violence are making big news these days, but Puerto Vallarta is many hundreds of miles away. Imagine not going to visit the Florida Keys because of reports of violence in a bad section of New York City. Still, Puerto Vallarta is no longer the innocent of years gone by; pickpocketing and the occasional mugging can be a concern, and precaution is in order here as elsewhere. Store only enough money in your wallet or bag to cover the day's spending. And don't flash big wads of money or leave valuables like cameras unattended. Leave your passport and other valuables you don't need in your hotel's safe.

Bear in mind that reporting a crime to the police is often a frustrating experience unless you speak good Spanish and have a great deal of patience. If you're victimized, contact your local consulate or your embassy in Mexico City.

# Essentials

One of the most serious threats to your safety is local drivers. Although pedestrians have the right-of-way, drivers disregard this law. And more often than not, drivers who hit pedestrians drive away as fast as they can without stopping, to avoid jail. Many Mexican drivers don't carry auto insurance, so you'll have to shoulder your own medical expenses. Pedestrians should be extremely cautious of all traffic, especially city bus drivers, who often drive with truly reckless abandon.

If you're on your own, consider using only your first initial and last name when registering at your hotel. Solo travelers, or women traveling with other women rather than men, may be subjected to *piropos* (flirtatious compliments). Piropos are one thing, but more aggressive harassment is another. In the rare event that the situation seems to be getting out of hand, don't hesitate to ask someone for help. If you express outrage, you should find no shortage of willing defenders.

##  Taxes

Mexico charges an airport departure tax of $18 or the peso equivalent for international and domestic flights. This tax is included in the price of your ticket, but check to be certain. Traveler's checks and credit cards aren't accepted at the airport as payment for this, but U.S. dollars are.

Puerto Vallarta and environs have a value-added tax of 16%, called IVA (*impuesto al valor agregado*). It's often waived for cash purchases, or it's incorporated into the price. When comparing hotel prices, be sure to find out whether yours includes or excludes IVA and any service charges. Additionally, Jalisco and Nayarit charge a 2% tax on accommodations,

the funds from which are used for tourism promotion. Other taxes and charges apply for phone calls made from your hotel room.

## ⊙ Time

Puerto Vallarta, Guadalajara, and the rest of Jalisco State fall into Central Standard Time (the same as Mexico City). Nayarit and other parts of the northwest coast are on Mountain Standard Time.

However, Nuevo Vallarta, Bucerías, La Cruz de Huanacaxtle, Punta Mita, and most of the Riviera Nayarit have been adjusted to stay in the same time zone as Puerto Vallarta, avoiding the confusions of past years. Bear in mind that Mexico does observe daylight saving time, but not on the same schedule as the United States.

## 🕑 Tipping

When tipping in Mexico, remember that the minimum wage is just under $5 a day. Waiters and bellmen may not be at the bottom of that heap, but they're not very far up, either. Those who work in international chain hotels think in dollars and know, for example, that in the United States porters are tipped about $2 a bag; they tend to expect the equivalent.

## Tipping Guidelines for Puerto Vallarta

| | |
|---|---|
| Bartender | 10% to 15% of the bill |
| Bellhop | 10 to 30 pesos (roughly 80¢ to $2) per bag, depending on the level of the hotel |
| Hotel Concierge | 30 pesos or more, if he or she performs a service for you |
| Hotel Doorman | 10 to 20 pesos if he helps you get a cab |
| Hotel Maid | 10 to 30 pesos a day (either daily or at the end of your stay); make sure the maid gets it, and not the person who checks the minibar prior to your departure |
| Hotel Room-Service Waiter | 10 to 20 pesos per delivery, even if a service charge has been added |
| Porter/Skycap at Airport | 10 to 20 pesos per bag |
| Restroom Attendant | 5 pesos |
| Taxi Driver | cab drivers aren't normally tipped; give them 10 to 20 pesos if they help with your bags |
| Tour Guide | 10% of the cost of the tour |
| Valet Parking Attendant | 10 to 20 pesos but only when you get your car |
| Waiter | 10% to 15%; nothing additional if a service charge is added to the bill |

# Great Itineraries

Each of these itineraries fills one day. Together they touch on some of PV's quintessential experiences, from shopping to getting outdoors to just relaxing at the best beaches and spas.

## THE ZONE

Head south of downtown to the Zona Romántica for a day of excellent shopping and dining. Stop at Isla del Río Cuale for trinkets and T-shirts, and have an island breakfast overlooking the stream at the River Cafe.

■TIP→ **Most of the stores in the neighborhood will either ship your oversize prizes for you or expertly pack them and recommend reputable shipping companies.**

Crossing the pedestrian bridge nearest the bay, drop nonshoppers at Los Muertos Beach. They can watch the fishermen on the small pier, lie in the sun, sit in the shade with a good book, or walk south to the rocky coves of **Conchas Chinas Beach,** which is good for snorkeling when the water is calm. Meanwhile, shoppers head to **Calle Basilio Badillo** and surrounding streets for folk art, housewares, antiques, clothing, and accessories. End the day back at Los Muertos with dinner, drinks, and live music.

■TIP→ **Some of the musicians at beachfront restaurants work for the restaurant; others are freelancers. If a roving musician (or six) asks what you'd like to hear, find out the price of a song. Fifty pesos (around $4) is typical.**

## DOWNTOWN

Puerto Vallarta hasn't much at all in the way of museums, but with a little legwork, you can get a bit of history. Learn about the area's first inhabitants at the tiny but tidy **Museo del Cuale** (closed Sunday), with information in English. From the museum, head downtown along the newest section of the **malecón,** which crosses the river. About four blocks north, check out the action in the main plaza and Los Arcos amphitheater. At the **Iglesia de Nuestra Señora de Guadalupe,** you can pay your respects to the patron saint of the city (and the country).

Strolling farther north along the malecón is like walking through a sculpture garden: Look for the statue of a boy riding a sea horse (it's become PV's trademark), and *La Nostalgia,* a statue of a seated couple, by noted PV artist Ramiz Barquet. Three figures climb a ladder extending into the air in Sergio Bustamante's *In Search of Reason.* One of the most elaborate sculptures is by Alejandro Colunga: *Rotunda del Mar* has more than a dozen fantastic figures—some with strange, alien appendages—seated on chairs and pedestals of varying heights.

## A DAY OF GOLF AND STEAM

Puerto Vallarta is one of Mexico's best golfing destinations. And what better way to top off a day of play than with a steam, soak, and massage? At the southern end of the Costalegre, Tamarindo has a great course (18 holes) and a very good spa. The closest spas to the greens of Marina Vallarta and the Vista Vallarta are those at the Westin Regina and the Marriott, which has gorgeous new facilities. The El Tigre course is associated with the Paradise Village resort, whose reasonably priced spa is open also to those who golf at Mayan Palace, just up the road.

■TIP➜ **Ask your concierge (or look online) to find out how far ahead you can reserve, and then try for the earliest possible tee time to beat the heat. If the course you choose doesn't have a club pool, you can have lunch and hang at the pool at the resorts suggested above or get a massage, facial, or other treatment (always reserve ahead).**

## A DIFFERENT RESORT SCENE

If you've got wheels, explore a different sort of beach resort. After breakfast, grab beach togs, sunscreen, and other essentials for a day at a beach north of town. Before heading out, those with a sweet tooth should make a pit stop at PV's Pie in the Sky, which has excellent pie, chocolate, and other sugar fixes. (There's another Pie in the Sky in Bucerías, as well as a Los Chatos cake and ice-cream shop.)

About an hour north of PV, join Mexican families on the beach at **Rincón de Guayabitos,** on attractive Jaltemba Bay. Play in the mild surf; walk the pretty, long beach; or take a ride in a glass-bottom boat to **El Islote,** an islet with a small restaurant and snorkeling opportunities. Vendors on Guayabitos beach sell grilled fish, sweet breads, and chilled coconuts and watermelon from their brightly colored stands.

On the way back south, stop in the small town of **San Francisco** (aka San Pancho) for dinner. You can't go wrong at La Ola Rica. In high season and especially on weekend evenings, they will probably have live music.

■TIP➜ **Take a water taxi out for a look at El Islote, where with luck you might spot a whale between December and March.**

# Helpful Phrases in Spanish

## BASICS

| | | |
|---|---|---|
| Hello | Hola | oh-lah |
| Yes/no | Sí/no | see/no |
| Please | Por favor | pore fah-vore |
| May I? | ¿Puedo? | Pweh-doh |
| Thank you | Gracias | Grah-see-as |
| You're welcome | De nada | day nah-dah |
| I'm sorry | Lo siento | lo see-en-toh |
| Good morning! | ¡Buenos días! | bway-nohs dee-ahs |
| Good evening! | ¡Buenas tardes! (after 2pm) | bway-nahs-tar-dess |
| | ¡Buenas noches! (after 8pm) | bway-nahs no-chess |
| Good-bye! | ¡Adiós!/¡Hasta luego! | ah-dee-ohss/ah -stah lwe-go |
| Mr./Mrs. | Señor/Señora | sen-yor/sen-yohr-ah |
| Miss | Señorita | sen-yo-ree-tah |
| Pleased to meet you | Mucho gusto | moo-cho goose-toh |
| How are you? | ¿Cómo estás? | koh-moh ehs-tahs |

## NUMBERS

| | | |
|---|---|---|
| one | un, uno | oon, oo-no |
| two | dos | dos |
| three | tres | tress |
| four | cuatro | kwah-tro |
| five | cinco | sink-oh |
| six | seis | saice |
| seven | siete | see-et-eh |
| eight | ocho | o-cho |
| nine | nueve | new-eh-vey |
| ten | diez | dee-es |
| eleven | once | ohn-seh |
| twelve | doce | doh-seh |
| thirteen | trece | treh-seh |
| fourteen | catorce | ka-tohr-seh |
| fifteen | quince | keen-seh |
| sixteen | dieciséis | dee-es-ee-saice |
| seventeen | diecisiete | dee-es-ee-see-et-eh |
| eighteen | dieciocho | dee-es-ee-o-cho |
| nineteen | diecinueve | dee-es-ee-new-ev-eh |
| twenty | veinte | vain-teh |
| twenty-one | veintiuno | vain-te-oo-noh |
| thirty | treinta | train-tah |
| forty | cuarenta | kwah-ren-tah |
| fifty | cincuenta | seen-kwen-tah |
| sixty | sesenta | sess-en-tah |
| seventy | setenta | set-en-tah |
| eighty | ochenta | oh-chen-tah |
| ninety | noventa | no-ven-tah |
| one hundred | cien | see-en |
| one thousand | mil | meel |
| one million | un millón | oon meel-yohn |

## COLORS

| | | |
|---|---|---|
| black | negro | neh-groh |
| blue | azul | ah-sool |
| brown | café | kah-fehg |
| green | verde | ver-deh |
| orange | naranja | na-rahn-hah |
| red | rojo | roh-hoh |
| white | blanco | blahn-koh |
| yellow | amarillo | ah-mah-ree-yoh |

## DAYS OF THE WEEK

| | | |
|---|---|---|
| Sunday | domingo | doe-meen-goh |
| Monday | lunes | loo-ness |
| Tuesday | martes | mahr-tess |
| Wednesday | miércoles | me-air-koh-less |
| Thursday | jueves | hoo-ev-ess |
| Friday | viernes | vee-air-ness |
| Saturday | sábado | sah-bah-doh |

## MONTHS

| | | |
|---|---|---|
| January | enero | eh-neh-roh |
| February | febrero | feh-breh-roh |
| March | marzo | mahr-soh |
| April | abril | ah-breel |
| May | mayo | my-oh |
| June | junio | hoo-nee-oh |
| July | julio | hoo-lee-yoh |
| August | agosto | ah-ghost-toh |
| September | septiembre | sep-tee-em-breh |
| October | octubre | oak-too-breh |
| November | noviembre | no-vee-em-breh |
| December | diciembre | dee-see-em-breh |

## USEFUL WORDS AND PHRASES

| | | |
|---|---|---|
| Do you speak English? | ¿Habla Inglés? | ah-blah in-glehs |
| I don't speak Spanish. | No hablo español | no ah-bloh es-pahn-yol |
| I don't understand. | No entiendo | no en-tee-en-doh |
| I understand. | Entiendo | en-tee-en-doh |
| I don't know. | No sé | no seh |
| I'm American. | Soy americano (americana) | soy ah-meh-ree-kah-no (ah-meh-ree-kah-nah) |
| What's your name? | ¿Cómo se llama ? | koh-mo seh yah-mah |
| My name is ... | Me llamo ... | may yah-moh |
| What time is it? | ¿Qué hora es? | keh o-rah es |
| How? | ¿Cómo? | koh-mo |
| When? | ¿Cuándo? | kwahn-doh |
| Yesterday | Ayer | ah-yehr |
| Today | hoy | oy |
| Tomorrow | mañana | mahn-yah-nah |
| Tonight | Esta noche | es-tah no-cheh |
| What? | ¿Qué? | keh |

| | | |
|---|---|---|
| What is it? | ¿Qué es esto? | keh es **es**-toh |
| Why? | ¿Por qué? | pore **keh** |
| Who? | ¿Quién? | kee-**yen** |
| Where is . . . | ¿Dónde está . . . | **dohn**-deh es-**tah** |
| . . . the bus station? | la central de autobuses? | lah sehn-**trahl** deh ow-toh-**boo**-sehs |
| . . . the subway station? | estación de metro | la es-ta-see-**on** del **meh**-tro |
| . . . the bus stop? | la parada del autobus? | la pah-**rah**-dah del ow-toh-**boos** |
| . . . the terminal? (airport) | el aeropuerto | el air-oh-**pwar**-toh |
| . . . the post office? | la oficina de correos? | la oh-fee-**see**- nah deh koh-**rreh**-os |
| . . . the bank? | el banco? | el **bahn**-koh |
| . . . the hotel? | el hotel? | el oh-**tel** |
| . . . the museum? | el museo? | el moo-**seh**-oh |
| . . . the hospital? | el hospital? | el ohss-pee-**tal** |
| . . . the elevator? | el elevador? | ehl eh-leh-bah-**dohr** |
| Where are the restrooms? | el baño? | el **bahn**-yoh |
| Here/there | Aquí/allí | ah-**key**/ah-**yee** |
| Open/closed | Abierto/cerrado | ah-bee-**er**-toh/ ser-**ah**-doh |
| Left/right | Izquierda/derecha | iss-key-**eh**-dah/ dare-**eh**-chah |
| Is it near? | ¿Está cerca? | es-**tah sehr**-kah |
| Is it far? | ¿Está lejos? | es-**tah leh**-hoss |
| I'd like . . . | Quisiera . . . | kee-see-**ehr**-ah |
| . . . a room | un cuarto/una habitación | oon **kwahr**- toh/**oo**-nah ah-bee-tah-see-**on** |
| . . . the key | la llave | lah **yah**-veh |
| . . . a newspaper | un periódico | oon pehr-ee-**oh**- dee-koh |
| . . . a stamp | un sello de correo | oon **seh**-yo deh korr-**eh**-oh |
| I'd like to buy . . . | Quisiera comprar . . . | kee-see-**ehr**-ah kohm-**prahr** |
| . . . soap | jabón | hah-**bohn** |
| . . . suntan lotion | bronceador | brohn-seh-ah-**dohr** |
| . . . envelopes | sobres | **so**-brehs |
| . . . writing paper | papel | pah-**pel** |
| . . . a postcard | una postal | oo-nah pohs-**tahl** |
| . . . a ticket | un billete (travel) | oon bee-**yee**-teh |
| | una entrada (concert etc.) | oona en-**trah**-dah |
| How much is it? | ¿Cuánto cuesta? | **kwahn**-toh **kwes**-tah |
| It's expensive/ cheap | Es caro/barato | es **kah**-roh/ bah-**rah**-toh |
| A little/a lot | Un poquito/mucho | oon poh-**kee**-toh/ **moo**-choh |
| More/less | Más/menos | mahss/**men**-ohss |
| Enough/too (much) | Suficiente/ | soo-fee-see-**en**-teh/ |
| I am ill/sick | Estoy enfermo(a) | es-**toy** en-**fehr**-moh(mah) |

| | | |
|---|---|---|
| Call a doctor | Llame a un medico | **ya**-meh ah oon med-ee-koh |
| Help! | Ayuda | ah-**yoo**-dah |
| Stop! | Pare | **pah**-reh |

**DINING OUT**

| | | |
|---|---|---|
| I'd like to reserve a table . . . | Quisiera reservar una mesa . . . | kee-**syeh**-rah rreh- sehr-**bahr** oo-nah **meh**-sah . . . |
| . . . for two people. | para dos personas. | **pah**-rah dohs pehr-**soh**-nahs |
| . . . for this evening. | para esta noche. | **pah**-rah **ehs**-tah **noh**-cheh |
| . . . for 8 PM | para las ocho de la noche. | **pah**-rah lahs **oh**-choh deh lah **noh**-cheh |
| A bottle of . . . | Una botella de . . . | oo-nah bo-**teh**-yah deh |
| A cup of . . . | Una taza de . . . | oo-nah **tah**-sah deh |
| A glass of . . . | Un vaso (water, soda, etc.) de... | oon **vah**-so deh |
| | Una copa (wine, spirits, etc.) de... | oona **coh**-pah deh |
| Bill/check | La cuenta | lah **kwen**-tah |
| Bread | Pan | pahn |
| Breakfast | El desayuno | el deh-sah-**yoon**-oh |
| Butter | mantequilla | man-teh-**kee**-yah |
| Coffee | Café | kah-**feh** |
| Dinner | La cena | lah **seh**-nah |
| Fork | tenedor | ten-eh-**dor** |
| I don't eat meat | No como carne | noh koh-moh **kahr**-neh |
| I cannot eat . . . | No puedo comer . . . | noh **pweh**-doh koh-**mehr** |
| I'd like to order . . . | Quiero pedir . . . | **kee**-yehr-oh peh-**deer** |
| I'd like . . . | Me gustaría . . . | Meh goo-stah-**ee**-ah |
| I'm hungry/thirsty | Tengo hambre/sed | **Tehn**-goh **hahm**-breh/seth |
| Is service/the tip included? | ¿Está incluida la propina? | es-**tah** in-cloo-**ee**- dah lah pro-**pee**-nah |
| Knife | cuchillo | koo-**chee**-yo |
| Lunch | La comida | lah koh-**mee**-dah |
| Menu | La carta, el menú | lah **cart**-ah, el **meh-noo** |
| Napkin | servilleta | sehr-vee-**yet**-ah |
| Pepper | pimienta | pee-mee-**en**-tah |
| Plate | plato | **plah**-toh |
| Please give me . . . | Me da por favor . . . | meh dah pohr fah-**bohr** |
| Salt | sal | sahl |
| Spoon | cuchara | koo-**chah**-rah |
| Sugar | ázucar | ah-**su**-kar |
| Tea | té | teh |
| Water | agua | **ah**-gwah |
| Wine | vino | **vee**-noh |

# Festivals and Events

## JANUARY

**El Día de los Santos Reyes.** El Día de los Santos Reyes (January 6) was the day of gift-giving in Latin America until Santa Claus invaded from the North. Although many families now give gifts on Christmas or Christmas Eve, Three Kings Day is still an important celebration. The children receive token "gifts of the Magi." *Atole* (a drink of finely ground rice or corn) or hot chocolate is served along with the *rosca de reyes,* a ring-shape cake. The person whose portion contains a tiny baby Jesus figurine must host a follow-up party on Candlemass, February 2.

## FEBRUARY

**Festival de Música San Pancho.** The three-day Festival de Música San Pancho is an amalgam of the area's best regional musicians; snowbirds also participate. The free jamboree is usually held on the last weekend in February. The event has featured bluegrass, blues, jazz, funk, and standards in addition to cumbia and Mexican classics. San Pancho is 50 minutes north of downtown Puerto Vallarta. ⊕ *sanpanchomusicfestival.com.*

**Campeonato Nacional Charro Vallarta** National Charro Championship *Charros* (cowboys) and "Escaramuzas" (Charro Ladies) from all over Mexico compete in the four-day Campeonato Nacional Charro Vallarta. In addition to rope and riding tricks, there are mariachis, a parade, and exhibitions of charro-related art. ⊕ *centrodeeventosvallarta.com.*

## MAY

**Restaurant Week.** Restaurants lower their prices for two weeks at the beginning of low season during Restaurant Week, also known as the May Food Festival.

## JUNE

**Día de la Marina.** June 1 is Día de la Marina. Like other Mexican ports, PV celebrates Navy Day with free boat rides (inquire at the Terminal Marítima or the XII Zona Naval Militar, just to the south). Watch colorfully decorated boats depart to make offerings to sailors lost at sea. ⊠ *Puerto Vallarta.*

## JULY AND AUGUST

**San Antonio de Padua.** Barra de Navidad celebrates its patron saint, San Antonio de Padua, the week preceding July 13 with religious parades, mass, street parties, and fireworks. ⊠ *Barra de Navidad.*

**Cristo de los Brazos Caídos.** Cristo de los Brazos Caídos is honored August 30–September 1 in much the same way as St. Anthony. ⊠ *Puerto Vallarta.*

## SEPTEMBER

**Celebration of Independence.** The Celebration of Independence is held on September 15 and 16, beginning on the evening of September 15 with the traditional *Grito de Dolores.* It translates as "Cry of Pain," but it also references the town of Dolores Hidalgo, where the famous cry for freedom was uttered by priest Miguel Hidalgo. Late in the evening on September 15 there are mariachis, speeches, and other demonstrations of national pride. On September 16, witness parades and charros on horseback through the main streets of town. ⊠ *Puerto Vallarta.*

## OCTOBER

**Historic Center artWalk.** One of the most traditional events in downtown Vallarta is the Historic Center artWalk, which showcases artwork at several dozen galleries. The galleries stay open late, sometimes offering an appetizer or snack, wine, beer, or soft drinks. Browse among the paintings, jewelry, ceramics, glass, and folk art while hobnobbing with some of PV's most respected artists. If you don't have a map, pick one up from one of the perennially participating galleries, which include Galería Córsica I & II, Galería Colectika, Galería Pacífico, Galería Caballito de Mar, The Loft, and Galería de Ollas. This walk is held every Wednesday from 6 pm to 10 pm, from the last week of October until late May. ⊠ *Puerto Vallarta* ⊕ *www.vallartaartwalk.com.*

**Bucerías Art Walk.** North of Nuevo Vallarta, Bucerías Art Walk is on Thursday nights from 7 to 9 pm during high season: from the last week of October until late April. Participating galleries are on Boulevard Lázaro Cárdenas 62 around Calle Galeana. ⊠ *Puerto Vallarta* ⊕ *www. thebuceriasartwalk.com.*

## NOVEMBER AND DECEMBER
**International Gourmet Festival.** The International Gourmet Festival is one of PV's biggest events. ⊠ *Puerto Vallarta* ☎ *322/222–2247* ⊕ *www.festivalgourmet.com.*

**Home Tours.** Mid-November through the end of April, three-hour villa tours by the International Friendship Club get you inside the garden walls of some inspiring PV homes. English-speaking guides lead groups on air-conditioned buses Tuesday and Wednesday, from December to March. Tours depart at 10:30 am. Proceeds benefits local charities. ⊠ *Sea Monkey Restaurant, Calle Aquiles Serdan 174* ☎ *322/222–5466* ⊕ *ifctoursforvallarta. com* ⌨ *35 USD; 700 MXN per person.*

**Fiestas de la Virgen de Guadalupe.** Puerto Vallarta's most important celebration of faith—and also one of the most elaborate spectacles of the year—is Fiestas de la Virgen de Guadalupe, designed to honor the Virgin of Guadalupe, the city's patron saint and the patroness of all Mexico. Exuberance fills the air as the end of November approaches and each participating business organizes its own procession. The most elaborate ones include allegorical floats and papier-mâché *matachines,* or giant dolls (for lack of a better phrase), and culminate in their own private mass. Groups snake down Calle Juárez from the north or the south, ending at the Cathedral in Old Vallarta. ⊠ *El Centro.*

# Contacts

##  Air

**AIRLINES Aeroméxico.**
☎ *800/237–6639 in U.S.
and Canada, 55/5133–
4000 in Mexico, 322/221–
1204 in PV* ⊕ *www.aer-
omexico.com.* **Air Canada.**
☎ *888/247–2262 in U.S.
and Canada, 55/ 9138–
0280 in Mexico* ⊕ *www.
aircanada.com.* **Alaska
Airlines.** ☎ *800/252–7522
in Mexico* ⊕ *www.
alaskaair.com.* **American
Airlines.** ☎ *800/433–7300
in U.S., 01800/904–6000 in
Mexico, 322/221–1038 in
PV* ⊕ *www.aa.com.* **Delta
Airlines.** ☎ *800/221–1212
in U.S., 55/5279–0909 in
Mexico* ⊕ *www.delta.com.*
**Frontier.** ☎ *801/401–9000
in U.S.* ⊕ *www.flyfrontier.
com.* **Interjet.** ☎ *55/1102–
5555 in Mexico, 866/285–
9525 in U.S.* ⊕ *www.
interjet.com.mx.* **United
Airlines.** ☎ *800/864–8331
for U.S. and Mexico res-
ervations, 322/2210–3264
in Puerto Vallarta* ⊕ *www.
united.com.* **Volaris.**
☎ *55/1102–8000 in Mexi-
co City, 01800/122–8000
in Mexico* ⊕ *www.volaris.
com.mx.*

**AIRPORT INFORMATION
Aeropuerto Internacional
de la Ciudad de México
(Benito Juárez).** (*MEX*).
☎ *55/2482–2424,
55/2482–2400* ⊕ *www.
aicm.com.mx.* **Aeropuerto
Internacional Gustavo Díaz
Ordáz.** (*PVR*). ✉ *Tepic Hwy.
Km 7.5* ☎ *322/221–1298*

⊕ *www.aeropuer-
tosgap.com.mx/es/
puerto-vallarta-3.*

##  Bus

**BUS CONTACTS Central
Camionera.** ✉ *Bahia
Sin Nombre 363, Las
Mojoneras* ☎ *322/290–
1009.* **Estrella Blanca.**
☎ *01800/507–5500 toll-
free in Mexico* ⊕ *www.
estrellablanca.com.mx.*
**ETN.** ☎ *01800/800–0386
toll-free in Mexico,
322/290–0997 in PV*
⊕ *www.etn.com.mx*
✉ *Plaza Parabien, Av. Tepic sur 1508, Loc. 5, Nuevo
Vallarta* ☎ *322/297–7552*
⊕ *etn.com.mx.* **Primera
Plus.** ☎ *322/290–0716
in PV, 322/187–0492 in
NV* ⊕ *primeraplus.com.
mx.* **Transporte del Pacifico
(TAP).** ☎ *322/290–0119
in PV* ⊕ *tap.com.mx.*
**Vallarta Plus.** ✉ *Palma
Real 140, Marina Val-
larta* ☎ *322/221–3636,
322/306–3071* ⊕ *www.
vallartaplus.com.*

##  Car

**MAJOR RENTAL AGEN-
CIES Alamo.** ☎ *800/522–
9696 in U.S., 322/221–
3040 in PV* ⊕ *www.alamo.
com.* **Avis.** ☎ *800/331–
1084 in U.S., 322/221–1112
in PV* ⊕ *www.avis.com.*
**Budget.** ☎ *800/472–3325
in U.S., 322/221–1210 in*

*PV* ⊕ *www.budget.com.*
**Hertz.** ☎ *800/654–3001
in U.S., 999/911–8040
in PV* ⊕ *www.hertz.
com.* **National Car Rental.**
☎ *800/227–7368 in U.S.,
322/226–0069 in PV*
⊕ *www.nationalcar.com.*

##  Taxi

**TAXI COMPANY Sitio
Bucerías.** ☎ *329/298–
0714.* **Sitio Valle Dorado.**
☎ *322/297–5407.*

## 📍 Visitor Information

**Puerto Vallarta Tourism
Board & Convention and
Visitors Bureau.** ✉ *Independencia #123, ground
fl., Col. Centro, Vallarta*
☎ *322/ 222–0923 in U.S.,
01800/719–3276 in Mexico*
⊕ *www.visitpuertovallarta.
com.*

# Chapter 3

# PUERTO VALLARTA

Updated by
Luis Domínguez

| ◉ Sights | 🍴 Restaurants | 🏨 Hotels | 🛍 Shopping | 🍸 Nightlife |
|----------|---------------|-----------|------------|-------------|
| ★★★★☆ | ★★★★★ | ★★★★★ | ★★★★★ | ★★★★★ |

# WELCOME TO PUERTO VALLARTA

## TOP REASONS TO GO

★ **Legendary restaurants:** Eat barbecued snapper with your feet in the sand or chateaubriand with a killer ocean view.

★ **Adventure and indulgence:** Ride a horse, mountain bike, go four-wheeling in the mountains, dive into the sea, and relax at an elegant spa all in one day.

★ **Natural beauty:** Enjoy the physical beauty of Mexico's prettiest Pacific resort town, where cobblestone streets disappear into emerald green hills overlooking the vast, sparkling bay below.

★ **Authentic art:** PV's artists and artisans—from the Huichol tribe to expats—produce an array of exceptional folk art treasures and fine art.

★ **Diverse nightlife:** Whether you're old, young, gay, straight, mild, or wild, PV's casual and unpretentious party scene has something to entice you after dark.

★ **Mexico at its best:** From the picturesque beach town to the unparalleled luxury, PV has it all.

The original town, Old Vallarta, sits at the center of 42-km (26-mile) Bahía de Banderas, Mexico's largest bay, in Jalisco State. From here, the Sierra Madre foothills dive into the sea. Mountain-fed rivers nourish tropical deciduous forests as far north as San Blas, in Nayarit State. South of PV the hills recede from the coast, and the drier tropical thorn forest predominates south to Barra de Navidad.

**1 Zona Romántica.** South of the Cuale River, the Zona Romántica (Romantic Zone, including Co. E. Zapata) has PV's highest density of restaurants and tourist-oriented shops.

**2 El Centro.** Rising abruptly from the sea are the hilly, cobblestone streets of El Centro (Downtown), lined with white-washed homes and shops.

**3 Zona Hotelera.** Facing a busy avenue, the Zona Hotelera (Hotel Zone) has malls, businesses, and high-rise hotels.

**4 Marina Vallarta.** The shopping centers and deluxe hotels of Marina Vallarta are sandwiched between a golf course and the city's main yacht marina.

**5 Olas Altas.** On the southern edge of PV are the upscale residential neighborhoods of Amapas and Conchas Chinas, located on both sides of Highway 200.

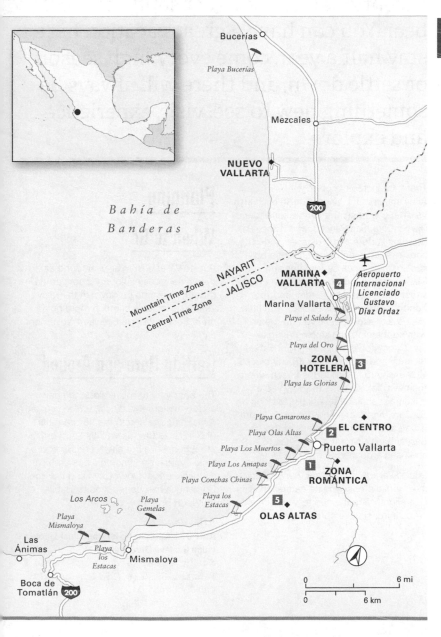

Bucerías

Playa Bucerías

Mezcales

**NUEVO VALLARTA**

200

*Bahía de Banderas*

NAYARIT

JALISCO

Mountain Time Zone

Central Time Zone

**MARINA VALLARTA** 4

Marina Vallarta

*Playa el Salado*

Aeropuerto Internacional Licenciado Gustavo Díaz Ordaz

*Playa del Oro*

**ZONA HOTELERA** 3

*Playa las Glorias*

*Playa Camarones*

*Playa Olas Altas*

2 **EL CENTRO**

*Playa Los Muertos*

Puerto Vallarta

*Playa Los Amapas*

1

**ZONA ROMÁNTICA**

*Playa Conchas Chinas*

*Playa los Estacas*

5

**OLAS ALTAS**

*Los Arcos*

*Playa Gemelas*

*Playa Mismaloya*

Las Ánimas

*Playa los Estacas*

Mismaloya

Boca de Tomatlán 200

0 ———————— 6 mi

0 ———————— 6 km

Puerto Vallarta is so much more than just another beach destination with exceptional climate, vast sands, and cold beer. You can have a great vacation here, stay half a year, come every high season, or settle down, and there will always be something new to see, visit, experience, and explore.

There are incredible petroglyphs in Altavista, about 1½ hours north of Puerto Vallarta; charming and picturesque towns like Sayulita, San Pancho, and Bucerías, loved by surfers and artists; ecological conservation zones with endangered species near Boca de Tomates and in the Marina area; various crocodile sanctuaries; and a botanical garden and zoo. Puerto Vallarta itself is packed with little places to discover once you get bored with sunbathing and sipping margaritas. The malecón has been refurbished recently and you can walk 15 city blocks all the way to Los Muertos beach where the new pier is. Along the way you'll encounter sculptures, shops, folkloric dancers, and more. The Romantic Zone is one of the trendiest areas of the city. Basilio Badillo Street is the place to eat and hang around with friends.

Puerto Vallarta is constantly reinventing itself while preserving its natural charms as a slightly chaotic, fun town that never stops surprising visitors.

# Planning

## When to Go

Puerto Vallarta is an all-year-round destination as far as exploring is concerned, though prices do go down in the rainy season and there is much more going on in Puerto Vallarta between November and May.

## Getting Here and Around

The best way to move along the bay and to explore it is by car, which you can rent. Things to see in the northern part of Banderas Bay, as well as southern attractions, are not always easily accessible by bus, and finding a bus stop can be a challenge. Downtown and the Zona Romántica can be reached by public transport or simply on foot.

### AIR

**AIRPORT Aeropuerto Internacional Licenciado Gustavo Díaz Ordaz.** ⊠ *Carr. a Tepic Km 7.5, Área Militar de Vallarta, Puerto Vallarta* ☎ *322/221–1298* ⊕ *aeropuertos-gap.com.mx.*

## AIRPORT TRANSFERS

Puerto Vallarta International Airport, officially named the Gustavo Díaz Ordaz International Airport, is well connected to the biggest airports in Mexico, the United States, and Canada. It also has a couple of connections with Europe, mainly in the United Kingdom, and other destinations during the high season. What started as a small airport with local flights had to expand quickly due to high demand from international tourists. To process out from the airport you can go to official taxi counters and buy a ticket to your zone. It is a safe but costly option (around $35). You can also get out of the airport and get on a public bus that will take you toward downtown or catch a cheaper taxi right there. Uber also operates in Puerto Vallarta and your trip to the city center will cost you around $6. Private Airport Transfers are also available in a wide range of options and prices; usually is better to make these arrangements before arriving to PV.

## BOAT

There is no public water transportation system in Puerto Vallarta but there are many water taxis and private companies with small boats and mini ferries that will take you to various beaches and islands. The most popular water destination is Yelapa and you can get there from Los Muertos Beach for about $11 or from Boca de Tomatlán for $6. The trip from Los Muertos Beach will be longer. The water taxis from Boca de Tomatlán also go to Las Animas, Quimixto, and Pizota. If you want to go to Islas Marietas, there are some companies that will take you there from Punta Mita. The access is limited to 116 people per day, so make your reservation early. If you want to go on a fishing tour, go to Marina Vallarta. There are plenty of companies that organize this type of tour, or simply a day out to sea on a yacht.

**CONTACTS Marina Vallarta.** ⊠ *Mástil 12, Marina Vallarta* ☎ *322/221–0275* ⊕ *marina-vallarta.com.mx.*

## BUS

Apart from urban buses there is a bus network that connects Puerto Vallarta with other cities. The fare ranges $1–$3 depending on the distance. If you want to travel north, take an ATM bus in front of Walmart (Boulevard Francisco Medina Ascencio 2900). They will take you to Nuevo Vallarta, Punta Mita, Bucerías, Valle de Banderas, and La Cruz de Huanacaxtle. There is always an employee with a clipboard that will be happy to help you get on the right bus. At the same bus stop, you will find white and green buses that will take you to San Francisco, Sayulita, and Rincón de Guayabitos. The buses heading to Mismaloya and Boca de Tomatlán are to be found at the South Terminal located at Constitución and Basilio Badillo. The bus to El Tuito leaves from the corner of V. Carranza and Aguacate and it stops at the Botanical Gardens. There are also intercity, often luxurious, buses that will take you to Manzanillo, Guadalajara, Mexico City, Mazatlán, and Aguascalientes. The price range is $21–$65 depending on the company and destination. They leave from the main bus terminal close to the airport.

**CONTACTS Terminal de Autobuses de Puerto Vallarta.** ⊠ *Bahía Sin Nombre 363, Puerto Vallarta* ☎ *322/290–1009.* **Vallarta Plus.** ⊠ *Av. Palma Real 140, Puerto Vallarta* ☎ *322/287–0300* ⊕ *vallartaplus.com.*

## CAR

Puerto Vallarta is not a complicated city to navigate by car; it's safe and easy, although you need to remember that people here don't follow lights and signs as strictly as in other countries. There is only one main street that crosses the city, so it's really difficult to get lost if you plan to only visit tourist spots. For left turns, however, be advised that sometimes you make them from left lanes, and sometimes from right lanes.

Sculptures stand against a stunning view of the ocean at La Rotonda del Mar on El Malecón.

In downtown areas, it's easiest to park in a garage rather than to try and find a free spot. Watch for careless scooter drivers and pedestrians crossing the street at any point. If you plan to rent a car, remember that the third-party liability insurance is obligatory now and it raises the price dramatically. It is less expensive to buy insurance online in advance.

**CONTACTS Europcar Renta de Autos en Puerto Vallarta Aeropuerto.** ✉ *Aeropuerto Internacional Licenciado Gustavo Díaz Ordaz, Puerto Vallarta* ☎ *322/209–0921* ⊕ *europcar.com.mx.* **Thrifty Car Rental.** ✉ *Blvd. Francisco Medina Ascencio 7926, Puerto Vallarta* ☎ *322/221–2984* ⊕ *thrifty. com.mx.*

## PUBLIC TRANSPORT

The public transportation in Vallarta improved over the last few years although it may still be very different from the ones in the U.S., Canada, or Europe and it is limited to public buses only. There are many new vehicles, clean natural gas powered, some are even equipped with a/c. However, drivers' personality is still clearly expressed through loud music and interior decorations, usually handmade by a loving wife. It might also be challenging sometimes to find a bus stop, the best solution is to look for a group of people on the street, usually near a corner. However, some bus drivers will stop anywhere when somebody stops them. The fare is 50¢, and you can transfer for just 25¢, plus get a third transfer for free. You can also buy a Smart Card at the terminals in Plaza Caracol, Sam's Club, Plaza Pitillal, and Cetram Ixtapa.

**CONTACTS UnibusPV.** ✉ *República de Ecuador 630, Puerto Vallarta* ☎ *322/276–4146* ⊕ *unibuspv.com.mx.*

## TAXI

If you prefer taxis to Ubers, look for city yellow cabs. Always ask your driver about the fare to your destination before you enter the taxi. If it doesn't sound reasonable, look for another one. There are designated taxi stops but you might get a cab practically anywhere. You don't have to tip as it's included in the fare. There are also special Federal licensed white taxis that can only give service from the airport to hotels and condos.

**CONTACTS Taxis Plaza Marina.** ⊠ *Blvd. Francisco Medina Ascencio s/n, Marina Vallarta* ☏ *322/221–2435.* **Taxi Sitio 23.** ⊠ *San Salvador 632, Puerto Vallarta* ☏ *322/222–9401.*

# Activities

Puerto Vallarta is a town that has a lot to offer in terms of activities. Water sports like snorkeling, scuba-diving, whale-watching, or fishing are popular. PV is also a mountain town, which means ATVs, canopy zip-lines, or bird-watching are also possible here. Including the Riviera Nayarit, the place is a paradise for golf-lovers with seven courses just in the Banderas Bay's surrounding area.

## BEACHES
Throughout the region, from the Riviera Nayarit to the Costalegre, long, flat beaches invite walking, and reefs and offshore breaks draw divers, snorkelers, and surfers. In some places, nontouristy hideaways with little to distract you beyond waves lapping the shore may be accessible by land or by sea. Omnipresent seafood shanties are perfect vantage points for sunsets on the sand. Although Pacific Mexico's beaches aren't the sugar-sand, crystal-water variety of the Caribbean, they're still lovely. The water here is relatively unpolluted, and the oft-mountainous backdrop is majestic. PV sits at the center of horseshoe-shape Bahía de Banderas (Banderas Bay), the second-largest bay in North America (after the Hudson). Exquisitely visible from cliff-side hotels and restaurants, the bay's scalloped coast holds myriad coves and small bays perfect for shelling, sunning, swimming, and engaging in more strenuous activities. At Zona Hotelera beaches and a few popular stretches of sand north and south of PV proper,

you can parasail, take boat rides, or Jet Ski; some beaches lend themselves to kayaking, boogie boarding, paddle surfing, or snorkeling. Foothills that race down to the sea are crowded with palms and cedars, and the jungle's blue-green canopy forms a highly textured background to the deep-blue ocean. Dozens of creeks and rivers follow the contours of these hills, creating estuaries, mangrove swamps, and other habitats. South of Cabo Corrientes the mountains recede from the coast. Lovely yet lonely beaches and bays are fringed, as elsewhere in and around PV, by dry, tropical thorn forest with a variety of plants. Several species of whales cruise down in winter, and turtles spawn on the beaches from late summer into fall.

## FISHING
Some experts consider Puerto Vallarta to be the best fishing spot in the Mexican Pacific, although people from Nayarit and Baja California might disagree. The waters in and around the Banderas Bay are filled with mahimahi, marlin, sailfish, and yellowfin tuna. There are plenty sportfishing charters offering great deals starting at around $300; you can find them all around town but most of them are centered on the Marina from where most fishing trips depart.

## GOLF
Puerto Vallarta features a couple of decent golf courses (Marina and Vista). Marina Vallarta is the easiest choice as it's in the middle of town and quite near actually from the airport. Vista Vallarta provides a more challenging course and some of the best views of the city, the bay, and the Sierra Madre.

# Hotels

Centered on the middle of a large bay, Bahía de Banderas, Puerto Vallarta is the traditional hub for area beach hotels. Look for smaller budget hotels downtown, and oceanfront high-rise hotels to the north in the Hotel Zone (Zona Hotelera), and Marina Vallarta. Having reached critical mass, Puerto Vallarta's hotel scene is more about upgrading than building new properties. In the Centro and Zona Romántica neighborhoods, expect refurbished budget and moderately priced hotels (with the exception of luxury property Hacienda San Angel). Continue north into Zona Hotelera for condos, timeshares, and high-rises. Areas directly to the north and south of the city continue to add vacation properties.

## PRICES

*Hotel reviews have been shortened. For full information, visit Fodors.com.*

| What It Costs In U.S. Dollars | | | |
|---|---|---|---|
| $ | $$ | $$$ | $$$$ |
| **FOR TWO PEOPLE** | | | |
| under $50 | $50– $100 | $100– $350 | over $350 |

# Restaurants

First-time travelers come for the sun and sea, but it's PV's wonderful restaurants that create legions of long-term fans. You can pay L.A. prices for perfectly decorated plates but also get fresh-caught fish and hot-off-the-griddle tortillas for scandalously little dough. Enjoy a 300-degree bay view from a cliff-top aerie or bury your toes in the sand. Dress up or go completely casual. It's the destination's great variety of venues and cuisine that keeps returning foodies blissfully content. During the past 30 years, immigrant chefs have expanded the culinary horizons beyond seafood and Mexican fare. You'll find everything from haute cuisine to fish kebabs. Some of the most rewarding culinary experiences are found outside of fancy restaurants and familiar chain eateries. Try the street-side tacos stalls and neighborhood fondas, humble spots serving bowls of chili-laced

pozole and seafood-heavy Mexican comfort food. The trend of the day is restaurant-lounges. Fifteen years ago, DeSantos (co-owned by the drummer of the Mexican rock band Maná) was the first to combine dining and dancing in a hip new way, with its noisy ground-floor bar-restaurant and pulsing dance club above. Today La Madalena, Mandala, and other lounges provide places to party with the locals beyond the dining rooms. For those who prefer dining alfresco (and wearing flip-flops), almost every popular beach has a palapa shanty or two selling fish fillets and snacks, sodas, and beer. Some offer the Pacific Coast specialty *pescado sarandeado* (butterflied red snapper rubbed with salt and spices and grilled over a wood fire) or the devilishly simple (and fiery hot) dish *aguachile*, which is a ceviche salad. The catch of the day may vary, but the white plastic tables and chairs in the sand are permanent fixtures.

*Restaurant reviews have been shortened. For full information, visit Fodors. com.*

| What It Costs In U.S. Dollars | | | |
|---|---|---|---|
| $ | $$ | $$$ | $$$$ |
| **AT DINNER** | | | |
| under $5 | $5–$10 | $10–$20 | over $20 |

# Shopping

It's hard to decide which is more satisfying: shopping in Puerto Vallarta, or feasting at its glorious restaurants. There are enough of both to keep a bon vivant busy for weeks. Puerto Vallarta's highest concentration of shops and restaurants shares the same prime real estate: El Centro. But as construction of hotels, timeshares, condos, and private mansions marches implacably north up the bay, new specialty stores and gourmet groceries follow the gravy train. To the south, the Costalegre is made up primarily of modest seaside towns and self-contained luxury resorts, and shopping opportunities are rare. More than a half-dozen malls line "the airport road," Boulevard Francisco M. Ascencio, which connects downtown with the Hotel Zone and Marina Vallarta. There you'll find folk art, resort clothing, and home furnishing stores amid supermarkets, and in some cases bars and banks. Galerías Vallarta is the largest of these shopping malls while La Isla is by far the most sophisticated. At these two shopping centers you will find the usual shopping and entertainment options as in most of North America's malls, including some of the most exclusive boutiques in town, ultramodern gyms, stylish beauty salons, a casino, food courts, and a couple of movie theater complexes (one of them VIP, at La Isla). A 15% value-added tax (locally called IVA, officially the impuesto al valor agregado) is levied on most larger purchases. (Note that it's often included in the price, and it's usually disregarded entirely by market vendors.) As a foreign visitor, you can reclaim this 15% by filling out paperwork at a kiosk in the Puerto Vallarta airport and other major airports around the country. That said, most visitors find the system tedious and unrewarding and avoid it altogether. You must make purchases at approved stores and businesses, and your merchandise must total $115 or more. Even if you plan to pay with cash or a debit card, you must present a credit card at the time of purchase and obtain a receipt and an official refund form from the merchant. Tax paid on meals and lodgings won't be refunded.

# Nightlife and Performing Arts

Outdoorsy Vallarta switches gears after dark and rocks into the wee hours. When the beachgoers and sightseers have been showered and fed, Vallarta kicks up its heels and puts the baby to bed. Happy hour in martini lounges sets the stage for an evening that might include a show, live music, or just hobnobbing under the stars at a rooftop bar. Many hotels have Mexican fiesta dinner shows, which can be lavish affairs with buffet dinners, folk dances, and even fireworks. Tour groups and individuals—mainly middle-age and older Americans and Canadians—make up the audience at the Saturday-night buffet dinner show at Playa Los Arcos and other hotels. Vaqueros (cowboys) do rope tricks and dancers perform Mexican regional or pseudo-Aztec dances. The late-late crowd gets down after midnight at dance clubs, some of which stay open until 6 am. The scene mellows as you head north and south of Puerto Vallarta. In Punta Mita (aka Punta de Mita), Bucerías, Sayulita, and San Francisco (aka San Pancho), local restaurants provide live music; the owners usually scare up someone good once or twice a week in high season. Along the Costalegre, tranquillity reigns. Most people head here for relaxation, and nightlife generally takes the form of stargazing, drink in hand. If you're visiting June through October (low season), attend live performances whenever offered, as they are few and far between. Although there's definitely crossover, many Mexicans favor the upscale bars and clubs of the Hotel Zone and Marina Vallarta hotels, while foreigners tend to like the Mexican flavor of places downtown and on the south side (the Zona Romántica), where dress is decidedly more casual.

# Tours

## Ecotours

**TOUR—SPORTS** | This company offers a bit of everything, from whale-watching to bird-watching, snorkeling in National Parks, to scuba diving in some of the most incredible places. ⊠ *Condominio Marina del Rey, Proa s/n Loc. 20, Marina Vallarta* ☎ *322/223–3130, 322/222–6606* ⊕ *www.ecotoursvallarta.com.*

## Ecotours de Mexico

**TOUR—SPORTS** | A PV–based operator (with the main office at Marina Vallarta) whose offerings include hiking, diving, snorkeling, kayaking, bird-watching, whale-watching, and turtle tours. Most tours start at $77. ⊠ *Proa s/n Loc. 20, Marina Vallarta* ☎ *322/209–2195* ⊕ *www.ecotoursvallarta.com.*

## Wildlife Connection

**TOUR—SPORTS** | Based in Puerto Vallarta's marina, this Mexican-owned company does what its name implies: it connects you with wildlife (specifically birds, turtles, dolphins, and whales) on seasonal trips. It also leads snorkeling and photography outings as well as cultural tours. Without a doubt the most popular tour is the one where you can swim with wild dolphins in the bay. Oh, and unlike in most other tours, most of these are led by real biologists. Tours start at $68. ⊠ *Paseo de la Marina Sur #214, Marina Vallarta* ☎ *322/225–3621* ⊕ *www.wildlifeconnection.com.*

# Visitor Information

Mexico in general, and Puerto Vallarta in particular, have carefully earned a reputation for going the extra mile to make visitors feel welcome and safe. At the airport you will easily find tourist information offices to help you with any issue you may have. Travelers need a valid passport to visit the country and will get a Tourist Permit upon arrival; make sure to keep this one in a safe place as you will need it once you leave the country.

**CONTACTS** **Mexican Tourism Board.** ☎ *800/446–3942 in U.S. and Canada, 555/278–4200* ⊕ *visitmexico.com.* **Puerto Vallarta Tourism Board & Convention and Visitors Bureau.** ⊠ *Lago Tangañica 222, Fluvial Vallarta, Col. Versalles* ☎ *322/224–1175, 888/384–6822 toll-free in U.S. and Canada* ⊕ *visitpuertovallarta.com.* **Secretaría de Turismo.** ☎ *553/002–6300, 800/006–8839 toll-free in Mexico* ⊕ *gob. mx/sectur.* **Visitor Information - Parque Hidalgo.** ⊠ *Av. México s/n, El Centro* ☎ *322/223–5791.* **Visitor Information - Parque Lázaro Cárdenas.** ⊠ *Pino Suárez y Venustiano Carranza s/n, Parque Lázaro Cárdenas, Zona Romántica* ☎ *322/223–5791.*

# Zona Romántica

The Romantic Zone is one of the hippest areas of Puerto Vallarta, popular not only with tourists but also with local residents, ensuring a buzz all year round. The area has many of Puerto Vallarta's must-sees.

The recent renovation of Basilio Badillo Street marked the beginning of its climb to fame. All the establishments got on board with the transformation and worked on reinventing their images to make the street bigger and brighter.

The oldest farmers' market in town is also in the Romantic Zone and takes place from 9:30 am to 2 pm at Lázaro-Cárdenas Park (only in high season). You can buy all kinds of freshly baked products, artisanal foods, handmade clothing, jewelry, and crafts.

It's also worth noting that the Zona Romántica is home to Vallarta's strong gay scene. Playa Los Muertos is widely known as Puerto Vallarta's gay beach, with a couple of beach clubs specifically dedicated to the LGBTQ community.

Several gay night clubs populate the streets of the Zona Romántica, too, and, by midnight, PV has nothing to envy the gay party capitals of the world.

Don't miss Los Muertos Pier. The spot was where the first wooden pier of Vallarta was built in the 1960s for the cast and crew of the film *The Night of the Iguana*. That ramshackle construction was replaced 30 years later by a concrete structure, which became the departure point for boats going to southern coastal destinations. In 2010, the city decided to renovate again. The result was the current sleek pier, resembling a soaring sail that projects 320 feet into the ocean. Apart from serving as a landing dock, it includes pedestrian pathways, plenty of seating, colorful lighting, and a waterfront promenade.

## GETTING AROUND
The best way to move around the Zona Romántica is on foot. The neighborhood is not that big and the streets are quite small, so a car only adds the hassle of parking. If you get tired of walking around what is also known as Old Town Vallarta, there are always available taxis that won't charge you much (as long as you stay inside the Zona Romántica).

**Parking:** The main parking spot in the Zona Romántica is the parking lot located below the Lázaro Cárdenas Park. It costs around 20 MXN ($1) per hour, and it also has public restrooms (5 MXN)

 **Sights**

### Los Muertos Pier
MARINA | There was a time when Los Muertos Pier was a sad piece of concrete extending a few meters into the sea, but that changed in 2013 when it was replaced by a beautifully designed pier that underwent years of renovations. The new pier was an instant hit and has become one of the most recognizable landmarks in Puerto Vallarta. It's perfect for a romantic walk, for reading a book

while listening to the sound of the waves, and for viewing at night when it lights up the buzzing Los Muertos Beach. Oh, and it also serves as a pier! You can get a boat from here to visit the amazing beaches south of Puerto Vallarta, such as Yelapa, Quimixto, and Las Animas. ✉ *End of Francisca Rodríguez St., Zona Romántica.*

 **Beaches**

Parallel to Zona Romántica, Playa los Muertos is PV's most popular beach, where restaurants and bars have music, vendors sell barbecued fish on a stick, and people cruise the boardwalk.

### ★ Playa los Muertos
BEACH—SIGHT | PV's original happening beach has nice bay views, and as action central, it's definitely the area's most engaging beach. Facing Vallarta's South Side (south of the Río Cuale), this flat beach hugs the Zona Romántica and runs about 1½ km (1 mile) south to a rocky point called El Púlpito. ■TIP➔ **The steps (more than 100) at Calle Púlpito lead to a lookout with a great view of the beach and the bay.**

Joggers cruise the cement boardwalk early morning and after sunset; vendors stalk the beach nonstop, hawking kites, jewelry, and serapes as well as hair-braiding and alfresco massage. Bar-restaurants run the length of the beach; the bright blue umbrellas at the south end belong to Blue Chairs resort, the hub of PV's effervescent gay scene.

The surf ranges from mild to choppy with an undertow; the small waves crunching the shore usually discourage mindless paddling. There are lifeguards on the beach, but the service isn't consistent. The Los Muertos Pier underwent a recent face-lift and it's now one of PV's main landmarks and a prime spot for romantic night walks. **Amenities:** lifeguards; water sports; food and drink.

For shaded surf-side relaxation, grab a table under an umbrella at Playa Olas Altas.

**Best for:** partiers; surfing; sunset. ✉ *Zona Romántica.*

### Playa Olas Altas
**BEACH—SIGHT | FAMILY** | The name means "high waves beach," but the only waves suitable for bodysurfing, boogie boarding, or, occasionally, surfing small waves are near the Cuale River, at the north end of this small beach. Although "Olas Altas" more often refers to the neighborhood of bars and businesses near the ocean south of the Río Cuale, it is also the name of a few blocks of sand between Daiquiri Dick's restaurant and the Río Cuale. The beach attracts fewer sunbathers than Los Muertos but is otherwise an extension of that beach, and it gets lively during holidays with sunbathers and impromptu snack stands and shaded tables on the sand. There are good views of the recently renovated Los Muertos Pier and spectacular lighting at night. Facing Olas Altas Beach near Lázaro Cárdenas plaza are open-air stands selling beach accessories, small grocery stores, and beach-facing bar-restaurants.

**Amenities:** food and drink; parking.
**Best for:** sunset; swimming. ✉ *Zona Romántica.*

##  Restaurants

Many excellent restaurants are packed into this tourist-heavy neighborhood. As throughout Vallarta, they are mainly casual places where a sundress or a pair of slacks is about as dressed up as most people get. Seafood and Mexican fare are the specialties at taco stands and at the restaurants facing Los Muertos beach. Pizza joints and Italian eateries are also popular, and there are plenty of places for dessert and coffee, too.

### Andale
**$ | AMERICAN** | Although many have been drinking rather than eating at this local hangout for years, the restaurant serves dependable cuisine (fajitas, burgers, fries), with daily lunch specials and nightly drink specials. The bar has a friendly atmosphere; the interior is cool, dark, and informal. **Known for:** outdoor dining;

attentive service; party spot after 10 pm. $ *Average main: 130 MP* ✉ *Av. Olas Altas 425, El Centro* ☎ *322/222–1054* ⊕ *www.andales.com.*

### Archie's Wok

$$ | ASIAN | Dishes at this extremely popular pan-Asian restaurant include Thai garlic shrimp, *pancit* (Filipino stir-fry with pasta), and Singapore-style (lightly battered) crispy fish. The spinach and watercress salad with feta, pecans, and a hibiscus dressing is healthy, refreshing, and perfect for a late lunch (the restaurant opens only after 2 pm). **Known for:** vegetarian dishes; Puerto Vallarta staple; great service. $ *Average main: 200 MP* ✉ *Calle Francisca Rodríguez 130, Zona Romántica* ☎ *322/222–0411* ۞ *Closed Sun. and Sept.*

### Café de Olla

$ | MEXICAN | Repeat visitors swear by the enchiladas and carne asada at this earthy restaurant. A large tree extends from the dining-room floor through the roof, local artwork adorns the walls, and salsa music often plays in the background. **Known for:** traditional Mexican cuisine; Raicilla (moonshine); packed at breakfast and dinner. $ *Average main: 130 MP* ✉ *Calle Basilio Badillo 168–A, Zona Romántica* ☎ *322/223–1626* ▭ *No credit cards* ۞ *Closed Tues. and Sept. 15–Oct. 15.*

### ★ Daiquiri Dick's

$$$ | INTERNATIONAL | Locals come frequently for breakfast; visitors come for the great service and consistent Mexican and international cuisine. The lunch-dinner menu has fabulous appetizers, including superb lobster, and shrimp tacos with a drizzle of béchamel sauce, and perfect, tangy jumbo-shrimp wontons. **Known for:** homemade orange-almond granola; grilled fish on a stick; sunset views. $ *Average main: 220 MP* ✉ *Av. Olas Altas 314, Zona Romántica* ☎ *322/222–0566* ⊕ *www.ddpv.com* ۞ *Closed Sept. and Tues. May–Aug.*

### El Brujo

$ | MEXICAN | It's on a noisy street corner, but the seriously good food and generous portions make this a local favorite. The *molcajete*—a sizzling black pot of tender flank steak, grilled green onion, and soft white cheese in a delicious homemade sauce of dried red peppers—is served with a big plate of guacamole, refried beans, and made-at-the-moment corn or flour tortillas. **Known for:** simple atmosphere; creamy huitlacoche (black corn fungus); seafood. $ *Average main: 130 MP* ✉ *Venustiano Carranza 510, at Naranjo, Zona Romántica* ☎ *322/223–2036* ۞ *Closed 2 wks in late Sept.–early Oct.*

### Fredy's Tucan

$ | CAFÉ | FAMILY | Even in low season, Fredy's, next door to the Hotel Posada de Roger, is packed full of Mexican families, gringo friends, and local business people. Your mug of coffee will be refilled without having to beg; service is brisk, professional, and friendly. **Known for:** great breakfast; fruit smoothies; closes at 3 pm daily. $ *Average main: 80 MP* ✉ *Calle Basilio Badillo 245, Zona Romántica* ☎ *322/223–0778* ⊕ *fredystucan.com/es/* ▭ *No credit cards* ۞ *No dinner.*

### Kaiser Maximilian

$$ | EUROPEAN | Viennese entrées dominate the menu, which is modified each year when the restaurant participates in PV's culinary festival. The adjacent café (open 8 am–midnight) has sandwiches, excellent desserts, and 20 specialty coffees—all of which are also available at the main restaurant. **Known for:** classic European cuisine; apple strudel; stylish setting. $ *Average main: 300 MP* ✉ *Av. Olas Altas 380, Zona Romántica* ☎ *322/223–0760* ⊕ *kaisermaximilian.com* ۞ *Closed Sun.*

### La Palapa

$$$ | INTERNATIONAL | This large, welcoming, thatched-roof eatery is open to the breezes of Playa Los Muertos and filled with wicker-covered chandeliers,

**At Hacienda Alemana, guests can choose to dine alfresco.**

art-glass fixtures, and lazily rotating ceiling fans. The menu meanders among international dishes with modern presentation: roasted stuffed chicken breast, pork loin, seared yellowfin tuna drizzled in cacao sauce. **Known for:** Puerto Vallarta's original beach restaurant; seafood enchilada; beach club. [$] *Average main: 300 MP* ✉ *Calle Púlpito 103, Playa Los Muertos, Zona Romántica* ☎ *322/222–5225* 🌐 *www.lapalapapv.com.*

**La Piazzetta**

**$$** | **ITALIAN** | Locals come for the Naples-style pizza, cooked in a brick oven and with a crust that's not too thick, not too thin. There's also great pasta and a good variety of entrées, like salmon with caviar, and lemon and broccoli with fettuccine in cream sauce served piping hot. **Known for:** large patio; great pizzas; LGTBQ-friendly. [$] *Average main: 130 MP* ✉ *Calle Rodolfo Gómez 143, at Av. Olas Altas, Zona Romántica* ☎ *322/222–0650* 🌐 *lapiazzettapv.com* 🕓 *Closed Sun. No lunch.*

**Langostino's**

**$** | **SEAFOOD** | Right on the beach just north of the pier at Playa Los Muertos, Langostino's is a great place to start the day with a helping of Mexican rock music, cranked up to a respectable volume. For lunch or dinner, the house favorite at this professional and pleasant place is surf and turf (called *mar y tierra*), and the three seafood combos are a good value. **Known for:** beachside dining; good music; ceviche. [$] *Average main: 100 MP* ✉ *109 M. Dieguez, at Los Muertos Beach, Zona Romántica* ☎ *322/222–0894* 💳 *No credit cards* 🕓 *Closed Aug. 20–Sept. 15.*

**The Pancake House**

**$$** | **AMERICAN** | **FAMILY** | Your child will most certainly find something he or she likes on this Pancake House menu. There are 12 kinds of pancakes—including the "Oh Henry," with chocolate bits and peanut butter—and eight kinds of waffles. **Known for:** kid-friendly breakfast spot; delicious smoothies; cash-only. [$] *Average main: 150 MP* ✉ *Calle Basilio Badillo*

*289, Zona Romántica ☎ 322/222–6272 🌐 www.thepancakehouse.com.mx 💳 No credit cards ⌚ No dinner.*

## Hotels

The Romantic Zone, aka Colonia Emiliano Zapata, is PV's party central. LGBTQ and straight bars are interspersed with diminutive boutiques and restaurants. Los Muertos and Amapas beaches face the fray, a convenient place to party, eat, and drink. Moderately priced hotels overlook the sand, with budget options a few blocks away. New parking structures provide parking, as most hotels here do not. Taxis and buses make exploring surrounding areas a snap.

**Boana Torre Malibu**

**$$ | RENTAL** | Located just a few meters from Playa Los Muertos, this hotel is at the center of PV's gay scene. **Pros:** large swimming pool; English- and French-speaking staff; gay tours. **Cons:** not beachfront; swimming pool area can get too noisy; ground floor rooms don't have ocean views. [$] *Rooms from: $125 ✉ Amapas 325, Zona Romántica ☎ 322/222–6695 🌐 boanaresort.com 🛏 35 condos 🍴 No meals.*

**Casa Cúpula**

**$$$ | HOTEL** | This popular, up-to-date boutique hotel is located a 10-minute walk from the beach and the Zona Romántica, catering largely to an LGBTQ clientele. **Pros:** themed pool parties; salt-water zen pool at the spa; oh-so-comfy beds and pillows. **Cons:** challenging location up a hill, though not a far walk to attractions; some rooms might get too noisy for some tastes; limited food options. [$] *Rooms from: $150 ✉ Callejón de la Igualdad 129, Zona Romántica ☎ 322/223–2484, 866/352–2511 🌐 www.casacupula.com 🛏 20 rooms 🍴 No meals.*

**★ Hacienda Alemana Frankfurt**

**$$ | B&B/INN** | Rooms here have king-size beds, 32-inch TVs, and double-pane windows to keep out noise. **Pros:** excellent on-site German restaurant; centric location; great for couples or solo travelers. **Cons:** no ocean views; furniture and design a bit outdated *biergarten.*; no spa or fitness center. [$] *Rooms from: $145 ✉ Calle Basilio Badillo 370–378, Zona Romántica ☎ 322/172–7205 🌐 www.haciendaalemana.com 🛏 10 rooms 🍴 Free Breakfast.*

**Hotel Eloísa**

**$ | HOTEL** | A block from the beach and overlooking Lázaro Cárdenas Park, this hotel offers great city- and mountain views from the rooftop, which has a pool and party area. **Pros:** suites have small kitchenettes; large pool on roof; centric location. **Cons:** no parking; mainly older a/c units; not at the beach. [$] *Rooms from: $60 ✉ Calle Lázaro Cárdenas 179, Zona Romántica ☎ 322/222–0286, 322/222–0286 🌐 www.hoteleloisa.com 🛏 58 rooms 🍴 Free Breakfast.*

**Hotel Gaviota Vallarta**

**$ | HOTEL** | Simple rooms in this six-story low-rise have somewhat battered colonial-style furnishings; some have tiny balconies but only a few on the top floors have a partial ocean view. **Pros:** moderately priced rooms a block from the beach; centric location; salsa club next door. **Cons:** poor pool placement; unattractive furnishings; very small parking lot. [$] *Rooms from: $50 ✉ Francisco I. Madero 176, Zona Romántica ☎ 322/222–1500 🌐 www.hotelgaviota.com 🛏 109 rooms 🍴 No meals.*

**Hotel Posada de Roger**

**$$ | HOTEL** | If you hang around the pool or the small shared balcony overlooking the street, it's not hard to get to know the other guests—many of them savvy budget travelers from Europe and Canada. **Pros:** great location; tinkling fountain and quiet courtyard; excellent breakfast restaurant next door. **Cons:** no in-room safes; cramped rooms; get-what-you-pay-for beds. [$] *Rooms from: $92 ✉ Calle Basilio Badillo 237, Zona Romántica*

☎ 322/222–0836 ⊕ www.hotelposada-deroger.com ⬦ 47 rooms ⧉ No meals.

### Hotel Tropicana

**$$ | HOTEL |** This is a reasonably priced, well-landscaped, bright white hotel at the south end of Playa Los Muertos. **Pros:** good beach access; great Zona Romántica location; nice pool and landscaping. **Cons:** no bathtubs; outdated furnishings; wristbands required for all guests. $ *Rooms from: $75* ✉ *Calle Amapas 214, Zona Romántica* ☎ *322/226–9696* ⊕ *www.tropicanavallarta.com* ⬦ *205 rooms* ⧉ *No meals.*

### Hotel Yasmín

**$ | HOTEL |** This budget hotel is a colorful example of traditional Mexican design. **Pros:** very inexpensive; close to Zona Romántica action; pleasant courtyard garden with pool, coffee, tables, and chaise lounges. **Cons:** dark rooms; low ceilings; small bathrooms. $ *Rooms from: $55* ✉ *Basilio Badillo 168, Zona Romántica* ☎ *322/222–0087* ⊕ *www.hotelyasminpv.com* ▭ *No credit cards* ⬦ *27 rooms* ⧉ *No meals.*

### ★ Playa Los Arcos Beach Resort & Spa

**$$$ | RESORT | FAMILY |** This hotel is recommended for its location: right on the beach and in the midst of Zona Romántica's restaurants, bars, and shops. **Pros:** great Zona Romántica location; nightly entertainment with theme-cuisine buffet; ocean views from most rooms. **Cons:** small bathrooms; some rooms have tired furnishings; extremely busy (and noisy) area. $ *Rooms from: $220* ✉ *Av. Olas Altas 380, Zona Romántica* ☎ *322/226–7100, 800/648–2403 in U.S., 888/729–9590 in Canada, 01800/327–7700 toll-free in Mexico* ⊕ *www.playalosarcos.com* ⬦ *169 rooms* ⧉ *No meals.*

## ⓨ Nightlife

Like any resort destination worth its salt—the salt on the rim of the margarita glass, that is—PV has an enormous variety of watering holes. Bars on or

overlooking the beach sell the view along with buckets of beer. Martini bars go to great lengths to impress with signature drinks, and sports bars broadcast Canadian hockey and Monday-night football. Hotels have swim-up bars and lobby lounges

### Andale

**BARS/PUBS |** Most nights, crowds spill out onto the sidewalk as partiers shimmy out of the narrow saloon, drinks in hand, to the strains of Chubby Checker and other vintage tunes. For a laugh, intoxicated or less inhibited patrons sometimes take a bumpy ride on the burro just outside Andale's door (a handler escorts the burro). ✉ *Av. Olas Altas 425, Zona Romántica* ☎ *322/222–1054* ⊕ *www.andales.com.*

### Apaches

**BARS/PUBS |** PV's original martini bar, Apaches is the landing zone for expats reconnoitering after a long day, and a warm-up for night owls. When the outside tables get jam-packed in high season, the overflow heads into the narrow bar and the adjacent, equally narrow bistro. It opens at 4 pm; happy hour is 5 to 7. If you're traveling alone, this is the place to make friends of all ages. ✉ *Av. Olas Altas 439, Zona Romántica* ☎ *322/429–8885.*

### Blue Chairs

**GATHERING PLACES |** In addition to its famous beach scene, Blue Chairs, at the south end of Los Muertos Beach, has the popular **Blue Sunset Rooftop Bar,** which is the perfect place to watch the sunset. It has daily late-afternoon and evening entertainment, and is open to the public between 3 and 11 pm; after that, it's hotel guests only. ✉ *Malecón 4, Zona Romántica* ☎ *322/222–5040* ⊕ *www.bluechairsresort.com.*

### Burro's Bar

**BARS/PUBS |** Right on the sand across from Parque Lázaro Cárdenas, this restaurant-bar has bargain brewskis and equally inexpensive fruity margaritas by the pitcher. The seafood is less than inspired, but nachos and other munchies are good accompaniments to the drinks. Watch the waves and listen to Bob Marley and the Gipsy Kings among lots of gringo couples and a few middle-age Mexican vacationers. It opens daily from 9 am to 10 pm. ⊠ *Av. Olas Altas 280 at Calle Lázaro Cárdenas, Zona Romántica* ☎ *322/222-0112.*

### Café San Angel

**CAFES—NIGHTLIFE** | A classic of the Olas Altas/Zona Romántica scene, Café San Angel used to be the place where one used to go for a coffee, grab a book (English or Spanish), and enjoy the slow pace of Vallarta's afternoons. Today it has evolved into a lively mix between a breakfast spot and a trendy burger grill. They still have books and sofas, but the pace is not as slow as it used to be. ⊠ *Av. Olas Altas 449, at Calle Francisca Rodriguez, Zona Romántica* ☎ *322/223-1273.*

### Garbo

**BARS/PUBS** | This isn't necessarily the kind of place where you'll strike up a conversation with the guy on the next barstool; rather, it's an upscale place to go with friends for a sophisticated, air-conditioned drink or two. A musician plays piano or gentle jazz on weekend nights at 10:30 during high season, less often the rest of the year. Garbo, renowned for its martinis, Is primarily a gay club, but is straight friendly and is open nightly from 6 pm to 2 am. ⊠ *Púlpito 142 at Av. Olas Altas, Zona Romántica* ☎ *322/223-5753.*

### J&B Dance Club

**DANCE CLUBS** | Originally located in the Hotel Zone, J&B has now moved with all its Latin rhythms to the Zona Romántica. It's the best club in town for salsa, hands down. The crowd varies but tends toward the 30s–40s age group and because J&B is serious about dancing, it feels young at heart. It's a favorite of locals and upbeat expats alike. ⊠ *Francisco I. Madero #178,*

*Zona Romántica* ☎ *322/224-4616* ⊕ *zamittizj8.wlx.com/jhdancingclub* ☞ *Closed Sun.*

### La Noche

**BARS/PUBS** | This charming martini lounge has red walls and a huge, eye-catching chandelier. Gringo-owned, it attracts a crowd of gay 20- to 40-year-old men (a mix of foreigners and Mexicans). Electronica and house music are the favorites. But, to get back to the martinis, the house makes excellent cocktails, and they're not too expensive, either. Make sure to visit the spectacular rooftop garden. Open from 8 pm to 4 am. ⊠ *Calle Lázaro Cárdenas 263, Zona Romántica* ☎ *322/222-3364* ⊕ *lanochepv.com*

### ★ Los Muertos Brewing Company

**BARS/PUBS** | If you love a good beer, Los Muertos Brewing Company is for you. The first craft brewery in Puerto Vallarta offers a relaxed atmosphere and the best beer on tap in town. It's a mix between the typical cantina and the traditional sports bar and they have a selection of rock and pop both in English and Spanish. Young gringos love it, and it's also getting attention from locals who come for the pizzas and stay for the beer. It's open every day from noon until midnight. ⊠ *Calle Lázaro Cárdenas 302, Zona Romántica* ☎ *322/222-0308* ⊕ *losmuertosbrewing.com.*

### Mantamar Beach Club Bar & Grill

**BARS/PUBS** | This gay, adults-only beach club located right on Los Muertos Beach is one of the best party spots in the Zona Romántica. Featuring a gorgeous infinity pool, restaurant, bar, several Jacuzzis, and stunning views of the Banderas Bay, Mantamar has it all. A flying pool and private areas showcase how extravagant this place can get. It closes at 11 pm, but it's a great place to start the fiesta. ⊠ *Malecón 169, Zona Romántica* ☎ *322/222-6260* ⊕ *mantamarvallarta.com.*

**Pie in the Sky Vallarta**
CAFES—NIGHTLIFE | FAMILY | Come for the excellent coffee as well as *the* most scrumptious pies, cookies, and cakes. There's free Wi-Fi. ⊠ *Calle Aquiles Serdan 242, L–3, Zona Romántica* ☎ *322/223-8183* ⊕ *www.pieinthesky.com.mx.*

★ **Roxy Rock House**
MUSIC CLUBS | Puerto Vallarta's only rock house is a very energetic club that features live music every night at 11 pm. Roxy is an institution in this town and one of the very few places that attracts all kinds of visitors—you'll find nationals and foreigners of all ages on the premises, and they are not afraid to sing and dance. It's open from 9 pm to 6 am every day. ⊠ *Ignacio L. Vallarta 217, Zona Romántica* ☎ *322/105-8515* ⊕ *www. roxyrockhouse.com.*

**Sapphire Ocean Club & Suites**
BARS/PUBS | A great place for sunbathing and enjoying great gourmet food with tasteful lounge music playing in the background, Sapphire is not as spectacular (nor as crowded) as the other big beach club in the area, Mantamar. Here, the swimming pool is smaller, but more intimate, and customers have access to free Wi-Fi, lounge chairs, umbrellas, a bottle of water upon arrival, and Oshibori towels. It closes at sunset. ⊠ *Malecón 1, Zona Romántica* ☎ *322/223-3264* ⊕ *sapphire.mx.*

**Steve's Bar**
BARS/PUBS | With NASCAR on Sunday morning, NFL on Monday night, hockey, indispensable motocross, and welterweight fights, Steve's is a sports mecca. Five feeds and nine television sets guarantee simultaneous broadcasts of many sporting events from various continents. There are piles of board games, too, and the burgers and fries couldn't be better. ⊠ *Calle Basilio Badillo 286, Zona Romántica* ☎ *322/222-0256* ⊕ *www. stevesbarpv.com.*

## ⊕ Performing Arts

★ **Act II Entertainment**
CABARET | A breath of fresh air in the nightlife scene of Puerto Vallarta, Act II is a multigenre theater, cabaret, and sophisticated bar all in one. On the top floor of a little shopping center in Zona Romántica, it offers a great diversity of shows, both on the "Main Stage" and in the more intimate "Red Room." Altogether, it's an excellent option for a different kind of night out in Puerto Vallarta. ⊠ *Calle Insurgentes 300 at Basilio Badillo, 2nd fl., Zona Romántica* ☎ *322/222-1512* ⊕ *actiientertainment.com.*

**The Palm Cabaret and Bar**
CABARET | With 20 years of history in Puerto Vallarta, The Palm is a household name in PV's gay scene. The drag queen shows have no equivalent in the area, but music shows are also of high quality. They're closed during the summer. ⊠ *Olas Altas 508, Zona Romántica* ☎ *322/222-0200* ⊕ *thepalmcabaret.com.*

## 🛍 Shopping

**A Page in the Sun**
BOOKS/STATIONERY | Folks read books they've bought or traded at this outdoor café by the Hotel Eloisa, and there are almost always people playing chess. The large selection of tomes is organized according to genre and then alphabetized by author. ⊠ *Calle Lázaro Cárdenas 169, Zona Romántica* ☎ *322/222-3608* ⊕ *apageinthesun.com.*

★ **Cassandra Shaw Jewelry**
JEWELRY/ACCESSORIES | It's hard to ignore the huge, chunky rings, bracelets, and necklaces here. In the back of the shop there are more delicate items of pure silver set with various stones in artful ways. All are unusual. ⊠ *Calle Basilio Badillo 276, Zona Romántica* ☎ *322/223-9734* ⊕ *cassandrashaw.com.*

★ **Gallería Dante**

ART GALLERIES | Classical, contemporary, and abstract works are displayed and sold in this 6,000-square-foot gallery—PV's largest—and sculpture garden. Check out the marvelous large-format paintings of indigenous people in regional costumes by Juana Cortez Salazar, whimsical statues by Guillermo Gómez, and the work of nearly 60 other talented artists. A classic in the art scene of Puerto Vallarta. ⊠ *Calle Basilio Badillo 269, Zona Romántica* ☎ *322/222-2477* ⊕ *www. galleriadante.com* ⊗ *Closed Sun.*

**Lucy's CuCú Cabana**

CRAFTS | At this very small shop you can buy inexpensive, one-of-a-kind folk art from Guerrero, Michoacán, Oaxaca, and elsewhere. Note that Lucy closes during lunch. ⊠ *Calle Basilio Badillo 295, Zona Romántica* ☎ *322/222-1220* ⊗ *Closed in Sept.*

**Mundo de Azulejos**

CERAMICS/GLASSWARE | Buy machine- or handmade tiles starting at about 13 MXN ($1) each at this large shop. You can get mosaic tile scenes (or order your own design), a place setting for eight, hand-painted sinks, or any number of soap dishes, cups, saucers, plates, or doodads. Around the corner and run by family members, Mundo de Cristal has more plates and tableware in the same style. ⊠ *Av. Venustiano Carranza 374, Zona Romántica* ☎ *322/222-5402* ⊕ *www.talavera-tile.com.mx* ⊗ *Closed Sun.*

**Mundo de Cristal**

CRAFTS | Come for the glassware from Jalisco and Guanajuato states, in sets or individual pieces. Also available are Talavera place settings and platters, pitchers, and decorative pieces. Look in the back of the store for high-quality ceramics with realistic portrayals of fruits and flowers. You can have your purchase packed and shipped. ⊠ *Av. Insurgentes 333 at Calle Basilio Badillo, Zona Romántica*

☎ *322/222-4157* ⊕ *mundodecristal.com. mx* ⊗ *Closed Sun.*

**Mundo de Pewter**

CRAFTS | Relatives of the owners of Mundo de Cristal and Mundo de Azulejos own this shop. Attractive, lead free items in modern and traditional designs are sold here at reasonable prices. The practical, tarnish-free pieces can go from stovetop or oven to the dining table and be no worse for wear. ⊠ *Av. Venustiano Carranza 358, Zona Romántica* ☎ *322/222-8503* ⊗ *Closed Sun.*

★ **Myskova Beachwear Boutique**

CLOTHING | This boutique has its own extensive line of bikinis, cover-ups, yoga pants, and some items for children (sunglasses, bathing suits, flip-flops). There's a small line of jewelry, and Brazilian flip-flops for adults in a rainbow of colors. The shop is open daily until 11 pm. ⊠ *Calle Basilio Badillo 278, Zona Romántica* ☎ *322/222-6091* ⊕ *www.myskova.com. mx.*

**Talavera Etc.**

CERAMICS/GLASSWARE | Here you can buy reproductions of tiles from Puebla churches and small gift items or choose made-to-order pieces from the catalog. Note that hours are limited. ⊠ *Av. Ignacio L. Vallarta 266, Zona Romántica* ☎ *322/222-4100* ⊕ *www.talaveraetc. com.*

★ **Xocodiva**

FOOD/CANDY | Exquisite truffles and molded chocolates are all stylishly arranged on immaculate glass shelves at this classic Canadian chocolatier. The chocolate itself is European; among the different mousse fillings are some New World ingredients, including lime, coconut, cinnamon, Kahlúa, espresso, and a few dozen more. Stop by after dinner for a fab dessert. During holidays, out come the molded Santas or Day of the Dead skulls, some packaged as pretty gifts. ⊠ *Aquiles Serdan 368, Zona Romántica* ☎ *322/113-0352* ⊕ *xocodiva pv.com* ⊗ *Closed Sun.*

## Activities

### Canopy El Edén

**TOUR—SPORTS** | The daily trips to the spirited Mismaloya River and an adjacent restaurant are 3½-hour adventures. You zip along 10 lines through the trees and above the river. They have expanded their operations, and now offer other kind of tours, too, such as ATVs, city tours, and even an interesting boat tour. ✉ *Clemente Orozco s/n, Zona Hotelera* ☎ *322/128–9346* ⊕ *canopyeleden.mx.*

### Wild Treks Adventures

**TOUR—SPORTS** | This company with years of experience in Vallarta leads daily ATV tours that head into the hills behind Vallarta, Sayulita, or beyond. Those that stop at Rancho Las Pilas include a brief tequila-making tour and tasting, but lunch there is optional and not included in the price. A four-hour tour combines this ATV trek with a canopy tour through River Canopy, along the Cuale River. ✉ *Calle Basilio Badillo 400, Zona Romántica* ☎ *322/222–8944* ⊕ *www.wildtreksadventures.com.*

# El Centro

Downtown Puerto Vallarta is the main attraction of the whole Banderas Bay, with lots of things to do and explore. If your last visit to Puerto Vallarta was a few years ago, you won't recognize the city. It still has that old charm, but it has been enhanced with some 21st-century improvements.

The new malecón is the most noticeable change. It has been totally renovated, closed to traffic, and embellished with big planters full of colorful flowers, bushes, and palm trees. Now you can rent a bike for two or three, and even a stroller or a wheelchair. The malecón extends from Hotel Rosita to the new pier and maintains all the old, well-known establishments as well as the entertainment:

street performers, Papantla birdmen, sand sculptures, and many others. Almost all the clubs and bars took advantage of the renovating period to update their businesses.

The Church of Our Lady of Guadalupe is an obligatory stop in the historic center. Recently it got a new crown and looks splendid over the city skyline. After your visit, relax at the main square just one block from the parish where you can eat an ice cream. On Sunday there is live music and dancers performing the traditional danzón.

You'll spot art galleries all over the city and, in the high season, you can attend an art walk. From November to April, stroll from one gallery to the next and enjoy local art together with a free cup of wine, a shot of tequila, and some appetizers. The participating galleries are labeled on the outside walls and you can get a free map along the way. Be sure to check ahead on which days you can chat with the artists.

The natural island on the Cuale River with restaurants, a museum, an art gallery, and countless shops and souvenir stands is another must-see. If you want to buy some more crafts at affordable prices go to the Municipal Market on the north side of the island. It has lots to choose from: pottery, jewelry, embroidered clothing, and many food stands.

### GETTING AROUND

Driving in and around El Centro can be challenging, at the very least. There are not many streets, but those that do exist are small and many of them still of the cobblestone variety, so you might imagine that this would be a pleasant drive around a sleepy Mexican beach town. However, bus drivers, annoying parking rules, and lack of road signs make it hard for those not experienced enough in the art of driving in Mexico. So, to get to and from downtown, a taxi is your best bet, but once in El Centro walking is the best option.

**Parking:** The underground parking lot below popular Parque Hidalgo is your best choice, it is located just before the start of the malecón. It's safe and will cost no more than 20 MXN per hour ($1). Otherwise, you may park on the streets, just make sure that parking is allowed in there.

### QUICK BITES

One of the most traditional dishes of the state of Jalisco is the famed *torta ahogada* (a pork meat sandwich drowned in tomato and really spicy sauce), and **Mamá Martha** (✉ *Uruguay 263*) have the best in town with *bolillos* (baguettes) brought directly from Guadalajara every day specially for this little place located just before actually getting into El Centro. For a wide range of Mexican *antojitos* (typical Mexican corn-based snacks) you may want to drop by **Cenaduría Doña Raquel** (✉ *Leona Vicario 131*), an authentic old-school establishment where traditional Mexican food tastes as it's supposed to.

### TOURS

**Puerto Vallarta Tours**

**TOUR—SPORTS** | This company offers tours that are available from other area operators, but we recommend it for its all-in-one website, English-speaking operators and crew, and the convenience factor: through this one operator, you can book everything from canopy tours, ATVs, deep-sea fishing, and mountain biking to cruise tours, cultural tours, and bullfighting. ✉ *Manuel M. Dieguez 404, Zona Romántica* ☎ *322/222-4935, 866/217-9704 toll-free in U.S.* 🌐 *www.puertovallartatours.net.*

**★ Vallarta Food Tours**

**$$$** | **MEXICAN** | Not sure where to start? Why not sample a bit of everything? [$] *Average main: 1000 MP* ✉ *1193–A Av. Mexico, Colonia 5 de Deciembre, El Centro* ☎ *322/222–6117* 🌐 *vallartafoodtours.com* 🕒 *No dinner.*

## Sights

El Centro might be the best-known neighborhood in the Banderas Bay region, but it's hard to find, besides the revamped malecón, a sight that's worth visiting. The area is a sight in itself, with cobblestone streets, typical white houses with red tile roofs, and a nostalgic atmosphere that recalls a bygone era.

**Church of Our Lady of Guadalupe**

**BUILDING** | The Church of Our Lady of Guadalupe is dedicated to the patron saint of Mexico and of Puerto Vallarta. The holy mother's image, by Ignacio Ramírez, is the centerpiece of the cathedral's slender marble altarpiece. The brick bell tower is topped by a lacy-looking crown that replicates the one worn by Carlota, short-lived empress of Mexico. The wrought-iron crown toppled during an earthquake that shook this area of the Pacific Coast in October 1995 but was soon replaced with a fiberglass version, supported, as was the original, by a squadron of stone angels. This was replaced with a newer and larger rendition in October 2009. ✉ *Calle Hidalgo 370, between Iturbide and Zaragoza, El Centro* ☎ *322/223–1226* 🌐 *parroquiadeguadalupevallarta.com.*

**Cuale Museum** (*Archaeological Museum*)

**MUSEUM** | Pre-Columbian figures and Indian artifacts are on display at the Cuale Museum. There's a general explanation of Western Pacific cultures and shaft tombs and abbreviated but attractive exhibits of Aztatlán and Purépecha cultures and the Spanish conquest. ✉ *Western tip of Isla Río Cuale, El Centro* 🎟 *By donation.*

**El Malecón**

**PROMENADE** | **FAMILY** | "El Malecón" of Puerto Vallarta is its flagship attraction. The construction started in 1936 and it went through a complete renovation in 2011. Now, it's closed to traffic and pedestrians can stroll for almost a kilometer (0.6 mile) through a gorgeous palm-filled promenade. The walk starts at

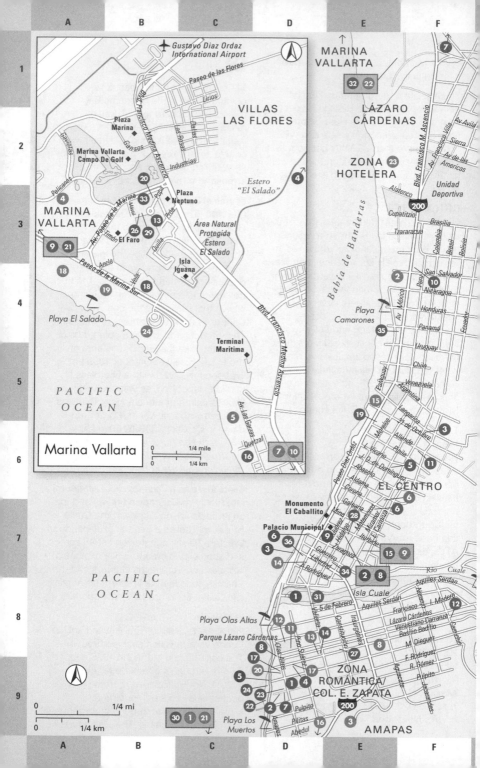

G          H          I

ÓLIMPICA

La Lagunilla

Rio Nilo

Rio Amazonas

Bio de la Plata

Río Grande

Río Dabubio

Río Po

Río Nazas

COL. 5 DE
DICIEMBRE

Urano

Libr…

Rivera del Rio

Benito Juarez

BENITO
JUAREZ

# Puerto Vallarta

## KEY

🔴 Sights
🔴 Restaurants
🔴 Hotels
⤢ Beach

A section of El Malecón, the iconic waterfront boardwalk that extends down the coastline to Los Muertos beach.

the "Rosita Hotel" and continues till the amphitheater across the main square. Enjoy the 10 sculptures on your way and the Voladores de Papantla (ancient Mesoamerican tradition involving bungee-jump-like "flying people"). ⊠ *Paseo Díaz Ordaz s/n, El Centro.*

### Museo Naval de Puerto Vallarta
**MUSEUM** | This small museum managed by the Mexican Navy has a permanent exhibition about Mexico's relationship with the sea, from the times of the Spanish conquest through modern times. You'll see interesting pieces of antique artillery and silver jewelry, and learn about the history of the Nao de China, a Spanish sailboat that used to navigate the Pacific all the way to China and the Philippines in the 16th and 17th centuries. ⊠ *Zaragoza 4, Puerto Vallarta* ☎ *322/223–5357* ⊕ *sic.gob.mx* ✉ *45 MXN* ⊙ *Closed Mon.*

### Parroquia de Nuestra Señora de Guadalupe
**RELIGIOUS SITE** | The construction of this landmark of Puerto Vallarta, started in 1903 and it wasn't finished until 1963, when a replica of the crown used by the Empress Carlota (there was a time when Mexico had Empresses) was put on top of the building. The crown had to be replaced a few years ago, because an earthquake destroyed the original one. On Saturday at 5 pm there is a mass in English, while on Sunday at 10 am they do a bilingual one. ⊠ *Hidalgo 370, El Centro* ☎ *322/222–1326* ⊕ *parroquiade-guadalupevallarta.com.*

### Plaza de Armas
**PLAZA** | **FAMILY** | The Plaza de Armas or Main Square is a perfect spot to relax. Enjoy an ice cream by the gazebo or a Mexican snack sold by stall vendors in one of the many benches around. The city hall is on one side, the Parish of Our Lady of Guadalupe on the other and, in the background, the malecón. On Thursday and Sunday at 6 pm, everybody dances to the sound of "danzón" while listening to the Municipal Bands. ⊠ *Independencia s/n, El Centro.*

## Beaches

The only functional beach at El Centro is Playa Camarones and it's recognized as one of the best in all of Banderas Bay, as it includes lifeguards, toilets, and easy access. Sadly, the beach right in front of the malecón has become too rocky and people can't even walk through it now as they used to do years ago.

**Playa Camarones**

**BEACH—SIGHT** | A long, flat brown sand beach whose name translates to Shrimp Beach, Playa Camarones was the first urban beach in the country to receive the Playa Limpia (Clean Beach) certification by the federal government. The certification means that the beach will always have a lifeguard present, trash bins, clean bathrooms, and handicap accessibility. Its location attracts many locals: parallel to the malecón between the Hotel Rosita and the Buenaventura Hotel. The shore is always changing—it could be rock-strewn in the morning and clear later when the tide goes out. Watch for whales in winter, too, from trendy beachfront El Solar Bar or from the Barracuda Restaurant next door. Although the waves are gentle, there are strange currents here, which should discourage all but strong swimmers. **Amenities:** lifeguards; food and drink; parking (no fee); toilets; water sports. **Best for:** sunset; surfing; walking. ✉ *El Centro.*

## Restaurants

Comprising the *malecón* (seawalk) and the half-dozen blocks behind it, El Centro has plenty of upscale restaurants. Parking is limited mainly to the street; many of the better restaurants offer valet parking. Café des Artistes, Trio, Vitea, and others offer a variety of cuisines and elegant yet casual dining, which is what Puerto Vallarta diners demand. At the other end of the spectrum, downtown PV has a great assortment of bargain eateries, including those offering tacos (in street stands and sit-down restaurants) and diners catering to locals with excellent prices on changing daily specials.

**Barcelona Tapas**

**$$$** | **SPANISH** | One of the best all-around restaurants in El Centro, this place offers great food and excellent service. The restaurant is air-conditioned in summer; the rest of the year the windows are taken off to let the breeze in. **Known for:** best tapas in town; outstanding view of the bay; fresh sangria. [$] *Average main: 350 MP* ✉ *Calle Matamoros 906, El Centro* ☎ *322/222–0510* 🌐 *www.barcelonatapas.net* ⏲ *No lunch.*

**★ Café des Artistes Bistro Gourmet**

**$$$** | **INTERNATIONAL** | Style and sophistication is what you get when eating at Café des Artistes. Owned and managed by famous French Chef Thierry Blouet, this restaurant is top-shelf when talking about gourmet cuisine in Puerto Vallarta. **Known for:** crème brûlée; cigar bar; hosts and participates in festivals and events throughout the year. [$] *Average main: 300 MP* ✉ *Av. Guadalupe Sánchez 740, El Centro* ☎ *322/226–7200* 🌐 *www.cafedesartistes.com* ⏲ *No lunch.*

**Chez Elena**

**$$** | **MEXICAN** | Frequented in its heyday by Hollywood luminaries and the who's who of PV, this downtown restaurant still has a loyal following. The casual patio ambience is simple, but the wholesome food is satisfying, and the portions are generous. **Known for:** delicious osso buco; amazing views; longtime favorite of the area. [$] *Average main: 145 MP* ✉ *Calle Matamoros 520, El Centro* ☎ *322/222–0161* 🌐 *www.chezelena.com* ⏲ *Closed June–Sept. No lunch.*

**El Andariego**

**$$** | **MODERN MEXICAN** | Locals come here for weekend brunch. They serve truly authentic *huevos rancheros* and all those delicious dishes that make traditional Mexican cuisine so hard to resist. **Known for:** murals depicting PV; diverse menu; favorite of tourists and locals alike. $ *Average main: 200 MP* ✉ *Av. México 1358, at San Salvador, El Centro* ☎ *322/222–0916.*

**★ El Arrayán**

$$ | MEXICAN | Some call it the best in town, others say it's the best restaurant in PV, period. Here you can find the things *abuelita* (grandma) still loves to cook, with a few subtle variations. $ *Average main: 200 MP* ✉ *Calle Allende 344, at Calle Miramar, El Centro* ☎ *322/222–7195* ⊕ *www.elarrayan.com.mx* ☯ *No lunch. Closed Tues. and Sept.*

**Hacienda San Angel Gourmet**

$$$$ | INTERNATIONAL | Ivy climbs blond, hacienda-style columns, and chandeliers bathe in a romantic light in the second-floor dining room of this stunningly restored boutique hotel and restaurant. The chef has a restrained hand when it comes to salt and spices; recipes are straightforward yet neither bland nor boring. **Known for:** cabrería (a choice cut of beef on the bone) served over mashed potatoes and sautéed spinach; breathtaking sunset views; 12-piece mariachi. $ *Average main: 400 MP* ✉ *Calle Miramar 336, El Centro* ☎ *322/222–2692* ⊕ *www.haciendasanangel.com* ☯ *Closed Aug. and Sept.*

**La Bodeguita del Medio**

$$ | CARIBBEAN | Near the malecón's north end, this world-famous franchise restaurant with a fun-loving atmosphere has a bit of a sea view from its second-floor dining room and a Caribbean flavor. Like its Havana namesake, La Bodeguita sells Cuban rum and cigars, and the music (canned during the day, live at night)—like the cuisine—is pure *cubano*. Try the mojito, a signature Havana drink of lime juice, sugar, white rum, and muddled fresh mint leaves. **Known for:** fresh mojitos; sea views; live music in the evening. $ *Average main: 120 MP* ✉ *Paseo Díaz Ordáz 858, El Centro* ☎ *322/223–1585.*

**Planeta Vegetariano**

$ | VEGETARIAN | Those who stumble upon this hogless heaven can "pig out" on tasty, meatless *carne asada* and a selection of main dishes that changes daily. Choose from at least three healthful main dishes, plus beans, several types of rice, and a soup at this casual buffet-only place. **Known for:** the best vegetarian restaurant in town; vegan pancakes; cold-pressed green juice (with grapefruit, celery, nopal, spinach, and parsley). $ *Average main: 85 MP* ✉ *Iturbide 270, El Centro* ☎ *322/222–3073* ⊕ *planetavegetariano.com* ⊟ *No credit cards.*

**River Cafe**

$$$ | INTERNATIONAL | At night, candles flicker at white-skirted tables with comfortable cushioned chairs, and tiny white lights sparkle in palm trees surrounding the multilevel terrace. This riverside restaurant is recommended for breakfast and for the evening ambience. **Known for:** location on a river island; gluten-free options; wedding venue. $ *Average main: 170 MP* ✉ *Isla Río Cuale, Loc. 4, Zona Romántica* ☎ *322/223–0788* ⊕ *www.rivercafe.com.mx.*

**★ Trio**

$$$ | INTERNATIONAL | Trio is simply Puerto Vallarta's best restaurant. The kitchen often stays open until midnight, and during high season the restaurant opens the back patio, second floor, and rooftop terrace. **Known for:** German chef-owners; warm chocolate cake; wide liquor selection. $ *Average main: 150 MP* ✉ *Calle Guerrero 264, El Centro* ☎ *322/222–2196* ⊕ *www.triopv.com* ☯ *No lunch.*

**Vitea Oceanfront Bistro**

$$ | FRENCH | When chefs Bernhard Güth and Ulf Henriksson, of Trio, needed a challenge, they cooked up this delightful (and quite intimate) seaside bistro. The decor of the open, casual venue is as fresh as the food. **Known for:** sunset views; spicy shrimp tempura; outstanding wine list. $ *Average main: 110 MP* ✉ *Libertad 2, north of Cuale River on*

*the malecón, El Centro* ☎ *322/222–8703* 🌐 *www.viteapv.com* ⏲ *Closed 1 wk in late Sept.*

## Hotels

At the north end of downtown, moderately priced and four- to five-star hotels stretch north from the boardwalk along a manicured (and seasonally rocky) beach. A sunset stroll on the malecón is easily accessible from these hotels, as are bustling downtown's activities, galleries, shops, and restaurants. North of the Cuale River, El Centro has fewer hotels than the Zona Romántica, which is just across the bridge and within easy walking distance. The area does have the city center's only luxury hotel, Hacienda San Angel, which is situated just far enough away from Zona Romántica for the walk to be notable (but still not prohibitive).

**Dulce Vida**
$ | **RENTAL** | Hidden four blocks off the busy malecón, this '60s-era villa has apartments of various sizes filled with modern Mexican art and comfortable, if well-worn, furniture. **Pros:** red-tile pool and tropical gardens; ocean-view terraces; friendly staff helps book tours. **Cons:** booked for weeks and months at a time in high season; some rooms better than others; minimum week-long stays during high season. [$] *Rooms from: $80* ✉ *Calle Aldama 295, El Centro* ☎ *322/138–0632, 780/651–1611* 🌐 *www.dulcevida.com* 💳 *No credit cards* 🛏 *7 suites* 🍴 *No meals.*

**Hacienda San Angel**
$$$$ | **HOTEL** | Each room is unique and elegant at this pricey boutique hotel in the hills five blocks above the malecón. **Pros:** the most elegant lodging in downtown Puerto Vallarta; concierge service; excellent bay views. **Cons:** short but steep walk from the malecón; 5% service fee (in addition to taxes) plus 10% fee for using a credit card; fewer amenities than hotels of comparable price point. [$] *Rooms from: $435* ✉ *Calle Miramar 336, at Iturbide, El Centro* ☎ *322/222–2692, 877/815–6594* 🌐 *www.haciendasanangel.com* 🛏 *20 suites* 🍴 *Free Breakfast.*

**Hotel Rio Malecón Puerto Vallarta**
$ | **HOTEL** | Located in downtown Puerto Vallarta and just a block from the beach, Hotel Rio offers quaint traditional accommodations as well as some modern rooms. **Pros:** a block from the boardwalk; two on-site restaurants; kitchenettes in some rooms. **Cons:** some rooms need an upgrade; traffic noise may be a problem for some guests; no elevator. [$] *Rooms from: $80* ✉ *Morelos 170, El Centro* ☎ *322/222–0300* 🌐 *hotelrio.com.mx* 🛏 *47 rooms* 🍴 *No meals.*

**Hotel Rosita**
$$ | **HOTEL** | What started as a sleepy 12-room hostelry—Puerto Vallarta's very first—is now a busy 115-room downtown hotel. **Pros:** old-fashioned value near downtown; Sunday brunch buffet under $10. **Cons:** no bathtubs; older floors and furnishings; so-so beach; Wi-Fi in lobby only. [$] *Rooms from: $75* ✉ *Paseo Díaz Ordaz 901, El Centro* ☎ *322/176–1110* 🌐 *www.hotelrosita.com* 🛏 *115 rooms* 🍴 *Free Breakfast.*

## Nightlife

You can dance salsa with the locals, groove to rock in English or *en español*, or even tango. Things slow down in the off-season, but during school vacations and the winter, clubs stay open until 3, 5, or even 6 am. Except those that double as restaurants, clubs don't open until 10 pm. ■ **TIP→ Clubs don't usually fill up before midnight, but arriving around 10 pm could save you a cover charge.**

Have a late and leisurely dinner, take a walk on the beach and get some coffee, and then stroll into the club cool as a cucumber at 12:30 am or so.

Most of Puerto Vallarta's live music is performed in restaurants and bars, often on or overlooking the beach. ■TIP→ Musical events happening anywhere in Vallarta are listed in Bay Vallarta (⊕ www.bayvallarta. com). This twice-monthly paper lists who is playing in El Centro, the Zona Hotelera Norte, Marina Vallarta, and even as far north as the Riviera Nayarit. More detailed than most similar publications, Bay Vallarta lists showtimes, venues, genres, and cover charges. Live music is much less frequent in the smaller towns to the north and south of PV; to find out what's happening there, ask in tourist-oriented bars, restaurants, or hotels.

### Cervecería Unión

BARS/PUBS | A favorite with the locals, this is a delightful place to have a quality beer and enjoy some of the best oysters in town. In fact, it's the only oyster bar on the malecón, and it offers a wide array of handcrafted beers, both Mexican and international. With a nice location, Cervecería Unión is a relaxing, large spot with full ocean views. It's open from 8 am to midnight. ⊠ Paseo Díaz Ordaz 610, El Centro ☎ 322/223–0929.

### ★ El Solar

BARS/PUBS | This oceanfront bar is just the way a beach bar is supposed to be—small, hip, and laid-back—making it a real pleasure to enjoy a beer while watching the waves of Playa Camarones. There's live music on Friday night and a DJ on Saturday. There is always a good vibe in this place, and, if you feel like having a bite, you can always ask the waiter to bring you some food from their next-door sister restaurant, Barracuda. ⊠ Calle Paraguay 1290, El Centro ☎ 322/222–4034.

### La Bodeguita del Medio

DANCE CLUBS | People of all ages come to salsa and drink mojitos made with Cuban rum at this wonderful Cuban bar and restaurant with a friendly vibe. The small dance floor fills up as soon as the house sextet starts playing around 9:30 pm. There's no cover. ⊠ Malecón 858, El Centro ☎ 322/223–1585 ⊕ labodeguitadelmedio.com.mx.

### La Regadera

BARS/PUBS | Talent at this karaoke spot varies; it's open Monday through Saturday (except during low season, when the schedule is less consistent) after 9 pm. Come practice your standard Beatles tunes or hip-hop before your next official recording session. ⊠ Calle Morelos 666, El Centro ☎ 322/222–5735 ⊕ laregaderapv.com.

### La Vaquita

DANCE CLUBS | La Vaquita is arguably the hippest of all the El Centro clubs. A mostly young crowd packs the place every weekend, dancing to the rhythms of house, techno, Latin, pop, and rock music. The location is outstanding, with great ocean views. Here it's customary to enjoy your favorite drink in a litro, a one-liter (a little more than 2 pints) Styrofoam glass, with a straw. It opens every day from 7 pm to 6 am. ⊠ Paseo Diaz Ordaz 610, El Centro ☎ 331/400–2533 ⊕ www.facebook.com/ LaVaquitaPuertoVallarta.

### Mandala

DANCE CLUBS | If you were to choose just one of the malecón nightclubs, Mandala may be a good choice. It's the most stylish club in the whole El Centro area, and throws some of the best parties, too. The music is mostly electronic, with lots of house and techno. The cover varies according to the night of the week and the season of the year, but it's in line with the rest of the nightclubs along the malecón. ⊠ Paseo Diaz Ordaz 633, El Centro ☎ 322/142–9111 ⊕ mandalanightclub.com.

### P'yote Lounge

PIANO BARS/LOUNGES | Keeping with the glamorous style of Café des Artistes, this small but classy bar is the perfect place to enjoy a cocktail or martini before heading to the theater or to a nightclub. P'yote Lounge is a celebration of the

Huichol, the indigenous people of the Jalisco/Nayarit region, and is named after the psychotropic cactus central to the Huichol vision of the world. ✉ *Café des Artistes, Av. Guadalupe Sánchez 740, El Centro* ☎ *322/226–7200* ⊕ *www.cafedesartistes.com.*

### Sky Mandala

**DANCE CLUBS** | The sister nightclub of Mandala has its entrance just around the corner and it's on a gorgeous rooftop terrace with stunning views of the malecón and the Pacific Ocean. It's a bit more exclusive than Mandala and offers a more intimate kind of atmosphere, with a small dance floor and an open design that makes the most of its location. House, techno, and Latin beats will play out all night long. ✉ *Morelos 633, El Centro* ☎ *322/108–9948* ⊕ *www.facebook.com/SkyMPV.*

### Zoo Bar

**DANCE CLUBS** | Ready to party? Then head here for DJ-spun techno, Latin, reggae, and hip-hop. The adventurous can dance in the cage. It attracts a mixed crowd of mainly young locals and travelers, though after midnight the median age plunges. It's open until 6 am when things are hopping. The restaurant fills with cruise-ship passengers early in the evening. ✉ *Paseo Díaz Ordaz 630, El Centro* ☎ *322/150–4152* ⊕ *facebook.com/zoodancebarpv/.*

## 🎭 Performing Arts

Most hotels have lounge music, and many hotels have buffet dinners with mariachis, folkloric dancers, and *charros* (elegantly dressed horsemen, who, in this case, perform mostly roping tricks). All-inclusive hotels generally include nightly entertainment in the room price. Drag shows are crowd-pleasers.

### Cinépolis

**FILM** | Until Cinemex showed up, this was PV's newest movie theater. Next to Soriana department stores at the south entrance to El Pitillal, it has 15

screens and shows movies in English and Spanish. Tickets are about 59 MXN ($3), less on Wednesday. ✉ *Plaza Soriana, Av. Francisco Villa 1642–A, El Centro* ☎ *552/122–6060* ⊕ *cinepolis.com.*

### ★ Teatro Vallarta

**THEATER** | The biggest cultural center in Puerto Vallarta, Teatro Vallarta is in a modern building with an outstanding sound system that qualifies it to screen New York Met operas. It offers a bit of everything: national theater companies that are happy to include this beach town in their yearly circuit; sporadic international ballet performances or touring musicians; local conferences; dance contests; and all kinds of other events. ✉ *Calle Uruguay 184, El Centro* ☎ *322/467–8888* ⊕ *teatrovallarta.com.*

## 🛍 Shopping

### Alfarería Tlaquepaque

**CERAMICS/GLASSWARE** | This is a large store with a ton of red-clay items traditional to the area—in fact, their predecessors were crafted before the 1st century AD. Rustic pottery and glazed ceramic pieces come in traditional styles at reasonable prices. ✉ *Av. México 1100, El Centro* ☎ *322/223–2121* ⊕ *at.com.mx* ⌚ *Closed Sun.*

### ★ Galería de Ollas

**CERAMICS/GLASSWARE** | The 300 or so potters from the village of Mata Ortiz add their touches to the intensely—sometimes hypnotically—geometric designs of their ancestors from Paquimé. At this shop pieces range from about $60 to $10,000, with an average of about $400. Stop in during an afternoon walk through downtown. ✉ *Calle Corona 176, El Centro* ☎ *322/223–1045* ⊕ *www.galeriadeollas.com.*

### Galería Indígena

**CRAFTS** | The assortment of handicrafts here is huge: Huichol yarn paintings and beaded bowls and statuettes, real Talavera ceramics from Puebla, decorative pieces in painted wood, and many other items. The owner likes offering customers a drink of water or other refreshment, no strings attached. ⊠ *Av. Juárez 628, El Centro* ☎ *322/223–0800* ☾ *Closed Sun.*

**Galería Pacífico**
ART GALLERIES | Open since 1987, Pacífico features the sculpture of Ramiz Barquet, who created the bronze *Nostalgia* piece on the malecón. Brewster Brockmann paints contemporary abstracts; Marco Alvarez, Alejandro Mondria, and Alfredo Langarica are other featured artists. During the summer months the gallery can be visited only by appointment. ⊠ *Calle Aldama 174, 2nd fl., El Centro* ☎ *322/222–1982* ⊕ *www.galeriapacifico. com.*

**La Casa del Habano**
TOBACCO | The Cuban cigars for sale here start at around 75 MXN ($4) each and top out at about 4,000 MXN ($200) for a Cohiba Siglo VI (by order only; they don't keep these in stock). The owner claims that 95% of the cigars sold in Vallarta are fake Cubans, but his are the genuine article. You can smoke your stogie downstairs in the casual lounge while sipping coffee or enjoying a shot of Cuban rum. ⊠ *Aldama 170, El Centro* ☎ *322/223–2758* ⊕ *lacasadelhabanopv. com.mx* ☾ *Closed Sun.*

**Mercado Isla Río Cuale**
CRAFTS | FAMILY | Small shops and outdoor stands sell an interesting mix of wares at this informal and fun market that divides El Centro from Colonia E. Zapata. Harley-Davidson kerchiefs, Che paintings on velvet, and Madonna icons compete with the usual synthetic lace tablecloths, shell and quartz necklaces, and silver jewelry amid postcards and key chains. The market is partially shaded by enormous fig and rubber trees and serenaded by the rushing river; a half-dozen cafés and restaurants provide sustenance. ⊠ *Isla Cuale, between Ignacio L. Vallarta and Juarez, El Centro.*

**Plaza Caracol**
SHOPPING CENTERS/MALLS | This shopping mall is lively and full on weekends and evenings, even when others are dead. Its anchors are the Soriana supermarket and the second-floor casino. Surrounding these are tiny stores dispensing electronics, ice cream, fresh flowers, and more. This is also a good place for manicures and haircuts. Adding to the commercial center's appeal is the six-screen Cinemex movie theater. ⊠ *Bd. Francisco M. Ascencio, Km 2.5, Zona Hotelera* ☎ *322/224–3239* ⊕ *plazacaracol.mx.*

**Pueblo Viejo Mercado de Artesanías**
CRAFTS | Flowers, piñatas, produce, and plastics share space in indoor and outdoor stands with souvenirs and lesser-quality crafts. Upstairs, locals eat at long-established, family-run restaurants. ⊠ *Agustín Rodríguez 110, El Centro.*

★ **Sergio Bustamante**
ART GALLERIES | Internationally known Sergio Bustamante—the creator of life-size brass, copper, and ceramic animals, mermaids, suns, and moons—has a team of artisans to execute his never-ending pantheon of creative and quirky objets d'art, such as pots shaped like human torsos that sell for more than $1,000. Paintings, purses, shoes, and jewelry are sold here as well. ⊠ *Av. Juárez 275, El Centro* ☎ *322/223–1405* ⊕ *coleccionsergiobustamante.com.mx.*

 **Activities**

El Centro is the place to walk around and marvel at the beauty of Puerto Vallarta and the simplicity of its way of life. There is no better thing than to stroll along the malecón and take in the views and sculptures, or stop in at its many shops and restaurants. That said, there is must to do outside of this, although you will find many vendors offering tours in and around PV all over the area.

### Vista Vallarta

**GOLF** | Some of the best views in the area belong to the aptly named Vista Vallarta. There are 18 holes designed by Jack Nicklaus and another 18 by Tom Weiskopf. The greens fee for the course, which is a few miles northwest of the Marina Vallarta area, is $209. A shared cart and tax are included. ⊠ *Circuito Universidad 653, El Centro* ☎ *322/290-0030* ⊕ *clubcorp.com.*

# Zona Hotelera

Puerto Vallarta is a tourist destination with all kinds of accommodations to enjoy, but you will find the greatest concentration of hotels in the Hotel Zone. Zona Hotelera, as the locals call it, stretches along Francisco Medina Ascencio Avenue, from the Puerto Vallarta Maritime Terminal to the Sheraton Buganvilias Resort. The creation of the Hotel Zone moved the tourist accommodations outside the downtown boundaries, allowing the historic center to remain relatively untouched.

Although most of the hotels are not brand new, they are all on the beach and offer spectacular ocean views over Banderas Bay, making them highly popular among Vallarta visitors. The latest additions to the area are numerous skyscrapers with oceanfront exclusive condominiums that are often available for short-term vacation rentals.

Zona Hotelera is loved by joggers. They often start their route at the beginning of the river walk, located between Plaza Peninsula and the Holiday Inn, and continue to a calm residential area called Fluvial Vallarta across the street. Another option is to follow Medina Ascencio to the city's public stadium, Agustin Flores Contreras, at the very end of the Hotel Zone (in front of the Sheraton Buganvilia Resort). Medina Ascencio is partially closed at certain hours on Sunday, when cars are replaced by bicyclists, walkers, and joggers.

Beach lovers will enjoy the many interconnected beaches of the Hotel Zone. There are several points of access along Medina Ascencio Avenue. The best idea is to park your car between Plaza Peninsula and La Isla shopping center.

## GETTING AROUND

The Zona Hotelera covers the coastal road from the Marina all the way to El Centro, which is quite a large area. That disqualifies navigating on foot, unless you know exactly where are you going and it's close enough to avoid getting a taxi or bus. This is the section in PV where using a car is recommended. The road is wide and cars move at normal 21st-century speed. Here, it's also easier to find a proper bus stop. Likewise, taxi stations can be found every second block or you can simply stop one of the many cabs riding through the streets.

**Parking:** Parking in the Hotel Zone is not that difficult as roads in this part of Vallarta are modern and definitely wider than in El Centro and Zona Romántica. As it is a commercial area, most businesses provide their own parking space, so you'll have no problems for parking here.

## QUICK BITES

Not actually a stall, as it has tables and chairs, but neither a restaurant, **Tacos Mar y Tierra** (*Blvd. Francisco Medina Ascencio 1956*) is the place to go if you want to eat like the locals do. Either by day (quesadillas and shrimp tacos) or by night (beef tacos), it will not disappoint. For an informal bite on any given evening, nothing like **Food Park PV** (*Blvd. Francisco Medina Ascencio 2450*). Here, you will find a variety of snacks, beer, live music and good vibes, all in a refreshing outdoors atmosphere.

*Continued on page 97*

3

Puerto Vallarta ZONA HOTELERA

# THE ART OF THE HUICHOL

Updated by
Georgia de Katona

The intricately woven and beaded designs of the Huichols' art are as vibrant and fascinating as the traditions of its people, best known as the "Peyote People" for their traditional and ceremonial use of the hallucinogenic drug. Peyote-inspired visions are thought to be messages from God and are reflected in the art.

Like the Lacandon Maya, the Huichol resisted assimilation by Spanish invaders, fleeing to inhospitable mountains and remote valleys. There they retained their pantheistic religion in which shamans lead the community in spiritual matters and the use of peyote facilitates communication directly with God.

Roads didn't reach larger Huichol communities until the mid-20th century, bringing electricity and other modern distractions. The collision with the outside world has had pros and cons, but art lovers have only benefited from their increased access to intricately patterned woven and beaded goods. Today the traditional souls that remain on the land—a significant population of perhaps 6,000 to 8,000—still create votive bowls, prayer arrows, jewelry, and bags, and sell them to finance elaborate religious ceremonies. The pieces go for as little as $5 or as much as $5,000, depending on the skill and fame of the artist and quality of materials.

(loft) Huichol yarn painting, National Museum of Anthropology, (top) Huichol art, Puerto Vallarta

# UNDERSTANDING THE HUICHOL

When Spanish conquistadors arrived in the early 16th century, the Huichol, unwilling to work as slaves on the haciendas of the Spanish or to adopt their religion, fled to the Sierra Madre. They lived there, disconnected from society, for nearly 500 years. Beginning in the 1970s, roads and electricity made their way to tiny Huichol towns. Today, about half of the population of perhaps 7,000 continues to live in ancestral villages and *rancheritas* (tiny individual farms).

## The Power of Prayer

They believe that without their prayers and offerings the sun wouldn't rise, the earth would cease spinning. It is hard, then, for them to reconcile their poverty with the relative easy living of "free-riders" (Huichol term for nonspiritual freeloaders) who enjoy fine cars and expensive houses thanks to the Huichols efforts to sustain the planet. But rather than hold our reckless materialism against us, the Huichol add us to their prayers.

## THE PEYOTE PEOPLE

Visions inspired by the hallucinogenic peyote cactus are considered by the Huichol to be messages from God and to help in solving personal and communal problems. Indirectly, they provide inspiration for their almost psychedelic art. Just a generation or two ago, annual peyote-gathering pilgrimages were done on foot. Today the journey is still a man's chief obligation, but they now drive to the holy site at Wiricuta, in San Luis Potosi State.

## SHAMANISM

A Huichol man has a lifelong calling as a shaman. There are two shamanic paths: the path of the wolf, which is more aggressive, demanding, and powerful (wolf shamans profess the ability to morph into wolves); and the path of the deer, which is playful. A shaman chooses his own path.

## BEADED ITEMS

The smaller the beads, the more delicate and expensive the piece. Items made with iridescent beads from Japan are the priciest. Look for good-quality glass beads, definition, symmetry, and artful use of color. Beads should fit together tightly in straight lines, with no gaps.

## YARN PAINTINGS

Symmetry is not necessary, although there should be an overall sense of unity. Thinner thread results in finer, more costly work. Look for tightness, with no visible gaps or broken threads. Paintings should have a stamp of authenticity on the back, including artist's name and tribal affiliation.

## PRAYER ARROWS

Collectors and purists should look for the traditionally made arrows of brazilwood inserted into a bamboo shaft. The most interesting ones contain embroidery work, or tiny carved icons, or are painted with copal symbols indicative of their original intended purpose, for example protecting a child or ensuring a successful corn crop.

Huichol bird, Jalisco

# HOW TO READ THE SYMBOLS

Spiders that come out at dawn are thought to welcome the rising sun.

The **deer** is the animal manifestation of the god Kahumari, who intercedes in heaven on earthlings' behalf.

Anything with **horns** or **antlers** symbolizes communion and oneness with God.

Yarn painting

■ The trilogy of **corn, peyote,** and **deer** represents three aspects of God. According to Huichol mythology, peyote sprang up in the footprints of the deer. Depicted like stylized flowers, peyote represents communication with God. Corn, the Huichol's

Corn symbol

staple food, symbolizes health and prosperity. An image drawn inside the root ball depicts the essence of God within it.

■ The **double-headed eagle** is the emblem of the omnipresent sky god.

■ A **nierika** is a portal between the spirit world and our own. Often in the form of a yarn painting, a nierika can be round or square.

■ **Salamanders** and **turtles** are associated with rain; the former provoke the clouds. Turtles maintain underground springs and purify water.

■ A **scorpion** is the soldier of the sun.

■ The Huichol depict raindrops as tiny **snakes;** in yarn paintings they descend to enrich the fields.

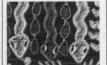

Snakes

**Jose Benictez Sánchez,** (1938—2009) may be the elder statesman of yarn painters and has shown in Japan, Spain, the U.S., and at the Museum of Modern Art in Mexico City.

Peyote

Scorpion

# TRADITION TRANSFORMED

The art of the Huichol was, for centuries, made from undyed wool, shells, stones, and other natural materials. It was not until the 1970s that the Huichol began incorporating bright, zingy colors, without sacrificing the intricate patterns and symbols used for centuries. The result is strenuously colorful, yet dignified.

## YARN PAINTINGS
Dramatic and vivid yarn paintings are highly symbolic, stylized visions of life.

## MASKS AND ANIMAL STATUETTES
Bead-covered wooden or ceramic masks and animal statuettes are other adaptations made for outsiders.

## PRAYER ARROWS
Made for every ceremony, prayer arrows send petitions winging to God.

## VOTIVE BOWLS
Ceremonial votive bowls, made from gourds, are decorated with bright, stylized beadwork.

## WOVEN SHOULDER BAGS
Carried by men, the bags are decorated with traditional Huichol icons.

For years, Huichol men as well as women wore **BEADED BRACELETS**; today earrings and necklaces are also made.

Diamond-shape **GOD'S EYES** of sticks and yarn protect children from harm.

# 👁 Sights

As its name suggests, the Hotel Zone is all about big resorts and the beaches in front of them. However, there are a few other interesting spots to visit such as the Estero El Salado or the lesser-known river walk that stretches along the Pitillal river.

### Estero El Salado

**NATURE PRESERVE** | El Salado Estuary is a natural reserve set in the middle of Puerto Vallarta. There is impressive biodiversity found in this place, considering it's in an urban area. They offer boat tours across the estuary, where you will see crocodiles roaming free in their habitat, as well as several species of water birds. ✉ *Blvd. Francisco Medina Ascencio s/n, Zona Hotelera* ☎ *322/201–7361* ⊕ *esterodelsalado.org.*

### Parque Lineal Río Pitillal

**NATIONAL/STATE PARK | FAMILY** | The Parque Lineal Río Pitillal is basically a scenic path along the Pitillal river, starting at Avenida Francisco Villa (right in front of Cinépolis) and extending all the way to the beach. There is a nice pathway perfect for bikes and trolleys, benches, picnic tables, and even a lookout that shows a nice and different perspective of the city. ✉ *Río Pitillal, between Francisco Villa and the beach, Zona Hotelera.*

# 🏖 Beaches

The beaches in the Hotel Zone can be lively during holidays and high season but have less to recommend them the rest of the year. Beach erosion is a problem here, and some of the hotels' beaches have little or no sand at high tide.

### Playa del Holi

**BEACH—SIGHT | FAMILY** | The high-rise-backed Zona Hotelera beach goes by several monikers—mainly Playa del Holi but also Playa Peninsula. Most people, however, just refer to each piece of beach by the hotel that it faces.

Interrupted here and there by breakwaters, this fringe of gray-beige sand is generally flat but slopes down to the water. Winds and tides sometimes strew it with stones that make it less pleasant. **Amenities:** food and drink; parking; water sports. **Best for:** walking; sunset. ✉ *Zona Hotelera.*

# 🍴 Restaurants

### El Coleguita Mariscos Marina Vallarta

$ | **SEAFOOD** | The ambience at this patio restaurant facing the boats and the marina is casual and festive; the crowd hums with contentment while other restaurants nearby scorningly have been drained of clientele. There is live music (mainly mariachi) most days. **Known for:** free tequila shots; great service; live music. 💲 *Average main: 115 MP* ✉ *Loc. 17, Calle Popa s/n, Marina Vallarta* ☎ *322/221–2116* ⊕ *mariscoselcoleguita. com* 🚫 *No credit cards* 🕑 *Closed Tues.*

### Mariscos 8 Tostadas Versalles

$ | **SEAFOOD** | The original Mariscos 8 Tostadas establishment (nowadays there are a few others in the bay), it's widely considered the best seafood restaurant in PV. Not a flashy place, it's clean, offers good service, and the dishes are simply delicious. **Known for:** the best aguachile in town; fresh ceviche; relaxed atmosphere. 💲 *Average main: 120 MP* ✉ *Niza 134, Zona Hotelera* ☎ *322/224–9225* 🚫 *No credit cards* 🕑 *Closed 2 wks in Sept. No dinner.*

# 🛏 Hotels

The creation of the Hotel Zone moved the tourist accommodations outside the downtown boundaries, which has kept the historic center relatively untouched. Although most of the hotels are not brand new, they are all beachfront with spectacular ocean views over Banderas Bay, which makes them highly popular among Vallarta visitors. The latest additions to the area are numerous skyscrapers with exclusive oceanfront condominiums that are often available for short-term vacation rentals.

**Fiesta Americana Puerto Vallarta All-Inclusive & Spa**
$$$ | **HOTEL** | **FAMILY** | This storied resort rises above a deep-blue pool that flows beside palm oases. **Pros:** across from Plaza Caracol, with its shops, grocery store, and Cinemex; lots of on-site shops; kids' club. **Cons:** no ocean view from the second and third floors; not the best beach in town; good at most things, great at nothing. [$] *Rooms from: $300* ✉ *Blvd. Francisco M. Ascencio, Km 2.5, Zona Hotelera* ☎ *322/226–2100, 443/310–8137 in U.S.* 🌐 *www.fiestaamericana.com* 🛏 *291 rooms* 🍴 *All-inclusive.*

**Hilton Puerto Vallarta Resort**
$$$ | **ALL-INCLUSIVE** | **FAMILY** | The Hilton Puerto Vallarta has spacious and modern rooms, good design, and the best beach in the hotel zone. **Pros:** right on the beach; kids' club; adults-only section. **Cons:** unimpressive meals; charge for Wi-Fi; charge for parking. [$] *Rooms from: $250* ✉ *Av. de las Garzas 136, Zona Hotelera* ☎ *322/176–1176* 🌐 *hiltonhotels.com* 🛏 *259 rooms* 🍴 *All-inclusive.*

**Secrets Vallarta Bay Puerto Vallarta**
$$$ | **ALL-INCLUSIVE** | This modern, adults-only resort enjoys a privileged location close enough to downtown, but still in the Hotel Zone and the array of shopping, dining, and nightlife options that the area has to offer. **Pros:** state-of-the-art spa; high-quality all-inclusive service; adults-only. **Cons:** not much privacy at beach; no parking; bathrooms separated only by curtain. [$] *Rooms from: $300* ✉ *David Alfaro Siqueiros 164, Zona Hotelera* ☎ *866/467–3273* 🌐 *secretsresorts.com* 🛏 *271 suites* 🍴 *All-inclusive.*

**Sheraton Buganvilias Resort & Convention Center**
$$$ | **RESORT** | **FAMILY** | Marking the start of the Hotel Zone, the Sheraton was the first one of the big-name resorts built in Puerto Vallarta and ever since it has maintained its status as a Vallarta household name. **Pros:** excellent Sunday Champagne brunch; gym and spa; daily supervised activities for kids. **Cons:** so-so beach; some facilities are outdated; faces busy and rather unattractive boulevard. [$] *Rooms from: $250* ✉ *Blvd. Francisco M. Ascencio 999, Zona Hotelera* ☎ *322/226–0404, 877/743–7282* 🌐 *www.sheratonvallarta.com* 🛏 *473 rooms* 🍴 *All-inclusive.*

## Nightlife

For years, when talking about nightlife in Vallarta everything was about the downtown clubs and maybe an indie local in the Zona Romántica, but that whole narrative changed with the arrival of Strana and La Santa to the heart of the Hotel Zone. These couple of nightclubs are undoubtedly the two best in town and their sole presence serve to bring new life to the whole area.

**La Madalena**
**BARS/PUBS** | A cool, although a bit posh, bar with the largest TV screen in Puerto Vallarta, locals come here for "pre-copa" (predrinks) and to watch big soccer matches or boxing fights. ✉ *Francisco Medina Ascencio 2025, Zona Hotelera* ☎ *322/135–9982.*

**La Santa**
**DANCE CLUBS** | The trendiest club in town and a favorite of locals and foreigners, La Santa has two different dance floors, one playing electronic and house music and the other mixing a variety of pop and rock in English and Spanish. There is a stylish swimming pool in the second room, where things can sometimes get a bit out of control. It has some great parties, but can get a bit too crowded at times. ✉ *Francisco Medina Ascencio 2468, at Fluvial Vallarta, Zona Hotelera* ☎ *322/182–1803* 🌐 *facebook.com/LaSantaPtoVallarta.*

### Nine Ninety 9

**BARS/PUBS** | Located just outside the Sheraton Buganvilias Resort, Nine Ninety 9 could be described as a classy sports bar with fine cuisine. ⌧ *Francisco Medina Ascencio 999, Zona Hotelera* ☏ *322/226–0404* ⊕ *facebook.com/nineninety9.vallarta.*

### ★ Strana

**DANCE CLUBS** | This stylish nightclub seems to be a bit small, but it features an enormous dance floor. The lights and sound systems are state-of-the-art, which is highly appreciated by the world-famous DJs that come here to mix it up. They play mostly Electronic Dance Music (EDM), but, as the night goes on, you'll also hear some '80s and '90s pop-rock hits. It's open from Thursday to Saturday after 10 pm. ⌧ *Francisco Medina Ascencio 2125, Zona Hotelera* ☏ *322/108–4358* ⊕ *facebook.com/StranaPV.*

##  Performing Arts

### Cinemex Plaza Caracol

**FILM** | This easy-to-access movie theater is in the heart of the Hotel Zone, on the second floor at the south end of the Plaza Caracol mall. The latest movies are shown on its 10 screens. Tickets are around 50 MXN (less than $3), with a 25% Wednesday discount. ⌧ *Plaza Caracol, Av. de los Tules 178, Zona Hotelera* ☏ *555/257–6969* ⊕ *cinemex.com.*

### Cinépolis VIP La Isla

**FILM** | Leather reclining sofas with trays and blankets are just the beginning of the VIP experience, which is rounded out by full gourmet menus and alcoholic drinks. ⌧ *Francisco Medina Ascencio 2479, La Isla Shopping Village, Zona Hotelera* ☏ *552/122–6060* ⊕ *cinepolis.com.*

##  Shopping

Shopping in the Zona Hotelera is quite different than in El Centro or Zona Romántica. Here, you will find sophisticated boutiques at big, modern shopping malls such as La Isla and Galerías Vallarta. This is not the place to look for original art works or traditional handicrafts.

### La Isla Shopping Village

**SHOPPING CENTERS/MALLS** | The largest, newest, and most modern shopping mall in Puerto Vallarta, La Isla features top-shelf boutiques, gourmet restaurants, and VIP cinema theaters. Its only con is that it's outdoors, which makes it hard to walk around it in the heat of the summer or during rainy days. ⌧ *Francisco Medina Ascencio 2479, Zona Hotelera* ☏ *322/688–1453* ⊕ *facebook.com/LaIslaPuertoVallartaOficial.*

##  Activities

Along the beach you will get plenty of opportunities to practice the water sport of your choice. Offices for most tour operators can also be found around the commercial area of Zona Hotelera, just like the Skydive Vallarta branch at Plaza Peninsula.

### Canopy Tour de Los Veranos

**TOUR—SPORTS** | Los Veranos was the first canopy tour company to establish itself here and has extended the number of services it offers, now including ATV and city tours as combos. After the descent you may want to enjoy its restaurant, sip some tequila, or go on a fantastic nature hike. ⌧ *Blvd. Francisco Medina Ascencio 2735, Loc. 5, Zona Hotelera* ☏ *322/223–0504, 800/396–9168 in U.S.* ⊕ *www.canopytours-vallarta.com.*

### Skydive Vallarta

**FLYING/SKYDIVING/SOARING** | During the winter season particularly, but also year-round, you'll frequently see skydivers landing at the beach in Nuevo Vallarta. Thrill seekers at Skydive Vallarta will take off at the airport in Puerto Vallarta and fly for about 25 minutes before jumping in tandem at around 9,000 feet, with three jumping schedules to choose from. ✉ *Plaza Peninsula, Blvd. Francisco Medina Ascencio 2485, Zona Hotelera* ☎ *322/189–3909* ⊕ *skydivevallarta.mx.*

# Marina Vallarta

Marina Vallarta is a beachfront model tourist community located next to the Puerto Vallarta International Airport, between a golf course and a marina. It was created at the end of the 1980s and was quickly "copied" by other tourist destinations such a Cancún, Los Cabos, Mazatlán, and Ixtapa. It functions almost as a self-sustainable entity, where tourists can find absolutely everything they may need during vacation including restaurants, bars, shops, and the Plaza Marina shopping center with a Mega Soriana supermarket.

Marina Vallarta is a pleasant area to visit on a lazy afternoon. If you arrive by car, you will first notice a big whale sculpture at the main entrance, designed by Octavio González in the 1990s and sponsored by local Marina businessmen. You may park your car at the Nima Bay building, which has numerous shops, cafés, and restaurants that cater to both tourists and locals. Nima Bay opens to a marina promenade, where the main attraction is a lighthouse with a bar at the top, at the end of Timón Street. The promenade stretches along modern vessels and offers numerous restaurants for breakfast, lunch, and dinner. This is also an ideal place to go on a fishing tour. Renting a boat is extremely easy, and you will surely be approached by many people offering you one.

If you come with your own boat, Marina Vallarta rents many slips on a daily, weekly, or monthly basis with all basic services such as electricity, satellite TV,

honey barge, water, laundry services, an 88-ton travel lift, and security. For more information contact the Harbormaster: ☎ *322/221–0722.*

Sports lovers will appreciate the 18-hole golf course designed by Joe Finger that offers a typical Vallarta experience with stellar ocean and mountain views.

## GETTING AROUND
The Marina area is ideal for bike-lovers. One can get everywhere in a bike without too much effort, which might not be the case if you'd like to walk from a resort to one of the many restaurants around the Nima Bay building. Driving is also a good option, although maybe a bit unnecessary if you are staying inside the Marina. Taxis are all over the area, but to get a bus you might need to go first to the Medina Ascencio Boulevard.

**Parking:** There is plenty of parking space on the streets; however, in the area surrounding the most popular restaurants it might get tricky to find a free spot during lunch time.

## QUICK BITES
The best fish and shrimp tacos in town are served at **Marisma** (*Corner of Popa and Quilla*). It started in a little stall away from the big restaurants of the Marina seawalk, has now overtaken most of them, at least in reputation among the locals. For coffee and desserts there is nothing more *Vallartense* than **Repostería Los Chatos** (*Plaza Neptuno Loc. 11*). Any local can recite their phone number by memory, as it advertised heavily on the radio and it's been the same number for decades. If you are going to try the famous Mexican *pan dulce* this is the place to do it.

 **Beaches**

The thing about Marina Vallarta beaches is that is hard to actually get to them. The big resorts of the area block most public accesses, so these are beaches mostly for the tourists staying here. However, if you really want to see it, there is a small road called Paseo Bocanegra at the north end of the golf course that goes all the way to the beach. Just be careful to avoid crocodiles and the security staff from the golf club.

**Playa el Salado**

**BEACH—SIGHT** | At Marina Vallarta, Playa El Salado—facing the Grand Velas, Sol Meliá, Marriott, Mayan Palace, and Westin hotels—is sandy but in spots very narrow. During fine weather and on weekends, and daily during high season, you can rent Jet Skis and pack onto colorful banana boats for bouncy tours of 10 minutes or longer. In late summer and early fall, there are opportunities to view turtle-protection activities. **Amenities:** food and drink; water sports; lifeguards. **Best for:** sunset; windsurfing; walking. ✉ *Marina Vallarta.*

## 🍴 Restaurants

Many of Marina Vallarta's restaurants face the boats at this area's main attraction: the yacht harbor. Interspersed with shops and storefronts selling fishing charters and canopy tours, the restaurant scene is easy to negotiate, with no busy boulevards or rushing traffic. After their meals, diners can take a spin around the marina or look at the shops here or at Plaza Neptuno, which abuts it. It's also an easy walk to the Hotel Zone facing the beach, where international brand-name hotels offer their own fine-dining opportunities.

**The Coffee Cup**

**$** | **CAFÉ** | Early risers and those heading off on fishing charters will appreciate the daily 5 am opening time, and closing time isn't until 10 pm. The café, which is filled with wonderful art for sale, has fruit smoothies, coffee in many manifestations, and tasty frappes with Oreo cookie bits, or frosting-topped carrot cake. **Known for:** all-day breakfast bagel; box lunches to go; free Wi-Fi for customers. [$] *Average main: 65 MP* ✉ *Paseo de La Marina 14–A, Marina Vallarta* ☎ *322/221–2517.*

**La Barra Cerveceria**

**$** | **PIZZA** | In Marina Vallarta, an upscale place to go for snacks and beer is La Barra Cerveceria, which sells pizza as well. Part of the worldwide craft beer trend, this place has differentiated itself by offering something for everyone. **Known for:** great beer; 2-for-1 specials; wood-oven pizzas. [$] *Average main: 100 MP* ✉ *Av. Paseo de la marina sur s/n L 1-E, zona comercial Hotel Vamar Vallarta, Marina Vallarta* ☎ *322/209–0909* 🌐 *labarracerveceria.com.*

**La Cevichería**

**$$$** | **SEAFOOD** | **FAMILY** | La Cevichería is one of the best seafood restaurants in the Marina Vallarta area. Not as tasty as other places in town, it is definitely more stylish. **Known for:** famous aguachile; shrimp and beer; constantly changing its name. [$] *Average main: 150 MP* ✉ *Paseo de la Marina 121, Marina Vallarta* ☎ *322/221–1050.*

**Porto Bello**

**$$$** | **ITALIAN** | A classic of Vallarta's dining scene, yachties, locals, and other return visitors attest that everything on the menu here is good. Since there are no lunch specials and the Italian menu is the same at dinner, most folks come in the evening. **Known for:** elegant atmosphere; gorgeous patio overlooking the marina; fusilli with artichokes. [$] *Average main: 500 MP* ✉ *Calle Popa s/n, Marina Vallarta* ☎ *322/221–0003* 🌐 *www.portobellovallarta.com* 🕒 *Closed Mon.*

**★ Sonora Grill Prime**

**$$$$** | **STEAKHOUSE** | One of the most sophisticated restaurants in Puerto Vallarta and a favorite of meat lovers, Sonora Prime Grill is a renowned chain that serves high-quality steaks, imported directly from the northern Mexican state of Sonora. **Known for:** the best steaks in town; impressive international wine list;

veggie carpaccio. $ *Average main: 400 MP* ⊠ *Paseo de la Marina 121, Marina Vallarta* ☎ *322/221–3124* ⊕ *sonoragrillprime.com.*

##  Hotels

Although its newness relative to the rest of Puerto Vallarta makes it feel a little homogenous, this small enclave of luxury hotels gives off a quiet, subdued vibe that more than makes up for it. This is the closest of the PV subdivisions to the airport. The Marriott, Westin, and other brand names face a narrow beach that pales in comparison to the properties' sparkling swimming pools and high-end spas. These high-rise hotels are near a beautiful if low-key private marina (faced with shops, bars, and eateries) and the Marina Vallarta Golf Course, and most offer standard accommodations as well as all-inclusive plans.

### Casa Velas

**$$$$ | RESORT |** A luxurious all-inclusive resort without the hassle of mass tourism, everything at Casa Velas feels classy and personal. **Pros:** large elegant suites; surrounded by a golf course; adults only. **Cons:** not beachfront; jet noise from nearby airport; overzealous timeshare salespeople. $ *Rooms from: $550* ⊠ *Calle Pelícanos 311, Marina Vallarta* ☎ *322/226–8670, 877/418–3011* ⊕ *hotelcasavelas.com* ➥ *80 suites* ⦿ *All-inclusive.*

### Crown Paradise Club Vallarta

**$$$ | RESORT | FAMILY |** This is an all-inclusive resort designed for families with a pirate-theme water park as its main attraction. **Pros:** on the beach; great for families with kids; clubs for babies, kids, and teenagers. **Cons:** not the ideal place if you want to chill out and relax; unimpressive rooms; there is no spa, just an open air palapa with a massage bed. $ *Rooms from: $160* ⊠ *Av. de las Garzas #3, Zona Hotelera* ☎ *322/226–6800*

⊕ *www.crownparadise.com* ➥ *252 rooms* ⦿ *All-inclusive.*

### Marriott Puerto Vallarta Resort & Spa

**$$$$ | RESORT | FAMILY |** The Marriott is hushed and stately in some places, lively and casual in others. **Pros:** lovely spa; turtle sanctuary; good Asian restaurant. **Cons:** unimpressive beach; some facilities need an update; daily kids' club fee. $ *Rooms from: $254* ⊠ *Paseo de la Marina 455, Marina Vallarta* ☎ *322/226–0000, 888/236–2427 in U.S. and Canada* ⊕ *www.marriott.com/hotels/travel/pvrmx-marriott-puerto-vallarta-resort-and-spa* ➥ *433 rooms* ⦿ *No meals.*

### Meliá Puerto Vallarta All-Inclusive Beach Resort

**$$$ | RESORT | FAMILY |** The sprawling, all-inclusive Meliá, on the beach and close to the golf course, is popular with families. **Pros:** lots of activities for small children; giant pool; several dining options. **Cons:** small beach diminishes further at high tide; lots of children; fee for the kids' club. $ *Rooms from: $170* ⊠ *Paseo de la Marina Sur 7, Marina Vallarta* ☎ *322/226–3000, 888/956–3542 in U.S.* ⊕ *melia.com* ➥ *318 rooms* ⦿ *All-inclusive.*

### Westin Resort & Spa, Puerto Vallarta

**$$$ | RESORT | FAMILY |** There's not a bad vantage point anywhere at the Westin, whether you're gazing out to the leafy courtyard or down an orange-tile, brightly painted corridor lined with Mexican art. **Pros:** fabulous beds and pillows; great spa; pet-friendly. **Cons:** small beach; no ocean views from lower floors; not the best location in town. $ *Rooms from: $225* ⊠ *Paseo de la Marina Sur 205, Marina Vallarta* ☎ *322/226–1100, 888/236–2427 in U.S. and Canada* ⊕ *www.marriott.com* ➥ *280 rooms* ⦿ *No meals.*

##  Nightlife

The bars and cantinas in and around the Nima Bay building have brought new life to what used to be a sleepy part of town.

Nowadays, the place is buzzing with young people (mostly locals) that hop from one bar to the other. During high season (November to May), the Marina organizes a farmers' market on Thursday evenings, which brings together expats and locals alike and the restaurants along the seawalk are filled with happy visitors.

### Almacén Cocktail

**BARS/PUBS** | This high-end cocktail bar is frequented by young affluent locals. The atmosphere is sophisticated and stylish, and the design of the place is quite impressive. From Thursday to Sunday it gets really busy and it's a good spot to kick off the night. ⊠ *Calle Popa s/n, Edif. Nima Bay, Marina Vallarta* 🕾 *322/221– 2188* ⊕ *almacencocktail.com.*

### El Faro

**BARS/PUBS** | Here you can admire the bay and marina from atop a 110-foot light-house. It's mainly an expat retiree crowd (think yachters) and opens daily after 6 pm. During high season, especially on weekends, there's mellow music (including Mexican folk, or trova) after 10 pm. ⊠ *Paseo de la Marina 245, Marina Vallarta* 🕾 *322/168–5876.*

### La Federal Vallarta

**BARS/PUBS** | A hipster version of a typical Mexican cantina, La Federal is arguably the best place to go for some drinks before heading to the club. A stylish place with dishes such as *pulpo zarandeado* (grilled octopus) and *atún sellado en costra de ajonjolí* (seared tuna in sesame crust) available. Recognized as the top bar in the Marina. ⊠ *Paseo de la Marina 121 L–9, Edif. Nima Bay, Marina Vallarta* 🕾 *322/221–2662* ⊕ *lafederalcantina.com.*

## 🎭 Performing Arts

### Cinemex Galerías Vallarta

**FILM** | Across from the cruise-ship pier in the Liverpool shopping complex is the newest of Puerto Vallarta's movie theaters. It has 10 screens and 55 MXN ($3) tickets. The nearly PV-wide Wednesday discount of 25% means prohibitively large crowds at this particular theater; we suggest coming on a full-price day. ⊠ *Galerías Vallarta, Blvd. Francisco M. Ascencio 2920, L–234, Zona Hotelera* 🕾 *555/257–6969* ⊕ *cinemex.com.*

## 🛍 Shopping

Marina Vallarta is a good place to look for fine, exotic furniture and interior design accessories. A few good spas in the area are also worth a try. Besides that, the Marina area also features a couple of big shopping malls.

### Galerías Vallarta

**SHOPPING CENTERS/MALLS** | This is the main shopping mall in the whole Puerto Vallarta–Riviera Nayarit area, offering 73,000 square feet of shopping distributed on two floors and a magnificent view of the arriving cruise ships. This mall and the surrounding shops are mainly visited by cruise-ship passengers and Mexican out-of-towners looking for everything from sporting goods to clothing to housewares. Galerías Vallarta has two escalators; restaurants; parking; a 12-theater cinema; and a fast-food court with the ubiquitous McDonald's, Dominos Pizza, Chili's, and Starbucks. ⊠ *Av. Francisco M. Ascencio 2920, Marina Vallarta* 🕾 *322/209–0923* ⊕ *www.galerias.com/ galeriasVallarta.*

### Ohtli Spa

**SPA—SIGHT** | The modern Ohtli spa and its high-tech gym offer 22,000 square feet of elegant pampering. Come early before a treatment to enjoy the cold pool, steam, sauna, and other elements of the separate men's and women's spa facilities. Treatment rooms are adorned with Huichol art and interior gardens to maintain a spiritual and nature-oriented mood. Many of the treatments—like the hydrating tequila-coconut body treatment—use local ingredients. The signature exfoliation treatment contains agave essence. ✉ *Marriott Tower B, Paseo de la Marina 435 Norte, Marina Vallarta* ☎ *322/226–0076* ⊕ *www.marriott.com.*

### Plaza Marina

**SHOPPING CENTERS/MALLS** | One long block south of the airport, this mall has several banks with ATMs, a dry cleaner, a photo-developing shop, a pharmacy, a café, an Internet café, and several bars and shops. The whole place is anchored by the Mega Soriana supermarket and a McDonald's. ✉ *Av. Francisco Medina Ascencio s/n, Marina Vallarta* ☎ *322/221–0060* ⊕ *plazamarina.com.*

### Plaza Neptuno

**SHOPPING CENTERS/MALLS** | This small mall in the heart of the marina district is home to a number of fine-home-furnishing shops, several classy clothing boutiques, and, just behind it, a few good, casual restaurants. ✉ *Blvd. Francisco Medina Ascencio s/n, Marina Vallarta* ☎ *322/221–0777.*

### Terra Noble

**SPA—SIGHT** | Your cares begin to melt away as soon as you enter the rustic, garden-surrounded property of this day-spa aerie overlooking Banderas Bay. Terra Noble is more accessible price-wise than some of the area's more elegant spas. After-treatment teas are served on an outdoor patio with a great sea view. Two-hour temazcal sweat-lodge rituals cleanse physically, mentally, and spiritually. ✉ *Col. 5 de Diciembre, Av. Tulipanes 595, El Centro* ☎ *322/223–0308* ⊕ *www.terranoble.com.*

## 🏃 Activities

If you are looking to rent a yacht or go on a fishing excursion this is where you want to go. The area has also some scuba diving shops and tour operators that will offer everything from whale-watching day trips to a visit to the Marietas Islands or one of the beaches south of Puerto Vallarta. Golf enthusiasts love staying in the neighborhood as the Marina Vallarta

Golf Club is located right here, with easy access and affordable greens fees.

### Marigalante

**TOUR—SPORTS** | **FAMILY** | A true sailing vessel, the Marigalante has a pirate crew that keeps things hopping for kids and teens with games, snorkeling, kayaking, or banana-boat rides during a seven-hour day cruise. The five-hour dinner cruise, with open bar, snacks, and pre-Hispanic show, is for adults only. Both tours cost $113 for adults and about half that for kids. Buy tickets online at a discount or from licensed vendors in town. The boat embarks from Terminal Marítima, across from Sam's Club. ✉ *Terminal Marítima, Blvd. Francisco Medina Ascencio, Marina Vallarta* ☎ *322/980–0667, 322/223–0875, 85/530–5733 in U.S. and Canada* ⊕ *pirateshipvallarta.com.*

### Marina Vallarta

**GOLF** | Joe Finger designed this 18-hole course; the $139 greens fee includes practice balls, tax, and a shared cart. It's the area's second-oldest course and is closest and most convenient for golfers staying in the Hotel Zone, downtown Puerto Vallarta, and Marina Vallarta. Although it's very flat, it's far more challenging than it looks, with lots of water hazards. Speaking of hazards, the alligators have a way of blending into the scenery. They might surprise you, but they supposedly don't bite. ✉ *Paseo de la Marina 430, Marina Vallarta* ☎ *322/221–0073* ⊕ *www.clubcorp.com/Clubs/Marina-Vallarta-Club-de-Golf.*

# Olas Altas

On the southern border of Puerto Vallarta, just behind the famous Los Muertos Beach and the new pier, you will find the upscale residential neighborhoods of Amapas and Conchas Chinas. They are located on both sides of Highway 200 and enjoy either the whitest beaches of the bay or the best panoramic ocean

Quinta Maria Cortez, just off Playa Conchas Chinas, has some of the most coveted palapas in town—not to mention tons of other amenities well worth the splurge.

views. The beaches are fun to visit and explore, with impressive boulders, little coves, and rocky grottos, and you can access them from the highway or on foot from Los Muertos Beach via a small trail. However, the lack of restaurants, showers, toilets, and other facilities don't make these beaches ideal for long stays.

The higher zones are incredible observation points and can be easily accessed through one of two entrances on the left side of the road. Simply take either of them and drive as high as you can, stopping whenever you feel like. At the top, turn round and get some spectacular shots of the bay or of the high-end villas.

## GETTING AROUND

Car is the only transportation option here. Olas Altas is basically a steep hill that goes from the Pacific Ocean to the top of the mountain in a very short distance; this quality of the terrain results in sinuous roads that go up and down the hill in a very challenging way for some cars,

not to mention someone trying to walk around the area.

**Parking:** There is no problem parking in this neighborhood as there is plenty of space on the street side and not as many cars as in other parts of town.

## QUICK BITES

This is a residential neighborhood with some interesting but rocky beaches and not many establishments around. However, if you happen to be hungry while in the area the place to go is **La Playita** (*Carr. a Barra de Navidad Km 2.5*). This restaurant of Hotel Lindo Mar is right at the beach and offers a menu of Mexican specialties and seafood. For a cocktail at sunset no better option than **El Set** bar located higher on the hill but in the same hotel. It has some of the best views in the whole Banderas Bay and a quiet but friendly atmosphere.

##  Beaches

### Playa Conchas Chinas
**BEACH—SIGHT** | This beach has a series of rocky coves with crystalline water. The individual coves are perfect for reclusive sunbathing and for snorkeling. It's accessible from Carretera 200 near El Set restaurant. You can walk—be it on the sand, over the rocks, or on paths or steps built for this purpose—from Playa Los Muertos all the way to Conchas Chinas. **Amenities:** Parking (no fee). **Best for:** swimming; snorkeling; sunset. ⊠ *Olas Altas.*

##  Restaurants

At the south end of Puerto Vallarta starts the Olas Altas neighborhood, a sprawling mix of steep hills, multilevel villas, and hard-to-find beaches. This area used to have more dining options, but now it's limited to the Restaurant La Playita and its bar El Set. Besides that, the best you can hope for is to catch one of those beach vendors selling fish roasted on a stick or grab a hotdog at one of the Oxxos in the area.

### Restaurant La Playita
**$$** | **INTERNATIONAL** | Open to the ocean air, this wood-and-palm exterior of this restaurant looks right at home on Conchas Chinas Beach. There are wonderful views of waves crashing on or lapping at the shore at its bar El Set. **Known for:** expansive weekend brunch buffet; spectacular ocean views; huevos Felix (scrambled eggs with fried corn tortillas). $ *Average main: 100 MP* ⊠ *Carr. a Barra de Navidad, Km 2.5, Playa Conchas Chinas, at Hotel Lindo Mar, Olas Altas* ☎ *322/221–5556.*

##  Hotels

South of the Zona Romántica and above Los Muertos and Amapas beaches is a mix of gay-friendly hotels, pretty villas, and other vacation rentals (like individual homes and condo complexes). The continuous beach stretches all the way to Playa Conchas Chinas.

### Buenaventura Grand Hotel & Spa
**$$** | **HOTEL** | **FAMILY** | Its location on downtown's northern edge is just a few blocks from the malecón, shops, hotels, and restaurants; rooms are cheerful, with wood furniture, bright white linens, and tastefully subdued accent colors. **Pros:** adults-only pool; good breakfast buffet; kids' club. **Cons:** balconies are small; rocky beach; noisy rooms and atmosphere in general. $ *Rooms from: $200* ⊠ *Av. México 1301, El Centro* ☎ *322/226–7000, 888/859–9439 in U.S. and Canada* ⊕ *www.hotelbuenaventura.com.mx* ⇥ *234 rooms* ⦵ *All-inclusive.*

### ★ Quinta Maria Cortez
**$$$** | **B&B/INN** | It takes a long walk up a steep hill at Playa Conchas Chinas to reach this B&B; rooms are furnished with antiques and local art; most have kitchenettes, or full kitchens, along with balconies. **Pros:** intimate, personable digs; quiet and classy; above lovely Conchas Chinas Beach. **Cons:** small property; frequently booked solid; away from all the action. $ *Rooms from: $200* ⊠ *Calle Sagitario 126, Olas Altas* ☎ *322/221–5317, 888/640–8100* ⊕ *www.quinta-maria.com* ⇥ *7 suites* ⦵ *Free Breakfast.*

# Chapter 4

# RIVIERA NAYARIT

4

Updated by
Federico Arrizabalaga

⊙ Sights    🍴 Restaurants    🛏 Hotels    🛍 Shopping    🍸 Nightlife
★★★★★    ★★★★★    ★★★★★    ★★★★☆    ★★★★☆

# WELCOME TO RIVIERA NAYARIT

## TOP REASONS TO GO

★ **Beaches for all tastes:** Riviera Nayarit has beaches with little surf; secluded, rocky beaches; and lively beaches.

★ **Fantastic local cuisine:** You'll find different flavors throughout the region as you travel along the Pacific coast.

★ **Surfing for all skill levels:** There are endless surf spots along this stretch of the ocean.

★ **Fun under the sun:** Outdoor activities include snorkeling, diving, surfing, turtle-watching, seed sea fishing, and sailing.

★ **Meet other travelers:** Bucerías and La Cruz de Huanacaxtle have a thriving population of expats and snow birds; Punta Mita is where the wealthy come to play; and Sayulita is a laid-back town that has experienced an influx of tourism in the past few years.

★ **Indulge in all-inclusive resorts:** There are dozens of all-inclusive beachfront hotels and resorts in Bahía de Banderas, the stretch of coastline between Punta Mita and Nuevo Vallarta.

**1 Bucerías.** With a population of about 9,000 residents (seasonal influxes double that number), Bucerías is your typical Mexican town with cobblestone streets, a main square, church, and a wide array of restaurants.

**2 La Cruz De Huanacaxtle.** Still a sleepy fishing village, La Cruz de Huanacaxtle has experienced a considerable influx of expats and snow birds from the United States and Canada. It's the last town in Bahía de Banderas before the winding road to Punta Mita starts.

**3 Punta Mita.** Punta Mita is officially a private peninsula on the north tip of Bahía de Banderas, home to the Four Seasons Punta Mita, the St. Regis Resort, and mansions. *Pangas* can be rented here to go whale-watching or to visit the Marietas Islands.

**4 Sayulita.** Hailed as a popular bohemian, off-the-beaten-path travel destination (many will argue that this is no longer true as the town does suffer from over tourism), Sayulita offers a variety of recreational activities such as horseback riding, hiking, jungle canopy tours, snorkeling, and fishing.

**5 San Pancho.** What used to also be a quiet beach town has become a popular destination among younger crowds.

**6 Jaltemba Bay.** Jaltemba Bay is a down-to-earth beach vacation area in Riviera Nayarit.

**7 Nuevo Vallarta.** This area just north of PV is composed mainly of golf courses, exclusive condos, and luxurious restaurants, and has the second-highest number of hotels in the country.

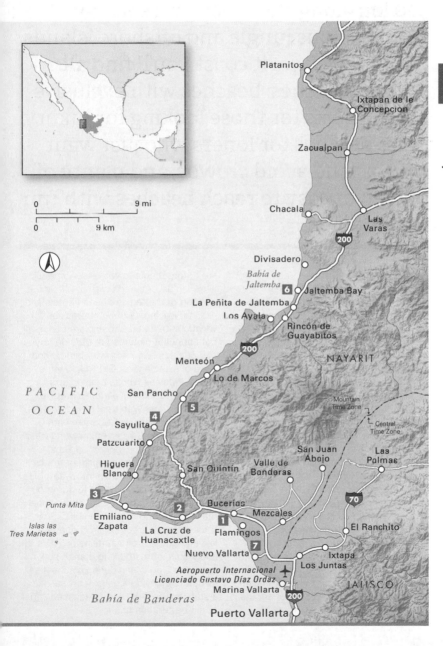

One of the most attractive destinations in Mexico, Riviera Nayarit extends about 300 km along the coast, preceded by mountainous jungle and offshore islands. Along the Nayarit coast you'll find all sorts of beaches: beaches with exclusive hotel resorts for those looking for luxury, quiet beaches for loners who just want to relax and avoid crowds, and plenty of hidden or easy to reach beaches with fun waves to ride.

To the already ample appeal of this region, you must add the Marietas Islands' beaches, hidden in a small volcanic archipelago protected by the UNESCO. The region also has mangroves, beautiful blue lakes with flamingos, and picturesque villages such as La Cruz de Huanacaxtle or San Pancho. Nayarit's southern border unfolds just 10 minutes north of the Puerto Vallarta International Airport, and its northern border is just 40 minutes west of the Tepic International Airport, making it reachable by air from two airports on opposite ends. Intense skies, emerald mountains, abundant vegetation, and endless beautiful golden beaches surprise visitors who are willing to leave the resort and head out to explore. Starting off at Banderas Bay, one of the largest and most beautiful tropical bays in the world, it plays host to a spectacular natural phenomenon year after year. Every winter, humpback whales arrive to give birth. Their magnificent breaches, jumps, and water spouts, along with glimpses of their newborns,

are unforgettable to witness. Authentic Mexican flavor blends with the luxurious comfort of the region's beach hotels and resorts, leaving a lasting impression for vacationers. Be sure to explore the small but abundant picturesque seaside towns and pueblos brimming with history and cultural experiences. Get to know the Huichol Indians whose beaded arts and crafts known as *alebrijes* provide Mexico visitors with treasures that often accompany them home. Swim with dolphins and sea lions, enjoy world-class golf courses, catch a wave on a surfboard, or land a tuna, sailfish, or trophy marlin while fishing. Dive into warm blue Pacific Coast waters home to numerous colonies of coral reefs, fish, and marine mammals of the Mexican Pacific. Soar through jungle treetops on canopy zip lines, conquer the mountains on ATVs, and watch a breathtaking orange sun meet the blue ocean during a sunset sail, all before enjoying a gourmet meal under a starlit sky in San Blas. Life just can't get much better than this.

## MAJOR REGIONS

Riviera Nayarit is divided into three major regions: **Bahía de Banderas**, **Sayulita and San Pancho,** and **the North.** Bahía de Banderas is the most populated of all, and includes Nuevo Vallarta, Bucerías, La Cruz de Huanacaxtle, and Punta Mita. This area accounts for 70% of the Nayarit's income and it is here that you'll find most of the all-inclusive hotels, restaurants, and activities. Sayulita and San Pancho are the second-most popular regions, and while they once were small fishing villages they have now become very popular among backpackers and travelers. To the north is San Blas, which marks the end of Riviera Nayarit.

# Planning

## Getting Here and Around

### AIR

Riviera Nayarit has no major airports, but Nuevo Vallarta (the southern limit of Riviera Nayarit), is just a 10-minute drive from the Puerto Vallarta International Airport (PVR). The airport has flights to several cities within Mexico and nonstop daily flights to many cities in the United States and Canada. Other destinations served by nonstop flights include Finland, the United Kingdom, and Panama.

### BUS

Several bus companies provide overland services within Riviera Nayarit and other destinations within Mexico. Basic ATM buses (Autotransportes Medina) travel between Nuevo Vallarta and Punta Mita with stops along the route (30 MXN for longest trip) throughout the day. Compostela-Pacifico buses provide service all the way to Sayulita. For comfortable long-distance travel within Riviera Nayarit, your options include Vallarta Plus, Primera Plus, and ETN. If you want to travel to San Blas by bus, which is not the best option in terms of comfort and convenience, Estrella Blanca is you best choice.

**CONTACTS Estrella Blanca.** ☏ 01800/507–5500 toll-free in Mexico ⊕ www.estrellablanca.com.mx. **Primera Plus.** ☏ 322/290–0716 in PV, 322/187–0492 in NV ⊕ primeraplus.com.mx. **Vallarta Plus.** ✉ Palma Real 140, Marina Vallarta ☏ 322/221–3636, 322/306–3071 ⊕ www.vallartaplus.com.

### CAR

There are many car rental companies once you land in Puerto Vallarta, and several within the Banderas Bay region, Sayulita, and San Pancho. Big name brands like Avis, Hertz, Budget, Enterprise, and National have a presence here, as well as other local suppliers that sometimes offer better rates than the big name brands. Prices vary $30–$75 per day for an economy car, and it's recommended that you purchase the additional insurance. Driving in Riviera Nayarit is not particularly complicated when compared to the big cities in Mexico, and in the smaller towns traffic is almost nonexistent. Perhaps the most complicated part of driving in the area (and Mexico) are the unmarked exit signs. Finally, the *policia de transito* (road police), while they're not as corrupt as they once were, will be on the lookout for infractions and will ask that you pay them a bribe (*mordida*) to be let off the hook. Remember to obey traffic laws and you should be fine.

### TAXI

If there's one thing Riviera Nayarit has plenty of when it comes to traveling, it's taxis. They are very easy to spot as most of them are yellow or white; just wave one down when needed and the car will come up to you. There are two things to bear in mind though when hailing a taxi: most of them work on a fixed price per destination so make sure you settle the price before the driver takes off; second, you'll notice that most of the cars are old Nissan Tsurus without a/c, making any summer taxi ride uncomfortable. There aren't many options when it comes to finding better vehicles, other than luck and location. Uber does exist and is often used in Puerto Vallarta, and while there are vehicles in Nuevo Vallarta and elsewhere in Banderas Bay, they may be difficult to find because they are often threatened by taxi drivers who don't appreciate their business. Hotel concierges often have phone numbers of Uber drivers who can be reached directly, and you'll get a better car and service than with a taxi, and there all also small businesses offering shuttle and limo cars.

## Hotels

Riviera Nayarit has all kinds of accommodations under the sun, and then some. From luxurious all-inclusive resorts to basic hotel rooms, fancy bungalows, and condos, the area has you covered. Prices vary greatly throughout the year, with high season being mid November to April, Easter, and August (when Mexicans are off for summer holiday). You'll find more options (and more tourists) than anywhere else in Nuevo Vallarta, the area closest to the Puerto Vallarta airport, and also the southern end of Riviera Nayarit. Prices here and in Bucerías tend to be slightly higher than in Sayulita or San Pancho, but there are many options. Your best bet is to book well in advance if you're visiting during the high season (hotels do sell out and condo prices on sites like Airbnb tend to skyrocket). Accommodation options beyond Bahía de Banderas or La Peñita de Jaltemba and all the way to San Blas drop in amount and value, but some destinations do have one or two four-star hotels.

## Restaurants

Food is a big deal in Riviera Nayarit, but if all you expect are beef tacos, burritos, and any of the other staple dishes Mexico is known for you are in for a big surprise. Seafood is a highlight of most local restaurants, whether Italian, Mexican, or Japanese. Ceviche, shrimp, mahimahi, tuna, oysters, and marlin are to be found one way or another at any restaurant, both expensive and affordable, and leaving the area without sampling any of them would be a big mistake. Try variations of ceviche, *tacos gobernador* (fish tacos), and *pescado zarandeado* (marinated and grilled fish) or *camarones al coco* (coconut breaded shrimp usually accompanied by tamarind or mango sauce). No matter where you are, you'll have somewhere to eat within walking distance of your hotel, and while eating at a restaurant with a/c will be more comfortable and pleasant don't neglect the small, no-frills taco joints. Locals will be pleased that you ventured out of the hotel to eat the food they eat.

### HOTEL AND RESTAURANT PRICES

*Hotel prices in the reviews are the lowest cost of a standard double room in high season. Restaurant prices in the reviews are the average cost of a main course at dinner, or if dinner is not served, at lunch.*

| WHAT IT COSTS In MXN | | | |
|---|---|---|---|
| $ | $$ | $$$ | $$$$ |
| **RESTAURANTS** | | | |
| under 50 MXN | 51–150 MXN | 151–250 MXN | over 251 MXN |
| **HOTELS** | | | |
| under 500 MXN | 501– 1500 MXN | 1501– 3000 MXN | over 3000 MXN |

---

## WHAT IT COSTS In USD

| | $ | $$ | $$$ | $$$$ |
|---|---|---|---|---|
| **RESTAURANTS** | under $3 | $3–$10 | $10–$15 | over $15 |
| **HOTELS** | under $25 | $25–$80 | $81–$160 | over $160 |

# Safety

Generally speaking, Riviera Nayarit is one of the safest destinations in all of Mexico. Drug cartels have little activity in the area (and those present remain undercover) and there's little to no violent crime for the most part. Like anywhere else it's best you don't carry valuables when walking around, and don't leave anything behind as odds are it'll be gone by the time you get back. Avoid driving at night as road safety decreases due to poor road conditions and aggressive or drunk drivers, and remain vigilant of your luggage when traveling by bus. Beware of the odd taxi driver that will try to scam you (Google Maps will show you the best way to reach your destination and which route you're taking). When swimming in the ocean be aware of current conditions (avoid swimming entirely if the sea is rough).

# Visitor Information

**CONTACTS Riviera Nayarit Visitors and Conventions Bureau.** ✉ *Paseo los cocoteros 55* ☎ *322/297–2516* ⊕ *www.rivieranayarit.com.*

# Beaches

At the northern end of Bahía de Banderas and farther into Nayarit State to the north are long, beautiful beaches fringed with tall trees or scrubby tropical forest. Only the most popular beaches like Rincón de Guayabitos or Nuevo Vallarta have much in the way of water-sports equipment rentals, but even the more secluded ones have stands or small restaurants serving cold coconut water, soft drinks, beer, and grilled fish with tortillas. Surfing is big in Sayulita and Punta Mita, where some of the best spots are accessible only by boat.

# Bucerías

*5 miles northwest of Nuevo Vallarta.*

Bucerías is your typical Mexican sea village that has grown with the influx of travelers throughout the years. A large number of them have decided to call Bucerías their permanent home (or at least home for the winter). Divided east–west by *Carretera Fed 200*, the western and more expensive side (closest to the ocean) is the preferred area by foreigners, while the east is home to many locals. Bucerías has a little bit of something for everyone, including art galleries, fine dining, small shops, large grocery stores, and fantastic breakfast joints, yet remains easily walkable. There is one all-inclusive resort, several hotels, and many condos to be rented both long and short term. All along Bucerías you'll find a beach, which locals are very proud of but visitors will not get too excited about, especially as you get closer to downtown. If you come for a visit you'll find that a week tends to go by before you even realize; it's one of those places where time flies by despite everything moving slowly.

### GETTING HERE AND AROUND
Reaching Bucerías is very easy once you're in Puerto Vallarta. All buses heading north will stop anywhere in Bucerías (just flag down the driver), *combis* (small white vans that carry passengers, faster than buses and with a/c) also stop here if you wave them down, and taxis run at around 400 MXN from the airport.

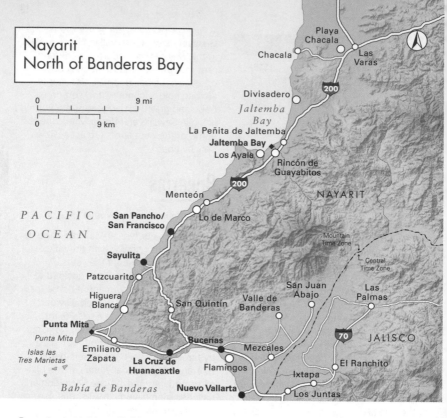

**Nayarit
North of Banderas Bay**

0 — 9 mi
0 — 9 km

Chacala

Playa Chacala

Las Varas

Divisadero

*Jaltemba Bay*

La Peñita de Jaltemba

**Jaltemba Bay**

Los Ayala

Rincón de Guayabitos

Menteón

NAYARIT

PACIFIC OCEAN

**San Pancho/ San Francisco**

Lo de Marco

Mountain Time Zone

Central Time Zone

**Sayulita**

Patzcuarito

Higuera Blanca

San Quintín

Valle de Banderas

San Juan Abajo

Las Palmas

**Punta Mita**

Punta Mita

Islas las Tres Marietas

Emiliano Zapata

**Bucerías**

Mezcales

JALISCO

**La Cruz de Huanacaxtle**

Flamingos

Ixtapa

El Ranchito

*Bahía de Banderas*

**Nuevo Vallarta**

Los Juntas

Bucerías is highly walkable, especially if you're here on vacation and stay on the beach side of town. The larger grocery shops (Mega, Chedraui, La Comer) will require a taxi to reach but shouldn't cost more than 100 MXN each way.

## ◉ Sights

Locals hang out at the central plaza, right in front of the local church, the Parish of Our Lady of Peace which is worth a visit. Other than this there's not much to see in terms of cultural attractions, but you may want to stop at the many art galleries you'll find along Calle Lázaro Cárdenas.

### Calle Lázaro Cárdenas

**NIGHTLIFE OVERVIEW | FAMILY** | During high season (December–April), this street is the place to go once the sun sets. There

are several restaurants, art galleries, and cafés. ✉ *Calle Lazaro Cardenas, Bucerías.*

### Parish of our Lady of Peace

**RELIGIOUS SITE** | It may not be as magnificent as other parishes, but it is probably the only architectural structure worth visiting in Bucerías. Mass is held here several times a day all year long, but it does get very hot in the summer months. ✉ *Av. Héroes de Nacozari s/n, Bucerías* ☎ *329/298–0408.*

### Plaza Central de Bucerías

**PLAZA | FAMILY** | This small plaza right in front of the Parish of our Lady of Peace is where local families come to hang out and spend time outdoors. Dozens of family-run taco stands are to be found, as well as a some basic restaurants and fresh juice shops. ✉ *Av. Mexico s/n, Bucerías.*

## Beaches

There is just one beach in Bucerías, but its beauty ranges from *meh* to fantastic depending on where you go. The southern part of the beach is wider, cleaner and definitely more visually attractive as there are just a few scattered buildings along it. Once you reach the Decameron Resort, the beach slowly becomes narrower, busier, and therefore dirtier. By the time you reach the plaza the beach is simply there, and while you can swim in it, you probably won't want to. During the high season (December–April), there's an entertaining water park with rafts and inflated games, ideal for families with active children; Wibit Adventures Water Park is a circuit of trampolines, climbing towers, slides, pyramids, tunnels, and more, all floating on the water off the beach.

**Bucerías Beach**
**BEACH—SIGHT | FAMILY** | The stretch of sand right in front of downtown Bucerías is not as appealing as what you'll find if you just walk about 200 meters south. The shorebreak can get a bit sketchy when there's a swell, so you might just want to walk toward Nuevo Vallarta before planting your beach umbrella.

## Restaurants

Fine Italian dining, superb local food, French crepes, and other international cuisine are all to be found in this small town. Visitors are often surprised by the variety and quality of the restaurants in Bucerías; diners come from Puerto Vallarta just to enjoy the great food in a peaceful environment, sometimes right next to the ocean. You'll also find taco joints, a sports bar, and simple mom and pop places where cheap food is available all throughout the day and late into the night. Note that during the high season most of the best restaurants will require a reservation.

★ **Casa Triskell**
**$$ | CAFÉ | FAMILY** | This midsize enclave is sure to satisfy anyone with a sweet tooth, particularly those fond of well-crafted French crepes. Try the orange-flavored "Suzette" or, if you're a chocolate fan, the full on "Tahitian" with ice cream, chocolate, and whipped cream. **Known for:** "moules et frites" night; sweet and savory crepes; dessert. [$] *Average main: 75 MP* ✉ *Calle Lázaro Cárdenas 500 B, Bucerías* ☎ *322/120–5041* 💳 *No credit cards.*

**El Brujo**
**$$ | MEXICAN** | This newer Bucerías branch of El Brujo is located right on the beach but with the same food and generous portions as the original location in Puerto Vallarta. The *molcajete*—a sizzling black pot of tender flank steak, grilled green onion, and soft white cheese in a delicious homemade sauce of dried red peppers—is served with a big plate of guacamole, refried beans, and made-at-the-moment corn or flour tortillas. **Known for:** large portions; beachside setting; delicious seafood. [$] *Average main: 140 MP* ✉ *Av. del Pacífico 202–A, Bucerías* ☎ *329/298–0406* 🕒 *Closed 2 wks late Sept.–early Oct.*

**Mark's Bar & Grill**
**$$$ | INTERNATIONAL** | You can dine alone at the polished black-granite bar without feeling too lonely, or catch an important ball game. But seemingly a world away from the bar and (muted) TV is the charming restaurant known for its delightful decor and international cuisine. **Known for:** solo dining; homemade pizza; musicians' hangout. [$] *Average main: 250 MP* ✉ *Lázaro Cárdenas 56, Bucerías* ☎ *329/298–0406* 🌐 *www.marksbucerias.com* 🕒 *No lunch.*

**Mezzogiorno**
**$$$ | ITALIAN** | This upscale Italian restaurant, the perfect spot for a celebratory dinner, is literally a stone's throw away from the ocean. They serve great pastas, pizzas, and chicken parmagiana,

but there are many more dishes to dive into. **Known for:** dinner for special occasions; next to the ocean; excellent wine selection. [$] *Average main: 240 MP* ✉ *Av. Pacifico 33, Bucerías* ✥ *It's the last restaurant along Av. Pacifico, and parking is easy. The road is unpaved, but not difficult* ☎ *329/298–0350* ⏲ *No lunch.*

**Sandrina's**

$$ | **MEDITERRANEAN** | **FAMILY** | The walls of this veteran, Canadian-owned restaurant and locals' favorite are covered in colorful paintings: portraits and tropical scenes and still life. The restaurant opens after 3 pm; it's very pleasant to dine on the back patio at night amid dozens of candles and tiny lights. **Known for:** Mediterranean and Greek cuisine; café only open during high season; romantic outdoor dining. [$] *Average main: 145 MP* ✉ *Av. Lázaro Cárdenas 33, Bucerías* ☎ *329/298–0273* 🌐 *www.sandrinas.com* ⏲ *Closed Tues. No lunch.*

**Tapas del Mundo**

$$ | **INTERNATIONAL** | Small plates of international cuisine are meant to be shared here. The cooks produce wonderful daily special dishes with ingredients found fresh that day, as well as the restaurant's staples, like shrimp with guajillo chilies served with homemade tortillas; goat cheese with herbs; Anaheim chilies stuffed with goat cheese; or stir-fried beef strips. **Known for:** breaded green olives; upstairs bar serving coffee and cocktails; jovial owner. [$] *Average main: 85 MP* ✉ *Corner of Av. Mexico and Av. Hidalgo, 2 blocks north of central plaza, Bucerías* ☎ *322/1180–1795* 💳 *No credit cards* ⏲ *Closed June–Sept. No lunch.*

## 🛏 Hotels

**Aventura Pacifico**

$$ | **RENTAL** | The condos at this boutique-style accommodation are a favorite among travelers and vacationers who return year after year. **Pros:** clean facilities; close to beach and restaurants; free Wi-Fi and VoiP calls to U.S. and Canada. **Cons:** road leading to hotel isn't well paved; dated furniture; somewhat noisy during Easter and when nearby hotel has a party. [$] *Rooms from: $105* ✉ *Calle Francisco I Madero 132, Bucerías* ☎ *329/298–2797* 🌐 *www.aventurapacifico.com* 🛏 *7 suites* 🍴 *No meals.*

**Decameron All-Inclusive Hotel & Resort**

$$$ | **RESORT** | This high-volume hotel is at the south end of long and lovely Bucerías Beach and has manicured grounds and a pool for each of its six buildings. **Pros:** excellent deal for all-inclusive (room-only and air packages, too); long beach great for walking or jogging; Spanish classes, yoga classes, and dance lessons plus many other activities. **Cons:** only a few Internet stations for hundreds of guests, and there's Wi-Fi only at the lobby; only one of six buildings has an elevator; loud entertainment music at night during high season. [$] *Rooms from: $140* ✉ *Calle Lázaro Cárdenas 150, Bucerías* ☎ *329/298–0226, 01800/011–1111* 🌐 *www.decameron.com* 🛏 *620 rooms* 🍴 *All-inclusive.*

**Hotel Carmelitas**

$ | **HOTEL** | In the heart of Bucerías, this small budget hotel is as unassuming as can be, and well maintained. **Pros:** low price; close to beach; quiet residential neighborhood. **Cons:** no views; no amenities; basic rooms. [$] *Rooms from: $21* ✉ *Francisco I. Madero 19, Bucerías* ☎ *329/298–0024* 💳 *No credit cards* 🛏 *12 rooms* 🍴 *No meals.*

**Hotel Palmeras**

$$ | **HOTEL** | A block from the beach, in an area with lots of good restaurants, "The Palms" has two floors of rooms surrounding a large, clean, rectangular pool. **Pros:** free Wi-Fi; inexpensive older rooms for bargain hunters; newer rooms have patios and ocean view. **Cons:** some rooms have odd layout; no parking; somewhat dated furniture. [$] *Rooms from: $143* ✉ *Lázaro Cárdenas 35, Bucerías* ☎ *329/298–1288, 647/722–4139*

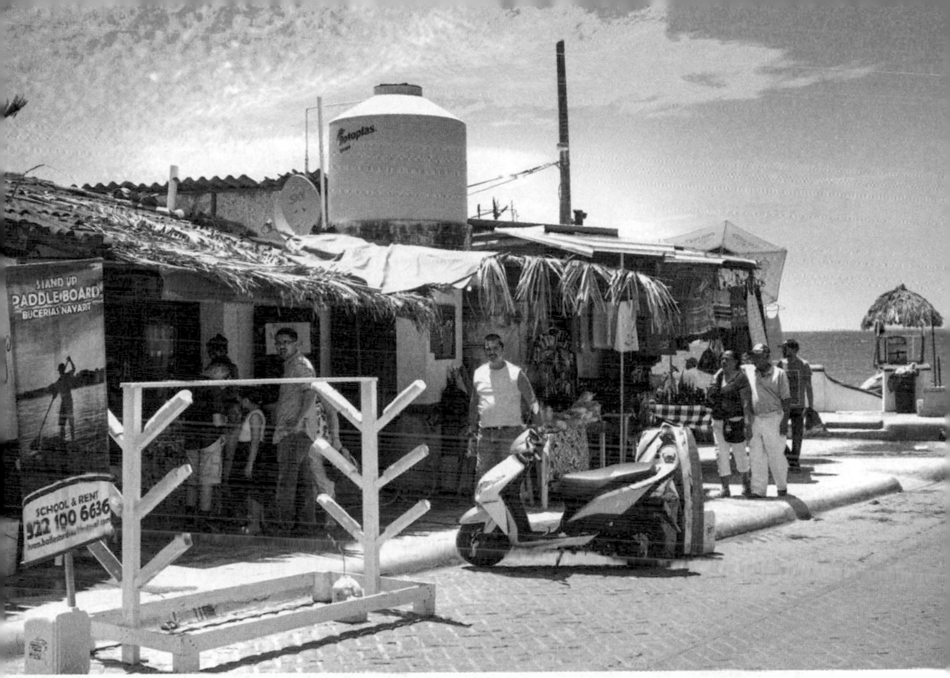

There are many places near the beach in Bucerías to rent paddleboards and other aquatic equipment.

*in U.S.* 🌐 *www.hotelpalmeras.com* 🛏 *21 rooms* 🍴 *No meals.*

**Marco's Place Suites & Villas**

**$$** | **HOTEL** | **FAMILY** | Despite its name, this property is a three-story motel. **Pros:** several different outdoor spaces for reading or relaxing; even least expensive room has kitchenette; budget-friendly. **Cons:** small rooms and tubs; street parking only; cash only. [$] *Rooms from: $148* ✉ *Calle Juventino Espinoza 6–A, Bucerías* ☎ *329/298–0865* 🌐 *www.marcosplacevillas.com* 💳 *No credit cards* 🛏 *18 rooms* 🍴 *No meals.*

## Nightlife

Forget huge clubs and wild parties: Bucerías's nightlife is more about a pleasant dinner followed by a nice dessert and a stroll along Lázaro Cárdenas street. Those looking to dance and listen to live music will have the time of their life at the Drunken Duck, where bands will play some Mexican music but mostly American oldies and greatest hits.

**The Bar Above**

**$$** | **CAFÉ** | This little place above Tapas del Mundo defies categorization. It's a martini bar without a bar that also serves varied desserts—the owners prefer a setting that encourages people to come converse with friends rather than hang out like barflies. [$] *Average main: 140 MP* ✉ *Corner of Av. Mexico and Av. Hidalgo, 2 blocks north of central plaza, Bucerías* ☎ *329/118–1795* 💳 *No credit cards.*

**Drunken Duck**

**BARS/PUBS** | Loud, live music and flowing drinks keep patrons happy late into the night, every night, during the high season. The food is also good, and includes tacos, burgers, and other bar basics. ✉ *Av. México 16, Bucerías* 🌐 *www.facebook.com/ddnayarit.*

**Jax Bar and Grill**

**BARS/PUBS** | Live music is played in this simple but fun grill in Bucerías. You can also enjoy burgers, steak, salads, and tacos here, as well as blues and good rock. ✉ *Av. Mexico 17, Bucerías* ✥ *Corner* *of Calle Miguel Hidalgo ⊕ www.facebook.com/JaxBucerias.*

##  Shopping

### Jan Marie's Boutique

**CRAFTS** | The gift items here include small housewares and tin frames sporting Botero-style paintings. The classy selection of Talavera pottery is both decorative and utilitarian. An extension half a block down the street has an even larger inventory, and the merchandise is larger, too, including leather settees, lamps, desks, and other furnishings as well as pieces from various parts of Mexico. Neither shop is for bargain hunters, but prices are reasonable given the high quality of the merchandise. ⊠ *Av. Lázaro Cárdenas 56 and 58, Bucerías* ☎ *329/298–0303.*

##  Activities

People come to Bucerías to hang out at the beach, eat good food, and chill out. You might be able to organize some horseback riding along the beach and there's a wave that sometimes breaks in town which can be surfed, but other than that tours and activities are done elsewhere in the bay.

# La Cruz De Huanacaxtle

*3 miles west of Bucerías.*

Between small hills and the ocean is La Cruz de Huanacaxtle, a fishing village founded in 1930 by the Chavez family. It's a typical sleepy Mexican seaside town, with just one stop light, an active fishing port, and since 2002, a bustling marina than can hold vessels up to 400 feet long. Locals are very proud of their town, as are the expats who now live here, too. The town has a couple of beaches, both within walking distance from anywhere in town, and during the winter season you'll spot dozens of sailboats that anchor just outside the marina and spend

the winter months there, or are taking a break before their ongoing voyage across the Pacific. It's not the kind of town where you come to party or engage in endless activities, but instead you come here to unwind and lose track of time. Go for a walk, read a book, check out the catch of the day, and head over to a cheap *cenaduría* for dinner, and you'll have covered most of what there is to do in town, unless you're here around Easter when the main plaza has live *banda* music every night and the whole town seems to gather here.

## GETTING HERE AND AROUND

To reach La Cruz (as locals call it) from anywhere else in the bay you can grab any of the buses or *combis* that head toward Punta Mita, or to Puerto Vallarta from Punta Mita. There are no designated stops, just wave them down wherever you are along the main road. The best way to get around is on foot or on a bicycle if you want to cover longer distances. Note that there are no large supermarkets in town, only *abarrotes* (small convenience stores).

##  Sights

While La Cruz does not have a plethora of entertainment or historical sights, there are some attractions worth checking out if you're in town. You'll find children playing and parents hanging out in the main square during the day, drinking an *agua fresca* (water with some natural fruit flavoring), engaged in some kind of conversation as older ladies walk in and out of the Parish of La Cruz de Huanacaxtle. Towards the ocean along the same road is the marina, worth a nice stroll and a stop for food at one of the very good restaurants. At the fish market, boats sell the fresh catch of the day each morning to restaurants, supermarkets, and anyone interested in buying. But in La Cruz, you're best off heading to one of the two beaches to lay down and sip fresh coconut water from a local vendor.

### La Cruz de Huanacaxtle Marina

**MARINA** | This modern marina may surprise visitors who arrive by land, as its modern design and large scale seems out of place. Boaters call it home for several months every winter, and it has a couple of very good restaurants. ✉ *Marina Riviera Nayarit La Cruz, La Cruz de Huanacaxtle* ☎ *329/295–5526* ⊕ *www. marinarivieranayarit.com.*

### Mercado del Mar

**OUTDOOR/FLEA/GREEN MARKETS** | **FAMILY** | Dozens of fishing boats arrive here every morning to sell their catch of the day. It's a great place to stock up on some fresh seafood. ✉ *Calle Del Mar, s/n, La Cruz de Huanacaxtle.*

### Parish of La Cruz de Huanacaxtle

**RELIGIOUS SITE** | This parish was recently upgraded and now has a/c and painted walls. It's not particularly beautiful, but still worth a visit. ✉ *Marlin 38, La Cruz de Huanacaxtle* ☎ *329/295–5622.*

##  Beaches

There are two beaches in La Cruz, each with its own distinct flavor. Tizate is at the southern end of town, right in front of some condos and two-story houses, with the marina to its right. While the beach is all right it's certainly not jaw-dropping, but surfers do get excited when there's a swell and the fantastic right breaks at the south end of the beach. Much more desirable is La Manzanilla, the other beach on the north side of town, right by the foothills. It's wide, clean, and very popular with local families who come here every day—and especially on the weekends—to swim in the calm water and eat fresh seafood at one of the many beachside *palapa* restaurants.

### Playa La Manzanilla

**BEACH—SIGHT** | **FAMILY** | This local beach is wide, busy, entertaining, and worth visiting if you're here for a while. It's particularly crowded on Sundays as locals flock here *en masse* to enjoy the ocean and snacks at various food stalls. There's a big parking lot right in front, and if you want a somewhat quieter place to relax, just walk south for a few dozen meters. **Amenities:** food and drink, parking **Best for:** swimming, snorkeling ✉ *La Cruz de Huanacaxtle.*

### Playa Tizate

**BEACH—SIGHT** | The surf here may not be consistent, but when it happens it is superb, which makes this a surfer favorite. The beach is adjacent to the fishing port of La Cruz, along the south side, and the area closest to the port is great for swimming even when the surf is big. Farther south it becomes nicer, but swimming gets trickier because of the rocks at the edge of the water. **Amenities:** watersports **Best for:** walking, surfing, swimming, solitude ✉ *La Cruz de Huanacaxtle.*

##  Restaurants

La Cruz de Huanacaxtle has more than two dozen restaurants and just as many (if not more) taco stands and *cenadurías* (unofficial restaurants that families set up in their porches). Most of them offer seafood and traditional Mexican cuisine, but you'll also find Italian and Greek food.

### ★ Fonda Coqui

**$** | **MEXICAN** | **FAMILY** | This new and basic but delicious family-run restaurant opened right in front of La Cruz's busiest joint (Tacos on the Street) but has managed to make a name for itself. Many say their *barbacoa* (slowly cooked goat meat stew) is the best in the bay, and their tamales, enchiladas, and tacos are nothing short of extraordinary. **Known for:** best barbacoa in the bay; espagueti poblano; family-run establishment. Ⓢ *Average main: 40 MP* ✉ *Huachinango L–14, La Cruz de Huanacaxtle* ☎ *322/295–6440* ▤ *No credit cards.*

### ★ Frascati

**$$$** | **ITALIAN** | **FAMILY** | Frascati is friendly and intimate while simultaneously sophisticated, with a lively soundtrack in the background. Choose your pasta (several are house-made) and then one of 12 toppings, including traditional sauces such as Bolognese, pesto, four cheese, and pomodoro, or something chef-inspired like the Arturito, a sauce of fresh tomatoes, cream, chicken, and basil. **Known for:** mixed seafood combo; upscale setting; romantic ambience. [$] *Average main: 175 MP* ✉ *39 Marlin, La Cruz de Huanacaxtle* ✣ *Inside de Marina, at its only building* ☎ *329/295–6185* 🌐 *www.frascatilacruz.com* 🕒 *Closed Mon.*

### La Cruz Inn

$$ | **INTERNATIONAL** | **FAMILY** | This restaurant, part of a small inn, might look like just another Mexican restaurant from the outside, but there is more than what meets the eye. The cuisine is mostly international, with Greek dishes like *gyros*. **Known for:** Mexican, Greek, and other international fare; excellent gyros; mostly foreign clientele. [$] *Average main: 110 MP* ✉ *Marlin 36, La Cruz de Huanacaxtle* ✣ *Right beside Parish of La Cruz de Huanacaxtle* ☎ *329/295–5849.*

### ★ Tacos on the Street

$ | **MEXICAN** | **FAMILY** | This small, no-frills restaurant offers what many claim to be the best tacos in all of Banderas Bay, but also the most expensive. The tender rib-eye meat that melts in your mouth is the secret to its success. **Known for:** handmade tortillas; carne asada tacos; best tacos in the area. [$] *Average main: 50 MP* ✉ *Huachinango St. 9, La Cruz de Huanacaxtle* ☎ *329/295–5056* 🌐 *www.facebook.com/tacosonthestreet* 💳 *No credit cards* 🕒 *Closed Mon. and Tues. No lunch.*

## Hotels

### B Nayar

$$$ | **HOTEL** | This four-star, all-suite hotel has its own beach club, an 18-hole golf course, pools, gym, restaurant, and a fantastic view. **Pros:** big suites; many facilities; great value for money. **Cons:** you'll need wheels to explore beyond the hotel; no cribs; no pets allowed. [$] *Rooms from: $153* ✉ *Blvd. Riviera Nayarit Km 1, La Cruz de Huanacaxtle* ☎ *329/295–5308* 🛏 *31 rooms* 🍴 *Free Breakfast.*

### Hotel Matlali

$$$$ | **RESORT** | Perched on a hill overlooking La Cruz, this brand new hotel and spa has 42 villas all tastefully decorated in Balinese style. **Pros:** brand new, elegant construction; good service; relaxed environment. **Cons:** limited Internet and phone reception; transportation needed to get anywhere; long walk uphill from the main road. [$] *Rooms from: $280* ✉ *Carr. Punta Mita Km 0.2, La Cruz de Huanacaxtle* ☎ *322/115–7703* 🌐 *www.matlali.com* 🛏 *42 suites* 🍴 *All-inclusive.*

### Villa Bella

$$ | **HOTEL** | **FAMILY** | The homey hotel is on a hill above quiet La Cruz de Huanacaxtle, just north of Bucerías, and offers garden-view or ocean-facing suites; several have a terrace overlooking the coast, and a large dining area/kitchen and living room. **Pros:** free airport pickup before 6 pm with at least three-night stay; lap pool; free afternoon cocktail Monday–Saturday. **Cons:** up a steep road (best for those with a car); rooms have lots of knickknacks; three-night minimum stay in high season. [$] *Rooms from: $73* ✉ *Calle del Monte Calvario 12, La Cruz de Huanacaxtle* ☎ *329/295–5161, 329/295–5154, 877/273–6244 toll-free in U.S., 877/513–1662 toll-free in Canada* 🌐 *www.villabella-lacruz.com* 🛏 *2 rooms, 4 suites* 🍴 *Free Breakfast.*

## Shopping

### ★ La Cruz de Huanacaxtle Farmers' Market

**CRAFTS** | This is arguably the best farmers' market in the whole Puerto Vallarta/Riviera Nayarit region. It offers a balanced combination of good quality Mexican handicrafts and jewelry, as well as clothes, lamps, hammocks, cigars, organic products, and lots of delicious food. Everything is in a delightful environment with stunning views of the Marina Riviera Nayarit and Banderas Bay, and there's live music in the background. It makes for a great way to spend a Sunday morning. ⊠ *Marina, La Cruz de Huanacaxtle* ⊕ *www.mercadohuanacaxtle.com.*

## 🏃 Activities

La Cruz is a mostly sleepy town, but there is plenty to do in the ocean, which is the biggest attraction in the area.

### Deep Sea Fishing

**BOAT TOURS** | The ocean within the bay limits and beyond is ideal for fishing, abundant in marine life, and without rough surf. There are many boats that can be chartered at the marina; just call or walk over and inquire about the options available when you're there. Marlin, tuna, mahimahi, and dorado are some of the bigger catches you can get. Be mindful of turtles and whales. ⊠ *Marina Vallarta, La Cruz de Huanacaxtle.*

### Fish TFC

**BOAT TOURS** | Guests have nothing but great things to say about their experience with Greg and Krisi's fishing charter service. The boat and equipment are top-notch, and their local knowledge is second to none. ⊠ *Carr. 200, La Cruz de Huanacaxtle* ✛ *Right in front of Arroyo Seco* ☎ *435/901–4564* ⊕ *www.fishtfc. com.*

### Snorkeling

**SNORKELING** | **FAMILY** | Grab your snorkeling gear and head over to the cove adjacent to La Manzanilla beach. The cove is easy to reach and you'll spot marine life including small fish and, if you're lucky, stingrays. ⊠ *La Manzanilla beach, La Cruz de Huanacaxtle* ✛ *North end of La Manzanilla beach.*

# Punta Mita

*10 miles west of La Cruz de Huanacaxtle.*

Punta Mita has been luring travelers for decades. At the very north tip of Banderas Bay is this exclusive peninsula where the sun shines 325 days a year, surfers ride waves at their many breaks, and the rich spend time relaxing at the Punta Mita estates. There's something for everyone in Punta Mita, except for heavy partiers who might find it too quiet for their liking.

### GETTING HERE AND AROUND

As with anywhere else in Banderas Bay, reaching Punta Mita is relatively easy with public transportation, albeit not the most comfortable. Buses and *combis* run here from other towns in the Bay every few minutes; just wave one down displaying a "Punta Mita" sign. Renting a car gives you more flexibility to check out the different beaches and towns; you can even stop in La Cruz or Bucerías along the way to Punta Mita. Taxis cost 500 MXN or more depending on where you go.

## 👁 Sights

Without a doubt, Punta Mita's best sights are its beaches. The area doesn't really have any cultural attractions per se, though you may want to explore a few towns such as El Anclote and Litibu. It's also easy and cheap to rent a *panga* boat here and visit the Marietas Islands, a national park where you'll find humpback whales in winter and blue-footed booby birds year-round.

## 🏖 Beaches

Regardless of your age or budget, you come to Punta Mita for the beaches. Some are best for surfing, others for lounging, but all have fine white sand and clear blue water. Note that only one of the beaches has access to food and other facilities.

### Burros

BEACH—SIGHT | FAMILY | Adjacent to the Grand Palladium Resort, you'll encounter rocks and sea urchins at this beach once you reach the water. Burros has one of the most consistent surf breaks in the area, and thus gets crowded with surfers. Nonsurfers also come hereto check out the action, and it is possible to go for a swim when the waves are small. During low tide you can make your way to the beach on the other side of the small cliff where there's a natural salt water pool. **Amenities:** watersports **Best for:** surfing, walking ⊠ *Punta Mita* ⊹ *Right before Grand Palladium gate, turn left along unpaved road. Get out of your car where it ends and follow trail to beach.*

### Destiladeras

BEACH—SIGHT | FAMILY | Favored by locals because of its long stretch of sand and beautiful color, Destiladeas is especially popular on weekends. You can reach the beach by bus or car, and there's unofficial parking at the top of the cliff where guards will look over your car for a price. **Amenities:** watersports, parking **Best for:** swimming, surfing, walking, sunset ⊠ *Along carretera La Cruz de Huanacaxtle-Punta Mita, Punta Mita.*

### El Anclote

BEACH—SIGHT | The water at this beach is almost always still, and even when surf is bigger, the many jetties keep the area safe for swimming (though swimmers should still take caution). Take a panga tour to the Marietas Islands; in winter, whale-watching is popular here. You'll also have plenty of dining options nearby. ⊠ *Av. El Anclote s/n, Corral del Risco (Punta de Mita).*

### La Lancha

BEACH—SIGHT | FAMILY | Regarded as one of the most beautiful beaches in all the bay, La Lancha requires some effort to get to, which means fewer crowds. To reach it, you'll need to walk for about 10 minutes along an overgrown trail that gets very muddy during the summer months. It's a great surfing beach for beginners when the waves are small, fantastic for advanced surfers when they are big, and the sand is ideal for families with small kids—just keep an eye on them if there's some surf. **Amenities:** watersports, **Best for:** surfing, sunset, swimming ⊠ *Km 15, Carr. Federal la Cruz de Huanacaxtle - Punta de Mita, Punta Mita* ⊹ *Across from Pemex station.*

## 🍴 Restaurants

Punta Mita has quite a few restaurants to choose from, including no-frills taco joints and traditional Mexican places, and a few upscale options.

### La Pescadora

$$$ | MEXICAN FUSION | As you walk into this restaurant you'll immediately notice that it's much more upscale than its peers. Seafood is the way to go, but they also have steak and some international dishes. **Known for:** worth the splurge; incredible beach views; seafood. $ *Average main: 280 MP* ⊠ *Av. El Anclote 10, Corral del Risco (Punta de Mita)* ☎ *329/291-5212* ⊕ *www.demitarg.com.*

### Restaurante El Coral

$$ | MEXICAN | FAMILY | El Coral serves generous portions of seafood in a relaxed environment facing the beach. It's a favorite among those heading out on a tour of the Marietas Islands, and for surfers who come to ride the waves at El Anclote. **Known for:** large portions of seafood; casual environment; stop before heading out to the Marietas Islands. $ *Average main: 140 MP* ⊠ *Av. El Anclote, Corral del Risco (Punta de Mita)* ☎ *329/291-6332* ⊕ *www.hotelelcoral.com.*

### Tuna Blanca

$$$ | INTERNATIONAL | A more casual iteration of its Puerto Vallarta location, Tuna Blanca faces the water at the north end

of Playa El Anclote. From the deck you'll have the best views of the ocean, Marietas Islands, and the left arm of Banderas Bay. **Known for:** small portions; five-course tasting menu; divine views. [$] *Average main: 250 MP* ✉ *Av. El Anclote 5, Punta de Mita, Punta Mita* ☎ *329/291–5415* 🌐 *www.tunablanca.com* 🕒 *Closed Mon. No lunch.*

## Hotels

Punta Mita is the priciest place to stay in Banderas Bay, but there are few lower-budget options, as well as Airbnbs. More affordable lodging options may require a car or taxi to get to.

**Casa de Mita**

$$$$ | **HOTEL** | Architect-owner Marc Lindskog has created a nook of nonchalant elegance, with updated country furnishings of wicker, leather, and wood; rock-floor showers without curtains or doors; and cheerful Pacific Coast architectural details. **Pros:** delicious food; nearly private beach; concierge service. **Cons:** little nightlife in vicinity; three-night minimum stay; strict cancellation policy. [$] *Rooms from: $700* ✉ *Playa Careyeros, Riviera Nayarit* ☎ *329/298–4114, 866/740–7999* 🌐 *www.casademita.com* 🛏 *8 rooms* 🍴 *All-inclusive.*

**Four Seasons Resort Punta Mita**

$$$$ | **RESORT** | **FAMILY** | The hotel and its fabulous spa perch above a lovely beach at the northern extreme of Bahía de Banderas, about 45 minutes from the Puerto Vallarta airport and an hour north of downtown Puerto Vallarta. **Pros:** beautiful beach; concierge service; excellent spa. **Cons:** staff trained to be overly solicitous; very expensive spa treatments; not all rooms have ocean views. [$] *Rooms from: $870* ✉ *Punta de Mita, Bahía de Banderas, Punta Mita* ☎ *329/291–6019, 800/819–5053 in U.S. and Canada* 🌐 *www.fshr.com/puntamita* 🛏 *168 rooms* 🍴 *No meals.*

**Hotel Basalto**

$$$ | **HOTEL** | This brand-new beachfront boutique hotel has just 10 rooms, plus a rooftop infinity pool and oceanfront views. **Pros:** hotel can organize tours and activities for guests; great food on-site; both ocean and mountain views. **Cons:** beachfront section only accessible in low tide; hotel road unpaved and bumpy; no shopping or restaurants nearby. [$] *Rooms from: $250* ✉ *Rinconada Careyeros 112, Punta Mita* ☎ *329/298–4283* 🛏 *10 rooms* 🍴 *Free Breakfast.*

★ **Hotel St. Regis Punta Mita**

$$$$ | **HOTEL** | The original St. Regis in Mexico (there's now a sister property in Mexico City) boasts a nouveau Mexican architectural style combining geometric simplicity with the warmth of giant palapa roofs and other natural elements. **Pros:** 80% of rooms have at least partial beach views; personal butlers perform services for all guests; impressive guest-to-employee ratio. **Cons:** rocky beach means no kayaking, swimming, or other water sports; three-night minimum stay (seven nights in high season); you'll need wheels to get anywhere outside the hotel. [$] *Rooms from: $1100* ✉ *Carr. 200, Km 19.5, Lote H4, Punta Mita* ☎ *329/291–5830* 🌐 *www.stregis.com/puntamita* 🛏 *119 rooms* 🍴 *No meals.*

**Marival Armony Resort Punta Mita**

$$$$ | **RESORT** | **FAMILY** | Marival Armony Resort facing Banderas Bay boasts modern tropical decor, seven international restaurants, a spa, kids' club, and five pools. **Pros:** beachfront property; incredible views from rooms; great for families but has an adults-only section, too. **Cons:** service faulty at times—still in the learning process; poolside food service can be an issue with kids; faulty Wi-Fi. [$] *Rooms from: $370* ✉ *Carr. A Punta de Mita Km 8.3 s/n Lote 5A, Punta Mita* ☎ *888/270–4980 toll-free U.S. and Canada, 329/291–7000* 🌐 *www.marivalarmony.com* 🛏 *268 rooms* 🍴 *All-inclusive.*

**W Punta de Mita**

**$$$$ | RESORT | FAMILY** | This secluded beachfront resort boasts spacious rooms with modern decor, a pool, six dining locations, and all the fun under the sun you can think of. **Pros:** great on-site restaurant; surfboards to rent at the hotel; beachfront suites. **Cons:** some rooms require considerable walking to get to; a heavy shorebreak can often make swimming dangerous; pool area can get loud. [$] *Rooms from: $320* ✉ *Km 8.5 Carr. Punta de Mita, Punta Mita* ☎ *329/226–8333* 🌐 *www.marriott.com/hotels/travel/pvrwh-w-punta-de-mita* 🛏 *119 rooms* 🍴 *No meals.*

## Activities

Surfing, whale-watching, mountain biking, stand-up paddleboarding, sailing, snorkeling, trekking, golf, diving... the list of things to do in Punta Mita is extensive and varied. Most of the activities are ocean-related, but if you don't mind being driven to the nearby mountains then you might have a new problem: there's simply too much to do but too little time. Don't try to saturate your agenda; instead pick some of your favorites and leave plenty of time for R&R.

**Accion Tropical**

**SURFING | FAMILY** | All surfers in the area know that the best waves are found along the beaches of Punta Mita on the northernmost tip of the bay. Accion Tropical is one of the most established surf businesses in the area and can hook you up with surf and SUP lessons, snorkeling tours, whale-watching, and more. All staff members are bilingual and will make sure you enjoy the sport of kings. ✉ *Av. Anclote 16, Riviera Nayarit* ☎ *329/291–6633, 329/295–5087, 322/131–6586* 🌐 *www.acciontropical.com.mx.*

**Four Seasons Punta Mita Golf**

**GOLF** | Nonguests are permitted to play the 195-acre, par-72, Jack Nicklaus–designed Pacífico course; however, they must pay the hotel's day use fee of 50% of the room rate (approximately $300 plus 28% tax and service charge), which covers use of a guest room and hotel facilities until dark. (Prices are in USD.) Reservations are essential. The green fee is $255 in the high season, including tax and the golf cart. The club's claim to fame is that it has perhaps the only natural island green in golf. Drive your cart to it at low tide; otherwise hop aboard a special amphibious vessel (weather permitting) to cross the water. There are seven other oceanfront links. The Bahía is another stunning 18-hole course. It has more undulating fairways and greens than the first course, but similarly spectacular ocean views—and a high price tag. ✉ *Punta Mita, Riviera Nayarit* ☎ *329/291–6000* 🌐 *www.fourseasons.com/es/puntamita/golf.*

**Sociedad Cooperativa Corral del Risco**

**TOUR—SPORTS | FAMILY** | Local fishermen at Punta Mita have formed this cooperative, which offers reasonably priced fishing trips, surfing, whale-watching excursions, diving, and snorkeling outings. All their boats are insured. Spot someone wearing a blue shirt with the Co-op's logo, or find them on the southern end of Avenida Anclote next to the jetty. ✉ *Riviera Nayarit* ☎ *329/291–6298* 🌐 *www.puntamitacharters.com.*

**Wildmex**

**SURFING** | Located by the Pemex gas station, this Wildmex location rents surfboards and offers surf lessons at La Lancha beach. They have four- and six-day surf packages and a week-long surf camp, as well; the latter includes accommodations, some meals, and airport transfer. The company also arranges horseback riding, fishing, yoga classes, and other activities. ✉ *Km 15, Carr. Federal la Cruz de Huanacaxtle - Punta de Mita, Punta Mita* ☎ *329/291–3726 cell* 🌐 *www.wildmex.com.*

The Puerto Vallarta area has some of the best golf options in Mexico, like the beautiful course at the Four Seasons Punta Mita.

# Sayulita

*11 miles north of La Cruz de Huanacaxtle.*

Once hailed as "off the beaten path," Sayulita is still a mecca for beginning surfers of all ages, but also attracts tourists to its numerous art galleries and casual and hipster cafés and restaurants. Over the past few years, larger economy hotels began competing against slightly pricier boutique hotels. Getting to Sayulita is fairly easy from the *carretera* (highway) Fed 200, and once you're in town you'll likely want to spend most of your time on the beach, the main plaza, or along Calle Delfines.

## GETTING HERE AND AROUND

You can reach Sayulita by bus from the southern towns in Riviera Nayarit and Puerto Vallarta. Trips cost 15–45 MXN. Limo and taxi rides are also available, but will be pricey. Once in Sayulita you don't need any kind of transportation as you can walk everywhere.

## TOURS

### Chica Locca Tours

**BOATING** | Gil and his team have been guiding sailing tours all around Banderas bay and beyond for many years, and are very well reputed. Tours include whale-watching, Los Arcos, and Yelapa, as well as private tours. The main office is in Sayulita and tickets include transportation to La Cruz marina, where all boats depart. Private tours start at $95 per adult. ⊠ *Av. Revolución Calle Delfines #44, Sayulita* ☎ *322/180–0597* ⊕ *chicaloccatours.com.*

## ◉ Sights

There's one thing that has put Sayulita on the map, and everything revolves around it: the beach. If spending days by the ocean, chilling out, and letting time go by sounds like your cup of tea, then Sayulita could be what you were looking for. Sayulita is not a cultural destination, and the church at the main square is the only sight worth checking out besides the town itself.

**Parroquia de Nuestra Señora de Guadalupe**
RELIGIOUS SITE | You'll find Sayulita's church at the main plaza, along with restaurants, taco stalls, and other eateries. Mass is held daily, and while small it does have some charm. ⊠ *Calle Jose Mariscal 14, Sayulita* ☎ *329/291–3747.*

##  Beaches

There are two main beaches in Sayulita: Sayulita Beach and Playa Los Muertos. At the former, you'll find restaurants right besides it and *palapas* selling drinks and fresh seafood as well asmany surf shops and stalls renting surfboards. Beyond the cape on southern (left) side of the beach is Playa Los Muertos, a gorgeous and secluded beach. Watch out for rip tides and a heavy shore break as there is no lifeguard on duty. ⚠ **A sewage problem at Sayulita Beach has caused swimmers to report sickness. As of April 2019, a sewage treatment plant has supposedly resolved this issue, but be advised when choosing to swim here.**

**Playa Los Muertos**
BEACH—SIGHT | FAMILY | Secluded and not as easy to reach, Playa Los Muertos is a great place to get away from it all and spend some quiet time in Sayulita (which is otherwise hard to get). Watch out for the rip currents as they can be mean, and there are not lifeguards here. **Amenities:** watersports **Best for:** swimming ⊠ *San Francisco.*

**Sayulita Beach**
BEACH—SIGHT | FAMILY | This is the main beach in town. Nowadays it's usually very busy; there are tons of restaurants and shops within walking distance, and the main surf break is right there, too, meaning it's full of surfers and surf schools. **Amenities:** watersports, food and drink, toilet **Best for:** partiers, swimming, surfing ⊠ *Sayulita, Sayulita.*

##  Restaurants

With such an influx of tourism there's no lack of places to eat in Sayulita, and many are in the lower- to mid-budget range. Seafood burritos, tacos, salads, and plenty of organic and healthy options abound all around town, most of them located along Calle Delfines. Don't expect any upscale restaurants; the vibe here is casual and laid-back.

**Calypso**
$$ | ECLECTIC | This second-story restaurant overlooks the town plaza from beneath an enormous palapa roof. Locals rave about the deep-fried calamari appetizer served with spicy cocktail and tangy tartar sauces; it's large enough for several people to share. **Known for:** large portions; reasonable prices; deep-fried calamari. Ⓢ *Average main: 115 MP* ⊠ *Av. Revolución 44, across from plaza, Sayulita* ☎ *329/291–3704* ☾ *No lunch.*

**★ ChocoBanana**
$$ | AMERICAN | FAMILY | One of Sayulita's pioneer restaurants has really gotten spiffy, beautifying its terrace restaurant with mosaic tile accents. BLTs and burgers, omelets and bagels, chicken with rice, and chai tea are some of what you'll find here, along with a good selection of vegetarian dishes. **Known for:** chocolate-covered bananas; laid-back atmosphere; large selection of vegetarian dishes. Ⓢ *Average main: 125 MP* ⊠ *Calle Revolución at Calle Delfín, on plaza, Sayulita* ☎ *329/291–3051* ▭ *No credit cards* ☾ *No dinner.*

**Don Pedro's**
$$ | INTERNATIONAL | FAMILY | Sayulita institution Don Pedro's has wonderful pizzas baked in a wood-fire oven, prepared by European-trained chef and co-owner Nicholas Parrillo. Also on the menu are consistently reliable seafood dishes, yummy Niçoise salad, and tapenade. **Known for:** second-floor dining room open in high season; Thursday live flamenco; Monday dance classes. Ⓢ *Average main:*

100 MP ⌧ *Calle Marlin 2, at the beach, Sayulita* 🕾 *329/291–3090* ⊕ *www.donpedros.com* ☾ *Closed Sept.*

## Tierra Viva

**$$ | MEXICAN FUSION | FAMILY** | Tierra Viva restaurant creates a unique dining experience with its innovative menu of international and tropical flavors. Patrons come here to enjoy fine and creative food from the Caribbean, Oaxaca, Puebla, and Veracruz in a serene location without having to overdress. **Known for:** slow but friendly service; surrounded by nature; fresh seafood. $ *Average main: 140 MP* ⌧ *Calle Marlin 10, Sayulita* 🕾 *322/356–1289* ⊕ *tierravivasayulita.com.*

#  Hotels

Accommodation in Sayulita has traditionally been basic and affordable, but in the past few years new hotels have appeared, catering to traveler demand for higher-quality options. All hotels in Sayulita are within walking distance of the beach, and what you end up choosing will mostly depend on your personal taste, not the location.

## Casa Amor

**$$$ | HOTEL** | What began as a hilltop home has slowly become an amalgam of unusual, rustic, but luxurious suites with indoor and outdoor living spaces. **Pros:** nice location across bay from Sayulita's main beach; staff arranges tours, transportation, and tee times; charming and unique lodgings at reasonable prices. **Cons:** many stairs to walk up; no phones or Wi-Fi in guest rooms; open-to-the-elements rooms can have creepy crawlies. $ *Rooms from: $180* ⌧ *Sayulita beach, south side, Sayulita* 🕾 *329/291–3010* ⊕ *www.villaamor.com* ⌲ *16 rooms* ⦿ *No meals.*

## Hotel Boutique OZ Sayulita

**$$$ | HOTEL** | Casual yet chic Hotel Boutique OZ is just a few blocks from the beach in a quieter part of town. **Pros:** new hotel; rooftop pool; spacious rooms. **Cons:** pricier than its competitors; may

be noisy despite being in quieter part of town; slow food service. $ *Rooms from: $275* ⌧ *61 Av. Revolución, Sayulita* 🕾 *329/298–8766* ⊕ *www.ozsayulita.com. mx* ⌲ *31 rooms* ⦿ *Free Breakfast.*

## Hotel Kupuri

**$$$ | HOTEL | FAMILY** | Hotel Kupuri is near to both the beach and downtown. **Pros:** fantastic location; comfortable rooms; very clean. **Cons:** no parking; rooms close to the restaurant might be somewhat noisy; spotty Wi-Fi. $ *Rooms from: $140* ⌧ *Gaviotas 12, Sayulita* 🕾 *322/291–3218* ⊕ *hotelkupuri.com/en/room* ⌲ *22 rooms* ⦿ *Free Breakfast.*

#  Nightlife

Sayulita may not have a big dance club, but it does have many bars that are open late into the night right on the beach as well as closer to downtown. Sayulita is very small, and at the end of the day you are better off walking around and checking out all the spots that are open until you find one that suits your groove.

## Don Pato

**GATHERING PLACES** | Don Pato serves craft beer in a lively setting, right in the middle of Sayulita. They also serve great food including burgers, enchiladas, and burritos. ⌧ *Calle Marlín 12, Sayulita* 🕾 *322/149–5836.*

## Yambak Bar

**BREWPUBS/BEER GARDENS** | Centrally located and open past midnight, Yambak Bar has a live DJ, and craft beer on tap. ⌧ *Calle Marlin #12 Centro, Sayulita* 🕾 *329/291–3756.*

#  Shopping

Sayulita has plenty of shops catering to all of its visitors. There are plenty of small boutiques selling handmade bikinis and beachwear, jewelry, souvenirs, and more. You'll also find handicrafts, and surf shops selling boards and other surfing gear.

**Banannie Jewelry**

JEWELRY/ACCESSORIES | With more than 17 years in Sayulita, Annie Banannie has become one of the most beloved residents in town. She's the shop owner, manager, and jewelry artist, working strictly in silver (no gold) and semi-precious exotic stones from all over the world. You will find great pieces with emeralds, sapphires, and rubies, among many other stones. ⊠ *Calle Pelicanos 50D, Riviera Nayarit* ☎ *329/291–3769.*

★ **Galería Tanana**

CRAFTS | The beauty of its glistening glass-bead (Czech) jewelry in iridescent and earth colors may leave you weak at the knees. Sometimes a Huichol artisan at the front of the store works on traditional yarn paintings, pressing the fine filaments into a base of beeswax and pine resin to create colorful and symbolic pictures. Money from sales supports the owner's nonprofit organization to promote cultural sustainability for the Huichol people. ⊠ *Av. Revolucion 22, Riviera Nayarit* ☎ *329/291–3889* ⊕ *www. thehuicholcenter.org.*

**La Hamaca**

CRAFTS | The inventory of folk art and utilitarian handicrafts is large, and each piece is unique. Scoop up masks and pottery from Michoacán, textiles and shawls from Guatemala, hammocks from the Yucatán, and lacquered boxes from Olinalá. ⊠ *Calle Revolución 110, Riviera Nayarit* ☎ *329/291–3039.*

 **Activities**

Surfing is what put this lively town in Rivieria Nayarit on the map. If riding waves is not your thing, Sayulita does offer quite a selection of outdoor activities, including horseback riding, mountain biking, bird watching, ATV tours, snorkeling and diving, sailing, and whale-watching. There are plenty of operators in town, but we recommend you shop around for prices as they change often. Note that activities

such as whale-watching or sailing will require a drive from Sayulita to Banderas Bay, which tour operators can sometimes provide.

**Wildmex (Sayulita)**

SURFING | Located right on the beach in Sayulita, Wildmex rents surfboards (as well as bicycles and kayaks) and gives surf lessons either at Sayulita or elsewhere around the bay, depending on conditions. It offers four- and six-day surf packages and a weeklong surf camp; the latter includes accommodations, some meals, and airport transfer. The company also arranges horseback riding, fishing, yoga classes, and other activities. ⊠ *Calle Pelícanos 150–G, Sayulita* ☎ *322/291–3726* ⊕ *www.wildmex.com.*

# San Pancho/ San Francisco

*5 miles north of Sayulita.*

Ten minutes north of Sayulita is the town of San Francisco, known to most people by its nickname, San Pancho. Its beach stretches between headlands to the north and south and is accessed at the end of the town's main road, Avenida Tercer Mundo. At the end of this road, on the beach, a couple of casual restaurants have shaded café tables on the sand where locals and visitors congregate. You'll sometimes see men fishing from shore with nets as you walk the 1½-km-long (1-mile-long) stretch of coarse beige sand. There's an undertow that should discourage less-experienced swimmers. A small reef break sometimes generates waves for surfing (especially in September), but this isn't your ideal surf spot. In fact the undertow and the waves, which are usually too big for family splashing and too small for surfing, have probably helped maintain the town's under-the-radar existence—until now. Popular with a hip crowd, San Pancho has just a few hotels but a growing number of good restaurants.

### GETTING HERE AND AROUND

Getting to San Pancho is relatively easy and affordable by bus or combi, particularly from nearby towns such as Sayulita. Taxis from the Puerto Vallarta airport can run at around 1,200 MXN and street taxis run at around 900 MXN. Compostela buses cost 40 MXN. The final option if coming from PV is to grab a bus to Sayulita and then hop on a taxi to San Pancho; or if you're coming from Guadalajara, travel by bus to Guayabitos or La Penita and then take a taxi from there to San Pancho.

### TOURS

**Diva Tours**

**ADVENTURE TOURS | FAMILY** | Snorkeling, sea kayaking, hiking, and surfing are just some of the activities Diva Tours can set you up with. Get in touch with them if you want to organize a single activity or a full day of nonstop action. ✉ *Mexico 20* ☎ *311/258–4017* 🌐 *divatours.net.*

## Sights

Most of the action in San Pancho happens either along the town's main street Avenida 3er (Tercer) Mundo or at the beach. Walk around town, check out the church on Calle Mexico, and finish off your visit at the beach and you'll have seen the whole town in just one morning. But you don't come to San Pancho to indulge in sightseeing. You come here to take things slowly, eat good food, wander around, and simply spend a day or more relaxing in a sleepy Mexican town right by the ocean with nothing to worry about.

## Beaches

**San Pancho Beach**

**BEACH—SIGHT | FAMILY** | There's only one beach in San Pancho, aptly called Playa San Pancho. Roughly about a mile long, it has fine sand and clean blue water, but also a strong undertow and shorebreak that can be dangerous when the swell builds up. Swimming is fantastic when the sea is calm, but do be careful if the ocean is rough. You can rent surfboards and surf the break on the south side of the beach, which tends to get busy with locals when the waves are pumping.

## 🍴 Restaurants

Restaurants are a highlight in San Pancho, which may come as a surprise given how small the town is. Besides the typical taco stands you can find anywhere in Mexico, great seafood, organic bistros, and Argentine meals are sure to offer something to your liking.

**Café de María**

**$ | CAFÉ | FAMILY** | There are three distinct menus for breakfast, lunch, and dinner. The two rooms of this renovated former home overlook the street just a few blocks from the beach. **Known for:** classic lunch sandwiches like BLTs; omelets and smoothies for breakfast; delicious carrot cake. [$] *Average main: 95 MP* ✉ *Av. Tercer Mundo at Calle América Latina, San Francisco* ☎ *311/258–4439* 💳 *No credit cards* 🕒 *Closed Wed.*

**★ La Ola Rica**

**$$ | INTERNATIONAL** | One of San Pancho's first upscale restaurants, "The Delicious Wave," has still got it goin' on. Small, medium-crust, wood-fired pizzas are just right for an appetizer (we recommend the brie pizza with caramelized onions) or, with a soup or salad, as a delicious dinner for one. **Known for:** excellent margaritas; inside a former home with fun decor; popular in summer. [$] *Average main: 95 MP* ✉ *Av. Tercer Mundo s/n, San Francisco* ☎ *311/258–4123* 🕒 *Closed Sun. No lunch.*

**Mar Plata**

**$$$$ | EUROPEAN** | Impressive second-story digs have views of the sea as well as a celestial seasoning of stars on the ceiling

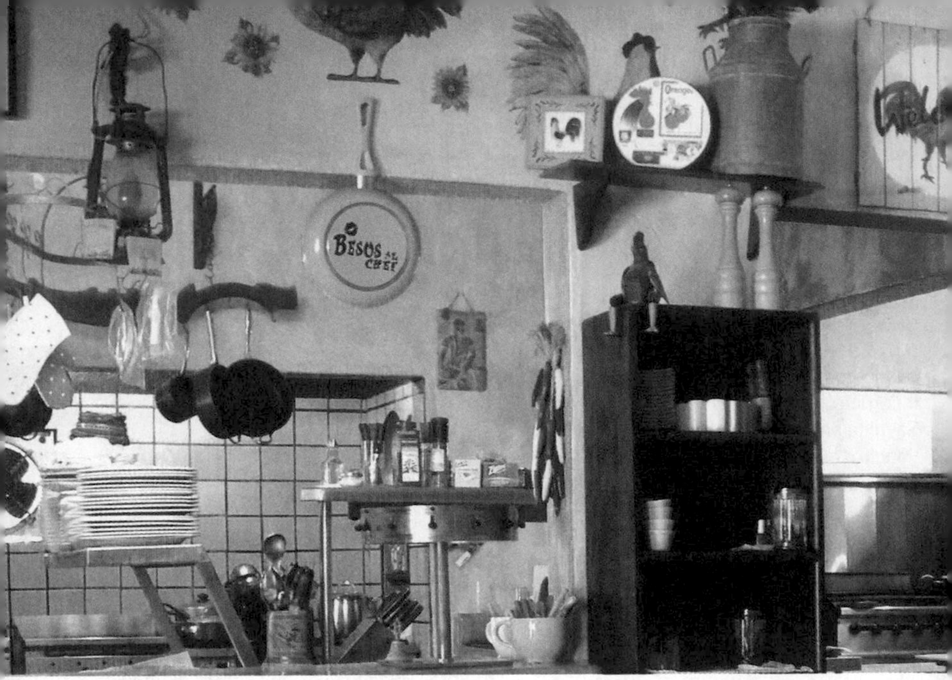


La Ola Rica has a delightfully homey feel.

in the form of tin lamps from Guadalajara. Dark-blue and deep terra-cotta walls juxtapose nicely; the huge space is saved from looking industrial by innovative installations and fixtures. **Known for:** live music on Sunday; occasional flamenco shows and tango classes; Argentine/Continental cuisine. [$] *Average main: 350 MP* ✉ *Calle de Palmas 130, Col. Costa Azul, San Francisco* ☎ *311/258–4424, 311/258–4425* 🌐 *www.marplata.com.mx* ⏲ *Closed Mon. and June–Sept. No lunch.*

## 🛏 Hotels

**Haramara Retreat**

**$$$$ | HOTEL** | With stunning views and acres of trees, as well as blissful breezes off the Pacific Ocean, Haramara Retreat is an oasis of tranquility just south of Sayulita. **Pros:** wonderful views; tranquil setting on a huge, tree-studded property; gifted body workers and yoga teachers. **Cons:** no Wi-Fi access; cab ride from Sayulita; limited cell phone coverage. [$] *Rooms from: $348* ✉ *Riviera Nayarit* ✥ *Off paved road from Sayulita to Punta Mita, about 2½ km (1½ miles) off Carr. 200* ☎ *329/291–1338 local number, 866/801–4084 toll-free in U.S.* 🌐 *www.haramararetreat.com* 🛏 *15 bungalows, 1 dorm-style room* 🍴 *All meals.*

**Villas Buena Vida**

**$$ | HOTEL** | On beautiful Rincón de Guayabitos Beach, this property has three-story units, breeze-ruffled palms, and manicured walkways. **Pros:** beautiful bay-side location; 5% cash discount; good for budget travelers. **Cons:** uninspired furnishings; unreliable Internet access in rooms via Wi-Fi; little hospitality. [$] *Rooms from: $50* ✉ *Retorno Laureles 2, Riviera Nayarit* ☎ *327/274–0231* 🌐 *www.villasbuenavida.com* 🛏 *45 rooms* 🍴 *No meals.*

## 🎟 Performing Arts

For the most part, nightlife in San Pancho is very limited to a few bars and restaurants that are open late. There is however, one attraction that is rather unique:

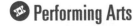

Entreamigos, a local foundations started by the Cirque du Soleil founder.

### Entreamigos

**GATHERING PLACES | FAMILY |** In 2011 the co-founder of Cirque Du Soleil and Creative Director, Gilles Ste-Croix and his wife Monique Voyer created "Entreamigos" with the children of a local community theater to raise money for their programs. This was made possible with the support of Cirque du Soleil who donated training equipment; friends and artists who came from Canada; the company Cirrus Cirkus; as well as over 100 local volunteers. Currently, more than 140 children are enrolled in Circo de los Niños programs. Apart from obtaining space for its school, Circo de los Niños operates a cultural center, open to proposals from individual performers and groups interested in participating in the project. There are annual fundraising shows every March, so if you're in town when it happens make sure you attend to support a good cause. ⊠ *Av. Tercer Mundo 13, San Francisco* ☎ *311/258–4377* ⊕ *entreamigos.org.mx.*

## 🏃 Activities

Despite being a very quiet town, San Pancho has quite a few activities to keep you busy. There's, of course, the beach with its surfing and sailing, but there's also 9-hole golf course Las Huertas, world-class polo venue La Patrona (with its own beach club open during the day to the public), hiking, mountain biking, turtle egg releases, yoga, and bird-watching. Note that during Easter and other holidays the beach does get busy.

### El Estar

**AEROBICS/YOGA | FAMILY |** El Estar holds yoga, meditation, and other classes for groups and individuals in a relaxing environment. ⊠ *Calle América Latina 32, San Francisco* ☎ *722/186–1364* ⊕ *elestar.org.*

### La Patrona Polo and Equestrian Club

**POLO | FAMILY |** It may come as a surprise but there is a very good and luxurious polo club in San Pancho, which of course comes with a big price tag. La Patrona is just a 10-minute drive from San Pancho itself, and the setting is nothing short of spectacular. It's surrounded by a lush jungle and lovely hills, and has a nice restaurant, too. ⊠ *Africa s/n, San Francisco* ☎ *322/146–7714* ⊕ *tierratropical.com.mx.*

### Las Huertas Golf Club

**GOLF |** This 9-hole, par 32 golf course may be challenging for even low-par golfers, making the tropical surroundings even prettier and more challenging, but a lot of fun. ⊠ *Las Huertas Golf Club, San Francisco* ☎ *311/258–4521* ⊕ *www.lashuertasgolf.com* ⅄ *par 9; 32 holes.*

# Jaltemba Bay

*18 miles north of San Pancho.*

Comprising just three towns (minute Los Ayala, Rincón de Guayabitos, and La Peñita), Jaltemba Bay may be just a 25-minute drive north from San Pancho along carretera Fed 200, but it feels worlds apart. Even before you exit the main road you'll notice tourism feels different here, but you may not be able to tell why. Following the Pacific Ocean along Jaltemba Bay with the view of Isla del Coral just a few hundred meters into the ocean, life is simple, time stops being as important, and visitors slowly grasp why these three towns are loved by locals and appreciated by the mostly Mexican tourists who flock here every year. It's not about going wild, joining tours, or staying in nice all-inclusive resorts, but instead about enjoying the simple things in life: the sun, the beach, fresh food, family and friends. It may take some time for you to adapt, but once you do, you'll begin to question why you didn't experience anything like this before.

### GETTING HERE AND AROUND

Roughly an hour and a half away from Puerto Vallarta's international airport, Jaltemba Bay can be reached by car or bus. Autocares Estrella Blanca and Autocares del Pacifico are two low-cost options, though the buses are pretty basic. You'll be awarded a much better travel experience if you head over to the *Terminal de Autobuses* (bus terminal) of Puerto Vallarta and buy tickets with either ETN, Primera Plus, or Vallarta Plus. Should you want to get there with your own car renting one at the airport is very easy, though you will get better deals if you book online in advance. The drive to La Peñita is very simple, just hope onto the carretera Fed 200 heading north as you leave the aiport and don't stop until you reach signs pointing to Guayabitos or La Peñita.

### TOURS

Like in most beach towns along Riviera Nayarit most activities revolve around the ocean, and Guayabitos or La Peñita are no exception. During the winter months, whale-watching tours abound, join a snorkeling tour to Isla del Coral or free turtle hatchings. For a really special trip many don't know about,hop on a boat to Bahia Rincón de Guayabitos, a small beach just past the cape on the south side where clear turquoise clean waters lead to a small beach you'd expect to find in the South Pacific or Caribbean.

**Fiesta Guayabitos**

**ADVENTURE TOURS** | **FAMILY** | This all-in-one tour operator can help organize tours to Tequila and Guadalajara, as well as Isla del Coral. You can also book banana boat experiences with them. ✉ *Av. Sol Nuevo s/n* ✥ *Rincon de Guayabitos* ☎ *327/274–0453* 🌐 *www.fiestaguayabitos.com.*

## 👁 Sights

The *tianguis* (traditional street market held every Thursday) in La Peñita is the place to start your visit as soon as you get here. You might not end up buying anything, but you will get a sense of what to expect in town. When done, walk along the short boardwalk and then make your way to Guayabitos. Visit the Church of Our Lady of Perpetual Help and look for your perfect spot on the beach to finish off the day. There's not much sightseeing to do in Jaltemba Bay, but what little there is to see plus all ocean-related activities are sure to keep you busy without overdoing it.

## ⛱ Beaches

The beaches in both Guayabitos and La Peñita have mellow surf and are ideal for families with kids. The white sand goes on for miles, and there are usually food and drink vendors along the way. Just 3 km off the beach is Isla del Coral, a small island that can be reached by *panga* where you can snorkel, swim, or simply enjoy a different perspective of this part of Mexico. Note that overnight camping is not allowed.

## 🍴 Restaurants

Traditional Mexican dishes and seafood are the way to go in Jaltemba Bay. There's a wide selection of places to choose from, and perhaps where you end up will depend more on where you are when you're hungry than anything else. Most restaurants have simple decor if any.

**Juan's Place**

**$$** | **MEXICAN** | **FAMILY** | A mix between a sports bar and a restaurant, the food here is legendary. Big burgers, ribs, hot dogs, and of course your share of Mexican seafood all come in generous portions. **Known for:** jovial host; delicious seafood; relaxed atmosphere. [$] *Average main: 240 MP* ✉ *Cedros 6, Rincón de Guayabitos* ✥ *Guayabitos* ☎ *322/158–6209* 💳 *No credit cards.*

At popular Rincón de Guayabitos beach, you'll share umbrella space with locals and visitors alike.

### Piña Loca

**$ | MEXICAN |** Come hungry to Piña Loca; all portions in this simple restaurant are huge, but without the huge bill to match. Try the fajitas in lava bowls, the *burrito norteño*, or the shrimp salad. **Known for:** plates are meant to be shared; fajitas served in lava bowls; shrimp salad. $ *Average main: 80 MP* ✉ *Tabachines 5, Rincón de Guayabitos* ☎ *327/274-1184* ▭ *No credit cards.*

### Restaurante Pineda

**$$ | MEXICAN | FAMILY |** Generous portions of delicious seafood is what patrons come to Restaurante Pineda for, though the beautiful ocean view is also a draw. Locals rave about the grilled octopus, oysters, and scallops, but the coconut breaded shrimp aren't too shabby either. **Known for:** pricey but worth it; large portions; raved-about seafood. $ *Average main: 130 MP* ✉ *Carr. Los Ayala 5,, Rincón de Guayabitos* ☎ *327/274-2143.*

### Salvador's

**$$$ | MEXICAN |** Shrimp lovers will find Salvador's the closest place to heaven on earth. Tuesday is "all you can eat shrimp" night. **Known for:** great location on the beach; excellent service; shrimp-lovers paradise. $ *Average main: 250 MP* ✉ *Tabachines Frente al Mar, 6, Rincón de Guayabitos* ☎ *322/151-7702* ▭ *No credit cards.*

##  Hotels

There are plenty of budget hotels in Jaltemba Bay, especially compared to Puerto Vallarta and Nuevo Vallarta.

### ★ Hotel Real Villas

**$$$ | HOTEL |** The rooms in this all-suite hotel are spacious and just a few meters from the ocean. **Pros:** all-suite hotel; full kitchen; towels for pool use. **Cons:** loud pool music; spotty Wi-Fi; room furniture beginning to look run down. $ *Rooms from: $142* ✉ *Retorno Pelicanos s/n, Rincón de Guayabitos* ☎ *327/274-0340* ⊕ *hotelrealvillas.com* ⤳ *44 rooms* ❍ *Free Breakfast.*

##  Nightlife

While La Peñita is definitely on the quieter side, Guayabitos does have some options for when it gets dark. You won't find big nightclubs but good bars with music (some of them live) that will keep you entertained 'til late in the night—or early in the morning.

### Nivel Zero Bar

**WINE BARS—NIGHTLIFE** | Serving a good mix of drinks and bar snacks, Nivel Zero also has live rock music daily. Themed parties happen often and young crowds find it a local favorite. ⊠ *Av. Sol Nuevo 320, Rincón de Guayabitos* ☎ *327/274–3332.*

##  Shopping

Without it being a shopping destination, Jaltemba Bay has some basic and general shopping options, most of them in Guayabitos. Beach attire, handcrafts, silver, and souvenirs are not difficult to find, with Avenida del Sol Nuevo in Guayabitos being your street of choice.

### La Peñita Tianguis Market

**OUTDOOR/FLEA/GREEN MARKETS** | **FAMILY** | The outdoor street market in La Peñita is fun, lively, and colorful. You'll find souvenirs, clothes, fruits, drinks, and more to entertain you. Make sure you stock up on fresh produce. The market is only open on Thursday from 7 am to 2 pm. ⊠ *Av. Bahia de Manzanillo Sur.*

##  Activities

Swimming, snorkeling off Coral Island, and sleeping on the beach are perhaps the best activities you can come across in Jaltemba Bay. The ocean in this part of Riviera Nayarit is calm most of the time, but if surfing is something you really want to do, head over to Chacala or Lo de Marcos. Remember that most visitors come here to relax and enjoy the simple side of life.

# Nuevo Vallarta

*15 km (9 miles) north of Puerto Vallarta.*

Nuevo Vallarta is one of the fastest growing beach destinations in Mexico and has the second-highest number of hotels in the country. With vast golf courses, exclusive condominiums, luxurious restaurants, marinas, and miles of golden beaches, this is a great place to try all kinds of water sports including surfing, scuba diving, kayaking, paddle- and kite-surfing. The hotels and resorts in the area also hide world-class spas and renowned restaurants.

Golf courses of Nuevo Vallarta are among the best in the world. El Tigre (par 72), designed by Robert von Hagge, has 18 holes and 144 sand traps distributed over 7,329 yards of Bermuda 419-covered terrain, and nine artificial lakes. Even the most experienced golfers find it challenging.

Massive Vidanta development has Nayar Golf Club, another spectacular course designed by Jim Lipe and redesigned by Jack Nicklaus. Here you get 6,936 yards with nine holes and fine Bermuda 417 grass.

Two marinas, Nuevo Vallarta Marina and Paradise Village Marina, are also worth a visit. They can accommodate around 500 vessels and the latter is certified as the cleanest marina in the country. Beautiful ships, natural surroundings, and luxurious properties alongside should be enough to attract your attention. But if not, the marinas are home to numerous bird species such as herons, ducks, pelicans, and seagulls, as well as enormous crocodiles that swim freely between boats. If you don't disturb them, you shouldn't be disturbed either.

Nature lovers can also enjoy turtle releases. Olive ridley and leatherback turtles come to the beaches of Nuevo Vallarta to lay their eggs, spurring the development of a turtle sanctuary near Bahia del Sol Resort that guarantees their protection. From August to January nightly releases are organized if any eggs have hatched. To participate, ask the reception staff at Bahia del Sol (☎ 322/297–9527) for details.

## TOURS
### Vallarta Adventures

Vallarta Adventures is one of PV's most respected tour operators and offers sea and land adventures; a particularly wonderful tour combines round-trip air transportation to the highlands with a visit to the former mining town of San Sebastián. Their main office is in Nuevo Vallarta, and many of their adventures start in this location. Some of their activities do involve animals in captivity (which are well taken care of) but most of their tours will take you around the bay. ✉ Paseo de las Palmas 39–A, Nuevo Vallarta ☎ 322/297–1212, 888/303–2653 in U.S. and Canada ⊕ www.vallarta-adventures.com.

## QUICK BITES

One of the best ice-cream shops in Nuevo Vallarta, **Yogurtime** (✉ Paseo las Palmas 32) offers scoops in cups, and excellent toppings. If you are looking for lunch and want to sit, you'll find a wide range of hot and cold seafood at **La Ola** (✉ Paseo las Palmas 32–1), which offers plenty of seating both indoors and outdoors (the tuna toast is perhaps the best starter).

# ◉ Sights

Nuevo Vallarta doesn't have much when it comes to cultural attractions, but it more than makes up for it with a beautiful endless beach, golf courses, plenty of restaurants, bars, and even a crocodile farm. There's much less traffic than in Puerto Vallarta, lots of places to ride a bicycle and even a freshwater channel where you can paddle surf—but watch out for crocodiles.

### El Cora Crocodile Sanctuary

ECOTOURISM | FAMILY | This crocodile farm takes care of reptiles and offers guided tours. The sanctuary is fun for kids, and is best visited in the morning or in the afternoon as temperatures can get very high during midday. ✉ Carr. Puerto Vallarta-Tepic Bucerías, Nuevo Vallarta ☎ 332/109–1125 ⊕ www.facebook.com/cocodrilarioelcora ✉ 20 MXP (Donation).

# ⚘ Beaches

One wide, flat, sandy beach stretches from the mouth of the Ameca River north for miles, past the Nuevo Vallarta hotels (including the new developments at the north end, called Flamingos) and into the town of Bucerías. The generally calm water is good for swimming and, when conditions are right, bodysurfing or boogie boarding. Activities are geared towards all-inclusive-hotel guests north of Paradise Village marina. Vendors on the beach rent water-sports equipment, as do most of the hotels.

### Playa Nuevo Vallarta

BEACH—SIGHT | FAMILY | Several kilometers of pristine beach face the hotels of Playa Nuevo Vallarta. In the fall, a fenced-off turtle nesting area provides relief for the endangered ocean dwellers. Jet Skis whiz by, kids frolic in the roped-off water nearest the beach, and waiters attend to vacationers lounging in recliners in front of their respective hotels. The wide, flat sandy stretch is perfect for long walks. In fact, you could walk all the way to Bucerías, some 8 km (5 miles) to the north. Most of the hotels here are all-inclusives, so guests generally move between their hotel pool, bar, and restaurant, and the beach in front. All-inclusive programs mean that only hotel guests may enter the bars and restaurants on the property. This beach recently received certification by the Mexican government as a "Clean Beach." **Facilities:** Banana-boat rides; Jet Skis; parasailing; lifeguards; parking; toilets; showers,

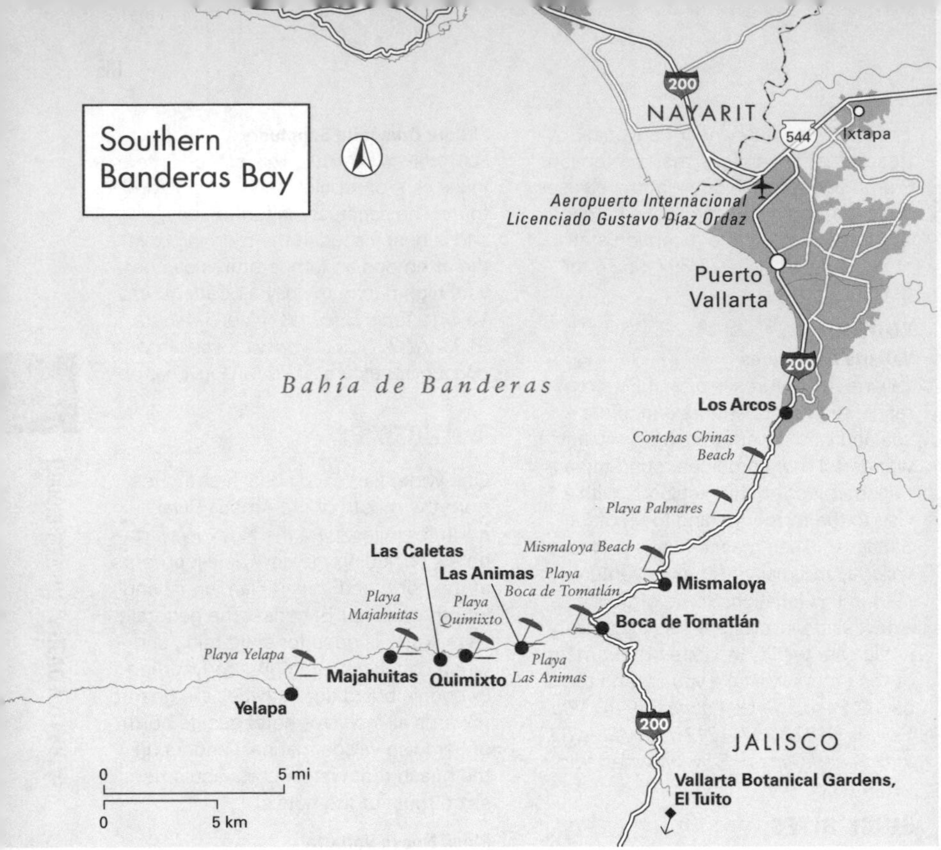
Southern Banderas Bay
NAYARIT
200
544
Ixtapa
Aeropuerto Internacional Licenciado Gustavo Díaz Ordaz
Puerto Vallarta
Bahía de Banderas
Los Arcos
Conchas Chinas Beach
Playa Palmares
Mismaloya Beach
Mismaloya
Las Caletas
Las Animas
Playa Boca de Tomatlán
Boca de Tomatlán
Playa Majahuitas
Playa Quimixto
Playa Yelapa
Majahuitas
Quimixto
Playa Las Animas
Yelapa
JALISCO
Vallarta Botanical Gardens, El Tuito
0
5 mi
0
5 km

trash bins. **Best for:** walking; swimming; sunset. ✉ *Nuevo Vallarta.*

## 🍴 Restaurants

It's difficult to beat Nuevo Vallarta's food scene, and despite the area having a small population there are tons of restaurants for all budgets and of all kinds: Italian, Lebanese, Mexican, international, Chinese, Japanese, and other types of restaurants are to be found here. There's also a handful of bars where you can enjoy beer and music late into the night. To sample traditional food at a low price, just cross Carretera Federal 200 and make your way to Valle Dorado where you'll find dozens of busy eateries with authentic burritos, tacos, and more.

**Buonissimo**

**$$ | MEXICAN FUSION | FAMILY** | This trendy but casual café also offers lunch and dinner, but it's the breakfast people come here for. Enchiladas, huevos al gusto, pastries, and good coffee are loved by patrons, though the pizzas and salads served later in the day and into the night are also tasty. **Known for:** Italian-style ice cream; enchiladas; pastries. [$] *Average main: 100 MP* ✉ *Paseo las Palmas 3, Nuevo Vallarta* ☎ *322/125–4967* 🌐 *www.buonissimogelato.com.*

**Dolce Vita**

**$$ | ITALIAN** | Fine Italian food can be found at any of the three locations of this well-known local business. Casual attire is expected, with the location in Nuevo Vallarta being somewhat fancier and ideal for either romantic dinners or family reunions. **Known for:** thin-crust pizzas;

excellent service; gluten-free pasta. $ *Average main: 165 MP* ⊠ *Av. Paseo las Palmas #2, Nuevo Vallarta* ☎ *322/297–0403* ⊕ *dolcevita.com.mx.*

### Eddie's Place Nopal Beach

$$ | **MEXICAN FUSION** | This restaurant is an institution among locals and visitors who know that in Nuevo Vallarta there's more than just all-inclusive hotels. Eddie's Place is one of the few expat meeting points in the area. **Known for:** great views of the marina; coconut shrimp with mango sauce; exquisite kebabs (hard to find anywhere else in PV). $ *Average main: 135 MP* ⊠ *Blvd. Nayarit 70 Loc. 1–3, Paseo de la Marina, Nuevo Vallarta* ☎ *322/297–1568* ▬ *No credit cards.*

### Fajita Republic

$$ | **MEXICAN FUSION** | **FAMILY** | A favorite among visitors, Fajita Republic serves big portions of Tex-Mex food at fair prices in a cozy yet relaxed environment. You'll mostly find tourists here, perhaps because the restaurant is just a short walk away from most of the hotels in Nuevo Vallarta. **Known for:** Aztec cheese; BBQ ribs; fajitas. $ *Average main: 130 MP* ⊠ *Paseo de los Cocoteros lote 8, Villa 8 Embarcadero 5, Nuevo Vallarta* ☎ *322/297–2267.*

### ★ La Ola

$$ | **MEXICAN** | **FAMILY** | Fresh seafood including ceviche, tuna, and shrimp are to be found in this relaxed restaurant. The friendly staff and owners and surf decor (and sand that's often dragged in by surfers from the beach) makes for a relaxed vibe. **Known for:** chill atmosphere; tuna toast, sashimi. $ *Average main: 105 MP* ⊠ *Av. las Palmas 8* ☎ *322/297–0280* ◷ *Closed Mon. No dinner.*

### Mr. Cream Pancakes and Waffles

$$ | **INTERNATIONAL** | **FAMILY** | Chilaquiles, pancakes, waffles, baked goods, omelets… whatever you want for breakfast, they have it. This brand-new restaurant in Nuevo Vallarta has been a total success and a great excuse to leave your nearby

hotel to eat good food any given morning. **Known for:** busy on Sunday; loved by locals and tourists; classic breakfast spot. $ *Average main: 115 MP* ⊠ *Av. Paseo de las Palmas 3 , Plaza 3.14, Nuevo Vallarta* ☎ *322/297–0201* ◷ *No dinner.*

### Rincón de Buenos Aires

$$$ | **ARGENTINE** | Restaurants are a hard sell in all-inclusive-dominated Nuevo Vallarta, but this one has managed to survive (it was formerly called La Porteña). The setting, an L-shaped covered patio with kids' play equipment in the center, is Mexican, but the food is pure Argentine flavor. **Known for:** mesquite-grilled meat; authentic Argentine cuisine; Italian dishes. $ *Average main: 205 MP* ⊠ *Blvd. Nayarit 25, between highway to Bucerías and El Tigre golf course, Nuevo Vallarta* ☎ *322/297–4950* ◷ *Closed Mon.*

### ★ Sonora al Sur

$ | **BARBECUE** | Throw in prime cuts from Sonora, Mexico's finest meat producing state, a chef that has found the secret to grilling the perfect BBQ, and very affordable rates and you'll get this local favorite. The all-you-can-eat buffet for less than $6 is an added bonus. **Known for:** all-you-can-eat buffet; local favorite; delicious BBQ. $ *Average main: 100 MP* ⊠ *Blvd. Nuevo Vallarta No. 64, Nuevo Vallarta* ☎ *322/297–0376* ▬ *No credit cards.*

##  Hotels

The beach in Nuevo Vallarta is dominated by large all-inclusive hotels and some condos. Most are in the high-end price range, but some can be rather affordable in shoulder seasons and summer, when foreigners leave the city due to excessive heat and humidity. Getting to any of the hotels is very simple as they're all on Paseo de los Cocoteros street, the avenue closest to the ocean that runs all along Nuevo Vallarta.

### Grand Velas All-Suites & Spa Resort

$$$$ | **RESORT** | In scale and majesty, the public areas of this property outshine all

other Nuevo Vallarta all-inclusive resorts. **Pros:** exceptionally beautiful rooms and public spaces; lovely spa; extremely long beach great for walking. **Cons:** Nuevo Vallarta location is far from Puerto Vallarta if you're looking for shops and restaurants (but 10 minutes by car from Bucerías); Wi-Fi is not included; restaurants need reservations. [$] *Rooms from: $780* ✉ *Paseo de los Cocoteros 98 Sur, Nuevo Vallarta* ☎ *322/226–8000, 888/261–8436 in U.S. and Canada* 🌐 *www.grandvelas.com* 🛏 *267 1-, 2-, and 3-bedroom suites* 🍴 *All-inclusive.*

**Krystal Reflect Nuevo Vallarta**
$$$ | **ALL-INCLUSIVE** | **FAMILY** | The Krystal Reflect is a beachfront hotel ideal for families and couples. **Pros:** new since 2019; luxurious but not extremely expensive; beachfront. **Cons:** food is mediocre; limited access to restaurants; loud music at night. [$] *Rooms from: $310* ✉ *Blvd. Costero # 800* ☎ *322/226–1050* 🌐 *www.reflectresorts.com/en_us/resorts/mexico/nuevo-vallarta.html* 🛏 *410 rooms* 🍴 *All-inclusive.*

**Marina Banderas Suites Hotel Boutique**
$$ | **HOTEL** | The very large and well-appointed suites in this boutique hotel overlook the marina in Nuevo Vallarta and, if you're in the rooms facing west, you'll see spectacular sunsets, too. **Pros:** very clean and tasteful rooms; magnificent views; close to restaurants and the largest tour operator in Vallarta. **Cons:** downtown Puerto Vallarta is a 20-minute drive away; no shops; slow Wi-Fi. [$] *Rooms from: $136* ✉ *Paseo de la Marina y 16 de Septiembre #42, Nuevo Vallarta* ☎ *322/297–6056* 🌐 *www.marina-banderas.com.mx* 🛏 *16 suites* 🍴 *Free Breakfast.*

**Marival Emotions Resort and Suites**
$$$$ | **RESORT** | Come here if you're looking for an all-inclusive bargain that includes a wealth of activities. **Pros:** value-priced; immaculately kept grounds; premium booze brands. **Cons:** most rooms have no tub or an uncomfortable square tub; musty smell in some rooms; cheap finishing touches like plastic chairs and fake plants. [$] *Rooms from: $343* ✉ *Paseo Cocoteros s/n, at Blvd. Nuevo Vallarta, Nuevo Vallarta* ☎ *322/226–8200* 🌐 *www.gomarival.com* 🛏 *495 rooms* 🍴 *All-inclusive.*

**Paradise Village Beach Resort & Spa**
$$$ | **RESORT** | **FAMILY** | This Nuevo Vallarta hotel and timeshare property is perfect for families, with lots of activities geared toward children. **Pros:** reasonably priced spa; fully loaded kitchen in all suites; wide range of accommodations. **Cons:** big cats caged in depressing zoo; timeshare-oriented; guests must bring cable for Internet access. [$] *Rooms from: $134* ✉ *Paseo de los Cocoteros 1, Nuevo Vallarta* ☎ *322/226–6770, 866/334–6080* 🌐 *www.paradisevillage.com* 🛏 *702 suites* 🍴 *No meals.*

**Vidanta Nuevo Vallarta**
$$$$ | **RESORTRESORT** | **FAMILY** | This hugely impressive hotel is an excellent choice for both families with kids or couples looking for a place to get away from it all. **Pros:** good service; lots of facilities; great for kids. **Cons:** the resort is huge and takes a long time to walk through; timeshare presentations are difficult to avoid and can be pushy; need transportation to get anywhere outside the hotel. [$] *Rooms from: $290* ✉ *Av. Paseo de las Moras s/n, Nuevo Vallarta* ☎ *322/226–4000* 🌐 *www.mayanresorts.com* 🛏 *789 suites* 🍴 *No meals.*

## 🍸 Nightlife

Nuevo Vallarta is pretty quiet when the sun sets as there aren't many night clubs or bars, but there are a few. These are mostly restaurants with music that remain open until late into the night, and most of the hotels are also open to the general public. If you want a loud and busy night vibe your best bet is to make your way to Puerto Vallarta, but if you want a place where to hang out there are some options.

### Wing's Army Nuevo Vallarta

**BARS/PUBS** | This unpretentious place filled a bar void in Nuevo Vallarta. Large TV screens show every major sporting event, and the second floor has a pool table. The bar fills with young locals, especially on Thursday when there is live music (mostly rock). A variety of chicken wings and other snacks are available, along with a wide array of beers, both national and international. It's open daily from 1 pm to 3 am. ⊠ *Av. Tepic Sur 1508, L–2 at Plaza Parabien, Nuevo Vallarta* ☎ *322/297–4929.*

##  Performing Arts

### Cinépolis Lago Real

**FILM** | In the new shopping mall of Nuevo Vallarta, Cinépolis Lago Real is a modern, well-designed complex and also the cheapest option to catch a movie in the whole Banderas Bay region. On Wednesday they offer a special discounted ticket price. ⊠ *Plaza Lago Real, Av. Tepic 430 Ote, Nuevo Vallarta* ☎ *322/297–6175.*

## 🔴 Shopping

### Grand Velas Spa

**SPA—SIGHT** | The spa at Nuevo Vallarta's most elegant all-inclusive resort has dramatic architectural lines and plenty of marble, stone, teak, and tile. The 16,500-square-foot facility has 20 treatment rooms and ample steam, sauna, and whirlpools. Lounge in the comfortable chaises near the "plunge lagoon" (with warm and cold pools) between or after treatments. Highlights of the extensive treatment menu are the chocolate, gold, or avocado wrap; Thai massage; cinnamon-sage foot scrub; and the challenging buttocks sculpt-lift. There's even a kids' spa menu. Adjoining the spa is an impressive fitness facility. ⊠ *Av. de los Cocoteros 98 Sur, Nuevo*

*Vallarta* ☎ *322/226–8000* ⊕ *www.grand-velas.com.*

### NV Bookstore

**BOOKS/STATIONERY** | It may be small, but this bookstore has the area's best-distilled selection of English-language books. There are guidebooks; books about Mexican culture, history, and arts; and best-selling titles to read around the pool. ⊠ *Paradise Plaza, 2nd fl., Nuevo Vallarta* ☎ *322/297–2274* ⊗ *Closed Sun.*

### Paradise Plaza

**SHOPPING CENTERS/MALLS** | It's the most comprehensive plaza in the Nuevo Vallarta Hotel Zone, with a food court, grocery store, several coffee and juice shops, an Internet café, a Starbucks, clothing and handicraft boutiques, and a bank. You will also find in here Riviera Nayarit's Conventions & Visitors Bureau on the second floor. ⊠ *Paseo de los Cocoteros 85 Sur, Nuevo Vallarta.*

### Paradise Village Mall

Paradise Village Mall has underground parking, which is very convenient if you have chores to do at the only mall you'll find near the beach. The mall has eateries, a supermarket, and shops where you can buy clothing and souvenirs. They will validate parking for two hours. ⊠ *Paseo de los Cocoteros Sur 85, Nuevo Vallarta.*

### Plaza Lago Real

**SHOPPING CENTERS/MALLS** | Nuevo Vallarta was in dire need of a proper, non-tourist-oriented shopping center, and that's exactly what Lago Real is—an unpretentious mall featuring a wide array of shops and services including Walmart, Cinépolis, Telcel, a food court, and several banks. ⊠ *Carr. Tepic 430 Ote, Valle Dorado, Nuevo Vallarta* ☎ *322/297–6175* ⊕ *www.lagoreal.mx.*

##  Activities

Most of the activities in Nuevo Vallarta involve the ocean in one way or another. Sailing and fishing can be enjoyed year-round, while high-wind sports like kite- and wind-surfing are best practiced March–June. Banana boating, jet-skiing, boogie boarding, and paddle surfing can be practiced at all times, while non-ocean activities may include bike riding, horseback riding, roller blading and anything you can think of along Paseo de Los Cocoteros.

## GOLF
### El Tigre
GOLF | This 18-hole course with 12 water features is at the Paradise Village hotel and condo complex. The greens fee of $210 includes a shared cart, bottled water, practice balls, and cold towels. After 2 pm it's $125. Don't be surprised if you see a guy driving around with tiger cubs in his truck: the course's namesake animals, tigers, are a passion of the club's director, Phil Woodrum. ✉ *Paseo las Garzas, Nuevo Vallarta* ☎ *322/226–8190, 866/843–5951 in U.S., 800/214–7758 in Canada* ⊕ *www.eltigregolf.com.*

### Los Flamingos Country Club
GOLF | Designed by Percy Clifford in 1978, PV's original course has been totally renovated. The 18-hole course in Los Flamingos development, at the northern extremity of Nuevo Vallarta, has new irrigation and sprinkler systems to maintain the rejuvenated greens. The high-season greens fee is $149, including a shared cart, tax, a bottle of water, and a bucket of balls. ✉ *Carr. 200, Km 145, 12 km (8 miles) north of airport, Nuevo Vallarta* ☎ *329/296–5006* ⊕ *www.flamingosgolf. com.mx.*

### Nayar Golf Course at Vidanta
GOLF | This par 70, nearly-7,000-yard course is a natural and technical masterpiece. The course features conditions to fit every player, and was recently redesigned by the celebrated group Nicklaus Design. It's challenging because of the constant, strong crosswinds coming off the ocean. Spotting iguanas is part of the fun and you can keep an eye on the crocodiles sunning in a neighboring sanctuary. The full 18-hole course runs at $225. The fee includes cart rental, taxes, use of the practice range, and return transportation to your hotel. Twilight fees (after 1 pm) cost $165. ✉ *Paseo de las Moras s/n, Fracc. Naútico Turístico, Nuevo Vallarta* ☎ *322/226–4000* ⊕ *www.vidantagolf.com/nuevo-vallarta.*

# Chapter 5

# SOUTH OF PUERTO VALLARTA

Updated by
Luis Domínguez

👁 **Sights**
★★★★★

🍴 **Restaurants**
★★★★★

🏨 **Hotels**
★★★★★

🛍 **Shopping**
★★★☆☆

🍸 **Nightlife**
★★☆☆☆

# WELCOME TO SOUTH OF PUERTO VALLARTA

## TOP REASONS TO GO

★ **Escape the crowds.** The southern part of Puerto Vallarta is well hidden, and tourists rarely visit.

★ **Enjoy pristine beaches.** The beaches here resemble the Caribbean: white sand, transparent water, and colorful marine life.

★ **Whale-watching from the coast.** You don't need to get on a boat; during the winter you can catch a glimpse of the whales even from a restaurant.

★ **Botanical gardens.** Admire their collection of orchids, treat yourself to a delicious breakfast, and swim in the river.

★ **Snorkeling in Los Arcos.** This protected marine reserve encompasses a couple of small island with reefs, underwater tunnels, and caves full of sea life.

★ **Las Caletas.** This is where John Huston spent almost two decades after filming *The Night of the Iguana*. The beach is still as secluded as in the '70s and only accessible by boat.

South of Puerto Vallarta offers a very different experience from the busy town. It's not about shopping, discos, and entertainment but more about enjoying the natural beauty of the area. Highway 200 south to Manzanillo will drive you through the southern part of Banderas Bay for about 25 km (15 miles) before it turns inland. To visit the southern beaches you will need to rent a boat or book a tour.

**1 Los Arcos.** Los Arcos Maritime Nature Reserve is situated just in front of Mismaloya. Apart from being a beautiful landmark, it is the best spot for diving, snorkeling, and SUP. Colorful fish, manta rays, dolphins, and skipjack tuna abound around the tiny islands. The biggest hotels and the finest restaurants in the zone are situated in the area.

**2 Mismaloya.** Mismaloya is the place that made Puerto Vallarta famous. Here, John Huston made his *The Night of the Iguana* movie in 1963 and suddenly PV became a world-famous tourist destination. Mismaloya Beach is still enchanting.

**3 Boca De Tomatlán.** Boca de Tomatlán is loved by PV locals. Take a short drive from downtown PV and suddenly you are in a sleepy fishing village. Enjoy the beach where the river meets the ocean, and delicious food from palapa restaurants.

**4 Vallarta Botanical Gardens.** It opened its doors in 2005 and quickly became one of the most important places to visit during your vacation in PV. It is the quickest way to get acquainted with the tropical dry forest biome and one of the best spots for bird-watchers.

**5 El Tuito.** A small town located an hour away from downtown Puerto Vallarta, El Tuito is a starting point for trips to Cabo Corrientes, but the town itself is worth visiting and will make you feel like you've gone back in time.

**6 Las Ánimas.** Las Ánimas beach is one of three beaches known as the Three Pearls. It's great for snorkeling and diving.

**7 Quimixto.** This is another beach that you can get to with a panga from Boca de Tomatlán. It is relatively narrow but with soft waves and good for swimming, famous for its falls a short walk inland.

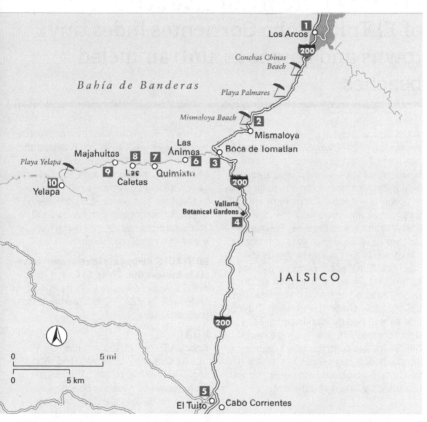

Los Arcos

*Conchas Chinas Beach*

*Bahía de Banderas*

*Playa Palmares*

*Mismaloya Beach*

Mismaloya

Las Ánimas

Boca de Tomatlan

Majahuitas

*Playa Yelapa*

Las Caletas

Quimixto

Yelapa

Vallarta Botanical Gardens

JALSICO

0            5 mi

0            5 km

El Tuito        Cabo Corrientes

**8 Las Caletas.** Las Caletas is a 1-km long, quaint beach with turquoise waters, a paradise on earth. John Huston hid there for more than 20 years after filming *The Night of the Iguana*. Currently it is the only of the southern beaches that is not public. It is now leased by Vallarta Adventures and included in their tours.

**9 Majahuitas.** A small beach accessible by boat from Los Muertos Beach or Boca de Tomatlán, Majahuitas is a great place for swimming, sun bathing, and hiking as well as spotting fish of all colors and numerous sea birds.

**10 Yelapa.** Accessible by boat from Los Muertos Beach or Boca de Tomat-lán, Yelapa offers the greatest number of attractions among the southern beaches of PV, and is also great for jungle hiking. The little town has some lodging options.

All the way to Mismaloya, the hotels of the Zona Hotelera Sur hug the beach or overlook it from cliff-side aeries. South of El Tuito, Cabo Corrientes hides tiny towns and gorgeous, untrammeled beaches.

While coastal Nayarit is jumping on the development bandwagon, the isolated beaches of Cabo Corrientes and those of southern Jalisco—some surrounded by ecological reserves—continue to languish in peaceful abandon. Things here are still less formal, and aside from the super-posh resorts like El Careyes, El Tamarindo, and Las Alamandas, whose beaches are off-limits to nonguests, words like "laid-back" still apply. Long sandy beaches are frequented by fishermen and local people relaxing at seafood shanties. They usually allow shelling, snorkeling, fishing, and trips to nearby islands and beaches only accessible by sea. Having a car is helpful for exploring multiple beaches, although local bus service is available if you have no problem with riding through the tropics without air-conditioning.

# Planning

## Getting Here and Around

The best way to get here and around is by car, though you can also get to some areas by a local bus. Some beaches will be only accessible by boat, and you will need to rent one or take a tour.

### AIR

Puerto Vallarta International Airport (PVR) is well connected with Canada and the United States, and in winter has some charter connections with Europe. You can rent a car at the airport and drive south. It will take you 13 km (8 miles) to cross the city, around 30 minutes. You can also get on a local bus at the airport and get to the main bus terminal in downtown to catch another bus that heads south. You can rent a taxi as well, but it's an expensive option.

**CONTACTS Aeropuerto Internacional Licenciado Gustavo Díaz Ordaz.** ⊠ *Carr. a Tepic Km 7.5, Área Militar de Vallarta, Puerto Vallarta* ☎ *322/221–1298* ⊕ *aeropuertos-gap.com.mx.*

### BOAT

Boca de Tomatlán, Las Ánimas, Quimixto, Las Caletas, Majahuitas, and Yelapa are all accessible by boat. You can get there from Los Muertos Beach or start from Boca de Tomatlán. Los Muertos water taxis leave every two hours and from Boca de Tomatlán every hour, and less frequently in the low season. The prices are around 90 MXN ($4.50) from Boca to Yelapa, and 160 MXN ($8) from Los Muertos to Yelapa. Get ready for a 50-minute ride from Los Muertos and a shorter one from Boca, although the trip can get longer depending on the number of stops requested by clients. Don't forget to ask about the latest returning boat; miss it and you will have to stay the night.

## BUS

Buses to the South of Puerto Vallarta will always leave from the southern part of town. The orange and white bus to Mismaloya and Boca de Tomatlán leaves from the corner of Basilio Badillo and Constitución Street. Boca de Tomatlán is the last stop and you can get off in Conchas Chinas, Hyatt Ziva, and in Mismaloya. It costs around 10 MXN (50¢) and reaches Mismaloya in 20 minutes, and Boca de Tomatlán in 30 minutes. The blue buses from the corner of Venustiano Carranza and Aguacate go to El Tuito and stop at Botanical Gardens. The trip takes about 50 minutes and costs 20 MXN, (just over $1).

**CONTACTS UnibusPV.** ✉ *Constitución 383, Zona Romántica* ☎ *322/276–4146* ⊕ *unibuspv.com.mx.*

## CAR

Traveling by car to reach South of PV is the best option. If you didn't bring your own vehicle you can rent one at the airport. Highway 200 is narrow and windy, but safe and with little traffic. It offers beautiful views and some spontaneous stops on the way to restaurants or local shops selling arts and crafts. If you plan to visit the southern beaches, leave your car in Boca de Tomatlán—there is plenty of free or inexpensive parking.

## TAXI

Uber operates in Mismaloya, and the trip costs between 170 to 220 pesos ($8–$11), and between 260 and 350 pesos ($13–$18) to Boca de Tomatlán. Taxis from the Hotel Zone are usually twice as expensive as an Uber. Remember to always ask for the price to your destination before getting in. If it sounds high, wait for another cab.

# Hotels

South of Puerto Vallarta offers many lodging options, from cheap rental rooms in Boca de Tomatlán and El Tuito, to big resorts and luxurious villas in Mismaloya and Conchas Chinas. There are also some boutique options in Boca de Tomatlán and Yelapa.

# Restaurants

The Mexican Pacific Coast is famous for its seafood and South of PV is no exception. You can enjoy delicious food in small street stands, cheap, palapa eateries with sea views, or at exclusive, gourmet restaurants.

## HOTEL AND RESTAURANT PRICES

*Hotel prices in the reviews are the lowest cost of a standard double room in high season. Restaurant prices in the reviews are the average cost of a main course at dinner, or if dinner is not served, at lunch.*

| WHAT IT COSTS In USD | | | |
|---|---|---|---|
| **$** | **$$** | **$$$** | **$$$$** |
| **RESTAURANTS** | | | |
| under $5 | $5–$10 | $10–$15 | over $15 |
| **HOTELS** | | | |
| under $50 | $50–$150 | $150–$350 | over $350 |

| WHAT IT COSTS In MXN | | | |
|---|---|---|---|
| **$** | **$$** | **$$$** | **$$$$** |
| **RESTAURANTS** | | | |
| under 95 MXN | 95–190 MXN | 191–285 MXN | over 285 MXN |
| **HOTELS** | | | |
| under 945 MXN | 945–2836 MXN | 2837–6620 MXN | over 6620 MXN |

# Safety

Puerto Vallarta and South of PV is one of the safest destinations in Mexico. It is safe to drive, safe to sunbathe and swim, safe to walk at night.

# Tours

South of PV offers many tour options from traditional jungle and river hiking, canopy, snorkeling, horseback riding, and ATV to distillery and coffee tours, food tours, and unforgettable shows on secluded beaches.

# Los Arcos

*9 km (5 miles) south of Puerto Vallarta.*

Los Arcos is an area that stretches for about 10 km (6 miles) from Conchas Chinas to Mismaloya on Highway 200. You'll find mostly steep beaches, luxurious villas, and a couple of resorts.

### GETTING HERE AND AROUND

Los Arcos is easily accessible by car, you just need to follow Highway 200. Walking is not recommended as the road is narrow with no space for pedestrians. You can take the local bus from Basilio Badillo but it won't stop everywhere. You can also try Uber or taxis to get to your destination in Los Arcos. If you are staying in one of the resorts, arrange for shuttle transportation before your arrival.

## ◉ Sights

The coast in Los Arcos is usually steep and rocky but there are some pleasant, yellow-sand beaches. Conchas Chinas beach is without a doubt one of the most beautiful ones in this area and loved by the locals for its small natural pools. Los Arcos Natural Reserve is a total must, perfect for diving and snorkeling. There is also a great lookout in the residential area of Conchas Chinas with spectacular views over Banderas Bay.

### Los Arcos

NATURE PRESERVE | Protected area Los Arcos is an offshore group of giant rocks rising some 65 feet above the water, making the area great for snorkeling and diving. Its waters are among the deepest in the area getting at around 1,600 feet. For reasonable fees, local men along the road to Mismaloya Beach run diving, snorkeling, fishing, and boat trips here and as far north as Punta Mita and Las Marietas or the beach villages of Cabo Corrientes. ⊠ *South of Puerto Vallarta.*

### Playa Palmares

BEACH—SIGHT | FAMILY | Playa Palmares was the first beach in the area that got the coveted international Blue Flag certification in 2014. This certification is an eco-award designed for beaches, marinas, and boating tourism operators; recipients of the Blue Flag comply with a series of stringent environmental, accessibility, and safety requirements. However, it lost the certification a few years back as it's hard for the local government to install all the facilities required. Palmares is connected to Punta Negra, but its waves are smaller, which make it a better fit for families. **Amenities:** toilets; showers; lifeguards; food and drink; parking (no fee). **Best for:** swimming; sunset. ⊠ *Carr. México 200, South of Puerto Vallarta.*

### Playa Punta Negra

BEACH—SIGHT | Seldom-crowded Playa Punta Negra is a favorite among locals for its waves. Just 5 km south of Conchas Chinas, the entrance to the beach is right on the highway and there is not a lot of parking space, which limits the amount of visitors to just a few cars at a time. **Amenities:** lifeguards; parking (no fee); food and drink. **Best for:** surfing; walking; sunset. ⊠ *Carr. Puerto Vallarta - Manzanillo km 5, South of Puerto Vallarta.*

#  Restaurants

There are not many dining options in Los Arcos. Most restaurants in the area are part of hotels or residential areas. There are some small eateries close to the Conchas Chinas beach, and that's it.

### Restaurante Los Girasoles

$$$ | SEAFOOD | Even though this ocean-front restaurant has seen better times, it still has a reputation as one of the best spots to eat South of PV. Part of the Girasoles Condominium Complex, it's right on the beach, offering customers extraordinary views of the Pacific Ocean and the legendary sunsets of the region. **Known for:** great ocean views; seafood salad; delicious margaritas. $ *Average main: 185 MP ⊠ Carr. Barra de Navidad 2354, South of Puerto Vallarta* ☎ 322/228–0350.

# Hotels

Los Arcos area is home to some of the most exclusive resorts south of PV. The villas in Conchas Chinas are slightly older than the ones in the north of PV, but you will fall in love with the style. All the hotels have beach access and spectacular ocean and jungle views.

### Costa Sur Resort & Spa

$$ | RESORT | FAMILY | A classic property leftover from the golden age of '80s Puerto Vallarta, the Costa Sur Resort & Spa has successfully reinvented itself a few times over. **Pros:** private ocean lagoon; two swimming pools; cute oceanfront restaurant. **Cons:** old building; narrow beach; limited services at spa. $ *Rooms from: $88 ⊠ Carr. a Barra de Navidad Km 4.5, South of Puerto Vallarta* ☎ 322/226–8050 ⊕ *costasurpuertovallarta.com* ⇄ *200 rooms* ❍ *Free Breakfast.*

### Garza Blanca Preserve Resort & Spa

$$$ | RESORT | Definitely one of the most exclusive resorts south of Puerto Vallarta, lavish luxury and outlandish design are everywhere to be found at this eco-conscious hotel. **Pros:** world-class spa; private jungle reserve; extraordinary restaurants. **Cons:** rocky beach; annoying timeshare pitches; fee for Wi-Fi in the rooms. $ *Rooms from: $200 ⊠ Carr. a Barra de Navidad Km 7.5, South of Puerto Vallarta* ☎ 322/176–0718, 877/845 3791 *toll-free in U.S. and Canada* ⊕ *garzablancaresort.com* ⇄ *165 rooms* ❍ *All-inclusive.*

### Grand Fiesta Americana Puerto Vallarta

$$$ | RESORT | An all-inclusive that's also adults-only, this resort has the modern design, luxury details, spacious rooms, diverse dining, quality outdoor facilities, and great location for the perfect romantic getaway. **Pros:** excellent wine-and-dine offer; private ocean lagoon; adults-only. **Cons:** feels too corporate at times; small beach; far from Puerto Vallarta's action. $ *Rooms from: $350 ⊠ Carr. Costera a Barra de Navidad Km 4.5, South of Puerto Vallarta* ☎ 443/310–8137 ⊕ *grandfiestamericana.com* ⇄ *443 rooms* ❍ *All-inclusive.*

### Hyatt Ziva Puerto Vallarta

$$$ | RESORT | FAMILY | One of the most recent additions to the impressive lodging offered in Puerto Vallarta, the Hyatt Ziva is private and secluded, but close enough to the action downtown. **Pros:** private beach; five infinity pools; six restaurants. **Cons:** average food; for anything outside the hotel you'll need a car; a bit pricey. $ *Rooms from: $350 ⊠ Carr. a Barra de Navidad, South of Puerto Vallarta* ☎ 322/226–5000 ⊕ *hyatt.com* ⇄ *335 rooms* ❍ *All-inclusive.*

# Activities

Apart from scuba diving and snorkeling tours in Los Arcos Ecological Reserve, the area offers some adrenaline-filled activities in the jungle. You can try zip-lines with ocean views, jungle hiking, swimming in the river and in the waterfall.

# South of Puerto Vallarta

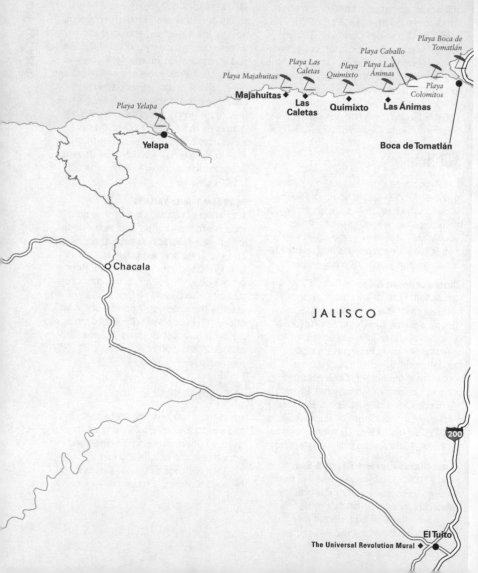

*Bahía de Banderas*

*Playa Boca de Tomatlán*

*Playa Caballo*

*Playa Las Caletas*

*Playa Quimixto*

*Playa Las Ánimas*

*Playa Majahuitas*

**Majahuitas** ♦

*Playa Colomitos*

**Las Caletas**

**Quimixto** ♦

**Las Ánimas** ♦

*Playa Yelapa*

**Yelapa** ●

**Boca de Tomatlán**

○ Chacala

JALISCO

200

**El Tuito** ●

The Universal Revolution Mural ♦

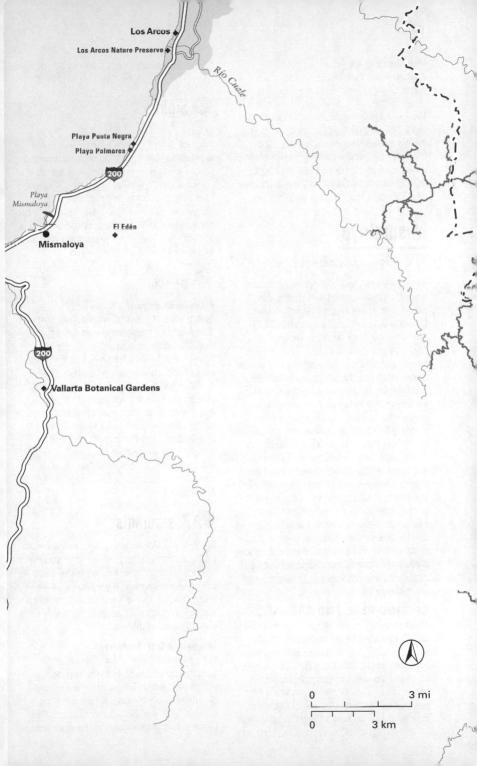

Los Arcos ◆

Los Arcos Nature Preserve ◆

*Río Cuale*

Playa Punta Negra

Playa Palmores ◆

200

*Playa Mismaloya*

El Edén ◆

**Mismaloya** ●

200

◆ **Vallarta Botanical Gardens**

| 0 | | | | 3 mi |

| 0 | | | | 3 km |

### Nogalito Ecopark
**ECOTOURISM | FAMILY |** El Nogalito is a place of extraordinary natural beauty, deep in the tropical rain forest of the Sierra Madres that surround Puerto Vallarta. This ecopark offers canopy zip-lines, hiking routes, temazcal healing ceremonies, and bird-watching tours. Most adventure tours start at $80. ✉ *Laurel 107, El Nogalito, South of Puerto Vallarta* ☏ *322/113–2152* ⊕ *nogalito.com.*

# Mismaloya

*12 km (7 miles) south of Los Arcos.*

Mismaloya is the first important stop after Conchas Chinas and this is the place that made Puerto Vallarta famous. Director John Huston chose this little hamlet as a setting for his movie *The Night of the Iguana* in 1963, and that is when and where it all started. The whole crew, including Elizabeth Taylor and Richard Burton, fell in love with the village, whose name in Náhautl means, "the place where they grab fish with their hands." It wasn't long after the movie came out that tourists started to come. A few year later, *Predator* with Arnold Schwarzenegger was filmed nearby in a jungle known as El Edén. Nowadays, the remains of the original sets are not accessible to the public (unless on a tour), but there is a large Barceló hotel on the beach, rustic palapa bars and restaurants, and a small village to explore with more spots to grab something to eat, if you are not looking for sophisticated restaurants.

### GETTING HERE AND AROUND
The best way to get to Mismaloya is by car heading south for about 10 km (6 miles) south. The road is beautiful and not busy at all. There is a dirt road leading to the beach next to the Barceló hotel and you can park there. If you want to get by bus, take one by the OXXO at the corner of Basilio Badillo and Constitución Street and you will get there in 20 minutes. The trip costs about 10 MXN (50¢).

##  Sights

### El Edén
**BODY OF WATER |** From Mismaloya there is a trail following the river deep into the jungle and up through the mountains; it's about 4 km (2.5 miles) long and it leads to a beautiful waterfall and natural pool known as El Edén. The trek could be a bit arduous for kids, but the nature around is impressive. There is a restaurant and an eco-park on-site. ✉ *Mismaloya.*

##  Beaches

### Playa Mismaloya
**BEACH—SIGHT |** It was in this cove that *The Night of the Iguana* was filmed. Unfortunately, construction of the big Hotel La Jolla de Mismaloya at the north end of the once-pristine bay has stolen its Shangri-La appeal. Nonetheless, the place retains a certain cachet. It also has views of the famous cove from two seafood restaurants on the south side of a bridge over the mouth of the Río Mismaloya. **Amenities:** food and drink; water sports; toilets. **Best for:** swimming; snorkeling. ✉ *South of Puerto Vallarta, Mismaloya.*

##  Restaurants

As every Mexican town, Mismaloya is a paradise for foodies. Street taco stands and local eateries will provide the best culinary experience. If you want something fancier, there are a couple of more elegant restaurants around the town with more gourmet dishes.

### Mismaloya Grill Restaurant
**$$$ | SEAFOOD |** For a fancy lunch with panoramic views of the bay and beach, visit Mismaloya Grill inside the La Jolla de Mismaloya condo complex. Formerly known as María Bonita Restaurant, this place has a long history in the area and

arguably is the best restaurant in town. **Known for:** gorgeous outdoor terrace overlooking the Mismaloya Bay; gourmet seafood; great shrimp tacos. $ *Average main: 180 MP* ⊠ *Carr. a Barra de Navidad Km 11, Mismaloya* 🕾 *322/228–0838* ⊘ *Closed Sun. and during summer.*

### Ramada Miramar

**$$ | SEAFOOD | FAMILY |** This restaurant is not by the beach; you will have to actually cross a little bridge over the Mismaloya river to get there, but the food is worth the trek. Ramada Miramar is what Mismaloya is all about: family, the jungle, and seafood. **Known for:** garlic mahimahi; lush vegetation surrounding the place; perfectly sized portions. $ *Average main: 140 MP* ⊠ *Paseo del Río 117, Mismaloya* 🕾 *322/121–0675* ⊘ *Closed Sun.*

### Restaurant Bar Las Gaviotas

**$$ | SEAFOOD |** Las Gaviotas is the perfect place to enjoy seafood and a cold beer with the Pacific ocean in the background. The tables and chairs are right on the beach. **Known for:** grilled fish; the best guacamole in Mismaloya beach; just steps from the ocean. $ *Average main: 120 MP* ⊠ *Paseo del Río Km 12, Playa, Mismaloya* 🕾 *322/113–0380* ⊘ *No dinner.*

##  Hotels

Lodging in Mismaloya will surprise you. There are private apartments, condos, houses, and villas, in addition to hotels. There is something for all tastes and budgets. Most places will have breathtaking ocean or jungle views.

### Barceló La Jolla de Mismaloya

**$$$ | RESORT | FAMILY |** Guests consistently give this hotel high marks for the classy suites, each with a brown-and-taupe color scheme and an ample terrace with a table and four chairs. **Pros:** recently redecorated and remodeled; concierge service; lots of on-site dining and activity options. **Cons:** least expensive rooms don't have ocean views; no bathtubs; crowded beach with lots of vendors.

$ *Rooms from: $250* ⊠ *Carr. a Barra de Navidad Km 11.5, Zona Hotelera Sur, Mismaloya* 🕾 *322/226–0660* ⊕ *barcelo.com* ⌁ *317 suites* ¶O¶ *All-inclusivo.*

### Casa Iguana All-Suites Hotel

**$ | HOTEL | FAMILY |** Palms and plants edge the walkways that line the swimming pool and goldfish ponds; balconies look down on this idyllic garden scene. **Pros:** experience village life not far from Puerto Vallarta's bars and restaurants; on-site grocery store; swimming pool and Jacuzzi. **Cons:** tiny gym; a cab or bus ride from nightlife, restaurants, and shops; not on the beach. $ *Rooms from: $55* ⊠ *Av. 5 de Mayo 455, Mismaloya* 🕾 *322/228–0186* ⊕ *casaiguana.com.mx* ⌁ *52 rooms* ¶O¶ *Free Breakfast.*

## 🏃 Activities

The beach in Mismaloya is not the most spectacular, as it is crowded with hotel guests, but there are other things to enjoy in town. You can visit the jungle set of the *Predator* movie, try some zip-lines, go on a hike, visit a tequila distillery, or swim in the Mismaloya river.

### Canopy El Edén

**ECOTOURISM |** A true slice of paradise on earth, El Edén shows why Puerto Vallarta and its surroundings are much more than just nice beaches. Fly over the lush canopy of the rain forest in superfast zip-lines while discovering the set of Arnold Schwarzenegger's film *Predator*. The place features a nice restaurant overlooking a river in the middle of the jungle, where guests can take a refreshing splash. ATVs and city tours are also available. ⊠ *Mismaloya* 🕾 *322/128–9346* ⊕ *canopyeleden.mx.*

# Boca De Tomatlán

*4 km (2 miles) south of Mismaloya.*

Boca de Tomatlán, a small fishing village, is the most important departure point for

Grab a boat ride right off the beach at Boca de Tomatlán.

reaching southern destinations accessible only by boat, such as Las Ánimas, Yelapa, or Quimixto. The village itself went through a couple of renovations recently, and even got a small malecón by the river. Boca de Tomatlán is very small, but offers beautiful views over the cove with dolphins coming for a visit in the winter season and a few palapa restaurants located on the beach, with delicious seafood and sun umbrellas for rent. It is a good place to spend a quiet day by the sea.

## GETTING HERE AND AROUND

Boca de Tomatlán can be reached by car, bus, or water taxi. Your own car is the cheapest and fastest option. You will reach town after about 25 minutes, 15 km (9 miles) away from PV, and there are many parking options close to the beach. You can also catch a C-01 bus leaving from the corner of Basilio Badillo and Constitución Street in downtown Vallarta. The ride costs about 20 pesos ($1). Water taxis leave from Los Muertos beach. Taxi and Uber drivers will also take

you to Boca de Tomatlán but the price will be higher at around 200–450 pesos ($10–$23).

##  Beaches

The beach in Boca de Tomatlán is its main attraction. It has been vastly improved over the last couple of years and now has a small Malecón and public washrooms and showers (for about 30¢).

**Playa Boca de Tomatlán**

BEACH—SIGHT | FAMILY | This V-shape, rocky bay lies at the mouth ("boca" means "mouth") of the Río Horcones, about 5 km (3 miles) south of Mismaloya. Water taxis leave from Boca to the southern beaches. As far as most visitors are concerned, this is mainly the staging area for water taxis with nowhere else to hang out. However, this dramatic-looking bay lined with palm trees does have rustic appeal. **Amenities:** food and drink; toilets; showers. **Best for:** swimming. ⊠ *Puerto Vallarta.*

#  Restaurants

There are five small restaurants on the beach that differ only by tablecloth color. They all serve delicious, fresh seafood and will bring your food or beer out to your table or towel on the beach. If you are looking for a gourmet experience visit Le Kliff restaurant at the entrance on top of the hill.

### Le Kliff

$$$$ | SEAFOOD | Perched on top of a hill overlooking the Boca de Tomatlán little cove, Le Kliff has an extraordinary setting; couples choose to get married here because of the views. Though it's a bit stuffy, this is a great place to impress a date. **Known for:** great views; lobster tail with hibiscus marmalade; weddings are held here. $ *Average main: 400 MP* ⊠ *Carr. a Barra de Navidad* ☎ *322/228–0300* ⊕ *lekliff.com.*

### ★ Rest & Bar Boca del Mar

$$$ | SEAFOOD | An excellent traditional Mexican seafood restaurant, Boca del Mar is just steps from the sea. The food is extraordinary (you can also take it to-go) but the service is even better. **Known for:** best restaurant in the Boca de Tomatlán beach; delicious pescado sarandeado (grilled fish); five-person mariscadas (seafood mix). $ *Average main: 280 MP* ⊠ *Pelicanos 535* ⊹ *On the beach* ⊕ *restbarbocadelmar.com* ⊟ *No credit cards.*

#  Hotels

There are no big hotels in Boca but there are many lodging options to choose from: bed-and-breakfasts, rental villas and condos, apartments, and small boutique hotels with more upscale amenities.

### ★ Villa Armonía Luxury Boutique Hotel

$$$ | HOTEL | This boutique hotel with huge suites and panoramic views is Boca's hidden gem. **Pros:** open-air showers; waterfall suite; steps from the beach.

**Cons:** away from Puerto Vallarta's attractions; no gym; unappealing swimming pool. $ *Rooms from: $260* ⊠ *Carr. a Barra de Navidad #5710* ☎ *322/102–3772* ⊕ *villaarmoniapv.com* ⤳ *9 suites* ⊙ *No meals.*

### Villa Lala Boutique Hotel

$$$ | HOTEL | Villa Lala is gorgeous little oceanfront hotel with only seven suites, but lots of personality. **Pros:** unique suites (two are treehouses); infinity pool; meters from Boca beach. **Cons:** long ride from airport; no fitness center; rocky beach. $ *Rooms from: $300* ⊠ *Carr. a Barra de Navidad Km 16 #5696* ☎ *322/294–2252* ⊕ *villalalapv.com* ⤳ *7 suites* ⊙ *No meals.*

#  Activities

### Boca Divers

ADVENTURE TOURS | Well-established tour company offering scuba, snorkeling, and kayak tours in Boca de Tomatlán and its nearby beaches. You will find here PADI-certified instructors. ⊠ *Pelícanos 518* ☎ *322/888–3886* ⊕ *bocadivers.net.*

# Vallarta Botanical Gardens

*8 km (5 miles) east of Boca de Tomatlán.*

Vallarta Botanical Gardens has become an obligatory stop on the PV map. It is internationally acclaimed and considered one of the best botanical gardens in North America. There are almost 3,000 species of plants, and visitors get to experience the real dry tropical forest habitat. There are also very few botanical gardens in the world where you can swim in a river.

## GETTING HERE AND AROUND

If you decide to get a bit away from the coast, following the same Highway 200 you will find yourself in one of the most beautiful places in Puerto Vallarta. This not-so-little paradise is about 30 minutes from Puerto Vallarta's historic district, and you can also get to the gardens by public transportation, catching the bus headed for "El Tuito" at the corner of Carranza and Aguacate streets in the Romantic Zone. The fare costs 20 MXN (around $1) and the bus departs every half hour.

### TOURS

Apart from jungle hiking, bird-watching, and swimming in the river, you can book one of two available tours. "Botanical Delights" combines nature lessons with culinary experiences, and "A Trip to Jaguar Country" shows you the jungle from the perspective of jaguars, a truly unique experience.

## Sights

You can spend the whole day in Vallarta Botanical Gardens, but no less than two hours. You can visit it independently, buy a tour, or explore it by bike. You can simply enjoy and learn about dry tropical forest habitat, watch hummingbirds and other birds, or visit the orchid sanctuary. There is also a small shop with plants, souvenirs, and arts and crafts.

**★ Vallarta Botanical Gardens**
**GARDEN** | Since its opening in 2005, the Vallarta Botanical Gardens has become a landmark of Puerto Vallarta and with good reason. The place is spectacular, set in the middle of the Sierra Madre mountains, just a few miles from the Pacific Ocean. In its 64 acres of land you will find extraordinary biodiversity, a vanilla plantation, hiking trails, plant conservatories, a scenic restaurant, and even a river of crystal clear waters. ✉ *Carr. a Barra de Navidad* ☎ *322/223–6182* 🌐 *vbgardens.org* 🎟 *206 MXN* 🕒 *Closed Mon.*

## Restaurants

There is one restaurant on the premises, with spectacular jungle views, beautiful Mexican decor and obviously, delicious Mexican food. You have to try their brick oven pizzas, handmade tortillas, and sauces.

**Restaurant La Hacienda de Oro**
**$$$** | **MEXICAN** | Located in the second floor of the main building in the Gardens, guests dine in an open-air terrace that overlooks the cliff below all the way to the river and the mountains in the background. The food is typically Mexican, with handmade corn tortillas and exquisite but spicy sauces. **Known for:** scenic views; only restaurant inside the Botanical Gardens; shrimp stuffed avocado. [$] *Average main: 260 MP* ✉ *Carr. a Barra de Navidad* ☎ *322/223–6184* 🌐 *vbgardens.org.*

# El Tuito

*20 km (12 miles) east of Vallarta Botanical Gardens.*

Continuing your trip south, you will soon get to El Tuito, the capital of Cabo Corrientes—still close enough to consider it a day trip from Puerto Vallarta (40 minutes from downtown). El Tuito is a very small but charming town with everything you might want to explore within two blocks of the plaza. All the buildings are painted with a mixture of local clays, which gives them a uniform orange look. Enjoy the day walking on the cobblestone streets and shopping for organic coffee, artisanal cheese, and delicious *Raicilla* (the local version of Tequila).

### GETTING HERE AND AROUND

El Tuito is about 50 minutes away from Puerto Vallarta. After traveling south for a bit more than 40 km (26 miles) on a winding Highway 200 you will get to El Tuito. It is so small that you can park your car somewhere around the main square and explore the village on foot. El Tuito is also easy to reach by bus. The blue buses from the corner of Venustiano Carranza and Aguacate in downtown PV go to El Tuito. The trip takes about 60 minutes and costs about 32 pesos ($1.65). The buses leave every half an hour. The last trip back is at 5:30 pm.

## Sights

There are a few things worth seeing in El Tuito. You could start with the main square with several restaurants with reasonable prices. Everything else to see will be within the radius of two blocks. Go and see the mural "Universal Revolution" from 1970 at the Cultural Center and the San Pedro Apostol Parish. You can also peep into local bakeries to see how pastries and bread are made in traditional brick ovens.

**The Universal Revolution Mural**
**LOCAL INTEREST** | The Cultural Center, a charming orange clay building, hides one of the main cultural attractions of El Tuito. After crossing its courtyard you will find a dramatic mural called "The Universal Revolution" decorating the main staircase. The work of art, painted by local artist David Edmundo Castillon Sánchez in 1970, shows part of the history of Cabo Corrientes and honors its past, present, and future. The mural occupies three walls and includes many historical characters. ✉ *H. Ayuntamiento de Cabo Corrientes, Portal Hidalgo 12, Casa de la Cultura de Cabo Corrientes, El Tuito* ☎ *322/269–0090.*

## Restaurants

El Tuito is a small town (practically a village) without any fine dining options. However, you can pamper your palate with local, Mexican food served in numerous eateries. You have to try the Panela and Oaxaca cheese sold at small stands, as well as *Raicilla.*

**El Patio de Mario**
**$** | **MEXICAN** | **FAMILY** | El Patio de Mario serves good traditional Mexican food, in a clean, calm environment with a gorgeous open patio and friendly staff. Forget what you know about Mexican food, come here and try their *birria* or *menudo* , exquisite soups of pre-Hispanic origins. **Known for:** central courtyard (patio); the best menudo in town; all main courses come with fried beans and rice (or salad). [$] *Average main: 80 MP* ✉ *Jalisco 6, El Tuito* ☎ *322/269–0604* 🕒 *No dinner.*

**Restaurant Valle Azul**
**$** | **MEXICAN** | **FAMILY** | This quaint restaurant is small but cozy, and serves traditional homemade dishes and wood oven pizzas. Sit on the outside tables and get a good view of the quiet life in the main square. **Known for:** exquisite chiles rellenos (stuffed peppers); cold beer; handmade tortillas. [$] *Average main: 100 MP* ✉ *Primero de Abril 6, El Tuito* ☎ *322/269–0646* 🕒 *Closed Tues.* 💳 *No credit cards.*

## Hotels

Lodging in El Tuito is quaint and inexpensive, and rentals are mostly private. You can rent a room for around 500 MXN ($25) or the whole house for 2,000 MXN ($100). They come with quaint Mexican decor and views over the lush jungle. You can also find a couple of simple hotels at the town.

**La Joya De Tuito Hotelito**
**$** | **B&B/INN** | **FAMILY** | This small hotel has just two rooms, but they very well could be the best rooms in town; the Frida Kahlo room features a design inspired by the iconic Mexican painter and a queen size bed, while the Day of the Dead theme La Catrina is a two-bedroom suite with three beds and a full bathroom. **Pros:** free Wi-Fi in rooms; chiropractic services; patio with beautiful mountain views. **Cons:** no air-conditioning; really small place; no restaurant. [$] *Rooms from: 45 MP* ✉ *Allende 3, El Tuito* ☎ *322/205–1979* 🌐 *lajoyadetuitobedandbreakfast.com* 🔑 *2 rooms* 🍴 *No meals.*

*Continued on page 162*

# MARIACHI: BORN IN JALISCO

By Sean Mattson

It's 4 AM and you're sound asleep somewhere in Mexico. Suddenly you're jolted awake by trumpets blasting in rapid succession. Before you can mutter a groggy protest, ten men with booming voices break into song. Nearby, a woman stirs from her slumber. The man who brought her the serenade peeks at her window from behind the lead singer's sombrero, hoping his sign of devotion is appreciated—and doesn't launch his girlfriend's father into a shoe-throwing fury.

Left and top right: Mariachis in traditional attire. Above: Mariachi strumming the guitarrón.

At the heart of Mexican popular culture, mariachi is the music of love and heartache, of the daily travails of life, and nationalistic pride. This soundtrack of Mexican tradition was born in the same region as tequila, the Mexican hat dance, and *charrería* (Mexican rodeo), whose culture largely defines Mexican chivalry and machismo.

Today, mariachi bands are the life of the party. They perform at weddings, birthdays, public festivals, restaurants, and city plazas. The most famous bands perform across the globe. Guadalajara's annual mariachi festival draws mariachis from around the world.

## WHY IS IT CALLED "MARIACHI"?

The origin of the word mariachi is a source of some controversy. The legend is that it evolved from the French word mariage (marriage), stemming from the French occupation in the mid-1800s. But leading mariachi historians now debunk that myth, citing evidence that the word has its origins in the Nahuatl language of the Coca Indians.

Flying mariachi skeleton formed out of paper, used to celebrate Day of the Dead.

## THE RISE OF MARIACHI

Historians trace the roots of mariachi to Cocula, a small agricultural town south of Guadalajara. There, in the 17th century, Franciscan monks trained the local indigenous populations in the use of stringed instruments, teaching them the religious songs to help win their conversion.

The aristocracy, who preferred the more refined contemporary European music, held early mariachi groups in disdain. But by the late 19th century, mariachi had become enormously popular among peasants and indigenous people in Cocula, eventually spreading throughout southern Jalisco and into neighboring states.

## MODERN MARIACHI INSTRUMENTS

Traditional mariachi groups consisted of two violins (the melody), and a vihuela and guitarrón (the harmony). Some long-gone groups used a tambor or drum, not used in modern mariachi. All members of the group shared singing responsibilities.

**THE FOLK HARP**
Longstanding mariachi instrument, used today by large ensembles and by some traditional troupes

### VIOLINS
Essential to any mariachi group

**TRUMPETS**
Added to the traditional mariachi lineup in the 1930s when mariachis hit the big screen, at the insistence of a pioneer in Mexican radio and television

### GUITARS
The round-backed vihuela is smaller and higher-pitched than the standard guitar

**THE GUITARRÓN**
A large-bellied bass guitar

5-string Vihuela      6-string guitar

In 1905, Mexican dictator Porfirio Díaz visited Cocula and was received with a performance of a mariachi group. Impressed, Díaz invited the group to Mexico City where, after a few years and a revolution, mariachi flourished. Over the next two decades, more groups followed to Mexico City. Mariachi groups gained more popularity by the 1930s, when Jorge Negrete and Pedro Infante began portraying mariachi musicians in their films. In 2011, UNESCO included mariachi on its List of Intangible Cultural Heritage of Humanity.

## MARIACHI STYLE

The mariachi *traje* (suit) consists of matching vest, *chaleco* (short jacket), and form-fitting pants, and *moño* (large bow tie). Simple *trajes* have soutache trim or embroidery; finer versions have suede patterns on the jacket with metal buttons down the pants legs. Trajes come in all colors, but formal costumes are black.

The modern mariachi's dress is an adaptation of *charro*, or Mexican cowboy attire, first worn by the members of an early mariachi group led by Cirilo Marmolejo and adopted for Mexican movies of the 1930s–50s. A complete formal outfit can cost as much as US$3,000.

Sombreros made from pressed rabbit fur are the highest quality.

*Botonaduras* (decorative buttons on the pants legs) can be simple, or ornate, made of silver or gold. A brooch on the front of the jacket often matches the botonadura.

Black leather *botínes* (half-boots) are standard mariachi footwear.

## WHERE AND HOW TO HEAR MARIACHI

### HIRE A MARIACHI GROUP

There may be no better way to thoroughly surprise (or embarrass) your significant other than with a mariachi serenade. Hiring a band is easy. Just go to Plaza de los Mariachis, beside Mercado Libertad in downtown Guadalajara. Negotiate price and either leave a deposit (ask for a business card and a receipt) and have the band meet you at a determined location, or, as Mexicans usually do, accompany the band to the unexpecting recipient.

### HIT THE INTERNATIONAL MARIACHI FESTIVAL

The last weekend of every August, some 700 mariachi groups from around the world descend upon Guadalajara for this event. Mexico's most famous mariachi groups—Mariachi Vargas de Tecalitlán, Mariachi los Camperos, and Mariachi de América—play huge concerts in the Degollado Theater, accompanied by the

### THE WORLD'S BEST MARIACHI BAND

The world's most *famous* mariachi band, Mariachi Vargas de Tecalitlán was founded in 1897, when the norm was four-man groups with simple stringed instruments. Started by Gaspar Vargas in Tecalitlán, Jalisco, the mariachi troupe shot to fame in the 1930s after winning a regional mariachi contest, which earned them the favor of Mexican president Lázaro Cárdenas. The group quickly became an icon of Mexican cinema, performing in and recording music for films. Now in its fifth generation, Mariachi Vargas performs the world over and has recorded more than 50 albums, and music for more than 200 films.

Jalisco Philharmonic Orchestra. The week-long annual charro championship is held simultaneously, bringing together the nation's top cowboys and mariachis.

The gabán (poncho) was worn traditionally for warmth.

## CATCH YEAR-ROUND PERFORMANCES

If you miss Guadalajara's mariachi festival you can still get your fill of high-quality mariachi performances on street corners, in city plazas, and at many restaurants. An estimated 150 mariachi groups are currently active in the City of Roses.

Restaurants, most notably Guadalajara's Casa Bariachi chain, hire mariachi groups, whose performance is generally included with your table (though tips won't be refused). On occasion, mariachis perform free nighttime concerts in Guadalajara's Plaza de Armas. Another venue, the Plaza de Mariachi, beside Guadalajara's landmark Mercado Libertad, is a longstanding attraction, albeit during the day—at night it's better known for crime than mariachi.

Tlaquepaque's El Parían, a former market turned series of bars around a tree-filled central patio, is a fantastic intimate setting for mariachi music. Between free performances in the central kiosk, you can request serenades at about $15–18 per song or negotiate deals for longer performances for your table.

## ALL ABOARD THE TEQUILA TRAIN!

To experience the Jalisco quartet of traditions—mariachi, charreria, folkloric dance, and tequila—in one adventure, take the Tequila Express. It includes a train ride from Guadalajara through fields of blue agave to a tequila-making hacienda, live mariachi music, all the food and drink you can handle, and a charro and folkloric dance performance.

## WORKING HARD FOR THE MONEY

It is becoming harder for mariachi groups to make a living at the trade. The increasing cost of living has made nighttime serenades, once a staple of a mariachi's diet of work, expensive ($200 and up) and out of the reach of many locals. Performers generally work day jobs to make ends meet.

## THE COWBOY CONNECTION

Mariachi and Mexican rodeo, or *charroada* (Mexico's official sport), go together like hot dogs and baseball. Both charreada and mariachi music evolved in the western Mexican countryside, where daily ranching chores like branding bulls eventually took on a competitive edge. The first of Mexico's 800 charro associations was founded in Guadalajara in 1920, and to this day holds a two-hour rodeo every Sunday. Throughout the competition, mariachi music is heard from the stands, but the key mariachi performance is at the end of a competition when female riders called *escaramuzas* perform synchronized moves, riding side-saddle in traditional ribboned and brightly colored western Mexican dresses.

**Villa Loma Alta**
$ | **B&B/INN** | **FAMILY** | Villas Loma Alta is a big, three-room house done in a contemporary Mexican style. **Pros:** comfy beds; nice outdoor terrace; living room with fireplace. **Cons:** shared kitchen; kitschy decor; lack of privacy. [$] *Rooms from: $65* ✉ *Pablo Ríos 71, El Tuito* ☎ *322/102–1402* 🌐 *villaslomaalta.com* 🛏 *3 rooms* 🍴 *No meals* 💳 *No credit cards.*

## Activities

El Tuito is a good place for a day trip while staying in PV. You can stroll around the main square admiring the local architecture and beautiful vegetation. You can also go on a culinary tour and try the local moonshine, Raicilla, and fresh panela cheese. Tour companies that have El Tuito in their offers usually include visiting an organic farm and trying local delicacies.

# Las Ánimas

*30 km (18 miles) west of El Tuito.*

Las Ánimas is one of the most popular beaches in South of PV because apart from being accessible by boat, you can also get there by hiking. This is also the beach with the most beach restaurants and bars. There is also an adventure park nearby to do something more active than just lying on the beach.

### GETTING HERE AND AROUND

The traditional way to get to this hidden beach is by water taxi from Los Muertos Pier or from Boca de Tomatlán. However, if you feel fit enough you can try jungle hiking from Boca de Tomatlán beach on a narrow trail. After about 40 minutes you will get to the Colomitos beach, cross it, climb a few stairs and continue your journey.

## Beaches

**Playa Caballo**
**BEACH—SIGHT** | For a truly romantic spot you might want to visit Playa Caballo, a spectacular secluded beach of turquoise blue waters, calm waves, and lush vegetation. There is nothing else. Get a water taxi at Boca de Tomatlán or, if you are up for the adventure, start walking from Boca through a small pathway across the jungle all the way to this "Horse Beach." You'll be there in hour and a half. **Amenities:** none. **Best for:** swimming; solitude; walking.

**Playa Colomitos**
**BEACH—SIGHT** | This little cove is set between two hills that seem to be closing in on this gorgeous beach that's been called "Mexico's smallest beach" (it extends for only 30 meters). Its waters vary between turquoise blue and emerald green, its sand has a golden tone, and the surrounding mountains provide it with a unique atmosphere. From Boca de Tomatlán get a water taxi or walk through the jungle for 40 minutes. **Amenities:** food and drink. **Best for:** solitude; snorkeling; swimming.

**Playa Las Ánimas**
**BEACH—SIGHT** | **FAMILY** | There's lots to do besides sunbathe at this beach and town 15 minutes south of Boca de Tomatlán. The brown-sand beach is named "The Souls" because pirate graves were reportedly located here many years ago. Because of its very shallow waters, Las Ánimas is a favorite of families with kids. They come by water taxi or as part of bay cruises. Some seafood eateries line the sand. **Amenities:** food and drink; water sports. **Best for:** swimming; walking; sunset.

## Restaurants

There are some palapa restaurants in Las Ánimas serving delicious, inexpensive seafood, and cold beer. None of them are too fancy, but you'll find everything you will need to make your stay on the beach unforgettable.

**Los Conos Restaurant Bar**
$$ | **SEAFOOD** | **FAMILY** | Los Conos Restaurant and Bar serves Latin and Mexican dishes and drinks, and specializes in seafood. Their tasty lemonade or cold beer will save your life if you decided on hiking to Las Ánimas from Boca do Tomatlán. **Known for:** right on the beach; lounge chairs for rent; tasty seafood. [$] *Average main: 120 MP* ✉ *Camino Playa Las Ánimas s/n* ☎ *322/122–3852* 🌐 *facebook.com/losconosrestaurant* 🕒 *No dinner.*

**Mike's Beach Club**
$$$ | **SEAFOOD** | Mike's Beach club is a cozy restaurant located on Las Ánimas beach with great service and delicious food at reasonable prices. You can spend the whole day at their beach club, enjoying access to all the services and cold cocktails served by very friendly staff. **Known for:** grilled octopus; it has its own water park; comfy hammocks. [$] *Average main: 250 MP* ☎ *322/236–5430* 🌐 *facebook.com/mikesbeachclublasanimas* 🕒 *No dinner.*

## Hotels

Hotels around Las Ánimas beach are luxurious, expensive, and very eco-friendly. All of them offer exclusive cottages, villas, and suites with deluxe Mexican décor, upscale amenities, and breathtaking ocean views.

**Casitas Maraika**
$$ | **HOTEL** | Located on Playa Caballito next to popular Las Ánimas beach it's only reachable by boat, guaranteeing a calm, secluded environment. **Pros:** hanging beds; gorgeous terraces with hammocks and ocean views; beach club. **Cons:** requires a water taxi to get there; mosquitoes can be an issue; rocky beach. [$] *Rooms from: $250* ✣ *On Playa del Caballo* ☎ *322/222–2502* 🌐 *casitasmaraika.com* 🛏 *6 casitas* 🍴 *No meals.*

**Hotelito Mio**
$$$ | **HOTEL** | Hotelito Mio is a quaint boutique hotel that is both luxurious and rustic, located on Playa Caballo next to Las Ánimas. **Pros:** long list of spa treatments; open-air palapa restaurant right on the beach; all villas include a bathtub. **Cons:** hard to get to; no fitness center; a bit pricey. [$] *Rooms from: $500* ✉ *Playa Caballo* ☎ *332/183–8803* 🌐 *hotelitomio.com* 🛏 *8 villas* 🍴 *Free Breakfast.*

## Activities

If relaxing on the beach with delicious Mexican dishes is not enough, you can head to the Adventure Park Las Ánimas, 200 meters from the seaside offering jungle games that will challenge your balance.

**Adventure Park Las Ánimas**
**ADVENTURE TOURS** | **FAMILY** | This fun park manages to mix beach and jungle like no other in the area. This Adventure Park offers a wide range of activities right on Las Ánimas beach, they have several zip-lines, a hanging bridge, a spiderweb, balancing beams and wood beams, and more. You may be climbing a rock and watching a whale at the same time, and they include your meal for the same price. The whole tour takes about five hours. Adventures range $39–$69. ☎ *322/178–2410* 🌐 *adventureparkpv.com.*

# Quimixto

*2 km (1 mile) south of Las Ánimas.*

Quimixto is the second destination most visited by water taxis from Boca de Tomatlán (after Yelapa) and one of the most untouched ones. PV locals love to unwind here and spend a lazy day away from civilization. It has a 10-meter-high waterfall, perfect for swimming, as well as options to hiking or go horseback riding. There's also a restaurant zone with simple Mexican treats and beverages.

## GETTING HERE AND AROUND

Quimixto beach can be reached by water taxi from Boca de Tomatlán (20 minutes) or Los Muertos Beach Pier (45 minutes), although Boca is a better option. At Los Muertos Beach, sometimes you need to wait for a bigger group that wants the taxi to stop in Quimixto. You can also book a cruise tour that will include the beach.

##  Sights

Quimixto beach has two parts. The section where the boats arrive is narrow and full of little rocks, not good for swimming or sunbathing, but there is another sandy part with the only permanent restaurant in the area, Los Cocos. The waves are soft, and the sand, as well. There is a small waterfall, part of La Puerta river, about 1½ km (1 mile) away from the beach. There are many seabirds and iguanas in the area, and you will spot some. There is also a small village nearby with a few stores and souvenir stands.

##  Beaches

### Cuale Waterfall

**BODY OF WATER** | The small waterfall can be reached on foot or you can take a horseback ride for about 150–400 MXN ($8–$23) depending on how well you haggle. You can enter the waterfall from the lower road for free or buy a drink and snack at the restaurant on top of the hill. You can also take a swim in the cold waters below the fall, which is refreshing in summer but quite cold in winter season.

### Playa Quimixto

**BEACH—SIGHT** | **FAMILY** | About 20 minutes by boat from Boca de Tomatlán, Quimixto has a narrow, rocky shoreline that attracts few bathers. Tour boats stop here, and their clients usually have a meal at one of the seafood eateries facing the beach. Horses are standing by to take passengers to Quimixto Falls

($10). During the full moon there's a fun, fast wave at Quimixto's reef, popular with surfers but, because of its inaccessibility, rarely crowded. **Amenities:** food and drink; toilets. **Best for:** surfing; walking.

##  Restaurants

Beach restaurants and bars can be opened and closed depending on the season, but Los Cocos bar is always there. You can expect home-style seafood dishes and there is delicious carne asada (barbecued meat) on Saturday.

### Los Cocos Restaurant and Bar

**$$** | **SEAFOOD** | **FAMILY** | Los Cocos Restaurant and Bar is the only permanent restaurant on Quimixto beach. You can spend the whole day on their loungers enjoying the beach, the ocean, delicious food, and refreshing micheladas. **Known for:** delicious coconuts; beach volleyball court; loungers and kayaks for rent. $ Average main: 130 MP ☎ 322/111–9209 ⊕ facebook.com/Los-Cocos-871133136255340.

##  Hotels

### El Grullo Naturista

**$$** | **HOTEL** | El Grullo is one of the two hotels located in Quimixto, but more than a hotel this is a wellness center, offering detox and healing natural therapies. **Pros:** wide array of detox and healing treatments; vegan menu; safe in all rooms. **Cons:** some rooms don't have air-conditioning; small bathrooms; remote. $ Rooms from: $200 ✉ Pez Volador 4, Quimixto ☎ 322/195–7010 ⊕ elgrullonaturista.com ⤴ 10 rooms ⦁○⦁ No meals.

### Xinalani Retreat

**$$$** | **HOTEL** | Xinalani is a world-class yoga retreat, with beautiful rooms, healthy food, and eco-friendly activities in the extraordinary setting of Quimixto beach. **Pros:** beach casitas include plunge pool; many holistic activities; all rooms enjoy ocean views. **Cons:** lots of stairs; no road access; spotty Wi-Fi. $ *Rooms from: $550 ⊠ Playa Xinalani, Quimixto* ☎ *322/221–5918, 619/730–2893 in U.S. and Canada ⊕ xinalaniretreat.com ⊸ 37 rooms* ⦿❙ *All-Inclusive.*

##  Activities

In Quimixto and the surroundings you can swim and sunbathe, but also go snorkeling, fishing, diving, and seabird watching. You can have a delicious meal at Los Cocos, or take a stroll through the village. There are always locals who offer a horseback ride to the waterfall instead of walking. It will cost you around $20 but less sweat.

### Puerto Vallarta Tours - Las Animas & Quimixto

**ECOTOURISM | FAMILY |** This tour provider has a snorkeling cruise tour that takes you to Los Arcos, Las Ánimas, and Quimixto. Once in Quimixto, you'll be able to go on a horseback ride to the waterfall. Tours start at $48. ⊠ *Puerto Vallarta* ☎ *322/222–4935, 866/217–9704 toll free in U.S. and Canada ⊕ puertovallartatours. net/kontiki-booze-cruise.htm.*

### Vallarta Adventures - Sea Safari & Horseback Riding

**BOAT TOURS | FAMILY |** This tour by Vallarta Adventures offers a bit of everything. It starts with a speedboat ride across the waters of the Banderas Bay all the way to Quimixto, where some downtime is scheduled to enjoy its gorgeous beach. The next step is a horseback ride to Quimixto's waterfall. Kayaking, snorkeling, and lunch are all included in this thrilling day-long trip. ⊠ *Av. Las Palmas 39, Vallarta Adventures Center, Nuevo Vallarta* ☎ *322/226–8413, 888/526–2238 ⊕ vallarta-adventures.com/en/tour/ sea-safari-and-horseback-riding.*

# Las Caletas

*2 km (1 mile) south of Quimixto*

Traveling south, you'll come upon this beach, most famous for its exclusive show by Vallarta Adventures, Rhythms of the Night, a Las Vegas–level spectacle. The show, which is actually a tour based on ancient traditions, starts in Nuevo Vallarta at Vallarta Adventures Center or at the Maritime Terminal. During the day, Vallarta Adventures also organizes sea lion encounters at the same beach.

### GETTING HERE AND AROUND

You can't get to Las Caletas on your own. It has been concessioned to Vallarta Adventures company since 1990 and they own all the facilities. The tour leaves from the Marine Terminal in Puerto Vallarta at 8:30 am, or from the Nuevo Vallarta Office at 8 am. You can also get to Las Caletas at sunset for the Rhythms of the Night dinner and show.

##  Sights

Apart from the beach itself, broken into four smaller beaches, Las Caletas is filled with beautiful places to see and enjoy. There is a natural reserve over a large extension of jungle, there is a spa, orchidarium, aviary, deer sanctuary, kids' adventure park (ages 4–11), and Teen Adventure Cove for participants in excellent physical condition.

##  Beaches

### Playa Las Caletas

**BEACH—SIGHT |** Legend has it that director John Huston discovered this secluded beach and lived here for years. The beach is a bit rocky, but its waters are crystal clear. It's hard to find a more beautiful place; the only problem is that it's private and exclusive: to visit Las Caletas you'll need to buy a tour, which takes away some of the magic.

##  Activities

The tour company will make sure you are not bored on their private beach, so there are plenty of activities options. You can simply relax in a hammock or try scuba diving, snorkeling with sea lions, paddle boarding, kayaking, or you might challenge yourself with some more adrenaline-filled activities. Las Caletas also offers options for kids such as arts and crafts, kids' adventure park, or cooking lessons (also for adults).

### Las Caletas Beach Hideaway Vallarta Adventures

**ADVENTURE TOURS | FAMILY |** This place is a piece of paradise, one over which the Vallarta Adventures company has the exclusive control. A visit will cost you $139 and include a bit of everything, from snorkeling and kayaking, to cooking classes, kids' adventure park, teen adventure cove, good food, and open bar. ☎ *322/226–8413, 888/526–2238 in U.S. and Canada ⊕ vallarta-adventures.com/ en/tour/caletas-beach-hideaway.*

# Majahuitas

*2 km (1 mile) south of Las Caletas.*

Majahuitas is a tiny cove with a beautiful beach. Unless you decide to stay at the Majahuitas resort located here, there are no services or facilities available, but you may simply enjoy the white-sand beach and crystalline water.

### GETTING HERE AND AROUND

Majahuitas as all the other beaches in the area is only accessible by boat. You can take a water taxi at Los Muertos Beach or in Boca de Tomatlán, or take a cruise tour that includes other beaches. The trip from Boca is around 20–30 minutes and the cost is around 50 MXN ($2.50).

##  Sights

Look for the local trees called "Majahua"—Seaside Mahoe that gave the name to the place, and grows in the sand. There are numerous caves with a variety of sea fauna, and December through March, humpback whales come to the area plus four different species of sea turtles, manta rays, and dolphins all year round.

### Majahuitas Caves

**CAVE |** The rock formations around the Majahuitas cave hide many sea caves inhabited by a wide range of marine creatures in different colors, shapes, and sizes. Moorish idols with striking black, white, and yellow bands are the most common residents in the area but you may also spot sea cucumbers, parrot fish, puffer fish, schools of surgeonfish, eels, and many other tropical fish.

##  Beaches

### Playa Majahuitas

**BEACH—SIGHT |** Between the beaches of Quimixto and Yelapa and about 35 minutes by boat from Boca de Tomatlán, this small beach is the playground of people on day tours. There are no services for the average José; the lounge chairs and toilets are for hotel guests only. Palm trees shade the white beach of broken, sea-buffed shells. The blue-green water is clear, and there's sometimes good snorkeling around the rocky shore. **Amenities:** none. **Best for:** snorkeling; swimming. ⊠ *Yelapa.*

##  Activities

What to do in Majahuitas? Lay down and relax, or swim. There are kayaks and snorkeling options, and you might find some someone to rent you the gear. If you are lucky, you might see and take pictures of dolphins, manta rays, or whales (only late November through March).

**Vallarta Adventures - Yelapa & Majahuitas**
**BOAT TOURS | FAMILY** | This boat tour stops at the beaches of Yelapa and Majahuitas. Activities include snorkeling in Majahuitas Cove, kayaking, and paddleboarding. Food and drinks are also included, as well as beach club access and a guided hiking to Yelapa's waterfall. The tour is from 9 am to 5 pm and costs $79. ✉ *Las Palmas 39, Nuevo Vallarta* ☎ *322/226–8413* 🌐 *vallarta-adventures.com/en/tour/yelapa-majahuitas.*

# Yelapa

*1 km (0.7 miles) south of Majahuitas.*

Yelapa is only 40 minutes away from PV but feels like a totally different world. In addition to being home to the biggest beach south of PV, Yelapa has many dining options and things to keep you entertained. The jungle is also magical, and the upper waterfall is worth the hike.

## GETTING HERE AND AROUND

Yelapa is only accessible by boat; don't let anyone convince you to hike. To get here, you need to take a boat from the pier in Los Muertos Beach (45 minutes) or from Boca de Tomatlán (30 minutes). The last boat back to PV leaves at 5:30 pm, so make sure not to miss it. The round trip costs 380 MXN (around $20). The town is not as small as you might expect and a walk from the beach to the farthest point can take about 35 minutes.

## TOURS

**MiraMar Yelapa**
**EXCURSIONS** | This family-run tour provider offers a different excursions than most PV-based companies. With them, you can go on a fishing trip departing from Yelapa (no need to go to Boca de Tomatlán or Puerto Vallarta). Excursions to the nearby waterfall and zip-line tours are also available. ✉ *Marlyn 19, Yelapa* ☎ *322/209–5230, 818/293–5272* 🌐 *miramaryelapa.com.*

## Beaches

**Playa Yelapa**
**BEACH—SIGHT** | The beach slopes down to the water, and small waves break right on the shore. In high season and during holidays, there are water-sports outfitters. From here you can hike 20 minutes into the jungle to see the small Cascada Cola de Caballo (Horse Tail Waterfall), with a pool at its base for swimming. **Amenities:** food and drink; water sports. **Best for:** swimming; walking. ✉ *Yelapa.*

## Restaurants

The small fishing villages and quaint towns south of Puerto Vallarta like Yelapa are known for their delicious no-fuss seafood and rustic, beachfront palapa bars and restaurants. Eating here is very informal and laid-back, and if you're not looking for a full meal, just grab a beach chair by the water and kick back with a cold drink and a light snack.

**La Cascada y Bosque**
**$$ | SEAFOOD** | La Cascada y Bosque, simply known in town as "Cascada" is a wonderful place for breakfast or lunch even when the waterfalls are just a water drop. Open daily from 9 to 5, the jungle setting here is spectacular and begs for a stroll before or after your meal. **Known for:** great waterfall views; live music; delicious ceviche. [$] *Average main: 130 MP* ✉ *Yelapa* ✥ *At waterfall* ☎ *322/209–5146* 🕓 *No dinner* 💳 *No credit cards.*

**Yelapa Yacht Club**
**$$ | SEAFOOD** | The Yacht Club is a restaurant and bar on the town beach, and it's not a yacht club at all. Their breaded fish fillet is famous among the villagers and tourists, as are their chicken dishes. **Known for:** lively spot in Yelapa; great parties; beautiful ocean views. [$] *Average main: 130 MP* ✉ *Bacalao 11, Yelapa* ☎ *322/209–5272* 💳 *No credit cards.*

#  Hotels

There are many lodging places in Yelapa but in high season we recommend reserving ahead of time as it can get really busy. Prices and amenities will vary, and everything depends on your budget. The higher you get in the hills, the quieter your stay will be. The beach hotels will give you sunshine, beach, and swimming, but you will have to hike to get to the shops. In-town rentals are for the ones that want to explore the town apart from the beach. Among the lodgings in the surrounding hills you will find upscale hotels and more exclusive rentals and retreats.

### Hotel Lagunita

**$$ | HOTEL |** These rustic, thatched huts with mosquito nets over the beds are the most popular lodging options in Yelapa. **Pros:** exceptionally fresh seafood and great cocktails; gorgeous pool with great views of the bay; Wi-Fi in common areas. **Cons:** need to take a water taxi to get there; casitas are very rustic; no air-conditioning. $ *Rooms from: $110* ✉ *Barcina 3, Yelapa* ☎ *322/209–5056* ⊕ *hotel-lagunita. com* ↻ *28 rooms* ⊓O⊦ *No meals.*

### Pura Vida Wellness Retreat

**$$ | HOTEL |** Pura Vida Wellness Retreat offers cabins in the southern part of Yelapa, situated on top of a hill with spectacular ocean views. **Pros:** infinity salt water chlorine-free pool; organic treats at the juice bar; thalassotherapy treatments. **Cons:** not all rooms have air-conditioning; need to take a water taxi to get there; some rooms are not fully enclosed and mosquitoes can be an issue. $ *Rooms from: $150* ✉ *Huachinango 64, Yelapa* ☎ *322/209–5214, 833/787–8432* ⊕ *puravidaecoretreat.com* ↻ *15 rooms* ⊓O⊦ *No meals.*

### Verana

**$$$ | HOTEL |** Understated luxury and an open-to-nature building design describe this eight-suite boutique property located in a jungle about an hour south of Vallarta. **Pros:** simple luxury; no electronic distractions; gorgeous infinity pool. **Cons:** accessible to Puerto Vallarta only by boat; five- to seven-night minimum depending on season; steep hike up from boat dock (ask for mule if needed). $ *Rooms from: $300* ✉ *Playa de Yelapa, Domicilio Conocido, Yelapa* ✛ *30-minute boat ride west from Boca de Tomatlán* ☎ *322/227–5420, 800/211–9316 in U.S. and Canada* ⊕ *verana.boutique-homes.com* ↻ *10 rooms* ⊓O⊦ *No meals.*

#  Activities

Enjoy the beach. Relax, swim, sunbathe, go snorkeling, kayaking, diving, and even parasailing. Catch one of the "pie ladies" and buy a different pie every day. Try the local version of tequila called Raicilla, but with moderation. Take a walk to the town or horseback ride. Visit the waterfalls and swim in their chilly waters.

### Kayak Yelapa

**KAYAKING |** Rent kayaks and paddleboards on Yelapa's main beach. ✉ *Yelapa Beach, Yelapa* ☎ *322/173–4787* ⊕ *facebook.com/ marksparadise.*

# Chapter 6

# COSTALEGRE

Updated by
Luis Domínguez

| ◉ Sights | 🍴 Restaurants | 🛏 Hotels | 🛍 Shopping | 🍸 Nightlife |
|---|---|---|---|---|
| ★★★★★ | ★★★★☆ | ★★★★★ | ★★★☆☆ | ★★★★☆ |

# WELCOME TO COSTALEGRE

## TOP REASONS TO GO

★ **Explore the most scenic coastal highway:** This road has jaw-dropping ocean views and plenty of secluded coves.

★ **Try the freshest fish and seafood:** Fresh oysters sprinkled with lemon from beach vendors are a must, as well as ceviche and *aguachile*, raw fish and shrimps cured in citrus juices and chile.

★ **Look up in the sky:** The sunsets and stargazing without any light pollution are unforgettable.

★ **Enjoy luxurious but natural hideaways:** Dense greenery hides boutique ranch-style haciendas and deluxe hotels favored by privacy-seeking celebrities.

★ **Search authentic local art and crafts:** Outpost local towns are full with regional handmade treasures sold at incredibly low prices.

★ **Bask in delicious weather:** The climate here is near perfect: never cold, and it only rains at night.

Costalegre (also spelled Costa Alegre) stretches for 232 km (144 miles) and connects the Banderas Bay in the North with the Bahía de Navidad (Christmas Bay) in its southernmost point. It is nestled between Puerto Vallarta, Manzanillo, and Colima and it's all about fishing villages, small, picturesque towns, and pristine beaches that are its most famous tourist spots.

**1 Mayto.** Fifteen kilometers of unspoiled beaches just two hours south from Puerto Vallarta, Mayto is the biggest turtle nesting spot and a great, wild beach for camping.

**2 Costa Majahuas.** A long coast with numerous pristine beaches, don't miss Chalacatepec with a pirate ship wreck on its shore.

**3 Bahía De Chamela.** Chamela Bay is a large 10 km bay spotted with small islands declared a protected nature sanctuary in 2001. Some are home to local birds and vegetation and some are simply huge rocks, but all of them incredibly quaint, colorful, and accessible by boat. The Bay boasts four charming beaches: Pérula, Fortuna, Chamela, and Rosadas.

**4 Costa Careyes.** Costa Careyes is now a private community and a resort at the same time with castles, villas, casitas, bungalows, and restaurants on the premises.

**5 Tenacatita Bay.** The Tenacatita Bay is one of the biggest bays in Mexico and very rich in seafood.

**6 Barra De Navidad.** Barra De Navidad is like the New York of Costa Alegre. You can enjoy fresh fish under local palapas and dance salsa at the beach bars.

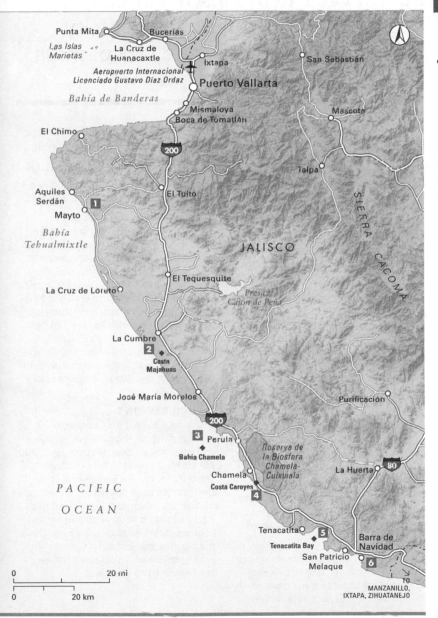

Punta Mita
Las Islas Marietas
Bucerías
La Cruz de Huanacaxtle
Ixtapa
San Sebastián
Aeropuerto Internacional Licenciado Gustavo Díaz Ordaz
Puerto Vallarta
Bahía de Banderas
Mismaloya
Boca de Tomatlán
Mascota
El Chimo
200
Talpa
Aquiles Serdán
1
El Tuito
Mayto
Bahía Tehualmixtle
JALISCO
SIERRA CACOMA
El Tequesquite
La Cruz de Loreto
Presa Cajón de Peña
La Cumbre
2
Costa Majahuas
José María Morelos
Purificación
200
3
Perula
Bahía Chamela
Reserva de la Biosfera Chamela-Cuixmala
La Huerta
80
Chamela
Costa Careyes
4
PACIFIC OCEAN
Tenacatita
5
Tenacatita Bay
Barra de Navidad
San Patricio Melaque
6
TO MANZANILLO, IXTAPA, ZIHUATANEJO

0          20 mi
0          20 km

Costalegre is a series of bays, white-sand beaches, and capes located south of Puerto Vallarta in Jalisco. The charm of Costalegre resides in its authenticity, its still quaint villages, and lack of mass tourism mentality.

This series of beach towns located in the southern part of the state of Jalisco lives in the shadows of Puerto Vallarta and Riviera Nayarit popularity, and that's been its blessing. With just a bunch of big resorts scattered here and there, this region feels more personal, more like the real Mexico, and not a staged version of it. However, this situation also has some obvious cons, as the quality of services and amenities available gets drastically reduced.

Costalegre has been for years a traditional destination for local tourism, as people from the nearby cities of Guadalajara and Colima drive to the area and rent low-cost apartments or stay at bungalows, in order to enjoy the wonders of nature in this part of the Mexican Pacific coastline. In recent years, however, the region has tried to change its usual low-budget destination tag and have invested heavily in roads, hotels, and facilities in general, looking to attract the attention of the international traveler. As a result, the area is now a rare mix of picturesque beaches with cars parked just a few steps from the sea, with exclusive high-end resorts and the customary array of luxuries attached to them such as golf courses and state-of-the-art spas.

The beaches in the region are varied and diverse. Some are pristine with breathtaking natural beauty, while others are too flat, with no waves and gray sand.

Fishing has been traditionally one of the main activities in the Costalegre, with Barra de Navidad leading the way in this area. There are good spots for the practice of snorkeling and scuba diving, specially around the Tenacatita Bay area.

There are two golf courses, one in Barra de Navidad, and the other at El Tamarindo, and there is even a polo club in Careyes. One of the most eclectic destinations in Mexico with no doubt, Costalegre offers a refreshing experience to the traveler that is bold enough to look for something different. It all depends on the kind of experience you are looking for, but if you want to try a different version of Mexico than the one available at Cancún, Cabo, and Puerto Vallarta, you will be surprised by the uniqueness of Costalegre.

## MAJOR REGIONS

Costalegre is not a single place, but a multidestination (think of Riviera Nayarit and you'll get an idea). It starts about 200 km south of Puerto Vallarta in Mayto. From there, you will find several other destinations each divided in their own set of different beaches. If you are not heading to a specific hotel in the region, the best way to move around is by car. There are big development plans for the area, which include an airport and a marina, but haven't materialized yet.

Costalegre is a series of unspoiled beaches and bays.

# Planning

## Getting Here and Around

### AIR

There is no international airport located on Costa Alegre but there are three airports to choose from not that far away. Guadalajara International Airport is the farthest but also the biggest one, so depending on your city of origin, it might be your best option. Guadalajara has frequent bus connections with Costalegre and the travel will take around 5–6 hours. You can also rent a car to get to your destination. The closest and the smallest airport is Playa de Oro International Manzanillo Airport (ZLO) situated between Manzanillo and Barra de Navidad. Although there are some international airlines that provide flights to and from Canada or the United States, the options are limited. There is no bus service at the airport so you will have to take a taxi or rent a car. If you are heading to a resort,

ask for their shuttle vans beforehand. You can share a taxi with other passengers to lower the cost or take it only to Cihuatlán and then use inexpensive local buses. Some people even walk 5 km to the highway and then stop a regional bus there.

Puerto Vallarta International Airport is our favorite choice. It is better connected with the world, and you will save on stops on your journey. If you arrive early, take a taxi (which tend to be expensive) or a public bus to the new bus terminal or to el Centro (downtown) and bus south. You can also rent a car at the airport.

Finally, a new airport for Costalegre is in the works, as there are big plans for this region. However, the lack of coordination between the state and federal governments has been a big obstacle that has derailed the projected airport several times.

**CONTACTS Aeropuerto Internacional de Guadalajara Miguel Hidalgo y Costilla.**
⊠ *Carr. Guadalajara - Chapala Km 17.5,*

*Guadalajara* ☎ *333/688–5248* ⊕ *aeropuertosgap.com.mx.* **Aeropuerto Internacional Licenciado Gustavo Díaz Ordaz.** ✉ *Carr. a Tepic Km 7.5, Área Militar de Vallarta, Puerto Vallarta* ☎ *322/221–1298* ⊕ *aeropuertosgap.com.mx.* **Aeropuerto Internacional Playa de Oro.** ✉ *Carr. Manzanillo - Barra de Navidad Km 42, Manzanillo* ☎ *314/333–1119* ⊕ *aeropuertosgap.com.mx.*

## BOAT

Although there is no official water transportation to Costalegre, the coast is extremely popular with cruisers, especially in winter months. You have cruiser anchorage in Ipala, Chamela, Cuastecomates, Melaque, and Barra de Navidad. The last one is believed to be one of the best marinas in Mexico. Costalegre was originally a place where people fished for a living, so it's no wonder that many local people will also offer unofficial water taxi services. *Pangas* can take you on a diving or fishing tour, or transport you from one beach location to another.

**CONTACTS Marina Puerto de la Navidad.** ✉ *Paseo del Pescador s/n* ☎ *314/337–9014* ⊕ *islanavidad.com.mx.*

## BUS

As Costalegre is a pretty remote place, regional buses are the best and the cheapest way to move from one place to another. There are six different companies that operate from Puerto Vallarta, Guadalajara, or Manzanillo, some of them offering first-class services. The buses from Puerto Vallarta leave from the main bus terminal at Venustiano Carranza in downtown PV. Check the stops as not all of them stop in every town. The cost depends on the company and distance ($17–$35). The whole trip from PV to Barra will take around 3½ hours, from Guadalajara 5–6 hours. The bus from Manzanillo to Puerto Vallarta will stop at almost any important spot and the whole trip takes almost five hours. You can also get to Costalegre from Mexico City but be prepared for a 14-hour trip.

**CONTACTS Primera Plus Barra de Navidad.** ✉ *Av. Veracruz 269, Barra de Navidad* ☎ *315/355–6111* ⊕ *primeraplus.com. mx.* **Terminal de Autobuses de Manzanillo (TAMA).** ✉ *Obras Marítimas, Col. Valle de las Garzas, Manzanillo* ☎ *314/336–8035.* **Terminal de Autobuses de Puerto Vallarta.** ✉ *Bahía Sin Nombre 363, Puerto Vallarta* ☎ *322/290–1009.*

## CAR

Costalegre is the perfect place to rent a car and discover piece by piece on a road trip. Taking into consideration poor public transport in the area, your own car will be your best option. If you don't bring your own car, you can rent one at Manzanillo or Puerto Vallarta airports. The coast road, Highway 200, is mountainous and winding so be prepared for a longer journey than what you would estimate by looking only at the distance. The roads are in good condition and the ocean views are really spectacular. It's impossible to get lost and there is very little traffic.

**CONTACTS Budget Rent a Car Aeropuerto de Manzanillo.** ✉ *Carr. a Aeropuerto Manzanillo, Manzanillo* ☎ *314/334–2270* ⊕ *budgetlac.com.* **National Car Rental - Aeropuerto de Puerto Vallarta.** ✉ *Blvd. Francisco Medina Ascencio 4172, Puerto Vallarta* ☎ *322/209–0390* ⊕ *nationalcar. com.mx.*

## TAXI

Nobody will stop you from taking a taxi but it is a costly option. You can take a taxi from Puerto Vallarta or Manzanillo that will eagerly get you to your destination in Costalegre but be prepared for a high fare, around $120 and a long trip of more than four hours. Avoid taking federal taxis from the airport as these are even more expensive. You can try to negotiate the price for longer arrangements but renting a car or using regional buses is a much cheaper option.

# Hotels

Although Costa Alegre is still considered an undiscovered treasure, it is becoming more and more popular among those looking for peace and seclusion. You will be surprised by the variety of options available. There are luxurious resorts, boutique hotels, budget hotels, private villas, Airbnb apartments and houses, RV parks, and camping spots. Unlike other Mexican tourist destinations, Costa Alegre's landscape and nature ensure the advantage of complete privacy and it's no wonder you will find all types of lodging from ranch-styled haciendas to deluxe design hotels. Driving on the highway, you would never guess that the dense greenery spotted by fuchsia bougainvilleas hides lavish amenities enjoyed by glittering clientele. You can also stay in eco-resorts or rustic huts, not always less expensive. You can find hotels as cheap as $20 in Melaque or Barra de Navidad but you may also pay around $630 per night in a deluxe hotel in Quemaro.

# Restaurants

When on the coast, eat fresh fish and seafood. Although you might find many different types of restaurants, we highly recommend focusing on the ones serving local specialties. Most of the biggest restaurants are located in Barra de Navidad, Melaque, and La Manzanilla, but you will also find some really fancy ones in Careyes. Smaller restaurants are located in all the Costalegre towns and beaches, and we highly recommend trying oysters from local beach vendors, served fresh, and seasoned with lemon and salt. Palapa restaurants and bars are also recommended if you want to get some local taste and vibe.

## HOTEL AND RESTAURANT PRICES
*Hotel prices in the reviews are the lowest cost of a standard double room in high season. Restaurant prices in*
*the reviews are the average cost of a main course at dinner, or if dinner is not served, at lunch. All prices in this chapter are in USD unless otherwise noted.*

| WHAT IT COSTS In USD | | | |
|---|---|---|---|
| $ | $$ | $$$ | $$$$ |
| **RESTAURANTS** | | | |
| under $5 | $5–$10 | $10–$20 | over $20 |
| **HOTELS** | | | |
| under $50 | $50–$100 | $100–$350 | over $350 |

# Tours

There are various tour companies operating in Costalegre. They organize all types of tours that can vary in duration, cost, and activities involved. You can book a tour to visit towns and cities around here, go snorkeling, or bird-watching. Some companies also offer diving, shopping, swimming with turtles, boat excursions to distant beaches, fishing, biking, and horse riding.

### Superior Tours Vallarta
**GUIDED TOURS** | Superior Tours offers a variety of interesting tours for the active, tequila lovers, anglers, and more, ranging from $20 to $750 per person. One tour specific to this region is the weekly Friday tour to Mayto and Tehuamixtle for a minimum of six passengers. They'll pick you up at a designated spot and will drive you to El Tuito, Mayto, and Tehuamixtle. You will be able to shop, swim, and eat on a day-long trip, while enjoying the best of this region south of Puerto Vallarta. ✉ *Calle Jazmín 158, Col. Villa Las Flores* ☎ *322/222–0024* ⊕ *superiortoursvallarta. com.*

### Vallarta Food Tours
**SPECIAL-INTEREST** | This company specialized in food tours around Puerto Vallarta, has a two-day, one-night tour that include stops in El Tuito, Mayto, and Tehuamixtle.

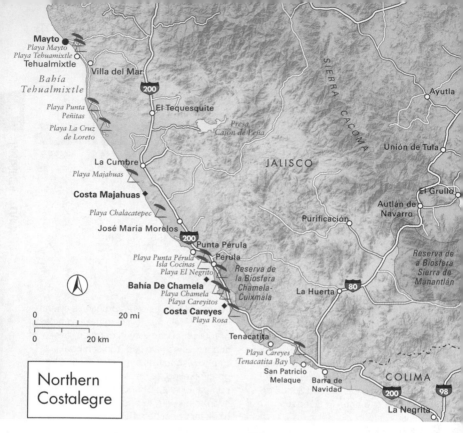

Mayto
Playa Mayto
Playa Tehuamixtle
**Tehualmixtle**
Villa del Mar
*Bahía Tehualmixtle*
200
Playa Punta Peñitas
El Tequesquite
Playa La Cruz de Loreto
La Cumbre
Playa Majahuas
**Costa Majahuas**
Playa Chalacatepec
José María Morelos
200
Punta Pérula
Playa Punta Pérula
Isla Cocinas
Playa El Negrito
Pérula
Reserva de la Biosfera Chamela-Cuixmala
**Bahía De Chamela**
Playa Chamela
Playa Careyitos
**Costa Careyes**
Playa Rosa
Tenacatita
Playa Careyes
Tenacatita Bay
San Patricio Melaque
Barra de Navidad
La Negrita
SIERRA CACOMA
JALISCO
Presa Cajón de Peña
Ayutla
Unión de Tula
El Grullo
Autlán de Navarro
Purificación
La Huerta
80
Reserva de la Biosfera Sierra de Manantlán
COLIMA
200
98

0    20 mi
0    20 km

**Northern Costalegre**

You'll get six different tastings for $200, and more importantly, you'll have a guide who will help you discover the secrets of this beautiful, but still sleepy, region. ⊠ *Puerto Vallarta* ☎ *322/222–6117, 866/630–0584 in U.S. and Canada* ⊕ *vallartafoodtours.com/food-tours/mayto.*

## Visitor Information

### Visitor's Information Center Costalegre
Tourism information office and website created by the Government of Jalisco to promote and provide useful information to visitors of Costalegre. ⊠ *Av. Veracruz 98, Barra de Navidad* ☎ *800/849–0322 toll-free in Mexico, 315/355–5100* ⊕ *costalegre.com.*

## Mayto

*96 km (59 miles) south of Puerto Vallarta.*

Mayto is probably the most spectacular of all the Costalegre beaches. Just imagine 15 km (9 miles) of white sand and extreme beauty, with nothing around but two small hotels at the entrance and sea turtle breeding grounds. You can camp and for an extra charge you will be allowed to use the restrooms at the little hotels. Don't forget to buy your own provisions beforehand, as there are no stores or restaurants in Mayto. If you book ahead, you may also participate in the release of newborn turtles.

### GETTING HERE AND AROUND
The trip from Puerto Vallarta to Mayto will take more than two hours. Head south on Highway 200 for about 43 km

(27 miles) until you reach Tuito. Then the fun off-road part starts for the next 30 km. If you start at Barra, take Highway 200 heading north, and after 194 km (120 miles) and about 3½ hours, you reach your destination.

## Sights

**Campamento Tortuguero Mayto**
**ZOO** | Mayto's Turtle Camp is a years'-long, well-run project from Universidad de Guadalajara that patrols the beaches of the area in search of turtle nests and their eggs, in order to save them from poachers. They constantly receive groups of students from schools from Puerto Vallarta, Guadalajara, and other cities. With some luck you might get to see a release of baby turtles into the sea. ✉ *Tehuamixtle* ☎ *322/232–7727.*

## Beaches

**★ Playa Mayto**
**BEACH—SIGHT** | If you have to choose just one beach in the whole Costalegre, this is the one. Difficult to reach, the unspoiled beauty of the place makes the adventure well worth it. The long wide beach invites for peaceful walks. Swimming might be risky here, though. Camping under the stars is highly recommended. **Amenities:** parking (no fee). **Best for:** solitude; sunset; walking. ✉ *Tehuamixtle.*

**Playa Tehuamixtle**
**BEACH—SIGHT** | **FAMILY** | Playa Tehuamixtle is a small stretch of beach, especially when compared with other beaches of the region. What makes it interesting is the ocean front restaurant and its dock, from where fishing boats take visitors on day trips to completely isolated beaches not reachable by car. Everything here is affordable, as locals are just happy to get visitors. **Amenities:** food and drink; parking (no fee). **Best for:** snorkeling; swimming. ✉ *Tehuamixtle.*

## Restaurants

Mayto is more about camping and turtle reservation than dining, but there are a couple of options to consider if you plan on staying there or visiting the area. The hotels on the beach serve delicious Mexican dishes at very fair prices. You don't have to be their guest to enjoy their cuisine. In Tehuamixtle you can also find smaller places to eat or street stands.

**Cande's Restaurant and Bar**
**$** | **SEAFOOD** | Cande's is the best and possibly only viable dining option in the whole Mayto-Tehuamixtle area. It enjoys an enviable location overlooking Tehuamixtle Bay, just a few steps from the pier, and serves just-caught seafood. **Known for:** freshest seafood in the region; stunning ocean views; cold beer always available. [$] *Average main: $5* ✉ *Tehuamixtle* ✣ *Right on pier* ☎ *331/036–6345* 🌐 *facebook.com/RestaurantCandesTehua.*

## Hotels

There are a couple of small hotels situated on the Mayto beach. They are very charming beach lodgings, some fancier than others. You can also rent a room at private houses nearby but the quality is obviously lower. There is also a nice hotel with a pool in Tehuamixtle, eight minutes away by car from Mayto, and some private rentals.

**Hotel Acantilado**
**$$** | **HOTEL** | The best place to stay in the fishing village of Tehuamixtle is the small but cozy and romantic Hotel Acantilado. **Pros:** sceney swimming pool; pet-friendly; can fish your own food and they'll cook it for you. **Cons:** faraway place; a bit expensive for what you get; balconies lack privacy. [$] *Rooms from: $80* ✉ *Gaviota, Tehuamixtle* ☎ *322/183–2005* 🌐 *hotelacantilado.com* 🛏 *8 rooms* 🍴 *No meals.*

**Hotel Mayto**

$ | **HOTEL** | **FAMILY** | This might be the largest building in Mayto and arguably the hotel with the best amenities; the manicured gardens and gorgeous swimming pool offer a quiet and refreshing area for those not ready to go down to the beach. **Pros:** on the beach; nice large swimming pool; pet-friendly. **Cons:** not much to do on-site; too isolated; unimpressive rooms. [$] *Rooms from: $60* ✉ *Estrella del mar 45, Tehuamixtle* ☎ *322/120–6206* 🌐 *mayto.mx* 🛏 *12 rooms* 🍴 *No meals.*

## Activities

There are surprisingly many things you can do in Mayto, if you like sports, you can try kayaking, surfing, beach and cliff walking, snorkeling, kite surfing, horse riding, or fishing. If you're interested in ecology, you can participate in night patrols and in releasing baby turtles, talk to the Turtle Camp and they will tell you how you can help.

# Costa Majahuas

*108 km (67 miles) south of Mayto.*

Here you will find Chalacatepec Beach and La Peñita Pintada (Painted Lil'Rock) that owes its name to a natural cavity with various ancient paintings. Both places are also famous for their turtle conservation programs.

### GETTING HERE AND AROUND

Get on Highway 200 from Puerto Vallarta and go south for about 130 km (80 miles). The whole trip takes about 2½ hours. From Barra de Navidad, you will get to your destination in less than two hours after about 105 km (65 miles) on Highway 200 heading north.

### TOURS

**Mex-Eco Tours**

**ECOTOURISM** | Mex-Eco Tours company offers interaction between tourists and cultural and environmental communities. In Costa Majahuas they offer a once-in-a lifetime experience of learning the basics of sea turtle conservation and participating in a hatchling release on Nature Reserve Camp. You can also book ATV, fishing, surfing, and paddling tours with them. ✉ *Gómez Farías 59–1, San Patricio–Melaque* ☎ *315/355–7027* 🌐 *mex-ecotours.com/sea-turtle.*

## Beaches

There are six beaches to visit on Majahuas Coast but Majahuas, Punta Peñita, La Cruz de Loreto, and Chalacatepec with its pirate wreck are the most important ones. La Cruz de Loreto offers tours to see ancient rock paintings.

**Playa Chalacatepec**

**BEACH—SIGHT** | Playa Chalacatepec is a true piece of unspoiled paradise. Miles of white-sand beach extend without any sign of human activity. However, this outstanding beauty could have its days numbered, as there are big projects for the area. Talk about building a "new Cancún" is commonplace, as the Chalacatepec lagoon provides a similar setting to that of the Caribbean resort town. Perfect for camping, just stay away from crocodiles. **Amenities:** none. **Best for:** walking; swimming; surfing; solitude. ✉ *Chalacatepec, Punta Pérula* ✣ *Take dirt road from Morelos.*

**Playa La Cruz de Loreto**

**BEACH—SIGHT** | La Cruz de Loreto is a little village located 6 km from the coast, where its namesake beach provides an amazing spectacle. The area is inside a nature reserve and home to an estuary, recognized by UNESCO as a birds' paradise. The area is worth visiting, mostly for day trips or camping, as there is no infrastructure at all. **Amenities:** none. **Best for:** solitude; swimming; sunset; walking. ✣ *6 km down dirt road from La Cruz de Loreto village.*

**Playa Majahuas**

**BEACH—SIGHT** | Right in the middle between La Cruz de Loreto and Chalacatepec, you'll find this magnificent white-sand beach that stretches for miles in parallel with the Estero Majahuas formed by the Tomatlán River. Basically, you have the sea on one side, then the beach and then the fresh water estuary on the other. This area has been targeted several times as a new tourism development due to its rare beauty. **Amenities:** none. **Best for:** swimming; solitude; walking. ✉ *Majahuas* ✥ *Between La Cruz de Loreto and Chalacatepec.*

**Playa Punta Peñitas**

**BEACH—SIGHT** | A few kilometers north of Playa La Cruz de Loreto, you will find this wide, breathtaking beach located between the waves of the Pacific Ocean and the warm waters of a gorgeous lagoon. Punta Peñitas is one more of the virgin beaches in the region, a favorite of surfers and camping enthusiasts. **Amenities:** none. **Best for:** solitude; sunset; surfing; swimming; walking. ✥ *South of Las Peñitas village and north of Playa La Cruz de Loreto.*

## Hotels

Beach camping may not be an option for everybody so Costa Majahuas offers a perfect hideaway in Las Alamandas luxury resort. There are big plans for the region, with a new small airport near Tomatlán for private jets and charter flights, and the Four Seasons Resort Tamarindo that will soon open its doors for glamorous clients.

**Hotel Rancho Santa María**

**$** | **HOTEL** | **FAMILY** | A few kilometers from the beach, this spacious hotel hosts weddings and events, and acts as a getaway destination for those who live in Tomatlán. **Pros:** outdoor swimming pool; free parking; Wi-Fi. **Cons:** noisy when there is an event; small bathrooms; no restaurant. [$] *Rooms from: $25* ✉ *Carr. a Cruz de Loreto Km 14* ☎ *332/045–7579* 🛏 *15 rooms* 🍴 *No meals.*

**★ Las Alamandas**

**$$$$** | **RESORT** | A luxury boutique resort hidden in the middle of nowhere, Las Alamandas is a top-notch hotel with tasteful Mexican design and decor. **Pros:** four private beaches; set inside a nature reserve; varied sports facilities. **Cons:** hard to get there; not much to do outside the resort; a bit pricey even for its category. [$] *Rooms from: $640* ✉ *Mexico 200 Km 82, Punta Pérula* ☎ *322/205–8054* 🌐 *alamandas.com* 🛏 *16 suites* 🍴 *No meals.*

## Activities

Beaches on Costa Majahuas are perfect for snorkeling and Punta Peñitas is the best for surfing. You can rent a board for $3 for the whole day. You can also see dolphins, sea turtles coming out of the ocean, and whales in winter season. Another option is to volunteer in the nature reserve camp and watch the turtles nest. Costa Majahuas is an ideal place for ecotourism for its swamp areas and river channels where you can watch crocodiles, wild ducks, herons, and other water birds. In La Cruz de Loreto, you can watch rock painting in La Peñita Pintada beach, or rent a panga (small boat) to explore El Ermitaño estuary. Horseback riding, sport fishing, mountain biking, and ATV tours are also available in the area.

# Bahía De Chamela

*25 km (15 miles) south of Costa Majahuas.*

Bahía de Chamela is an undeveloped bay with several islands accessible only by boat. They are exotic bird reserves, too, and great spots for snorkeling and diving.

### GETTING HERE AND AROUND

Go south toward Barra de Navidad on Highway 200 for 159 km (93 miles). The trip should take around 2 hours and 40 minutes. To get to Chamela Bay from Barra, head north via Manzanillo-Puerto Vallarta Highway 200. The 70 km (44 miles) will take about 75 minutes.

## Beaches

Chamela Bay is a hidden and secluded treasure. Its peaceful beaches and islands are spectacular and waiting to be explored. El Negrito, Chamela, Punta Pérula, and Isla Cocinas are the spots you should mark on your map.

**Isla Cocinas**

**BEACH—SIGHT** | Each of the nine islands set in front of Chamela Bay can be reached by boat. However, not all of them have such a beautiful beach as Isla Cocinas. Get a boat from Punta Pérula or Playa Chamela for as little as $15 and in 20 minutes you'll be sunbathing on one of the most extraordinary beaches you've ever seen. The island is uninhabited, so privacy and quiet is guaranteed. **Amenities:** none. **Best for:** swimming; solitude. ✉ *Costalegre.*

**Playa Chamela**

**BEACH—SIGHT** | **FAMILY** | The main beach in the Chamela Bay area, is long and wide, with several hotels and restaurants scattered here and there. You will also find lounge chairs and palapas for rent on the beach. The sea is good for kids and for swimming, as the islands in front of the coastline soften the surf in the bay. Boat trips to the islands are available. **Amenities:** parking (no fee); food and drink; water sports. **Best for:** swimming; snorkeling; walking ✉ *Costalegre.*

**Playa El Negrito**

**BEACH—SIGHT** | **FAMILY** | Also on Bahía de Chamela, this lovely beach is fringed in lanky coconut palms and backed by blue foothills. There are camping and RV accommodations and plenty of opportunities for shore fishing, swimming, and snorkeling. Almost every pretty beach in Mexico has its own humble restaurant; this one is no exception. **Amenities:** food and drink; parking (no fee). **Best for:** swimming; snorkeling; walking. ✉ *Costalegre.*

**Playa Punta Pérula**

**BEACH—SIGHT** | **FAMILY** | The handful of islands just off lovely Bahía de Chamela protects the beaches from strong surf. The best place on the bay for swimming is wide, flat Playa Punta Pérula. Fishermen here take visitors out to snorkel around the islands (about $40 for up to 10 people) or to fish ($20 per hour for one to four people); restaurants on the sand sell fresh fillets and ceviche. **Amenities:** food and drink; parking (no fee); water sports. **Best for:** swimming; snorkeling. ✉ *Costalegre.*

## Restaurants

El Negrito beach has some small beach palapa restaurants. Punta Pérula produces most of the fish and seafood consumed in Costalegre and you can be sure that your dish bought in many inexpensive seafood restaurants and taco stands will be always fresh. You should also try the locally produced ice cream "Nieve de Garrafa." Chamela offers more seafood and Mexican restaurants on the beach and inland.

**Restaurante La Sirenita**

**$$** | **SEAFOOD** | **FAMILY** | Punta Pérula beach is filled with this type of informal seafood restaurant, just steps from the sand. Look for a table with palapa by the beach for the ultimate local experience. **Known for:** camarones a la diabla (spicy shrimp); offering boat tours to Isla Cocinas; great views of the beach. [$] *Average main: $6* ✉ *Miguel Hidalgo s/n, Punta Pérula* ✥ *On beach between Tiburón and Miguel Hidalgo* ☎ *315/109–0345* ⏲ *No dinner* 💳 *No credit cards.*

Participating in a turtle-hatching tour (held from summer to late fall) will likely put you face-to-face with the adorable Lepidochelys olivacea, or olive ridley turtle, the smallest sea turtle species in the world.

### Scuba Jazz Cafe

$$ | CAFÉ | FAMILY | If you need a break from a seafood-intensive diet, this small, sophisticated café serves outstanding coffee, Mexican breakfasts, and classic burgers for lunch. They also have live music during the week. **Known for:** Atardecer Punta Pérula craft beer; live music; a nice break from typical seafood dishes. $ Average main: $6 ✉ Av. Independencia 43, Punta Pérula ☎ 322/121–2941 ⊕ facebook.com/scubajazzcafe ⊟ No credit cards.

##  Hotels

There aren't many places to stay in the bay although small hotels and B&Bs seem to sprout up every year. In Chamela you can camp anywhere on the beach, although it might be a good idea to ask the locals first. Punta Pérula offers some more hotels and RV parks.

### Hotel y Bungalows Playa Dorada

$$ | HOTEL | FAMILY | Widely considered as the best hotel in Pérula, Playa Dorada features 50 well-appointed accommodations distributed between rooms, suites, and bungalows. **Pros:** two swimming pools; oceanfront terraces; bungalows with kitchenette. **Cons:** restaurant opens only in high season; fee for kayaks and boogie boards; fee for umbrellas and lounge chairs. $ Rooms from: $50 ✉ Tiburón 40, Punta Pérula ☎ 315/333–9710 ⊕ playa-dorada.com ↝ 50 rooms ⊙ No meals.

### Mayar Chamela Bungalows

$$ | HOTEL | FAMILY | Located 50 meters from the beach, this hotel offer low-key lodging in bungalows at affordable rates. **Pros:** small-pet-friendly; free parking; kitchenettes in bungalows. **Cons:** not on the beach; restaurant only during high season; outdated rooms. $ Rooms from: $50 ✉ Carr. a Barra de Navidad Km 72, Costalegre ☎ 315/333–9711 ⊕ mayarchamela.mx ↝ 18 rooms ⊙ No meals.

### Villa Polinesia Wellness Resort

$$ | HOTEL | FAMILY | Villa Polinesia offers a diversity of colorful cabins by the beach

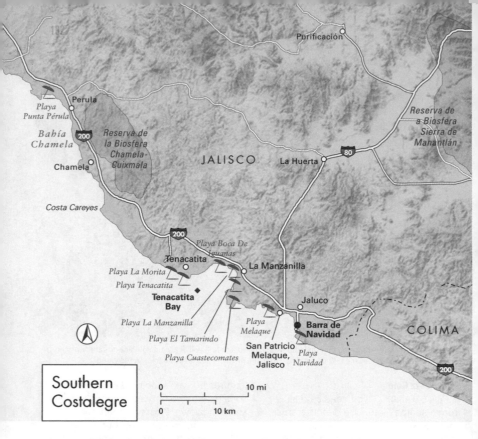

**Southern Costalegre**

0 ——— 10 mi

0 ——— 10 km

---

in a very laid-back environment. **Pros:** rooms with ocean views; Wi-Fi throughout the property; spa services. **Cons:** continental breakfast not included; cabins could use some restoration work; not all rooms include air-conditioning. $ *Rooms from:* $150 ✉ *Carr. a Barra de Navidad Km 71.5, Costalegre* ☎ *322/188–7631* ⊕ *villapolinesia.mx* ⇥ *40 rooms* ❄ *No meals.*

## 🏃 Activities

El Negrito beach is ideal for swimming and diving. Chamela offers all types of water sports, sport fishing, and exploring the nearby islands on a *panga* (skiff). Punta Pérula is a place to go fishing and make your private food tour. You can visit the Chamela Biological Station personally or on group tours.

### Pacific Adventures

**GUIDED TOURS** | Pacific Adventures offers this eight-hour tour starting at Melaque, in the south end of the Costalegre, and going all the way to the Chamela Bay, Careyes, and Isla Cocinas. You can snorkel, hike, paddle board, and even include a visit to a crocodile sanctuary. Food and drinks are included. ✉ *Gómez Farías 595, Barra de Navidad* ☎ *315/100–4999* ⊕ *pacificadventures.mx.*

### Tours Punta Pérula

**BOAT TOURS** | Tours Punta Pérula provides boat tours of Chamela Bay, day trips to Isla Cocinas, fishing expeditions, and all kind of water sports equipment for snorkeling, kayaking, and more. ✉ *Punta Pérula* ☎ *315/107–3720* ⊕ *facebook.com/ToursPuntaPerula/.*

# Costa Careyes

*14 km (8 miles) south of Bahía de Chamela.*

Costa Careyes is the luxurious part of Costalegre with a range of spas, aquatic sports facilities, and upscale accommodations. This large coast also hosts two Bermuda grass fields and stables for 150 polo horses. Cuixmala is a stunning private estate and an important ecological reserve. Located on 25,000 acres, the area has 1,200 plant species, 72 species of mammals, and 270 types of birds. There are also many small beaches with hidden grottos to explore and the estate offers plenty of activities to choose from, such as kayaking, snorkeling, and fishing.

## GETTING HERE AND AROUND

If you fly into Puerto Vallarta, the drive to Careyes will be around three hours. It's only 170 km (100 miles), but Highway 200 is winding and mountainous. The drive from Manzanillo should be one hour shorter, but the 100 kilometers (60 miles) will take around two hours.

## TOURS

Although there is no tour company, the concierge staff of Costa Careyes is always happy to help you arranging lots of sea and land activities. They can also give information about events and help you rent anything you may need.

### Costa Careyes Activities

ECOTOURISM | All the tours and activities must be arranged with the concierge staff of Costa Careyes accommodations. You can choose from sea, land, and nature activities or book all types of classes. There is a wide range of options for people with different physical abilities and interests. ⊠ *Careyes* ☎ *315/351–0240* ⊕ *careyes.com/activities.*

## VISITOR INFORMATION

### Costa Careyes Visitor's Information

As Costa Careyes is a resort and residential area, all the updated information about accommodation, dining, events, and tours can be consulted on their website. For more details on events you can contact the concierge staff at conciergе@careyes.com. ⊠ *Careyes* ☎ *315/351–0240* ⊕ *careyes.com.*

##  Beaches

Costa Careyes is surrounded by stunning green cliffs overlooking four golden sand beaches: Playa Rosa, Careyitos, Careyes, and Teopa. The first three constitute the Careyes Resort and residential area, while Teopa Beach, the biggest one, is a sea turtle preservation sanctuary.

### Playa Careyes

BEACH—SIGHT | FAMILY | This beach is named for the careyes (hawksbill) turtles that lay eggs here. It's a lovely soft-sand beach framed by headlands. When the water's not too rough, snorkeling is good around the rocks, where you can also fish. There's a small restaurant at the north end of the beach, and often you can arrange to go out with a local fisherman (about $20 per hour). **Amenities:** food and drink; parking (no fee). **Best for:** swimming; snorkeling. ⊠ *Costalegre.*

### Playa Careyitos

BEACH—SIGHT | Careyitos is one of the longest beaches in Costa Careyes and, paradoxically, maybe the most private as there are not many properties on its shore. Its waters are calm and inviting. It is a perfect place for camping. You may want to climb the Morro Prieto hill to reach a lookout that offers outstanding views of the area. **Amenities:** parking (no fee); food and drink; water sports. **Best for:** swimming; sunset; walking. ⊠ *Costalegre.*

### Playa Rosa

BEACH—SIGHT | FAMILY | This small cozy beach is a favorite among frequent visitors of Costa Careyes. Its waters have a gorgeous emerald green color and almost no waves, making it perfect for families with kids. Playa Rosa has three little islands and a couple of caves can be visited by boat, offering something different from most other beaches in the area. **Amenities:** food and drink; parking (no fee). **Best for:** swimming. ✉ *Costalegre.*

**Playa Teopa**

**BEACH—SIGHT | FAMILY** | Here, you can walk south from Playa Careyes along the dunes, although guards protect sea turtle nests by barring visitors during the summer and fall nesting seasons. A road from the highway at Km 49.5 gains access to Playa Teopa by car; ask the guard for permission to enter this way, as you'll need to pass through private property to gain access to the beach. **Amenities:** none. **Best for:** swimming; walking. ✉ *Costalegre.*

**Playa Rosa**

**BEACH—SIGHT | FAMILY** | This small cozy beach is a favorite among frequent visitors of Costa Careyes. Its waters have a gorgeous emerald green color and almost no waves, making it perfect for families with kids. Playa Rosa has three little islands and a couple of caves can be visited by boat, offering something different from most other beaches in the area. **Amenities:** food and drink; parking (no fee). **Best for:** swimming. ✉ *Costalegre.*

**La Copa del Sol**

**MEMORIAL** | This 35-foot-high, 88-feet in diameter, Burning Man-style sculpture is one of the defining sights of Costa Careyes. Created by Gian Franco Brignone, who also founded the Careyes community, it is a representation of a woman getting the gift of life directly from the sun (Copa del Sol means "Cup of the Sun"). During music festivals at Playa Teopa the Copa becomes a very popular meeting point. ✉ *Costalegre.*

## 🍴 Restaurants

There are seven restaurants in Costa Careyes, all of them inside the Careyes Resort. Playa Rosa Beach Club is perfect for a beach brunch or romantic dinner at sunset. Other restaurants specialize in meat and pizza, salads and panini, or Asian cuisine with a Mexican twist.

**La Coscolina**

**$$$ | MOROCCAN** | La Coscolina is a stylish restaurant with gorgeous Mexican decor and Moroccan flavors. Open from 8 am to 11 pm, its atmosphere changes several times during the day: fresh-pressed juices and salads dominate the early hours, while vegan options and handmade gelatos are served in the afternoon; and cocktails are enjoyed at night. **Known for:** the main café in town; weekend DJs during high season; delicious smoothies. [$] *Average main: 300 MP* ✉ *Paseo de los Artesanos s/n, Costalegre* ☎ *315/351–0630* 🌐 *www.careyes.com/restaurants* 🕒 *Closed Wed.*

**La Duna Restaurante & Sunset Bar**

**$$$ | SEAFOOD** | La Duna is right in front of Playa Careyes. During breakfast the cuisine is typically Mexican, while at lunch it goes more Mediterranean, and after 4 pm, La Duna becomes a sunset bar and social club. **Known for:** the best ceviche in Costa Careyes; local produce; memorable sunset views. [$] *Average main: 300 MP* ✉ *Carr. Barra de Navidad - Puerto Vallarta Km 53.5, Costalegre* ☎ *315/351–0000* 🌐 *www.careyes.com/restaurants.*

**Playa Rosa Beach Club**

**$$$ | MEDITERRANEAN | FAMILY** | A typical beach club with gourmet restaurant aspirations, Playa Rosa Beach Club offers a mix of Mediterranean and Mexican seafood in style. During the day, the place becomes a big social gathering for locals and visitors. **Known for:** gathering point for local socialites; direct access from private villas via a funicular; just-caught seafood dishes. [$] *Average main: 250 MP* ✉ *Carr. Melaque - Puerto Vallarta Km 53.5, Costalegre* ☎ *315/351–0462* 🌐 *www.careyes.com/restaurants* 🕒 *No dinner Tues.*

**Punto Como**

$$$ | **ITALIAN** | Located in a corner of buzzing Plaza de los Caballeros, Punto Como is an Italian steak house serving traditional Neapolitan pizzas and pastas. The place has an Italian-Mexican atmosphere, with classy design and excellent service. **Known for:** brick-oven pizzas; terrace provides the best seats to watch the open-air cinema; lively atmosphere. [$] *Average main: 350 MP* ✉ *Paseo de los Artesanos s/n, Costalegre* ☎ *315/351–2014* 🌐 *www.careyes.com/restaurants* ⏲ *Closed Mon.*

## Hotels

In Costa Careyes, lodging options include private villas, houses, castles, bungalows, residences, and casitas for rent. All rentals are managed by the Careyes concierge staff and prices depend on the season. However, don't expect anything under $320 per night. The private houses prices start at $3,000 per night and come equipped with a full staff. All lodging has ocean views and are a perfect spot for whale watching in winter season.

**Bungalows in Playa Rosa**

$$ | **HOTEL** | **FAMILY** | Located in the Playa Rosa area and just beside the trendy beach club of the same name, these bungalows have been called the world's smallest beach resort. **Pros:** ocean-front bungalows; has the perks of Careyes at half the price of a resort; Wi-Fi and air-conditioning. **Cons:** steps from a crowded beach by day; lack of privacy due to nearby beach club; small TVs. [$] *Rooms from: $200* ✉ *Carr. Barra de Navidad - Puerto Vallarta Km 53, Costalegre* ☎ *315/351–0320* 🌐 *careyes.com* 🛏 *3 bungalows* 🍴 *No meals.*

**Casitas de las Flores**

$$$ | **HOTEL** | **FAMILY** | Formerly known as Hotel Costa Careyes, Casitas de las Flores is a series of renewed condos part of the whole Careyes community face-lift. **Pros:** private splash pools in some casitas; access to private beach club; in-suite spa services. **Cons:** no swimming pool in common area; no fitness center; some casitas have obstructed ocean views. [$] *Rooms from: $300* ✉ *Carr. Barra de Navidad - Puerto Vallarta Km 53.5, Costalegre* ☎ *315/351–0320* 🌐 *careyes.com* 🛏 *4 condos* 🍴 *No meals.*

**★ Cuixmala**

$$$$ | **ALL-INCLUSIVE** | A favorite of models and celebrities, this spectacular resort nestled on top of a hill above a private beach and inside a wildlife reserve, Cuixmala is redefining what a luxury retreat looks like. **Pros:** private jet charter service; organic farm; exotic animal sanctuary. **Cons:** very expensive; no fitness center. [$] *Rooms from: $650* ✉ *Carr. Puerto Vallarta - Manzanillo Km 46, Costalegre* ☎ *315/351–6050* 🌐 *cuixmala.com* 🛏 *13 suites* 🍴 *All-inclusive.*

**El Careyes Club & Residences**

$$$$ | **RESORT** | El Careyes Club & Residences is an oceanfront integrally designed project that features a wide array of lodging options to choose from, from one- to five-bedroom suites, to private villas and luxurious bungalows. **Pros:** jet-setter atmosphere; all rooms with ocean views, some with jungle or garden views; private beach club. **Cons:** ultramodern design lacks Mexican style; too far from international airports. [$] *Rooms from: $450* ✉ *Carr. Barra de Navidad - Puerto Vallarta Km 53.5, Costalegre* ☎ *315/351–0000* 🌐 *careyes.com* 🛏 *35 suites* 🍴 *No meals.*

**Samadhi Nest**

$$ | **RESORT** | This eco- and wellness-focused retreat and hotel is for yogis and the spiritual-minded. **Pros:** concerts and dinners hosted on-site; extremely unique lodging experience; right on the beach of Teopa. **Cons:** closed June to November; minimum two-night stay; 2½ hours from PV airport. [$] *Rooms from: $250* ✉ *Costa Careyes, Costalegre* ☎ *314/102–1216* 🌐 *samadhinest.com* 🛏 *19 yurts* 🍴 *No meals.*

##  Nightlife

Nightlife in Costa Careyes is all about moonlight dinners, bonfires on the beach, and cocktail parties. Although the restaurant kitchens do have official closing hours, you're usually welcome to stay and sip your drinks late into the night.

### Casa de Nada Restaurant and Bar

TAPAS BARS | Casa de Nada Restaurant and Bar is located in Samahdi Nest. It offers a striking rustic look and vibe, but at the same time it feels bohemian and trendy. Dine with views over the dunes and the remote ocean in the horizon. It specializes in Mediterranean and vegetarian cuisine with a focus on tapas. After 11 pm cocktails are served. ✉ *Teopa Beach, next to Samadhi Nest, Careyes* ☎ *314/125–1060* ⊕ *careyes.com/ restaurants#casadenada.*

##  Activities

What can you do in Costa Careyes? Absolutely everything. The Careyes Resort offers three types of activities and classes: sea, land, and nature. You can try paddle boarding, ocean kayaking, snorkeling, scuba diving, fishing, and surfing. You can also arrange a coastal boat tour to admire the Careyes architecture. There are also horseback riding, polo, tennis, mountain biking and hiking, golf, spa services and yoga lessons available. Nature activities include bird-watching, dolphin spotting, and whale-watching in winter season. Costa Careyes is the only place on this side of the coast where the Hawksbill turtles come to nest and you can participate in releasing hatchlings.

### Costa Careyes Polo Club

SPORTS VENUE | FAMILY | Since its opening in 1990, the Costa Careyes Polo Club has received players from all over the world. For $500 you can play in one of their two regulation-size fields with green fees and horse rental included. ✉ *Carr.*

*Manzanillo-Puerto Vallarta, Costalegre* ☎ *315/351–0320.*

# Tenacatita Bay

*36 km (22 miles) south of Costa Careyes.*

Tenacatita Bay is one of the largest bays in Mexico and offers seven beautiful and not-so-developed beaches; La Manzanilla, Tenacatita, and Boca de Iguanas are the most famous ones. It is one of very few places in Mexico where, in winter months, you can observe both sunrise and sunset over the sea. The whole bay is famous for sports fishing, snorkeling, and diving.

### GETTING HERE AND AROUND

The best way to get to Tenacatita is by car. If Puerto Vallarta is your starting point, the distance is 203 km (123 miles) and the whole trip should take around 3 hours and 20 minutes on Highway 200. The drive from Manzanillo is much shorter: 90 km (55 miles), and can be done in 1 hour and 40 minutes. There are no local buses to Tenacatita, but you can get a taxi in Barra or Melaque.

### TOURS

**Danitours**

ECOTOURISM | Danitours offers a "Crocs and Mangroves" tour that covers a trip to La Manzanilla and the mangrove areas near Tenacatita. The tour starts in the village, and then takes you to a lagoon surrounded by mangroves where you will be able to see crocodiles in their natural habitat and plenty of water birds. ✉ *Progreso 40, Manzanillo* ☎ *314/872–4524* ⊕ *danitours.mx/croc.html.*

##  Beaches

As in most of the Costalegre area, the sights not to miss in Tenacatita Bay are its natural wonders. Tamarindo Beach, La Manzanilla, Boca de Iguanas, Punta Serena, Tenacatita, and El Tecuan are the most impressive beaches in the area.

## Did You Know?

Many travelers choose to skip captive dolphin swims due to the practice's ethical implications. In Puerto Vallarta, alternative options include wild dolphin swims and boat-based dolphin-watching tours —low impact on the dolphins and high impact on the participant.

Sierra de Manantlán Biosphere Reserve covers more than 12,000 hectares and is home to almost 3,000 plant species. Cuixmala is another environmental reserve in the area with jungle, lagoons, creeks and beaches.

**Playa Boca de Iguanas**

**BEACH—SIGHT** | **FAMILY** | This beach of fine gray-blond sand is wide and flat, and it stretches for several kilometers. Gentle waves make it suitable for swimming, boogie boarding, and snorkeling, but beware the undertow. It's a great place for jogging or walking on the beach. The place goes completely bananas every year during one weekend in August when the International Beach Festival Boca de Iguanas takes place. **Amenities:** food and drink; parking (no fee); showers; toilets; lifeguards. **Best for:** swimming; snorkeling; surfing; partiers. ✉ *Costalegre.*

**Playa El Tamarindo**

**BEACH—SIGHT** | This long beach of dark brown sand has a pier and not much more. It's semi-private as access is restricted to some of the most exclusive resorts in the area, and for that same reason it has become very popular among boat owners who come to enjoy its green emerald waters and unique beauty. **Amenities:** none. **Best for:** solitude; swimming; walking; sunset. ✉ *Costalegre.*

**Playa La Manzanilla**

**BEACH—SIGHT** | **FAMILY** | Informal hotels and restaurants are interspersed between small businesses and modest houses along the town's main street. The bay is calm and beautiful. At the beach road's north end, gigantic, rubbery looking crocodiles lie heaped together just out of harm's way in a mangrove swamp. The fishing here is excellent; boat owners on the beach can take you out for snapper and sea bass for $20 an hour. **Amenities:** food and drink; parking (no fee). **Best for:** swimming; walking; sunset. ✉ *Costalegre.*

**Playa La Morita**

**BEACH—SIGHT** | **FAMILY** | Near the north end of Playa Tenacatita, this pretty stretch of sand has a coral reef close to the beach, making it an excellent place to snorkel. Local fishermen take interested parties out on their boats, either fishing for tuna, dorado, or bonita or searching for wildlife such as dolphins and turtles. **Amenities:** food and drink; parking (no fee). **Best for:** snorkeling; swimming; walking. ✉ *Costalegre.*

**Playa Tenacatita**

**BEACH—SIGHT** | **FAMILY** | Dozens of identical seafood shacks line the shore; birds cruise the miles of beach, searching for their own fish. The water is sparkling blue. There's camping for RVs and tents at Punta Hermanos, where the water is calm and good for snorkeling, and local men offer fishing excursions ($40–$50 for one to four people) and tours of the mangroves ($20). **Amenities:** food and drink; parking (no fee); water sports. **Best for:** swimming; snorkeling; walking. ✉ *Costalegre.*

## 🍴 Restaurants

All the beach restaurants in Tenacatita have been demolished due to ownership disputes, but recently the restaurants beyond the beach area have been allowed to leave menus so that visitors can call and have food delivered to the beach. Take into consideration that there are no bathrooms at the beach. There are more dining options in La Manzanilla where beachside palapas offer all types of food.

**Magnolia's Kitchen & Drinks**

**$$** | **INTERNATIONAL** | Magnolia's serves seafood with a twist, and other types of cuisine. The open-air second floor is great for a romantic dinner. **Known for:** mezcal tastings; delicious flourless dark chocolate cake; American-owned. [$] *Average main: 120 MP* ✉ *Playa Blanca 43, Costalegre* ☎ *315/351–5114* 🌐 *facebook.*

*com/magnoliaslamanzanilla* ⏲ *Closed Fri.–Sun. No lunch.*

**Martin's**

$$ | **SEAFOOD** | **FAMILY** | Located in La Manzanilla, Martin's is one of the best restaurants by the beach in all the Tenacatita area. You can tell that the chef of this place goes the extra mile to serve more sophisticated seafood dishes than the other restaurants in town. **Known for:** great Caesar salad; flaming Monte Cristo coffee; live music on weekend nights. [$] *Average main: 100 MP* ✉ *Playa Blanca 70, Costalegre* ☎ *315/351–7315.*

**Restaurant Mia**

$$ | **SEAFOOD** | Set right on Boca de Iguanas beach, this restaurant serves the typical seafood dishes of the region. Breakfast and burgers are also available. **Known for:** quesadillas de camarón (shrimp quesadillas); great shrimp burger; has a beach and pool. [$] *Average main: 145 MP* ✉ *Playa Boca de Iguanas, Costalegre* ☎ *315/114–3901* 💳 *No credit cards.*

## Hotels

Due to some ownership disputes accommodation options have been limited but there are still pleasant lodgings available. Los Angeles Locos is one of the bigger hotels currently operating in the area, and Chantli Mare is a perfect option for visitors looking for more personal attention and service.

**Chantli Mare**

$$ | **B&B/INN** | This small inn by the sea is quite charming. **Pros:** beachfront; swimming pool; gourmet menu. **Cons:** not much to do; no gym; room terraces lack privacy. [$] *Rooms from: $150* ✉ *Carr. Manzanillo - Puerto Vallarta , Boca de Iguanas, Costalegre* ☎ *315/107–9957* 🌐 *chantlimare.com* 🛏 *6 rooms* 🍴 *Free Breakfast.*

**Coconuts by the Sea**

$$ | **B&B/INN** | A couple of friendly American expats run this charming cliff-top hideaway with gorgeous views of the ocean and Boca de Iguanas Beach below. **Pros:** homey apartments; great sea views; very nice beaches on Tenacatita Bay. **Cons:** its few rooms make last-minute reservations unlikely; long downhill walk to the beach; car is almost a must unless you're staying put. [$] *Rooms from: $150* ✉ *Playa Boca de Iguanas, Costalegre* ☎ *315/104–5014, 949/945–7465 in U.S. or Canada* 🌐 *www.coconutsbythesea.com* 🛏 *4 rooms* 🍴 *No meals.*

**Hotel Los Angeles Locos**

$$$ | **ALL-INCLUSIVE** | **FAMILY** | This old-school resort was recently transformed back into a trendy destination among mostly Mexican tourists. **Pros:** all rooms enjoy ocean views (full or partial); three tennis courts; theater and disco on-site. **Cons:** outdated design; no Wi-Fi in rooms; can get noisy at times. [$] *Rooms from: $150* ✉ *Carr. Puerto Vallarta - Manzanillo Km 20, Costalegre* ☎ *315/351–5020* 🌐 *hotellosangeleslocos.com* 🛏 *204 rooms* 🍴 *All-inclusive.*

**Hotel Punta Serena**

$$$ | **RESORT** | Perched on a beautiful headland, "Point Serene" enjoys balmy breezes and life-changing views from the infinity hot tub. **Pros:** gorgeous views from every room; temazcal (shaman-led steam healing ceremony); no kids. **Cons:** remote location; limited menu; cobblestone walkways and hills make walking difficult for some folks. [$] *Rooms from: $175* ✉ *Carr. Barra de Navidad- Puerto Vallarta (Carretera 200), Km 20, Costalegre* ✈ *196 km (122 miles) south of Puerto Vallarta, 20 km (12 miles) north of Barra de Navidad* ☎ *315/351–5020* 🌐 *hotelpuntaserena.com* 🛏 *24 rooms* 🍴 *All-inclusive.*

# 🏃 Activities

Water sports are the most popular activity in the area. Snorkeling, diving, and boogie boarding are recommended due to calm waters, "The Aquarium" at Playa Mora being the most famous spot. In La Manzanilla, you can rent a *panga* (small boat) and do a mangrove tour or go sport fishing with a guide. Some hotels offer golf, horseback riding, yoga, and kayaking.

**Caballos Aldo**
ECOTOURISM | Aldo organizes private horseback riding tours from La Manzanilla, Boca de Iguanas, and Melaque. ✉ *San Patricio–Melaque* ☎ *315/112–1194, 315/114–0794.*

# Barra de Navidad

*42 km (26 miles) south of Tenacatita Bay.*

Barra de Navidad is the biggest urban development in Costalegre. It offers all types of accommodations, including the exclusive Grand Bay Hotel, as well as plenty of palapa restaurants. In many of them you will be able to choose the fish you want for lunch from the restaurant's pools. A traditional pineapple filled with shrimp is a delicious must-have after a stroll down the local malecón.

## GETTING HERE AND AROUND

Barra de Navidad is the biggest town in Costalegre. It is only 60 km (37 miles) north of Manzanillo and 216 kilometers (134 miles) south of Puerto Vallarta. By car, you will get there in less than an hour from Manzanillo, but the drive from Puerto Vallarta will take almost four hours. Barra de Navidad is also easily available by bus from Guadalajara and the cost for a four-hour ride is around $35.

You can walk the length of the town in about 10 minutes. The main streets of Morelos and Veracruz have the most popular hotels and restaurants, and the beachside street Legazpi is also full of hotels, restaurants, and bars. There is a taxi rank at the corner of Legazpi and Sinaloa Street.

## TOURS

There are a few tour companies operating in Barra de Navidad or outside that offer exploring this fishing town and its surroundings. There are bike, ATV, and boat tours to visit the area, and many companies offer all types of activities in Barra and surroundings.

**Ecojoy Adventures**
ADVENTURE TOURS | Based in Barra de Navidad, Ecojoy Adventures offers a wide array of tours and services, including kayak tours, stand-up paddleboard lessons and tours, zip-line tours, horseback riding, bike tours, and even pet-friendly transportation services. Prices vary depending on the number of persons in your party and activities, but are on par with other outfitters in the region. Check their Facebook page for the most up-to-date pricing information. ✉ *Costa Occidental 13, Esq. Av. Veracruz, Barra de Navidad* ☎ *315/100–9240* ⊕ *ecojoyadventures.com.*

**Flip Flop Nomad Tours**
SPECIAL-INTEREST | Besides the great name, Flip Flop Nomad Tours has a unique offering of cultural day and multiday trips around Costalegre and other parts of Mexico. A refreshing option that stays away from the typical beach and adventure kind of tours, providing a different perspective of the region. Tours start around $70 per person for day tours. ✉ *Benito Juárez 71, San Patricio–Melaque* ☎ *315/355–9037* ⊕ *flipflopnomads.com.*

**The Only Tours Costalegre**
EXCURSIONS | One of the most renowned tour operators in the region, The Only Tours Costalegre have been offering day trips through this multidestination since 1997. From ATVs to snorkeling, to bird-watching and city tours to Puerto

Vallarta, Guadalajara, and Colima, this expat-owned company provides quality service. Contact owner for pricing. ✉ *Priv. Las Cabañas Lote 26, San Patricio–Melaque* ☎ *.315/355–6777* ⊕ *theonlytours. com.*

### VISITOR INFORMATION

**CONTACT Visitor's Information Center Costalegre.** ✉ *Av. Veracruz 98, Barra de Navidad* ☎ *800/849–0322 toll-free in Mexico, 315/355–5100* ⊕ *costalegre.com.*

##  Beaches

The Malecón is a good point to start to get the panoramic views of the bay. There is a centennial monument that commemorates the discovery of the Philippines by a Spanish expedition that departed from Barra de Navidad in 1554, and the "Nereida Triton" sculpture. A walk across the Legazpi street is excellent for shopping and experiencing the town vibe. The main attraction of Barra is its beach, but it can get very noisy. The waves are strong, making it excellent for surfing but not very safe for swimming. The downtown area gets busier in the evenings and there always seems to be some event taking place. There is also a small park "Jardín" between Legazpi and Veracruz streets with food stands and local performers.

### Playa Cuastecomates

**BEACH—SIGHT | FAMILY |** This small beach got the honor of becoming the first inclusivo beach in the Mexican Pacific. You'll see plenty of "floating chairs" for people who need assistance getting into the sea. There are also many non-motorized water sports options such as kayak, pedal boats, or snorkeling. The surrounding mountains give it a touch of mysticism. **Amenities:** food and drink; lifeguards; parking (no fee); toilets; water sports. **Best for:** swimming; snorkeling. ✉ *Costalegre.*

### Playa Melaque

**BEACH—SIGHT | FAMILY |** This long, coarse-white-sand beach is beautiful and has gentle waves. Restaurants, small hotels, homes, and tall palms line the beach, which slopes down to the water. Fishermen here will take anglers out in search of dorado, tuna, swordfish, and mackerel. The best swimming and boogie boarding are about half the length of town, in front of El Dorado restaurant. **Amenities:** food and drink; parking (no fee); water sports. **Best for:** surfing; swimming; snorkeling. ✉ *Costalegre.*

### Playa Navidad

**BEACH—SIGHT |** This is the main beach in Barra de Navidad, and it has a laid-back attitude just like the town where it's located. At any time but high tide you can walk between San Patricio and Barra, a distance of about 5 km (3½ miles). This is a sloping brown-sand beach where surfers look for swells near the jetty, where the sea enters the lagoon of Navidad. **Amenities:** food and drink; parking (no fee); water sports. **Best for:** swimming; surfing; sunset. ✉ *Costalegre.*

## 🍴 Restaurants

In Barra de Navidad there are plenty of street taco stands, beach-view palapa restaurants, lagoon-side eateries, and fine restaurants. Some quaint treasures are hidden in private patios in side streets so don't be afraid to go on your private cuisine exploration.

### ★ Barra Galeria de Arte & Restaurant

**$$$ | MEXICAN FUSION |** An art gallery that doubles as a gourmet restaurant, this place is classy and sophisticated, and as such it takes its time for every little entrée that serves. Usually they open only on Monday, Tuesday, and Thursday 5–10 pm, but during high season they may add an evening or two during the weekend. **Known for:** homemade recipes; art gallery; tequila tastings. Ⓢ *Average main: 185 MP* ✉ *Mazatlan 75, Costalegre*

☎ *315/109–6239* 🌐 *www.barragaleria-dearte.com* ⏲ *No lunch. Closed Wed., Fri.–Sun.*

**Sea Master**

$$ | **SEAFOOD** | Set on the side of Playa Navidad, Sea Master overlooks the Pacific Ocean, the origin of most of its menu. Widely recognized as one of the top restaurants in Barra, this is a place that tries hard to differentiate itself from the rest of seafood restaurants by the beach. **Known for:** gorgeous outdoor terrace overlooking the beach; live music on weekends; Sea Master Roll (fish stuffed with shrimp). [$] *Average main: 140 MP* ✉ *Veracruz 146, Costalegre* ☎ *315/355–8296* 🌐 *facebook.com/SeaMasterenBarra.*

**Simona's Alcatraz Bay**

$$$ | **GERMAN** | Overlooking the Navidad lagoon, Simona's offers a diverse menu enriched with German and Mexican influences. Dishes are always well plated, and the chef really delivers on food quality. **Known for:** beef goulash; lamb osso buco; German owner. [$] *Average main: 160 MP* ✉ *Veracruz 12, Laguna side, Costalegre* ☎ *315/355–8344* 🌐 *facebook.com/SimonaAlcatrazBay* ⏲ *Closed Mon. Closed in summer.*

## Hotels

There are numerous hotels of all types located in Barra de Navidad, as well as private rental villas, houses, beach bungalows, and rooms. The prices start at $23 per night and can go up to $340 for a night at the exclusive Grand Isla Navidad Resort.

**★ Grand Isla Navidad Resort**

$$$ | **RESORT** | Set in the spectacular end of a peninsula, this resort (hands-down the best hotel in the area) overlooks the Pacific Ocean to the west and the Navidad lagoon to the east. **Pros:** yacht rental is an option; three quality restaurants; 27-hole golf course and three tennis courts. **Cons:** pompous atmosphere; spotty Wi-Fi in rooms; unimpressive beach. [$] *Rooms from: $125* ✉ *Circuito de los Marinos s/n, Costalegre* ☎ *314/331–0500* 🌐 *islanavidad.com.mx* 🛏 *199 rooms* 🍴 *Free Breakfast; All-inclusive.*

**La Paloma Oceanfront Retreat**

$$ | **HOTEL** | Rates are reasonable considering these small studio apartments have all the creature comforts of home: the spacious kitchens come with juicers, blenders, toasters, and coffeemakers in addition to stoves and refrigerators; microwaves are available upon request. **Pros:** beside a beautiful bay; long beach perfect for walking and jogging; adults-only during winter. **Cons:** one-week minimum stay in high season; pay cash, Paypal, or bank deposit only; closed in May, Sept., and Oct.. [$] *Rooms from: $119* ✉ *Av. Las Cabañas 13, San Patricio–Melaque, Costalegre* ✥ *6 km (4 miles) north of Barra de Navidad* ☎ *315/355–5345* 🌐 *lapalomamexico.com* 💳 *No credit cards* ⏲ *Closed May, Sept., and Oct.* 🛏 *13 studio apartments* 🍴 *Breakfast.*

## Nightlife

Although Barra is a small town, it does provide nightlife and entertainment. Beach bars, discos, and bars with local Mexican and foreign musicians and bands get busy in high season (October through April), especially around Christmas, Easter, during Fiestas Taurinas in January, and during Jaripeo Carnaval Bailes in February.

**Backstage Bar and Bluewave Cafe**

**BARS/PUBS** | Backstage Bar is one of the few places in Barra where you can listen to great quality live music by Mexican, American, and Canadian artists. It's a popular place for locals, expats, and tourists to hang out (also during the day), as it offers classes and clubs (languages, books, games, etc.). Apart from cocktails and beer you can also got delicious, homemade dishes. ✉ *Av. Miguel López de Legazpi 200b, Barra de Navidad* 🌐 *www.facebook.com/Chynnasplace.*

# Buying a Timeshare

In Puerto Vallarta, timeshare sales-people are as unavoidable as death and taxes, and almost as dreaded. Although a slim minority of people actually enjoy going to one- to four-hour timeshare presentations to get the freebies that range from a bottle of $12 Kahlúa to rounds of golf, car rentals, meals, and shows, most folks find the experience incredibly annoying. For some it even casts a pall over their whole vacation.

The bottom line is, if the sharks smell interest, you're dead in the water. Timeshare salespeople occupy tiny booths up and down main streets where tourists and cruise passengers walk. In general, while *vallartenses* are friendly, they don't accost you on the street to start a conversation. Those who do are selling something. Likewise, anyone calling you *amigo* is probably selling. The best solution is to walk by without responding, or say "No thanks" or "I'm not interested" as you continue walking. When they yell after you, don't feel compelled to explain yourself.

Some sly methods of avoidance that have worked for others are telling the tout that you're out of a job but dead interested in attending a presentation. They'll usually back off immediately. Timeshare people are primarily interested in married couples. But our advice is still to practice the art of total detachment with a polite rejection and then ignore the salesperson altogether if he or she persists.

Even some very nice hotels allow salespeople in their lobbies disguised as the Welcome Wagon or informa-tion gurus. Ask the concierge for the scoop on area activities, and avoid the so-called information desk.

Timeshare salespeople often pressure guests to attend timeshare presenta-tions, guilt-tripping them ("My family relies on the commissions I get," for example) or offering discounts on the hotel room and services. The latter are sometimes difficult to redeem and cost more time than they're worth. And although it may be the salesperson's livelihood, remember that this is your vacation, and you have every right to use the time as you wish.

But if you do return to Puerto Vallarta frequently, a timeshare might make sense. Here are some tips for navigat-ing the treacherous waters:

■ Research before your vacation. Check out resale timeshares in the area, which makes it easier to deter-mine the value of what's offered.

■ Worthwhile timeshares come with the option of trading for a room in another destination. Ask what other resorts are available.

■ Timeshare salespeople get great commissions and are good at their jobs. Be brave, be strong, and sign on the dotted line only if it's what you really want. Remember there are plenty of good vacation deals out there that require no long-term commitment.

■ Buyer's remorse? If you buy a timeshare and want to back out, be aware that most contracts have a five-day "cooling-off period." Ask to see this in writing before you sign the contract; then you can get a full refund if you change your mind.

### Time Out Bar and Grill

**BARS/PUBS** | Time Out Bar and Grill offers live music in high season, usually late November through April, as well as special events. Check the events schedule on their website and buy the tickets early; no standing tickets available. ⊠ *Av. Miguel López de Legazpi 7, Barra de Navidad* ☎ *315/105–0809* ⊕ *timeoutbarandgrill.com.*

##  Shopping

Barra de Navidad is not a big city so don't expect malls and big plazas but it definitely has more shopping options than any other spot in Costalegre. Most of the little shops are located in the main streets of Morelos and Legazpi, where you can buy your groceries, fresh fish and seafood, and some local crafts. There is also a flea market every Thursday. It starts at the main square and goes for three or four blocks.

### Ancestral

**LOCAL SPECIALTIES** | Ancestral sells local handicrafts and 100% Mexican products of Náhuatl (ancient Aztecs) origins. You can even buy beautifully hand-painted bull skulls. From time to time, they also offer workshops, and embroidery, painting, and Náhuatl-language classes. ⊠ *Jalisco 4, Barra de Navidad* ☎ *315/355–0142.*

### Maitl Artesanías

**LOCAL SPECIALTIES** | Maitl Artesanías is a small shop with an eclectic selection of Mexican handicrafts, jewelry, and popular art. They have a variety of silver bracelets and rings with colorful gems and all kinds of pretty unique pieces. ⊠ *Miguel López de Legazpi 54, Barra de Navidad* ☎ *315/103–0652* ⊕ *facebook.com/ MaitlArtesanias.*

##  Activities

The best thing to do in Barra is to walk around, enjoy its food and local laid-back vibe, and admire the ocean views. You can also catch a boat at the pier or malecón and visit the lagoon, or go on a fishing tour. Boca de Iguanas, just 15 minutes away from Barra is a good surfing spot. There is also a golf course at Isla Navidad resort for the ones that look for more exclusive activities, far from the crowd.

Chapter 7

# GUADALAJARA

7

Updated by
Federico Arrizabalaga

| ⊙ Sights | 🍴 Restaurants | 🛏 Hotels | 👜 Shopping | Ⓨ Nightlife |
|:---:|:---:|:---:|:---:|:---:|
| ★★★☆☆ | ★★★★★ | ★★★★★ | ★★★★☆ | ★★★★☆ |

# WELCOME TO GUADALAJARA

## TOP REASONS TO GO

★ **Cultural heritage:** Guadalajara and its state may be the land of tequila and mariachi, but the city is also rich in history and tradition.

★ **Fascinating museums:** While Mexico City may have more museums than Guadalajara, the quality of museums here is right on par.

★ **Delicious food:** Often overlooked, Guadalajara has gifted the world with some of Mexico's most beloved dishes, drinks, and desserts.

★ **Mariachi:** The only thing more Mexican than tequila is the mariachi. Their songs speak about machismo, love, betrayal, death, politics, revolutionary heroes, and even animals.

★ **Great shopping:** Guadalajara is a savvy shopper's paradise. The main handicraft centers of Tlaquepaque and Tonalá feature pottery, hand-blown glassware, jewelry, furniture, and more.

★ **Tequila!:** It originates from the desert town of Tequila, about 45 minutes away from Guadalajara.

**1 Centro Histórico.** Also known as El Centro, it houses the city's biggest attractions including the twin-towered cathedral and the labyrinthine Mercado San Juan de Dios, Latin America's largest indoor market.

**2 Zona Minerva.** Also known as Zona Rosa (Pink Zone), this district west of the Centro Histórico is arguably the pulse of the city. At night a seemingly endless strip of the region's trendiest restaurants and watering holes lights up Avenida Vallarta east of Avenida Enrique Díaz de León. Victorian mansions, art galleries, a striking church, and two emblematic monuments—the Fuente Minerva (Minerva Fountain) and the Monumento Los Arcos—are scattered throughout the tree-lined boulevards.

**3 Tlaquepaque.** Local arts and handicrafts fill the showrooms and stores in this touristy town, where you'll find carved wood furniture, colorful ceramics, and hand-stitched clothing among other goods.

**4 Zapopan.** Mexico's former corn-producing capital is now a municipality of wealthy enclaves, modern hotels, and malls surrounded by hills of poor communities (as is much of metropolitan Guadalajara).

**5 Tequila.** The drive to tequila country is a straightforward and easy trip. Head west from Guadalajara along Avenida Vallarta for about 25 minutes until you hit the toll road junction (it will say Puerto Vallarta Cuota). The whole trip takes about an hour by car.

5 Tequila

15D

Antonio Escobedo  Amatitán

Volcán de Tequila

Ahualulco de Mercado

Guachimontones

4  6

Teuchitlán

Tala

San Nicolas  90

Ahuisculco

San Martín Hidalgo

80

Laguna Atatonilco

Cocula

Protected Area

80

Tecolotlán

Tamazuita

Atemajac de Brizuela

Los Guajes

Chiquilislán

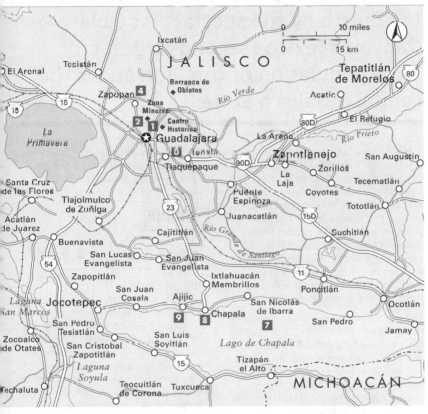

**6 Teuchitlán.** "The Place of the First God," (as Teuchitlán translates) is located within the shadow of the Tequila Volcano, 40 km (25 miles) west of Guadalajara.

**7 Around Lago De Chapala.** Mexico's largest natural lake is a one-hour drive southeast of Guadalajara. Surrounded by jagged hills and serene towns, Lake Chapala is a favorite Tapatío getaway and a haven for thousands of North American retirees.

**8 Chapala.** Chapala was a placid weekend getaway for aristocrats in the late 19th century, but when then-president Porfirio Díaz got in on the action in 1904, other wealthy Mexicans followed suit.

**9 Ajijic.** Ajijic has narrow cobblestone streets, vibrantly colored buildings, and a gentle pace—with the exception of the considerably congested main highway through the town's southern end.

Guadalajara rests on a mile-high plain of the Sierra Madre Occidental, surrounded on three sides by rugged hills and on the fourth by the spectacular Oblatos Canyon. Mexico's second-largest city has a population of 4 million and is the capital of Jalisco State.

This cosmopolitan if traditional and quintessentially Mexican city offers a range of activities. Shop for handicrafts, housewares, and especially fine ceramics in smart shops or family-owned factories. Dress up for drinks, dinner, and dancing in smart Zona Minerva, in downtown Guadalajara, or put on your comfy walking shoes to visit satellite neighborhoods of indigenous origin. For shoppers and metropolis lovers, this is a great complement to a Puerto Vallarta vacation.

The Guadalajara region's must-see sights can be found in four major areas: Guadalajara city itself, Zapopan, Tlaquepaque, and Tonalá. Each can be navigated on foot in a few hours, hitting the major sights, though to get a good feel for these places one must devote at least a day to each, and more to Guadalajara city.

In Guadalajara city, the historic Centro-Histórico houses many of the city's key tourist attractions, but several of the surrounding neighborhoods are also worth a visit. You'll find modern hotels, boutique shops, and some of the city's best cafés, bars, and restaurants in Zona Minerva, due west of the Centro Histórico, Plaza del Sol to the southwest, and Providencia to the northwest. Sample the Zona Minerva district by strolling down the Avenida Juárez–Avenida Vallarta corridor; Avenida Vallarta is shut to vehicular traffic from 8 am to 2 pm every Sunday for Via Recreativa, where locals and tourists gather to walk or bike.

# Planning

## Getting Here and Around

### AIR

Many major airlines fly nonstop from the United States to Guadalajara. Aeropuerto Internacional Libertador Miguel Hidalgo is 16½ km (10 miles) south of the city, en route to Chapala. Autotransportaciones Aeropuerto operates a 24-hour taxi stand with service to any place in the Guadalajara area; buy tickets at the counters at the national and international exits. Some hotels and airlines also offer airport pick-up shuttles; these need to be arranged in advance.

### BUS AND SUBWAY

Flying from your hometown to Guadalajara, then back home from PV can be a good deal; flying round-trip to Guadalajara from Puerto Vallarta is not. The bus is much cheaper, more scenic, and efficient. Luxury buses between PV and Guadalajara take 4½ hours and cost 45–55 USD. With one wide seat on one side of the aisle and only two on the other, ETN is the most upscale line and has about nine trips a day to and from PV, except Sunday, which has only one. Vallarta Plus and Primera Plus are two other very good options, slightly more affordable than ETN. Within Mexico, they accept advance reservations with a credit card. Estrella Blanca is an umbrella of different bus lines, many of which head straight for Guadalajara. TAP (Transportes del Pacifico) is a first-class line that serves major Pacific Coast destinations between Ixtapa/Zihuatanejo and the U.S. border, including service to Guadalajara, Puerto Vallarta, and Tepic. ■TIP→ **Most bus lines accept credit cards when buying at the counter or online.** Guadalajara's Nueva Central Camionera (New Central Bus Station) is 10 km (6 miles) southeast of downtown.

Most city buses (48¢) run from every few minutes to every half hour between 6 am and 9 pm; some run until 11 pm. ■TIP→ **The city's public transit buses are infamously fatal; drivers killed more than 100 pedestrians annually in the late 1990s before the government intervened. These poorly designed, noisy, noxious buses are still driven ruthlessly and cause at least a dozen deaths per year. Fortunately things have improved, and some areas now have new buses with a/c that are operated by trained drivers who have a fixed salary.**

Large mint-green Tur and red Cardinal buses are the safest, quickest, and least crowded and go to Zapopan, Tlaquepaque, and Tonalá for around 10 MXN. Wait for these along Avenida 16 de Septiembre.

Autotransportes Guadalajara–Chapala serves the lakeside towns from Guadalajara's new bus station (Central Camionera Nueva) and from the old bus station (Antigua Central Camionera); the cost is around 4 USD. It's 45 minutes to Chapala and another 15 minutes to Ajijic; there are departures every half hour from 6 am to 9:30 pm. Make sure you ask for

the *directo* (direct) as opposed to the *segunda clase* (second-class) bus, which stops at every little pueblo en route.

Guadalajara's underground *tren ligero* (light rail) system is clean and efficient. Trains run every 10 minutes from 5 am to midnight; a token for one trip costs about 40¢.

## CAR

Metropolitan Guadalajara's traffic gets intense, especially at rush hour, and parking can be scarce. Streets shoot off at diagonals from roundabouts (called *glorietas*), and on main arteries, turns (including U-turns and left turns) are usually made from right-side lateral roads (called *laterales*), which can be confusing for drivers unfamiliar with big city traffic. ■TIP→ **Ubiquitous and inexpensive, taxis and Uber are the best way to go in Guadalajara.**

## TAXI

Taxis are easily hailed on the street in the Centro Histórico, Zapopan, Tlaquepaque, and most other areas of Guadalajara. All cabs are supposed to use meters (in Spanish, *taxímetro*)—you can insist the driver use it or else agree on a fixed price at the outset. Many hotels have rate sheets showing the fare to major destinations and parts of town.

Taxi is the best way to get to Tonalá or Tlaquepaque (about $7). To continue from Tlaquepaque to Tonalá, take a taxi from Avenida Río Nilo southeast directly into town at the intersection of Avenida de los Tonaltecas ($4–$6; 5–10 minutes depending on traffic).

## Visitor Information

**CONTACTS Convention and Visitor Bureau Guadalajara.** ⊠ *Libertad 1725, Col. Americana, Centro Histórico Zapopan* ☎ *33/3122–7544* ⊕ *https://guadalajaramidestino.com/.* **Jalisco State Tourist Office.** ⊠ *Calle Morelos 102, Centro*

*Histórico Zapopan* ☎ *33/3668–1600,*
*01800/363–2200 toll-free in Mexico* ⊕ *vis-*
*ita.jalisco.gob.mx.* **Tlaquepaque Municipal**
**Tourist Office.** ✉ *Calle Morelos 288, top fl.,*
*Tlaquepaque* ☎ *33/1057–6212* ⊕ *www.*
*tlaquepaque.gob.mx/turismo.* **Tourist**
**Board of Zapopan.** ✉ *Av. Hidalgo #151,*
*Zapopan* ☎ *33/3818–2200* ⊕ *www.zapo-*
*pan.gob.mx.*

# When to Go

October to December is hands down the
best time to visit Guadalajara, a city that
can get swelteringly hot in spring and is
prone to heavy rain and flooding in summer. Winter is mild, but if you plan your
Guadalajara travel for autumn, you can
take advantage of the city-wide events
and fiestas that take place.

At roughly 5,100 feet (1500 meter), the
climate in Guadalajara is often described
as mild and springlike for most of the
year. However, with so much sun to go
around, daytime summer temperatures
in Guadalajara quickly rise to 86°F, often
reaching 95°F or more during the months
of April and May. December and January
tend to feature the coldest climate in
Guadalajara and while the temperatures
are still reasonable by day—averaging
around 77°F—they quickly drop sharply
as nighttime approaches, falling to
around 41°F, making packing for winter
travel somewhat tricky.

# Activities

### BIKING
Traffic in Guadalajara has become almost
unmanageable in the past few years, and
citizens have taken to scooters bicycles
(MiBici), and, as of late, electric scooters
like Lime. Fortunately local authorities
have noticed this trend and, seeing its
benefits, have created bicycle lanes
in many areas of the city, particularly
throughout the historical city center.

## GOLF
Golf clubs are less crowded on Wednesday and Thursday. You can rent equipment from a golf club for about $20 to
$30, and golf carts typically cost around
$40. Guadalajara's top golf clubs—El
Cielo and Santa Anita—are technically for
members only, but hotels can get you in.

# Hotels

There are more than 200 hotels in Guadalajara, ranging from basic and cheap
to luxurious, spread throughout the city.
It's best to stay close to where you'll be
spending the most time, as traffic around
the city can get tedious.

### PRICES
*Hotel reviews have been shortened. For*
*full information, visit Fodors.com.*

| What It Costs In U.S. Dollars | | | |
|---|---|---|---|
| $ | $$ | $$$ | $$$$ |
| **FOR TWO PEOPLE** | | | |
| under $25 | $25–$75 | $75–$150 | over $150 |

# Restaurants

*Restaurant reviews have been short-*
*ened. For full information, visit Fodors.*
*com. Restaurant prices are given in MXN*
*unless otherwise noted.*

| What It Costs In MXN | | | |
|---|---|---|---|
| $ | $$ | $$$ | $$$$ |
| **AT DINNER** | | | |
| under 45 MXN | 75–189 MXN | 190–280 MXN | over 280 MXN |

# Tours

The Tapatío Tour is Guadalajara's hop-on/hop-off bus, a convenient way to explore the city without having to rent a car and deal with complicated streets and traffic. Popular, too, are the free walking tours which are a great way to visit the city center on foot and learn about Guadalajara's past, present, and future. The famous Tequila Express train will take you to the town of Tequila where you'll learn and sample about Mexico's most popular export.

### Tapatío Tours

BUS TOURS | FAMILY | The Tapatío Tour is the local answer to hop-on/hop-off sightseeing buses (Tapatío is the name for a Guadalajara local). The double-decker bus stops at many areas within the city and has several packages available. Note that late afternoon showers are common in summer so make sure you're on the lower floor during these months. ⊠ *Av. 16 de Septiembre s/n, Guadalajara* ☎ *333/613–0887* ⊕ *www.tapatiotour.com.mx.*

# Shopping

The Centro Histórico is packed with shops as well as ambulatory vendors, who compete with pedestrians for sidewalk space. You'll find the most products under one roof at labyrinthine Mercado Libertad, one of Latin America's largest markets. Tlaquepaque and Tonalá are arts-and-crafts meccas. Shoe stores and silver shops are ubiquitous in Guadalajara.

Stores tend to open Monday through Saturday from 10 or 11 until 8 pm, and Sunday 10–2 pm; some close during lunch, usually 2–4 or 2–5, and others close on Sunday. Bargaining is customary in Mercado Libertad, and you can talk deals with some crafts vendors in Tlaquepaque and Tonalá. The ticketed price sticks just about everywhere else, with the exception of antiques shops.

Neighborhood street markets, called *tian guis* , also abound in Guadalajara. They take place at various times throughout the week, with a larger share on Sunday morning. Some focus on specific items like antiques or art, but many have a variety of vendors selling everything from chicken, homemade mole sauce, and fruits and vegetables to flowers, clothing, and housewares.

Tonalá's crafts market, Tlaquepaque's crafts and housewares shops, and Mercado Libertad are the region's top marketplaces. Allow yourself plenty of time and energy to explore all. El Trocadero is a weekly antiques market at the north end of Avenida Chapultepec. Feel free to drive a hard bargain.

# Nightlife

With the exception of a few well-established nightspots like La Maestranza, downtown Guadalajara quiets down relatively early. The existing nightlife centers on Avenida Vallarta, favored by the well-to-do under-30 set; Avenida Patria, full of bars for young people who party until early in the morning; or the somewhat seedy Plaza del Sol. Bars in these spots open into the wee hours, usually closing by 3 am. Dance clubs may charge a $15–$20 cover, which includes access to an open bar, on Wednesday and Saturday nights. Dress up for nightclubs; highly subjective admission policies hinge on who you know or how you are dressed (unfortunately). The local music scene is less formal and centers on more intimate digs.

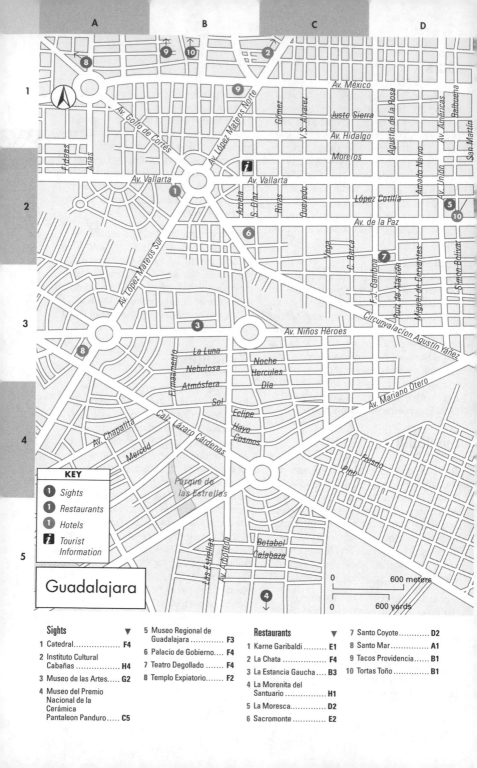

# Guadalajara

### KEY
- ① Sights
- ① Restaurants
- ① Hotels
- 🛈 Tourist Information

### Sights ▼

1 Catedral.................. **F4**

2 Instituto Cultural Cabañas ................. **H4**

3 Museo de las Artes..... **G2**

4 Museo del Premio Nacional de la Cerámica Pantaleon Panduro..... **C5**

5 Museo Regional de Guadalajara ............. **F3**

6 Palacio de Gobierno.... **F4**

7 Teatro Degollado ....... **F4**

8 Templo Expiatorio....... **F2**

### Restaurants ▼

1 Karne Garibaldi ......... **E1**

2 La Chata ................. **F4**

3 La Estancia Gaucha .... **B3**

4 La Morenita del Santuario ................ **H1**

5 La Moresca.............. **D2**

6 Sacromonte ............. **E2**

7 Santo Coyote............ **D2**

8 Santo Mar................ **A1**

9 Tacos Providencia...... **B1**

10 Tortas Toño .............. **B1**

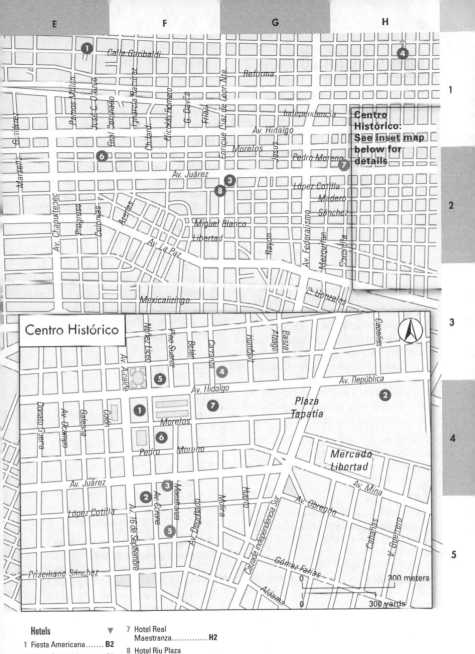

# Centro Histórico

The downtown core is a mishmash of modern and old buildings connected by a series of large plazas, four of which were designed to form a cross when viewed from the sky, with the cathedral in the middle. Though some remain, many colonial-era structures were razed before authorities got serious about preserving them. Conservation laws, however, merely prohibit such buildings from being altered or destroyed; there are no provisions on upkeep, as plenty of abandoned, crumbling buildings indicate.

Must-visit sights include the Palacio de Gobierno and the Instituto Cultural Cabañas; both have phenomenal murals by José Clemente Orozco. Even if you're not in the mood to shop, you should experience the bustling Mercado Libertad. Explore the district in the morning if you dislike crowds; otherwise, you'll get a more immediate sense of Mexico's vibrant culture if you wait for street performers and vendors to emerge around the huge Plaza Tapatía in the afternoon.

Allot at least three hours for the Centro Histórico, longer if you really want to absorb the main sights and stroll along the pedestrian streets.

## SAFETY

As in any major city, be aware of your surroundings, especially late at night. Take extra precautions when in El Centro (as it is also known).

## ◉ Sights

### Catedral
RELIGIOUS SITE | Begun in 1561 and consecrated in 1618, this downtown focal point is an intriguing mélange of baroque, Gothic, and other styles. Its emblematic twin towers replaced the originals, felled by the earthquake of 1818. Ten of the silver-and-gold altars were gifts from King Fernando VII for Guadalajara's financial support of Spain during the Napoleonic Wars. Some of the world's most magnificent *retablos* (altarpieces) adorn the walls; above the sacristy (often closed to the public) is Bartolomé Esteban Murillo's priceless 17th-century painting *The Assumption of the Virgin*. In a loft above the main entrance is a magnificent 19th-century French organ. ⊠ *Av. 16 de Septiembre, between Av. Hidalgo and Calle Morelos, Centro Histórico Zapopan* ☎ *33/3614–5504, 33/3614–3058* 🖭 *Free.*

### ★ Instituto Cultural Cabañas
MUSEUM | FAMILY | Financed by Bishop Juan Ruiz de Cabañas and constructed by Spanish architect-sculptor Manuel Tolsá, this neoclassical-style cultural center, also known as Hospicio Cabañas, was originally opened in 1810 as a shelter for widows, orphans, and the elderly. The Instituto's 106 rooms and 23 flower-filled patios now house art exhibitions. The main chapel displays murals by José Clemente Orozco, including *The Man of Fire*, his masterpiece. In all, there are 57 murals by Orozco, plus many of his smaller paintings, cartoons, and drawings. Kids can marvel at the murals, some which appear as optical illusions, and investigate the labyrinthine compound. The center was named a UNESCO World Heritage Site in 1997. ⊠ *Calle Cabañas 8, Centro Histórico Zapopan* ☎ *33/3668–1645* ⊕ *hospiciocabanas.jalisco.gob.mx* 🖭 *$7; free Tues.* ⊙ *Closed Mon.*

### ★ Museo del Premio Nacional de la Cerámica Pantaleon Panduro
MUSEUM | The museum is named after Pantaleon Panduro, who's considered the father of modern ceramics in Jalisco. On display are prizewinning pieces from the museum's annual ceramics competition, held every June. It's possibly the best representation of modern Mexican pottery under a single roof. You can request an English-speaking guide. ⊠ *Calle Prisciliano Sánchez 191, Guadalajara* ☎ *33/3639–5646* 🖭 *Free.*

**Museo Regional de Guadalajara**

**MUSEUM** | Constructed as a seminary and public library in 1701, this has been the Guadalajara Regional Museum's home since 1918. First-floor galleries contain artifacts tracing western Mexico's history from prehistoric times through the Spanish conquest. Five 19th-century carriages, including one used by General Porfirio Díaz, are on the second-floor balcony. There's an impressive collection of European and Mexican paintings. ✉ *Calle Liceo 60, Centro Histórico Zapopan* ☎ *33/3614–9957* 🎟 *$3.*

**Palacio de Gobierno**

**PUBLIC ART** | The adobe structure of 1643 was replaced with this churrigueresque and neoclassical stone structure in the 18th century. Within are Jalisco's state offices and two of José Clemente Orozco's most passionate murals, both worth the visit alone. One just past the entrance depicts a gigantic Father Miguel Hidalgo looming amid figures representing oppression and slavery. Upstairs, the other mural (look for a door marked "Congreso") portrays Hidalgo, Juárez, and other Reform-era figures. ✉ *Av. Corona 31, between Calle Morelos and Pedro Moreno, Centro Histórico Zapopan* ☎ *33/3614–4038* 🎟 *Free.*

**Teatro Degollado**

**ARTS VENUE** | Inaugurated in 1866, this magnificent theater was modeled after Milan's La Scala. The refurbished theater preserves its traditional red-and-gold color scheme, and its balconies ascend to a multitier dome adorned with Gerardo Suárez's depiction of Dante's *Divine Comedy.* The theater is home to the Jalisco Philharmonic. ✉ *Av. Degollado between Av. Hidalgo and Calle Morelos, Centro Histórico Zapopan* ☎ *33/3614–4773* 🎟 *Free.*

## 🍴 Restaurants

**★ La Chata**

**$$** | **MEXICAN** | At high meal times, travelers will find lines of locals and tourists alike extending out the door of this traditional Mexican restaurant in El Centro. While the decor is plain, the food is the best in the city. **Known for:** queso fundido; enchiladas; second location in West Guadalajara. [$] *Average main: $7* ✉ *Corona 126, between Avs. López Cotilla and Juárez, Centro Histórico Zapopan* ☎ *33/3613–1315* 🌐 *www.lachata.com.mx* 💳 *No credit cards.*

**La Morenita del Santuario**

**$** | **MEXICAN** | **FAMILY** | Tasty traditional Mexican food in a simple family-friendly restaurant is what locals and visitors come here for, and if there's one dish you should try it's the pozole. Prepared in many various ways, it always has to start with hominy and a protein as the base. **Known for:** pozole in three types of broth; traditional Mexican cuisine; suited to groups and families. [$] *Average main: $3* ✉ *Pedro Loza 527B, Guadalajara* ☎ *333/658–0466* 💳 *No credit cards.*

## 🛏 Hotels

**Holiday Inn & Suites Centro Histórico**

**$$** | **HOTEL** | **FAMILY** | This branch of the reliable international chain sits in the heart of historic Guadalajara. **Pros:** helpful business center; free Wi-Fi in rooms and public spaces; some free items in the minibar. **Cons:** small, old gym; no pool. [$] *Rooms from: $84* ✉ *Av. Juárez 211, Centro Histórico Zapopan* ☎ *33/3560–1200* 🌐 *www.holidaycentrogdl.com* 🛏 *45 rooms, 45 suites* 🍽 *No meals.*

**Hotel de Mendoza**

**$$** | **HOTEL** | Elegant with its postcolonial architecture, this hotel is on a calm side street a block from Teatro Degollado. **Pros:** great location; comfortable rooms; great architecture and staff.

**Cons:** standard rooms lack tubs; most rooms don't have balconies, little sound isolation. $ *Rooms from: $75* ✉ *Calle Venustiano Carranza 16, Centro Histórico Zapopan* ☏ *800/361–2600 toll-free in Mexico, 333/942–5151* 🖰 *104 rooms* 🍴 *No meals.*

### ★ Hotel Morales

$$ | **HOTEL** | After being abandoned for 30 years, this downtown hotel—originally a 19th-century rooming house—has been transformed into one of the city's most luxurious lodgings. **Pros:** Wi-Fi in rooms; double-paned windows keep out the noise; superb breakfast (surcharge). **Cons:** lobby restaurant isn't cozy; minor maintenance problems; somewhat dated. $ *Rooms from: $75* ✉ *Av. Ramón Corona 243, Centro Histórico Zapopan* ☏ *33/3658-5232* ⊕ *www.hotelmorales. com.mx* 🖰 *66 rooms* 🍴 *No meals.*

### ★ Hotel Real Maestranza

$$ | **HOTEL** | **FAMILY** | The centrally located Hotel Real Maestranza has a vintage vibe but brand-new rooms. **Pros:** free underground parking; comfortable rooms and pleasant common areas; fantastic breakfast buffet. **Cons:** some rooms may feel on the small side; spotty Wi-Fi; guests should take precaution in the surrounding area at night. $ *Rooms from: $105* ✉ *Calle Francisco Indelecio Madero 161, Guadalajara* ☏ *333/613–6101* ⊕ *realmaestranzahotel.com* 🖰 *78 rooms* 🍴 *No meals.*

##  Nightlife

Plaza de la Liberación is a good place to begin your night out before you move on to other areas of the city.

### ★ I Latina

**BARS/PUBS** | One of Guadalajara's hot spots, I Latina is where you will spot a cool, upscale local and international crowd having cocktails. Their food has long been considered the best cuisine in all of Guadalajara. ✉ *Av. Inglaterra 3128,*

*at López Mateos, Col. Vallarta Poniente, Centro, Guadalajara* ☏ *33/3647–7774* ⊕ *www.ilatinarest.com.*

### La Fuente

**BARS/PUBS** | Appealing and unpretentious, La Fuente opened in this location in 1950. The cantina draws business types, intellectuals, and blue-collar workers, all seeking cheap drinks, animated conversation, and live music. Above the bar, look for an old bicycle. It's been around since 1957, when, legend has it, one of a long list of famous people (most say it was the father of local newspaper Jesús Álvarez del Castillo) left the bike to pay for his drinks. The bar opens at 8—arrive soon after to avoid crowds. ✉ *Calle Pino Suarez s/n, at Hidalgo, Centro Histórico Zapopan* ⊘ *Closed Mon.*

### La Maestranza

**BARS/PUBS** | For some local color, stop at La Maestranza, a renovated 1940s cantina full of bullfighting memorabilia. ✉ *Calle Maestranza 179, between López Cotilla and Madero, Centro Histórico Zapopan* ☏ *33/3613–5878.*

## Did You Know?

In the 1500s, the roof of what would become today's Catedral de Guadalajara was made of thatch. The intervening 500 years brought fires, building relocations, earthquakes, and the reconstructions that come with them—but to what gorgeous architectural ends!

# 🛍 Shopping

Mercado San Juan de Dios (Mercado Libertad) should be your first stop, as it's one of Mexico's (and Latin America's) largest markets. You'll find many items here and food, though you might want to think twice before buying anything to eat. Besides the market there are many jewelry and handicraft shops of interest.

### Ana Lucia Pewter

**CRAFTS** | Ana Lucia Pewter sells beautiful locally made pewter items—from decorative tableware to picture frames— at ridiculously low prices. ⊠ *Calle Ermita 67, Guadalajara* ☎ *33/3683–2794* ⊕ *www. analuciapewter.com* ۞ *Closed Sun.*

### ★ Galería Sergio Bustamante

**ART GALLERIES** | Sergio Bustamante's work is in galleries around the world, but you can purchase his sculptures of human, animal, and fairy-tale creatures in bronze, ceramic, or resin for less at Galería Sergio Bustamante. You'll also find his designs in silver- and gold-plated jewelry. Don't expect a bargain, however; most pieces range from hundreds to thousands of dollars. ⊠ *Calle Independoncia 238, Tlaquepaque* ☎ *33/3639–5519, 33/3639–1272, 33/3659–7110* ⊕ *www. coleccionsergiobustamante.com.mx.*

### Instituto de la Artesanía Jalisciense

**CERAMICS/GLASSWARE** | The government-run Instituto de la Artesanía Jalisciense, on the northeast side of Parque Agua Azul, has exquisite blown glass and hand-glazed pottery typical of Jalisco artisans. Prices are fixed here. ⊠ *Calz. González Gallo 20, at Calz. Independencia Sur, Centro Histórico Zapopan* ☎ *33/3030–9050* ⊕ *www.artesaniasjalisco.gob.mx* ۞ *Closed Sun.*

### Mercado Libertad

**CRAFTS** | Better known as San Juan de Dios, this is one of Latin America's largest covered markets. Its three expansive floors, with shops organized thematically,

tower over downtown's east side. Fluctuating degrees of government intervention dictate the quantity of contraband electronics available. Avoid the food on the second floor unless you have a stomach of iron. Be wary of fakes in the jewelry stores. The market opens Monday–Saturday 10–8, but some stores close at 6; the few shops open on Sunday close by 3. ⊠ *Calz. Independencia Sur; use pedestrian bridge from Plaza Tapatía's south side, Centro Histórico Zapopan* ☎ *333/618–0506.*

# 🏃 Activities

### Atlas Country Club

**GOLF | FAMILY** | Atlas Country Club is an 18-hole, par-72 course designed by Joe Finger and is on the way to the airport. Greens fees are about $92 on weekdays, $104 on weekends and holidays. ⊠ *Carr. Guadalajara–Chapala, Km 6.5, El Salto, Guadalajara* ☎ *333/689–2620* ⊕ *country. atlas.com.mx.*

### El Cielo Country Club

**GOLF | FAMILY** | The private El Cielo Country Club, on a hill outside town, is an 18-hole, 6,765-yard, par-72 course blissfully removed from the city's din and with challenging holes and water features. For nonmembers it's $115 for 18 holes, including cart. ⊠ *Paseo del Cielo 1, Zapopan* ☎ *333/612–3535* ⊕ *www. elcielocc.com.*

# Zona Minerva

Also known as Zona Rosa (Pink Zone), this district west of the Centro Histórico is arguably the pulse of the city. At night a seemingly endless strip of the region's trendiest restaurants and watering holes lights up Avenida Vallarta east of Avenida Enrique Díaz de León. Victorian mansions, art galleries, a striking church, and two emblematic monuments—the Fuente Minerva (Minerva Fountain) and the Monumento Los Arcos—are scattered throughout the tree-lined boulevards.

The best way to get here from the Centro Histórico is by cab or private taxi. Museo de las Artes requires two hours when all its exhibits are open. Budget an hour for the Templo Expiatorio across the street.

### GETTING AROUND

Zona Minerva is easy to walk, but finding a parking spot can prove to be tricky. Once you've parked your wheels you're better off on foot.

## 👁 Sights

Zona Minerva's popularity is owed more to the chic bars, fancy restaurants, and fine shopping rather than cultural attractions. The area is named after the imposing statue of Minerva, the Roman goddess of knowledge, arts, and military strategy. Roughly 8 meters tall, it's in the middle of a large, busy roundabout.

**Museo de las Artes**
**MUSEUM** | The University of Guadalajara's contemporary art museum is in this exquisite early-20th-century building. The permanent collection includes several murals by Orozco. Revolving exhibits have contemporary works from Latin America, Europe, and the United States. ✉ *Av. Juárez 975, Centro Histórico Zapopan* ☎ *33/3134–1664* 🌐 *musa.udg.mx* 🎫 *Free* 🕒 *Closed Mon.*

**Templo Expiatorio**
**RELIGIOUS SITE** | The striking neo-Gothic Church of Atonement is Guadalajara's most breathtaking church. Modeled after Italy's Orvieto Cathedral, it has phenomenal stained-glass windows—observe the rose window above the choir and pipe organ. ✉ *Calle Díaz de León 930, at Av. López Cotilla, Centro Histórico Zapopan* ☎ *33/3825–3410* 🎫 *Free.*

## 🍴 Restaurants

Zona Minerva has many restaurants: simple, trendy, funky... they're all here. Some are easy to find, others require some planning to get to.

**Karne Garibaldi**
**$** | **MEXICAN** | **FAMILY** | In the *1996 Guinness Book of World Records,* this Tapatío institution held the record for world's fastest service: 13.5 seconds for a table of six. Lightning-fast service is made possible by the menu's single item: *carne en su jugo,* a combination of finely diced beef and bacon simmered in rich beef broth and served with grilled onions, tortillas, and refried beans mixed with corn. **Known for:** quick service; multiple locations; one item on the menu. [$] *Average main: $6* ✉ *Calle Garibaldi 1306, Zona Minerva* ☎ *33/3826–1286* 🌐 *www.karnegaribaldi.com.mx.*

**La Estancia Gaucha**
**$$$** | **ARGENTINE** | Guadalajara's gastronomic scene is one of the best in the country and there are many non-Mexican options. One of the best is La Estancia Gaucha, a delicious Argentinian restaurant with decades of success in the city. **Known for:** outstanding cava; steaks; Argentinian cuisine. [$] *Average main: $12* ✉ *Plaza Punto Sao Paulo, Av. de las Américas 1545, Col. Americana* ☎ *33/3817–1808* 🌐 *www.laestanciagaucha.com.mx* 🕒 *No dinner Sun.*

**La Moresca**
**$$$** | **ITALIAN** | While this modern Italian restaurant comes alive at night when it turns into a hip martini bar, don't pass up a meal before partaking in the revelry, it has the best Italian food in town. The twentysomething Tapatíos flock here for delicious pasta and pizza dinners, and stick around for the scene that follows. **Known for:** hip atmosphere; delicious pastas and pizzas; martini bar during later hours. [$] *Average main: $11* ✉ *Av. López Cotilla 1835, Zona Minerva* ☎ *33/3616–8277* 🕒 *Closed Sun.*

**Sacromonte**

$$$ | **MEXICAN** | If you're into trying local favorites, this is the place to order *la lengua*—the beef tongue—or the chicken mole, which has a sweet twist. The pork loin and barbecue ribs are also worth a taste. **Known for:** more tourists than locals; homemade flan; elegant decor. [$] *Average main: $10* ✉ *Pedro Moreno 1398, Col. Americana* ☎ *33/3825–5447* 🌐 *www.sacromonte.com.mx* 🕒 *No dinner Sun.*

**Santo Coyote**

$ | **MEXICAN FUSION** | One of the most sophisticated restaurants in Guadalajara, Santo Coyote offers top-notch Mexican-fusion cuisine, like delicious "tacos el negro" with lobster and traditional Mexican sopa de tortilla. Set in a wide indoor/outdoor space, the atmosphere couldn't be more spectacular with outstanding lighting, a huge palapa, and a beautiful garden. **Known for:** romantic setting; outdoor dining; fusion cuisine. [$] *Average main: $12* ✉ *Calle Lerdo de Tejada 2379, Col. Americana* ☎ *33/3343–2266* 🌐 *santo-coyote.com.mx.*

**Santo Mar**

$$$ | **SEAFOOD** | This elegant seafood restaurant is in the heart of the most exclusive commercial area in Guadalajara. Across the street from Santo Mar you'll find international boutiques such as Burberry, Hugo Boss, Adolfo Domínguez, Lacoste, Tous, and many others. **Known for:** some of the best seafood in Guadalajara; in a food court; upscale dining. [$] *Average main: $12* ✉ *Cento Comercial Andares, Blvd. Puerta de Hierro 4965, Col. Americana* ☎ *33/3611–2866* 🌐 *santomar.com.mx.*

**Tacos Providencia**

$ | **MEXICAN** | A true Tapatío (Guadalajara native) will tell you that these are the best tacos in town. Don't expect anything fancy; it's just a clean and functional taqueria where everything is about those exquisite tacos. **Known for:** local favorite; no-frills taqueria; tacos el pastor. [$] *Average main: $6* ✉ *Rubén Darío 534, Col. Americana* ☎ *33/3641–6049* 🌐 *www.facebook.com/TacosProvidencia* 🕒 *Closed Mon.*

**Tortas Toño**

$ | **MEXICAN** | One of Guadalajara's most famous dishes is the "Torta Ahogada," literally a drowned sandwich. It's a baguette filled with pork meat served in a kind of bowl with lots (and we are talking lots!) of hot tomato sauce on top of it, and Tortas Toño serves the best in town. **Known for:** the best "torta ahogada" in town; great for after a night of drinking; closes daily at 4 pm. [$] *Average main: $4* ✉ *Av. Tepeyac 605, Col. Americana* ☎ *33/3647–6208* 🌐 *www.tortastono.com.mx* 🕒 *No dinner.*

## Hotels

Trendy Zona Minerva has plenty of accommodation options.

**El Tapatío Hotel & Resort**

$$ | **HOTEL** | El Tapatío's colonial-style architecture, country-style design, expansive gardens, and spectacular panoramic views of the city create an unparalleled atmosphere. **Pros:** seven venues on the property for hosting events; close to the airport; swimming pool with a bar. **Cons:** no elevators; older hotel; isolated location. [$] *Rooms from: $60* ✉ *Carr. Chapala Km 6.5, Zona Minerva* ☎ *33/3837–2929, 01800/007–3845 toll-free in Mexico* 🌐 *www.hotel-tapatio.com* 🛏 *123 rooms* 🍴 *No meals.*

**Fiesta Americana**

$$ | **HOTEL** | The dramatic glass facade of this high-rise faces the Minerva Fountain and Los Arcos monument. **Pros:** arresting views from guest rooms; live music in lobby bar nightly; Wi-Fi in rooms. **Cons:** some rooms have unpleasant views of roof and generators; no swimming pool; rooms could use a refresh. [$] *Rooms from: $108* ✉ *Av. Aurelio Aceves 225,*

*Col. Vallarta Poniente, Zona Minerva ☎ 33/3818–1400 🌐 www.fiestamericana.com.mx 🛏 309 rooms 🍴 No meals.*

**Hilton Guadalajara**

**$$$ | HOTEL** | This AAA Four-Diamond award-winning hotel is located within Guadalajara's World Trade Center and just across the street from Expo Guadalajara, the city's convention center. **Pros:** set in the World Trade Center; complimentary Wi-Fi; top-notch spa. **Cons:** far from downtown; Mexican feeling is missing; small swimming pool. [$] *Rooms from: $110 ✉ Av. de las Rosas 2933, Zona Minerva ☎ 33/3678–0505, 33/3678–0511 🌐 www.hilton.com 🛏 450 rooms 🍴 No meals.*

**Hotel Plaza Diana**

**$$ | HOTEL** | At this modest hotel two blocks from the Minerva Fountain, the rooms are on the small side. **Pros:** free Wi-Fi; heated indoor pool; free airport shuttle. **Cons:** gym is on the small side; little water pressure; somewhat outdated. [$] *Rooms from: $83 ✉ Av. Agustín Yáñez 2760, Zona Minerva ☎ 33/3540–9700, 01800/248–1001 toll-free in Mexico 🌐 www.hoteldiana.com.mx 🛏 127 rooms, 24 suites 🍴 No meals.*

**Hotel Riu Plaza Guadalajara**

**$ | HOTEL** | One of the newest and trendiest hotels in the city, Hotel Riu enjoys a great location just one mile away from the Gran Plaza shopping mall and two miles from Expo Guadalajara, the city's convention center. **Pros:** central; great city views; well maintained. **Cons:** corporate atmosphere; noisy area; small pool. [$] *Rooms from: $110 ✉ Av. López Mateos 830, Zona Minerva ☎ 33/3880–7500 🌐 www.riu.com 🛏 550 rooms 🍴 No meals.*

**Quinta Real**

**$$$ | HOTEL** | Stone-and-brick walls, colonial arches, and objets d'art fill this luxury hotel's public areas. **Pros:** elegant rooms; stately grounds; in-room spa services. **Cons:** pricey rates; no on-site spa; some guests mention a slow breakfast. [$] *Rooms from: $160 ✉ Av. México 2727, at Av. López Mateos Norte, Zona Minerva ☎ 33/3669–0600, 866/621–9288 toll-free from U.S., 01800/500–4000 in Mexico 🌐 www.quintareal.com 🛏 76 suites 🍴 No meals.*

**★ Villa Ganz**

**$$$$ | HOTEL** | Staying in this neighborhood full of restaurants and nightlife yet away from the gritty historic center might be just the ticket. **Pros:** spacious rooms; romantic dining area in tree-shaded garden; great location. **Cons:** suites must be paid in full when booked; high-season cancellations charged 100% of room fee as well as tax; faulty Wi-Fi. [$] *Rooms from: $250 ✉ Av. López Cotilla 1739, Zona Minerva ☎ 33/3120–1416 🌐 www.villaganz.com 🛏 9 suites 🍴 Free Breakfast.*

## 🍸 Nightlife

This is perhaps one of the most bustling areas in the city at night, and close to the equally popular Avenida Chapultepec. Tons of restaurants and bars to choose from make it an ideal location for a night out, where you don't have to plan ahead. Just grab a taxi to the Zona Rosa (Pink Area, where the LGBT community tends to gather) and walk around until you find a restaurant or bar that suits your fancy.

**Kin Kin**

**DANCE CLUBS** | This underground club—it's literally in a basement—plays house and electronic music until the wee hours of the morning. Patrons love the unpretentious vibe and music, though drink prices are somewhat steep. *✉ Av. Mexico 2981 ☎ 331/075–4528 ☞ Closed Sun.–Tues.*

# Live Performance

**Plaza de Armas** The State Band of Jalisco and the Municipal Band sometimes play at the bandstand on Tuesdays around 6:30 pm. ⊠ *Av. Corona between Calle Morelos and Pedro Moreno, across from Palacio de Gobierno, Centro Histórico Zapopan.*

Small, triangular Plaza de los Mariachis, south of the Mercado Libertad, was once the ideal place to tip up a beer and experience mariachi, the most Mexican of music, at about $15 a pop. Now boxed in by a busy street, a market, and a run-down neighborhood, it's safest to visit in the day or late afternoon.

For about the same amount of money but a more tourist-friendly atmosphere, mariachis at El Parián, in Tlaquepaque, will treat you to a song or two as you sip margaritas at this enormous, partly covered conglomeration of 17 cantinas running diagonally from the town's main plaza. Once a marketplace dating from 1883, it has traditional *cazuela* drinks, which are made of fruit and tequila and served in ceramic pots.

**Ballet Folclórico de la Universidad de Guadalajara** After a brief stint at the newer Teatro Diana, the internationally acclaimed Ballet Folclórico of the University of Guadalajara has returned to perform its traditional Mexican folkloric dances and music in the Teatro Degollado most Sundays at 12:30 pm; tickets are $7–$30. ⊠ *Calle Belén s/n, Guadalajara* ☎ *33/3614–4773* ⊕ *www.ballet.udg.mx.*

**Orquesta Filarmónica de Jalisco** Though it's among Mexico's most poorly paid orchestras, the state-funded philharmonic manages remarkably good performances (usually pieces by Mexican composers mixed with standard orchestral fare). When in season (it varies), the OFJ performs Sunday afternoon and Wednesday and Friday evening at Teatro Delgollado. On the facing plaza, they hold an annual outdoor performance that helps kick off September's Mariachi Festival. ⊠ *Calle Belen at Morelos, Teatro Degollado, Guadalajara* ☎ *33/3030–9772* ⊕ *www.ofj.com.mx* ▨ *From $8.*

**Mazabel**

**BARS/PUBS** | This bar is most frequently visited by the lesbian community but everyone is welcome. Patrons love the decor, excellent drinks, and superb vibe it exudes. ⊠ *Av. Chapultepec Sur 480* ☎ *333/830–2185* ☞ *Closed Mon.*

 Shopping

Trendy Zona Minerva is one of the best places in the city if you want to walk around aimlessly hoping to find the perfect shop for whatever you don't know you are looking for until you find it. Handicrafts, clothing, books, and just about

anything coexist in this part of town. It might just take you a bit longer than what you want because of the walking, and the fantastic cafés that you'll stumble upon along the way.

**Galeria del Calzado**

**SHOES/LUGGAGE/LEATHER GOODS** | **FAMILY** | This medium-size mall is devoted exclusively to shoes. Most of them are from mid- and top-tier brands, though some deals are to be found. ⊠ *Av. Mexico 3225, Guadalajara* ☎ *33/3647–6422* ⊕ *www.galeriadelcalzado.com.mx.*

## Pandora

**JEWELRY/ACCESSORIES** | This highly popular jewelry store has a branch in the middle of the Minerva area. You'll find a bit of everything here, as well as hefty price tags. ✉ *Av. Adolfo López Mateos #2405, Guadalajara* ☎ *333/113–5687* ⊕ *stores. pandora.net.*

# Tlaquepaque

Local arts and handicrafts fill the show-rooms and stores in this touristy town, where you'll find carved wood furniture, colorful ceramics, and hand-stitched clothing among other goods. Pedestrian malls and plazas are lined with more than 300 shops, many run by families with generations of experience. One of Guadalajara's most exceptional muse-ums, which draws gifted artists for its annual ceramics competition in June, is also here.

But there's more to Tlaquepaque than shopping. The downtown area has a pleasant square and many pedestrian-on-ly streets, making this a good place to take a stroll, even if you're not interested in all the crafts for sale. There are several good restaurants, some with outdoor seating perfect for people-watching.

■**TIP➔ Many tourists come to Tlaquepaque via the Tapatío Tour, an open-air bus that leaves from Guadalajara's historic center.**

## GETTING AROUND

Getting around Tlaquepaque is easier on foot than it is with wheels. Besides it being a traffic-heavy area, the relatively large pedestrian only area is one of the main attractions. Plan on parking your car away from what your final destination will be, or even better get here with a public or private taxi.

## QUICK BITES

Chiles & Beer ✉ *Calle Donato Guerra 165* serves quick (or not) meals throughout the day, to be washed down with—you guessed it—beer. Their burgers are big and tasty, but it's the seafood that stands out, particularly the *aguachile*, a type of Mexican ceviche that hails from Sinaloa. The most classic version is made with fresh raw shrimp or fish, cucumber, red onion, lime juice, and chilies (typically serranos or jalapeños) that have been pulverized with water—hence the name. It's usually served with avocado and *tostadas*, and is a popular snack with beer and tequila.

## SAFETY

The streets in Tlaquepaque are busy at all times, and minor theft is common. Don't flash jewelry and expensive paraphernalia and you'll be fine.

##  Sights

Tlaquepaque is all about walking around, immersing yourself in the local scene and taking things as they come. Cultural attractions are lacking in this part of town, although the Regional Ceramic Museum is indeed fantastic.

### Museo Regional de la Cerámica

**MUSEUM** | The frequently changing exhibits at the Regional Museum of Ceramics are in the many rooms surrounding a central courtyard. Track the evolution of ceramic wares in the Atemajac Valley during the 20th century. The presentation isn't always strong, but the Spanish-lan-guage displays discuss six common pro-cesses used by local ceramics artisans, including *barro bruñido*, which involves polishing large urns with smoothed chunks of the mineral pyrite. Items in the gift shop are surprisingly uninterest-ing. ✉ *Calle Independencia 237, at Calle Alfareros, Tlaquepaque* ☎ *33/3635–5404* ⊕ *www.artesanias.jalisco.gob.mx* ✆ *Free* ☉ *Closed Mon.*

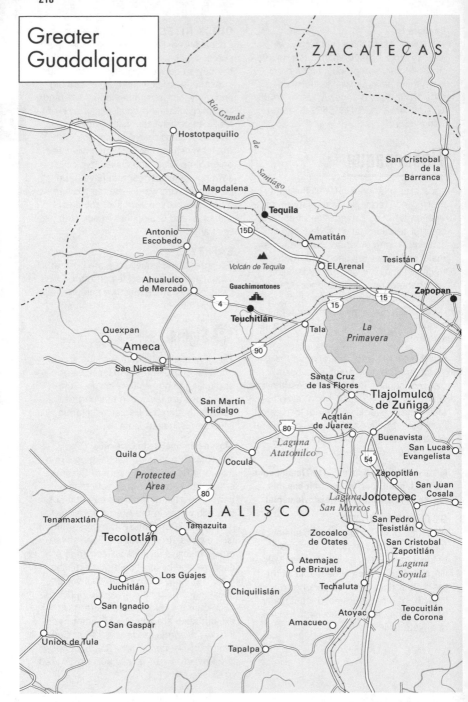

# Greater Guadalajara

ZACATECAS

Río Grande de

Santiago

Hostotpaquilio

San Cristobal de la Barranca

Magdalena

Tequila

Antonio Escobedo

15D

Amatitán

Tesistán

Volcán de Tequila

El Arenal

Ahualulco de Mercado

Guachimontones

Zapopan

4

Teuchitlán

15

15

Quexpan

Tala

La Primavera

Ameca

90

San Nicolas

Santa Cruz de las Flores

Tlajolmulco de Zuñiga

San Martín Hidalgo

Acatlán de Juárez

80

Buenavista

San Lucas Evangelista

Laguna Atatonilco

Quila

54

Cocula

Zapopitlán

Protected Area

San Juan Cosala

80

JALISCO

Laguna San Marcos

Jocotepec

Tenamaxtlán

San Pedro Tesistlán

Tamazuita

Zocoalco de Otates

Tecolotlán

San Cristobal Zapotitlán

Atemajac de Brizuela

Laguna Soyula

Los Guajes

Techaluta

Juchitlán

Chiquilislán

San Ignacio

Atoyac

Teocuitlán de Corona

San Gaspar

Amacueo

Union de Tula

Tapalpa

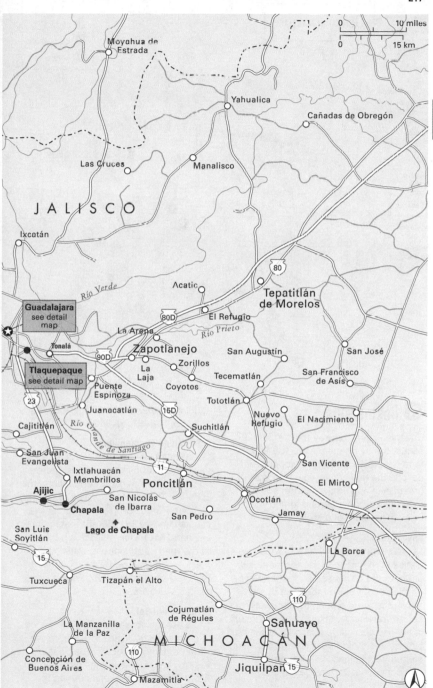

0          10 miles
0          15 km

Moyahua de
Estrada

Yahualica

Cañadas de Obregón

Las Cruces

Manalisco

J A L I S C O

Ixcatán

Río Verde

Acatic

80

Tepatitlán
de Morelos

Guadalajara
see detail
map

80D

El Refugio

Río Prieto

La Arena

Tonalá

90D

Zapotlanejo

San Augustín

San José

Tlaquepaque
see detail map

La
Laja

Zorillos

Tecematlán

San Francisco
de Asís

23

Puente
Espinoza

Coyotos

Tototlán

Juanacatlán

16D

Cajititlán

Río Grande de Santiago

Suchitlán

Nuevo
Refugio

El Nacimiento

San Juan
Evangelista

11

Ixtlahuacán
Membrillos

Poncitlán

San Vicente

El Mirto

Ajijic

San Nicolás
de Ibarra

Ocotlán

Chapala

San Pedro

Jamay

San Luis
Soyitlán

Lago de Chapala

15

La Barca

Tuxcueca

Tizapán el Alto

110

Cojumatlán
de Régules

Sahuayo

La Manzanilla
de la Paz

M I C H O A C Á N

Concepción de
Buenos Aires

110

Jiquilpan

15

Mazamitla

**Sights** ▼

1 Museo Regional de la Cerámica ... C3

**Restaurants** ▼

1 Casa Fuerte ....... C3

2 El Parián de Tlaquepaque ....... D4

3 El Rincón del Sol....... D5

**Hotels** ▼

1 El Tapatío Hotel & Resort....... B5

2 La Casa del Retoño ...... C4

3 La Villa del Ensueño..... B2

4 Quinta Don José.... C4

# 🍴 Restaurants

Cheap eats are the way to go in Tlaquepaque, but by no means will you find the food here lacking. Quite the opposite: despite the low prices, you'll discover great flavor and an even better environment; just wander around to find your culinary treasure of the day.

### Casa Fuerte

**$$** | **MEXICAN** | Relax with tasty Mexican dishes at the tables along the sidewalk or under the palms and by the fountain on the patio. You'll be tempted by the tables scattered around the sidewalk, but before you decide, take a peek at those in the oversize garden patio surrounding a magnificent old tree. **Known for:** chicken stuffed with huitlacoche; live music; outdoor dining. [$] *Average main: $13* ✉ *Calle Independencia 224, Tlaquepaque* ☎ *33/3639–6481, 33/3639–6474.*

### El Parián de Tlaquepaque

**$$** | **MEXICAN** | If you are looking for a traditional Mexican experience, there's no better place to go in Tlaquepaque than El Parián. This is not actually a restaurant but a large complex with a central patio shared by 18 different restaurants and bars. **Known for:** mariachis perform all day; party atmosphere; traditional Mexican experience. [$] *Average main: $6* ✉ *Calle Independencia 22, Tlaquepaque* ☎ *33/3330–5136.*

### El Rincón del Sol

**$** | **MEXICAN** | A covered patio invites you to sip margaritas while listening to live *trova* (romantic ballads). Musicians play Tuesday to Friday evenings between 7 and 9, and on weekends during the leisurely lunch hour (roughly 3 to 5). **Known for:** chiles en nogada; friendly staff; live music. $\boxed{\$}$ *Average main: $7* ⊠ *Av. 16 de Septiembre 61, Tonalá* ☎ *33/3683–1989, 33/3683–1940.*

##  Hotels

Tlaquepaque is far from being a destination for overnight stays. There are some conventional options should you choose to stay here, but no luxury properties.

### La Casa del Retoño

$$ | **B&B/INN** | On a quiet street several blocks from the shopping district is this B&B with clean and cheerful rooms overlooking a garden. **Pros:** quiet neighborhood; private terraces in some rooms; homey feeling. **Cons:** smallish rooms; lackluster garden; no a/c. $\boxed{\$}$ *Rooms from: $50* ⊠ *Matamoros 182, Tlaquepaque* ☎ *33/3639–6510, 33/3635–7636* ⊕ *www.lacasadelretono.com.mx* ↪ *9 rooms* ▯◎▮ *Free Breakfast.*

### La Villa del Ensueño

$$ | **B&B/INN** | A 10-minute walk from Tlaquepaque's center, this intimate B&B is near lots of shopping. **Pros:** hot tub; take-out food available from adjacent Mexican restaurant; friendly staff. **Cons:** only junior suites have bathtubs; no a/c; basic rooms. $\boxed{\$}$ *Rooms from: $95* ⊠ *Florida 305, Tlaquepaque* ☎ *33/3635–8792* ⊕ *www.villadelensueno.com* ↪ *20 rooms* ▯◎▮ *Free Breakfast.*

### Quinta Don José

$$$ | **B&B/INN** | One block from Tlaquepaque's main plaza and shopping area, this B&B has rooms of varying sizes and degrees of natural light; suites are spacious and face out to the pool. **Pros:** friendly bilingual staff; hearty continental breakfast; free Wi-Fi. **Cons:** pool is chilly; some rooms are small; traditional stoic Mexican decor. $\boxed{\$}$ *Rooms from: $100* ⊠ *Calle Reforma 139, Tlaquepaque* ☎ *33/3635–7522, 01800/700–2223*

*toll-free in Mexico, 866/629–3753 in U.S. and Canada* ⊕ *www.quintadonjose.com* ↪ *18 rooms* ▯◎▮ *Free Breakfast.*

##  Shopping

There are many boutique shops selling arts and crafts in Tlaquepaque. Some sell exclusive designs while others offer more common, but high-quality Mexican arts and crafts. This is not the place to hunt for bargains, but you will find quality and authenticity. Artesanías (*pottery*) are everywhere and make excellent souvenirs. A good place to start is the Mercado de Artesanías, which despite not offering the lowest prices, will allow you to get a feel for what you may be looking to get.

### Del Corazón de la Tierra

**LOCAL SPECIALTIES | FAMILY |** Excellent art pieces made by indigenous craftspeople are for sale here, including sculptures, paintings, and more. The art pieces are purchased by the store owners in small villages in the mountains and brought here for sale. ⊠ *Independencia 227, Guadalajara* ☎ *333/657–5682* ⊕ *delcorazondelatierra.mx.*

### Plaza de Artesanías

**LOCAL SPECIALTIES | FAMILY |** Handicraft markets are one of the best places to buy authentic local art and souvenirs at great prices. You can often bargain at this small market filled with great artwork and gifts. ⊠ *Calle Juárez 145, Centro, Guadalajara* ☎ *333/657–4595.*

# Zapopan

Mexico's former corn-producing capital is now a municipality of wealthy enclaves, modern hotels, and malls surrounded by hills of poor communities (as is much of metropolitan Guadalajara). Farther out, some farming communities remain. The central district, a good 25-minute cab ride from downtown Guadalajara, has two worthwhile museums, an aged church that's home to the city's most revered religious icon, and a pedestrian corridor punctuated by restaurants and watering holes popular with young Tapatíos.

### GETTING AROUND

Zapopan is a big area, and getting around is probably done best by taxi as public buses can be confusing. If you're planning on renting a car note that there are many one-way streets, and parking in some areas can be complicated.

### QUICK BITES

It's difficult to beat Cerveceria Chapultepec (✉ *Av. Guadalupe 1606 in Chapalita*) when it comes to finding a place for a quick snack and something to wash it down. Open throughout the day you'll find tacos, desserts, and many beers, and everything costs 20 MXN.

### SAFETY

Zapopan is generally very safe during the day, but once the sun sets some areas require that you stay alert. In recent years there has also been an increase in narcotics-related theft and crime, thus getting around with Uber (better than a taxi) is recommended—unless the taxi is a hotel partner.

## 👁 Sights

The word Zapopan derives from Nahuatl and means place of *zapotes* (any soft, edible fruit), and is one of the most touristy municipalities of Jalisco because of its strong religious, gastronomic, and historical attractions. You'll need about a day to visit every one of them, but it's better to give yourself even more time to linger and enjoy the local food and culture.

**Basílica de Zapopan**

**RELIGIOUS SITE** | This vast church with an ornate plateresque facade and *Mudejar* (Moorish) tile dome was consecrated in 1730. It's home to the Virgin (or Our Lady) of Zapopan: a 10-inch-high, corn-paste statue venerated as a source of many miracles. Every October 12 more than a million people crowd the streets around the basilica, where the Virgin is returned after a five-month tour of Jalisco's parish churches. It's an all-night fiesta capped by an early-morning procession. ✉ *Av. Hidalgo at Matamoros, Zona Zapopan Norte* ☎ *33/3633–6614* 🎟 *Free.*

**Museo de Arte de Zapopan**

**MUSEUM** | Better known by its initials, MAZ, the large and modern Art Museum of Zapopan is Guadalajara's top contemporary-art gallery. The museum regularly holds expositions of distinguished Latin American painters, photographers, and sculptors, as well as occasional international shows. ✉ *Andador 20 de Noviembre 166, at Calle 28 de Enero, Guadalajara* ☎ *33/3818–2575* 🌐 *www.mazmuseo.com* 🎟 *Free* 🕒 *Closed Mon.*

**Museo Huichol Wixarica de Zapopan**

**MUSEUM** | The Huichol Indians of northern Jalisco and neighboring states of Zacatecas and Nayarit are famed for their fierce independence and exquisite beadwork and yarn "paintings." This small museum has rather hokey mannequins wearing the intricately embroidered clothing of both men and women. Bilingual placards explain the Huichol religion and worldview. The gift shop sells a small inventory of beaded items, prayer arrows, and god's eyes. ✉ *Calle Eva Briseño 152, Centro Histórico Zapopan* ☎ *33/3636–4430* 🌐 *sc.jalisco.gob.mx/patrimonio/museos/museo-etnografico-huichol-wixarika* 🎟 *10 MXN.*

## 🍴 Restaurants

**Dona Gabina Escolastica**

**$$** | **MEXICAN** | **FAMILY** | Dona Gabina is a local staple. While pozole and enchiladas are among the most popular dishes, nothing on the menu here will disappoint. **Known for:** pozole and enchiladas; repeat customers; long lines. [$] *Average main: $6* ✉ *Javier Mina 237, Zapopan* ☎ *333/833–0883* 🕒 *Closed Mon.*

**La Moresca**
$$$ | **ITALIAN** | La Moresca serves great Italian food in a trendy, upscale setting. Unlike most restaurants in Zapopan, they are open on Sunday. **Known for:** reservations recommended; open on Sunday. [$] *Average main: $8* ✉ *Lopez Cotilla 1835, Guadalajara* ☎ *333/616–0412.*

**Little India Restaurant**
$$ | **INDIAN** | **FAMILY** | This highly acclaimed Indian food restaurant is not to be missed. What it lacks in character it makes up for in cuisine. **Known for:** mango chicken; beef madras; chai tea. [$] *Average main: $6* ✉ *Calle Miguel de Cervantes Saavedra 149, Zapopan* ☎ *333/630–9315* 🌐 *www.littleindia.com.mx* ⏲ *Closed Tues.*

## Hotels

Zapopan is one of the busiest and most popular areas in all Guadalajara, and many choose to stay here because of its central location, proximity to Chapalita, and for the sightseeing. There are many hotels to choose from, from the small and basic to larger, well-known names.

**Hard Rock Guadalajara**
$$$ | **HOTEL** | Chic rooms and a fantastic rooftop pool area are just two of the highlights of this new(ish) hotel in Guadalajara. **Pros:** great view from rooftop pool; new chic rooms; good buffet breakfast. **Cons:** very slow and small elevators; quirky electronics; train can be heard in some rooms at night. [$] *Rooms from: $135* ✉ *Av. Ignacio L. Vallarta 5145, Zapopan* ☎ *800/253–0114* 🌐 *www.hrhguadalajara.com* 🛏 *349 rooms* 🍴 *No meals.*

**Hyatt Regency Guadalajara Andares**
$$$$ | **HOTEL** | **FAMILY** | The modern, spacious rooms and flashy decor of this reputable brand are perfect for both business and leisure travelers. **Pros:** spacious rooms; kid-friendly; great location. **Cons:** mandatory valet parking; room menu lacks variety; service could be better. [$] *Rooms from: $240* ✉ *Blvd. Puerta de Hierro 4965, Guadalajara* ☎ *333/883–1234* 🌐 *www.hyatt.com/en-US/hotel/mexico/hyatt-regency-andares-guadalajara/gdlrg* 🛏 *257 rooms* 🍴 *No meals.*

**One Guadalajara Periférico Poniente**
$$$ | **HOTEL** | Basic but clean and modern rooms make this hotel a great option when on your way across or out of Guadalajara. **Pros:** good suburban location; clean rooms; functional facilities. **Cons:** few extras; lacks charm; small rooms. [$] *Rooms from: $95* ✉ *Periferico Poniente # 7306 Fracc. Ciudad Granja, Guadalajara* ☎ *333/777–9650* 🌐 *www.onehoteles.com/es/web/one-guadalajara-periferico-poniente* 🛏 *121 rooms* 🍴 *Free Breakfast.*

## Nightlife

Nightlife in Zapopan is nothing short of thriving even during working days. From night clubs to karaoke bars, pubs, trendy restaurants with music, there's sure to be something happening whenever you are there. Getting around from one to the other will require a car or taxi, so planning ahead could be wise.

**Barra Bar**
**MUSIC CLUBS** | Similar to their sister property in Puerto Vallarta, this chic, modern club has a live DJ who plays current tracks and some oldies to an audience that spans several generations. ✉ *Pab Av. Acueducto 2380 Loc. F Plaza 9, Guadalajara* ☎ *333/611–0126.*

**La Santa**
**DANCE CLUBS** | This huge nightclub plays music of all kinds (with a focus on house and techno) into the early morning. ✉ *Real de Acueducto 371, Guadalajara* ☎ *331/092–7901* ☞ *Closed Sun.–Wed.*

**Reyes Bar and Grill**
**BARS/PUBS** | Live Mexican music, drinks, and a good vibe are what draws crowds to this bar and grill. They also serve fantastic Mexican food with a modern twist.

# Tonalá

Among the region's oldest pueblos is bustling Tonalá, a unique place filled with artisan workshops small and large. Although it's been swallowed by ever-expanding Guadalajara, Tonalá remains independent and industrious. More geared to business than pleasure, it doesn't have the folksy character of nearby Tlaquepaque. There's a concentration of stores on Avenida Tonalá and Avenida de los Tonaltecas, the main drag into town, and many more shops and factories can be found spread throughout Tonalá's narrow streets. ■TIP➔The town has unusually long blocks, so wear your most comfortable shoes.

While Tonalá and its shops may not be as quaint or as touristy as Tlaquepaque, this is where you'll find the best bargains since most local goods—from furniture to glassware and ceramics—are made here. Most stores are open daily 10–5. On Thursday and Sunday, bargain-price merchandise is sold at a street market (Avenida Tonaltecas at Calle Benito Juárez 45400) packed with vendors from 9 am to 5 pm. Vendors set up ceramics, carved wood sculptures, candles, glassware, furniture, metal crafts, and more. Look for *vajilla* (ceramic place settings), but note that the more high-end ceramic offerings are sold at more formal stores.

✉ *Av. Real de Acueducto s/n, Guadalajara* ☎ *333/499–1859* ⊕ *www.reyescantina. com* ☞ *Closed Sun.–Tues.*

 **Shopping**

In addition to its food, Zapopan is well known for its shopping. Plaza Andares is the biggest with the most options, but there are small shops spread throughout Zapopan carrying everything under the sun.

### Gran Plaza

**SHOPPING CENTERS/MALLS | FAMILY** | Gran Plaza was the biggest shopping name in town until Andares stepped in. This mall carries designer brands with price tags to match. There's a food court and some restaurants, too. ✉ *Av. Vallarta No 3959, Guadalajara* ☎ *333/563–4083* ⊕ *www. lagranplazafashionmall.com.*

### ★ Plaza Andares

**SHOPPING CENTERS/MALLS** | The largest and most modern shopping mall in Guadalajara, Andares carries all styles of clothing in

more than 100 stores, including designer retail shops. Both an indoor and outdoor shopping area, you'll find ice-cream shops and other quick bites, as well as sit-down restaurants along the main entrance. Generally speaking, prices tend to be high here. ✉ *Blvd. Puerta de Hierro 4965, Guadalajara* ☎ *333/648–2280* ⊕ *andares.com.*

# Side Trips from Guadalajara

An hour's drive in just about any direction from Guadalajara will bring you out of the fray and into the countryside. Due south is Lake Chapala, Mexico's largest natural lake. Bordering it are several villages with large expat communities, including Chapala and Ajijic, a village of bougainvillea and cobblestone roads. Tequila, where the famous firewater is brewed, is northwest of Guadalajara. Teuchitlán, south of Tequila, has the Guachimontones Ruins.

The placid lakeside area around Chapala makes for a weeklong (expats would say lifelong) getaway, while Tequila and Teuchitlán are great for day trips.

# Tequila

The drive to tequila country is a straightforward and easy trip. Head west from Guadalajara along Avenida Vallarta for about 25 minutes until you hit the toll road junction (it will say Puerto Vallarta Cuota). The whole trip takes about an hour by car. Take either the toll road (*cuota*) or the free road (*libre*) toward Puerto Vallarta. The toll road is faster, safer, and costs about $10. You can also catch a bus to Tequila from the Antigua Central Camionera (Old Central Bus Station), northeast of the Parque Agua Azul on Avenida Dr. R. Michel, between Calle Los Angeles and Calle 5 de Febrero. Buses marked "Amatitán–Tequila" are easy to spot from the entrance on Calle Los Angeles.

Another option is to take the Tequila Express train from Guadalajara to Tequila and back for about 80 USD. One of the few passenger trains left in Mexico takes guests on an all-day tour starting and ending with free canned-tequila mixed drinks (like *palomas* and *sangrita*), accompanied by mariachi music. Upon arrival in Tequila, the tour takes visitors to a distillery to learn about the process of making the liquor; the day includes tastings at the distillery, a show of traditional Jalisco dancing and music, and a delicious all-you-can-eat-and-drink Mexican buffet.

## GETTING AROUND
Tequila is small enough to walk everywhere, though reaching the agave plantations will require a car or taxi. Most hotels are in the village, but some tequila distilleries have opened hotels, too.

## Tequila Express
One of the very few passenger trains in Mexico, this party train will take you from Guadalajara to Tequila and back in a day (1,300 MXN). It's not only a method of transportation, as you'll get to learn, sample, and drink Tequila for the better part of the day. ☎ *33/3880–9090* ⊕ *www.tequilaexpress.com.mx*.

## QUICK BITES
**Cafe D'Priss** (✉ *v. Av. Sixto Gorjon 141*) offers great coffee and bites for breakfast; their waffles are the best in town. Portions are reasonable and prices are low, making it a favorite among locals and visitors.

#  Sights

### José Cuervo Distillery
**WINERY/DISTILLERY** | Opened in 1/95, the José Cuervo Distillery is the world's oldest tequila distillery. Every day, 150 tons of agave hearts are processed into 80,000 liters of tequila here. Tours are given daily every hour from 10 to 4. The tours at noon and 3 pm are in English, but English-speakers can often be accommodated at other times. The basic tour, which includes one margarita cocktail, costs $8. It's $12 for tours with a few additional tastings as well as an educational catalog, or $20 if you want to add special reserve tequilas to your tasting. Tours including round-trip transportation can be arranged through the major hotels and travel agencies in Guadalajara. This is a good deal, including several tequila tastings, a complimentary margarita, and time for lunch for about $22. Call at least a day in advance to make arrangements. ■TIP➔ **Make sure to ask the guide for coupons for an additional margarita, as well as discounts at an area restaurant and in the gift shop.** ✉ *Calle José Cuervo 73, Tequila* ☎ *800/006–8630* ⊕ *www.mundocuervo.com*.

**Museo de los Abuelos**

**MUSEUM** | The Museo de los Abuelos or Sauza Museum has memorabilia from the Sauza family, a tequila-making dynasty second only to the Cuervos. The museum opens daily 10–3. Admission costs about 50 cents; for this low price they offer tours in English as well as Spanish, depending on the needs of the crowd. ✉ *Calle Albino Rojas 22, Tequila* ☎ *37/4742–0247* 🌐 *www.museolosabuelos.com.*

## 🍴 Restaurants

**Fonda Cholula**

$ | **MEXICAN** | This typical Mexican restaurant owned by José Cuervo serves decent quesadillas and other local favorites without leaving your wallet empty. The margaritas are quite tasty, too. **Known for:** owned by José Cuervo; reasonable prices; margaritas. [$] *Average main: $10* ✉ *Calle Jose Cuervo 3, Tequila* ☎ *37/4742–1079* 🌐 *www.grupolaposta.mx/fonda-cholula.html.*

**La Antigua Casona**

$$$ | **MEXICAN** | Food in this "Old House" is exquisite, the location is serene, and the service is very good, too. Located inside Hotel Solar de Las Animas, it's open to the public. **Known for:** part of Hotel Solar; refined atmosphere; tuna tostadas. [$] *Average main: $10* ✉ *Ramón Corona 86, Centro* ☎ *374/742–6700* 🌐 *www.hotelsolardelasanimas.com.*

# Teuchitlán

*50 km (28 miles) west of Guadalajara.*

Teuchitlán itself isn't much to see: a small Mexican town like many others, with a few small eateries surrounding a central plaza. But its main draw, the mysterious Guachimontones Ruins, is growing in popularity, and preservation efforts are moving apace. Near the ruins, there are nice lakeside restaurants with decent food and better atmosphere than in town; spending some time here after seeing the ruins makes for a lovely afternoon.

## 👁 Sights

**Guachimontones Ruins**

**ARCHAEOLOGICAL SITE** | For decades, residents in this sleepy village of sugarcane farmers had a name for the funny-looking mounds in the hills above town, but they never considered the Guachimontones to be more than a convenient source of rocks for local construction projects. Then in the early 1970s an American archaeologist asserted that the mounds were the remnants of a long-vanished, 2,000-year-old community. It took Phil Weigand nearly three decades to convince authorities in far-off Mexico City that he wasn't crazy. Before he was allowed to start excavating and restoring this monumental site in the late 1990s, plenty more houses and roads were produced with Guachimonton rock—and countless tombs were looted of priceless art.

This UNESCO World Heritage Site is most distinctive for its sophisticated concentric architecture—a circular pyramid surrounded by a ring of flat ground, surrounded by a series of smaller platforms arranged in a circle. The "Teuchitlán Tradition," as the concentric circle structures are called, is unique in world architecture. While little is known about the ancient settlement, Weigand believes the formations suggest the existence of a pre-Hispanic state in the region, whereas it was previously held that only socially disorganized nomads inhabited the area at the time. Similar ruins are spread throughout the foothills of the extinct Tequila Volcano, but this is the biggest site yet detected.

*Continued on page 232*

# TEQUILA AND MEZCAL—¡SALUD!

If God were Mexican, tequila and mezcal would surely be our heavenly reward, flowing in lieu of milk and honey. Before throwing back your first drink, propose a toast in true Mexican style and wave your glass accordingly—"¡Arriba, abajo, al centro, pa' dentro!" ("Above, below, center, inside!")

Historians maintain that, following Spanish conquest and the introduction of the distillation process, tequila was adapted from the ancient Aztec drink *pulque*. Whatever the true origin, Mexico's national drink long predated the Spanish, and is considered North America's oldest spirit.

When you think about tequila, what might come to mind are spaghetti-Western-style bar brawls or late-night teary-eyed confessions. But tequila is more complex and worldly than many presume. By some accounts it's a digestive that reduces cholesterol and stress. Shots of the finest tequilas can cost upward of $100 each, and are meant to be savored as ardently as fine cognacs or single-malt scotches.

Just one of several agave-derived drinks fermented and bottled in Mexico, tequila rose to fame during the Mexican Revolution when it became synonymous with national heritage and pride. Since the 1990s tequila has enjoyed a soaring popularity around the globe, and people the world over are starting to realize that tequila is more than a one-way ticket to (and doesn't necessitate) a hangover.

Harvesting agave in Jalisco.

## TEQUILA AND MEZCAL 101

Harvesting blue agave to make tequila.

### WHICH CAME FIRST, TEQUILA OR MEZCAL?

Mezcal is tequila's older cousin. Essentially, all tequila is mezcal but only some mezcal is tequila. The only difference between tequila and mezcal is that the tequila meets two requirements: 1) it's made only from blue agave (but some non-agave sugar can be added) and 2) it must be distilled in a specific region in Jalisco or certain parts of neighboring Guanajuato, Michoacán, Nayarit, and Tamaulipas. Unlike tequila, all mezcal must be made from 100 percent agave and must be bottled in Mexico.

### CHOOSE YOUR LIQUOR WISELY

Your first decision with tequila is whether to have a puro or a *mixto*. You'll know if a bottle is puro because it will say so prominently on the label; if the words "100% de agave" don't appear, you can be sure you're getting mixto. Don't be fooled by bottles that say, "Made from agave azul," because all tequila is made from agave azul; that doesn't mean that cane sugar hasn't been added. Popular wisdom holds that puro causes less of a hangover than mixto, but we'll leave that to your own experimentation.

Even among *puros*, there's a wide range of quality and taste, and every fan has his or her favorite. For sipping straight (*derecho*), most people prefer *reposado*, *añejo*, or *extra añejo*. For mixed drinks you'll probably want either a *blanco* or a *reposado*.

Herradura

# TEQUILA TIMELINE

Aztec ritual human sacrifice as portrayed on the Codex Magliabechiano.

| | |
|---|---|
| **Pre-Columbian** | Aztecs brew pulque for thousands of years; both priests and the sacrificial victims consume it during religious rituals. |
| **1600** | The first commercial distillery in New Spain is founded by Pedro Sanches de Tagle, the father of tequila, on his hacienda near the village of Tequila. |
| **1740** | Mezcal de Tequila earns an enthusiastic following and King Philip V of Spain grants José Antonio Cuervo the first royal license for a mezcal distillery. |

# THE MAKING OF MEZCAL

❶ To make both mezcal and tequila, the agave may be cultivated for as long as ten years, depending on growing conditions and the variety of plant.

❷ When the agave is ripe, the leaves, or *pencas*, are removed and the heavy core (called a *piña*, Spanish for "pineapple," because of its resemblance to that fruit) is dug up, ❸ cut into large chunks, and cooked to convert its starches into sugars.

❹ The *piñas* are then crushed and their juice collected in tanks; yeast is added and the liquid ferments for several days.

After the fermentation, the resulting *mosto* generally measures between 4 and 7 percent alcohol. ❺ Finally it's distilled (usually twice for tequila, once for mezcal). This process of heating and condensing serves to boost the alcohol content. ❻ And finally, the alcohol is aged in barrels.

While the process is the same, there are a few critical differences between tequila and mezcal: mezcal is made in smaller distilleries and still retains more of an artisanal quality; mezcal magueys are grown over a wider area with more diverse soil composition and microclimate, giving mezcals more individuality than tequila; and lastly, the *piñas* for mezcal are more likely to be baked in stone pits, which imparts a distinctive smoky flavor.

The World's Columbian Fair in Chicago, 1893.

**1800s** As the thirst for mezcal grows, wood (used to fire the stills) becomes scarce and distilleries shift to more efficient steam ovens.

**1873** Cenobio Sauza exports mezcal to the United States via a new railroad to El Paso, Texas.

**1893** *Mezcal de Tequila* (now simply called tequila) receives an award at Chicago's Columbian Exposition.

## TEQUILA COCKTAILS

**Margarita:** The original proportions at Rancho La Gloria were reportedly 3 parts tequila, 2 parts Triple Sec, and 1 part lime juice, though today recipes vary widely. In Mexico an orange liqueur called Controy is often substituted for the Triple Sec. The best margaritas are a little tart and are made from fresh ingredients, not a mix. Besides deciding whether you want yours strained, on the rocks, or frozen,

you have dozens of variations to choose from, many incorporating fruits such as strawberry, raspberry, mango, passion fruit, and peach. To salt the rim or not to salt is yet another question.

**Sangrita:** The name meaning "little blood," this is a very Mexican accompaniment, a spicy mixture of tomato and orange juice that's sipped between swallows of straight tequila (or mezcal).

**Tequila refresca:** Also very popular in Mexico, this is tequila mixed with citrus soft drinks like Fresca, or Squirt. Generally served in a tall glass over ice.

**Bloody Maria:** One to try with brunch, this is a bloody Mary with you-know-what instead of vodka.

### DID YOU KNOW?

Aging mezcal and Tequila imparts a smoothness and an oaky flavor, but over-aging can strip the drink of its characteristic agave taste.

**Tequila Sunrise:** Invented in the 1950s, this is a distant runner-up to the margarita, concocted from tequila, orange juice, and grenadine syrup. The grenadine sinks to the bottom, and after a few refills you might agree that the resulting layers resemble a Mexican sky at dawn.

---

# TEQUILA TIMELINE

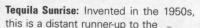

Mexican revolutionaries

**1910–1920** During the Mexican Revolution, homegrown tequila becomes a source of national pride, associated with the hard-riding, hard-drinking rebels.

**1930s** Federal land reforms break up the great haciendas and Mexico's agave production slumps by two thirds. To make up for the shortfall, the government allows distillers to begin mixing non-agave sugars into their tequila. This blander drink, called mixto, is better suited to American tastes and sales surge.

# TEQUILA AND MEZCAL VOCABULARY

**pulque:** an alcoholic drink made by the Aztecs

**mexcalmetl:** Nahuatl word for agave

**mixto:** a type of tequila that is mixed with non-agave sugars

**puro:** tequila made with no non-agave sugars

**reposado:** aged between two months and a year

**añejo:** aged between one and three years

**extra añejo:** aged longer than three years

**blanco:** tequila that is aged less than two months

**joven:** young tequila, usually a mixto with colorings and flavors

**caballito:** tall shot glass

**pechuga:** mezcal flavored with raw chicken breast

**cremas:** flavored mezcal

**aguamiel:** agave juice

**piña:** the agave core

**salmiana:** a type of agave

**pencas:** agave leaves

**mosto:** fermented agave before it is distilled

**gusano:** the larva found in mescal bottles

## WHAT'S WITH THE WORM?

Some mezcals (never tequila) are bottled with a worm (*gusano*), the larva of one of the moths that live on agave plants. Rumor has it that the worm was introduced to ensure a high alcohol content (because the alcohol preserves the creature), but the truth is that the practice started in the 1940s as a marketing gimmick. The worm is ugly but harmless and the best mezcals are not bottled *con gusano*.

Agave

| | |
|---|---|
| **Early 1940s** | The history of mixology was forever altered when Carlos Herrera invented the margarita for American starlet Marjorie King. |
| **2004** | The agave fields around Tequila become a UNESCO World Heritage Site. |
| **2006** | A one-liter bottle of limited-edition premium tequila sold for $225,000. The most expensive bottle ever sold according to The Guiness World Records. |

# CHOOSING A BOTTLE

Reposado (rested)

Silver

Añejo (mature)

Corralejo

## BUYING TEQUILA

There are hundreds of brands of tequila, but here are a baker's half dozen of quality *puros* to get you started; generally these distillers offer blanco, reposado, añejo, and extra añejo.

**Corralejo**—An award winner from the state of Guanajuato, made on the historic hacienda once owned by Pedro Sanchez de Tagle, "the father of tequila" and birthplace of Miguel Hidalgo, the father of Mexican independence.

**Corzo**—Triple distilled, these tequilas are notably smooth and elegant.

**Don Julio**—This award-winning tequila, one of the most popular in Mexico, is known for its rich, smooth flavor; the *blanco* is especially esteemed.

**Espolón**—A relative newcomer founded only in 1998, this distiller has already won several international awards.

**Herradura**—This is a venerable, popular brand known for its smoky, full body.

**Patrón**—Founded in 1989, this distiller produces award-winning tequilas. The *añejo* is especially noteworthy for its complex earthiness.

**Siete Leguas**—Taking their name ("Seven Leagues") from the horse of Pancho Villa, a general in the Mexican Revolution, these quality tequilas are known for their big, full flavor.

## TYPES OF TEQUILA AND MEZCAL

Three basic types of tequila and mezcal are determined by how long they've been aged in oak barrels.

*Blanco* (white) is also known as *plata* or silver. It's been aged for less than two months.

*Reposado* ("rested") is aged between two months and a year.

*añejo* ("mature") is kept in barrels for at least a year and perhaps as long as three. Some producers also offer an extra *añejo* that is aged even longer.

Herradura

Don Julio

Gusano Rojo

## BUYING MEZCAL

As for enjoying mezcal, it can be substituted in any recipe calling for tequila. But more often it's drunk neat, to savor its unique flavor. Like tequila, straight mezcal is generally served at room temperature in a tall shot glass called a *caballito*.

Some producers now add flavorings to their mezcals. Perhaps the most famous is *pechuga*, which has a raw chicken breast added to the still, supposedly imparting a smoothness and subtle flavor. (Don't worry, the heat and alcohol kill everything.) Citrus is also a popular add-in, and *cremas* contain flavorings such as peaches, mint, raisins, or guava, along with a sweetener such as honey or *aguamiel* (the juice of the agave).

Part of the fun of mezcal is stumbling on smaller, less commercial brands, but here are a few recognized, quality producers. Most make *blancos*, *reposados*, and *añejos*, and some offer extra *añejos*, flavored mezcals, and *cremas* as well.

**El Señorio**—Produced in Oaxaca the traditional way, with stone ovens and a stone wheel to crush the *piñas*.

**El Zacatecano**—Founded in 1910 in the northern state of Zacatecas; in a recent competitive tasting, their añejo was judged the best in its category.

**Gusano Rojo**—This venerable Oaxaca distillery makes the number-one-selling mezcal in Mexico. Yes, there's a worm in the bottle.

**Jaral de Berrio**—From Guanajuato, this distiller uses the *salmiana* agave. Their *blanco* recently garnered a silver medal.

**Real de Magueyes**—From the state of San Luis Potosí, these fine mezcals are also made from the local *salmiana* agave. Try the flavorful añejo.

**Scorpion**—More award-winning mezcals from Oaxaca. Instead of a worm, there's a scorpion in the bottle.

**Tequila isn't just about the local drink; you can easily spend an afternoon taking in the town's colonial architecture.**

Until late 2009, visitors had to find their way to the ruins by asking locals and driving up a hill on an unmarked dirt road. But a large visitor center and museum has been inaugurated, and there are signs along the highway and through the town of Teuchitlán directing visitors to the site. ✉ *Carr. Estatal 604, Guadalajara* 🌐 *www.guachimontones.org.*

## 🍴 Restaurants

**Restaurant Montecarlo**

**$$** | **MEXICAN** | This outdoor restaurant is one of a handful of eateries along the lakeside in Teuchitlán. While not fancy, it offers a variety of Mexican dishes, including fish, molcajetes, and fajitas, and provides a grand view of the lake teeming with fish and birds—including herons and pelicans (the section closest to the restaurant is now covered by vegetation). [$] *Average main: $8* ✉ *Calle Las Fuentes 5, Teuchitlan* ☎ *38/4733–0257* 🌐 *www.montecarloteuchitlan.com.mx.*

# Around Lago de Chapala

*48 km (30 miles) southeast of Guadalajara.*

Mexico's largest natural lake is a one-hour drive southeast of Guadalajara. Surrounded by jagged hills and serene towns, Lake Chapala is a favorite Tapatío getaway and a haven for thousands of North American retirees. The name probably derives from Chapalac, who was chief of the region's Taltica Indians when the Spaniards arrived in 1538.

The area's main town, Chapala, is flooded with weekend visitors and the pier is packed shoulder-to-shoulder most Sundays. Its malecón is often packed with local families and couples on the weekends. Eight kilometers (5 miles) west is Ajijic, a picturesque village that's home to the bulk of the area's expatriates. Farther west, San Juan Cosalá is popular for its thermal-water pools.

**GETTING AROUND**
You're going to need a car to get around the lake if you want to explore on your own, but there are taxis. Given how the towns are spread out and how easy it is to drive around during the day you'll be able to cover more distance and reach more points of interest if you have your own car; renting one in Guadalajara makes the most sense. If you don't plan on visiting many of the towns and prefer to stay in Ajijic or one of the others, you can take a bus and walk around town.

**TIMING**
While working days are pleasant and winters are mellow and fresh, weekends tend to be busy, and you're better off avoiding the area altogether during the Easter holidays. You'll find a big expat community here, and many small cafés and restaurants to spend some leisure time.

**CONTACTS Chapala Plus.** ☎ *33/3619–4777* 🌐 *chapalaplus.com.*

## Chapala

*45 km (28 miles) south of Guadalajara.*

Chapala was a placid weekend getaway for aristocrats in the late 19th century, but when then-president Porfirio Díaz got in on the action in 1904, other wealthy Mexicans followed suit. More and more summer homes were built, and in 1910 the Chapala Yacht Club opened. Avenida Madero, Chapala's main street, is lined with restaurants, shops, and cafés. Three blocks north of the promenade, the plaza at the corner of López Cotilla is a relaxing spot to read a paper or succumb to sweets from surrounding shops. The Iglesia de San Francisco (built in 1528), easily recognized by its blue neon crosses on twin steeples, is two blocks south of the plaza.

On weekends Mexican families flock to the shores of the (for now, at least) rejuvenated lake. Vendors sell refreshments and souvenirs, while lakeside watering holes fill to capacity.

**QUICK BITES**
For a quick bite **Tacos Las Palmas** (✉ *Libramiento Chapala- Ajijic 96*) offers a lot more than what the name suggests. Marlin, tuna, shrimp, and other staple items are served with local fruits and vegetables to produce mouthwatering dishes. The burritos are big and tasty, too.

### 🍴 Restaurants

**Restaurant Cazadores**
**$$** | **MEXICAN** | This grandly turreted brick building was once the summer home of the Braniff family, former owners of the defunct airline. The house specialty is *chamorro*, pork shank wrapped in banana leaves. **Known for:** a tad pricey; chamorro pork; patio dining overlooking the boardwalk. [$] *Average main: $11* ✉ *Paseo Ramón Corona 18, Chapala* ☎ *376/765–2162.*

### 🛏 Hotels

Accommodation in Chapala tends to be somewhat pricey.

**Hotel Villa Montecarlo**
**$$** | **HOTEL** | Built around a Mediterranean-style villa nearly a century old, this hotel has well-maintained grounds with plenty of places for picnics or for the kids to play. **Pros:** huge pools; extensive grounds; outdoor dining under a flowering tree. **Cons:** can be noisy; poor Wi-Fi; lacks maintenance. [$] *Rooms from: $95* ✉ *Paseo del Prado 20, Chapala* ☎ *37/676–52120* 🌐 *www.hoteles.udg.mx/montecarlo* 🔑 *47 rooms* 🍽 *No meals.*

**Lake Chapala Inn**

$$ | **B&B/INN** | Three of the four rooms in this restored mansion face the shore; all have high ceilings and whitewashed oak furniture. **Pros:** solar-heated lap pool; English-speaking host; sunny reading room. **Cons:** dated furnishings; square tubs not conducive to long soaks; breakfast finishes at 9:30 am. [$] *Rooms from: $90* ✉ *Paseo Ramón Corona 23, Chapala* ☎ *37/6765–4786, 37/6765–4809* 🌐 *www.chapalainn.com* 💳 *No credit cards* 🛏 *4 rooms* 🍴 *Free Breakfast.*

# Ajijic

*8 km (5 miles) west of Chapala; 47 km (30 miles) southwest of Guadalajara.*

Ajijic has narrow cobblestone streets, vibrantly colored buildings, and a gentle pace—with the exception of the considerably congested main highway through the town's southern end. The foreign influence is unmistakable: English is widely (though not exclusively) spoken, and license plates come from far-flung places like British Columbia and Texas.

The Plaza Principal (also known as Plaza de Armas) is a tree- and flower-filled central square at the corner of Avenidas Colón and Hidalgo. The Iglesia de San Andrés (Church of St. Andrew) is on the plaza's north side. In late November the plaza and its surrounding streets fill for the saint's nine-day fiesta. From the plaza, walk down Calle Morelos (the continuation of Avenida Colón) toward the lake and peruse the boutiques. Turn left onto Avenida 16 de Septiembre or Avenida Constitución for art galleries and studios. Northeast of the plaza, along the highway, the hub of local activity is the soccer field, which doubles as a venue for concerts.

### GETTING AROUND

You don't need a car to get around Ajijic as this is best done by foot. Stay away from heeled shoes at all times, as the treacherous cobble stones will do more harm than good, and riding bicycles is probably not a good idea either.

## Sights

Like Chapala, Ajijic is a small sleepy town that doesn't have much going on, but it is a great place to unwind. Walk over to the lake, then head to El Tepalo waterfall and you'll have covered what sightseeing there is to do.

**El Tepalo Waterfall**

**BODY OF WATER** | **FAMILY** | The waterfall is just a 40-minute walk from Ajiijc, and only visible during the rainy season, but the trek is definitely worth it if you want to spend some time in nature without people around you. ✥ *From Ajijic center turn right on Callejón el Tépalo. A sign there indicates where to start walking.*

**Lake Chapala**

**BODY OF WATER** | **FAMILY** | Ajijic is also set along Lake Chapala, Mexico's largest freshwater lake. Some boat tours are also available here, which will show you other points of view of the lake. Take some time to enjoy the peace and quiet, as this is what Tapatíos (Guadalajara citizens) come here for and you should, too.

## Restaurants

Perhaps the most striking aspect of Ajijic is the sheer number of restaurants this small village has. There's French, Thai, German, Argentinian, Mexican, and Italian cuisine, and upscale restaurants with a great atmosphere and quality food.

**Ajijic Tango**

$$ | **ARGENTINE** | Considered one of the top, if not *the* top, restaurants in Ajijic, this Argentine favorite has locals and

tourists waiting in a line down the block to get inside. Many go for the *arrachera* (flank steak), lamb, or carpaccio. **Known for:** Argentine cuisine; no reservations on weekends; flank steak and carpaccio. [$] *Average main: $10* ✉ *Calle Morelos 5, Ajijic* ☎ *37/6766–2458* 🌐 *www.ajijictango.com* 🕒 *Closed Tues.*

**Brew House**

$$ | **CAFÉ** | The only gastronomic brewery in Chapala, they offer craft beer and delicious food including burgers, burritos, tacos and salads. **Known for:** craft beer; ;. [$] *Average main: $7* ✉ *Calle De Las Flores 25, Ajijic* ☎ *376/766–5657* 🕒 *Closed Sun.*

**El Jardin de Ninette**

$$$ | **MEXICAN FUSION** | **FAMILY** | French, Mexican, and international fusion dishes are served in a nice indoor patio with a few tables and pleasant live music. It's all about the food here and chef Oscar will often step out to mingle with guests. **Known for:** fusion cuisine; local favorite; worth the splurge. [$] *Average main: $10* ✉ *Javier Mina 7, Ajijic* ☎ *376/766–4905* 🕒 *Closed Mon. No lunch Tues.–Thurs.*

**Johanna's**

$ | **GERMAN** | Come to this intimate bit of Bavaria on the lake for German cuisine like sausages and goose or duck pâté. Main dishes come with soup or salad, applesauce, and cooked red cabbage. **Known for:** delicious desserts like plum strudel; closes early; Bavarian cuisine. [$] *Average main: $10* ✉ *Blvd. Ajijic 118-A, Ajijic* ☎ *37/6766–0437* 💳 *No credit cards* 🕒 *Closed Mon.*

**La Bodega de Ajijic**

$$ | **ECLECTIC** | Eat on a covered patio overlooking a grassy lawn and a small pool at this low-key restaurant. In addition to Mexican standards, the menu has Italian pasta dishes. **Known for:** live music; friendly service; opens early (except Thursday). [$] *Average main: $11* ✉ *Av. 16 de Septiembre 124, Ajijic* ☎ *376/766–1002* 🕒 *Closed Sun.*

**Mom's Deli and Restaurant**

$ | **MEXICAN** | Mom's Deli and Restaurant ✉ is a fantastic stop for breakfast and during the day, serving fresh, delicious food in a pleasant though simple environment. Try the eggs Benedict and homemade muffins, and wash them down with a cup of perfectly roasted cup of coffee. **Known for:** perfectly roasted coffee; homemade pastries; no-frills environment. [$] *Average main: 3 MP* ✉ *Calle Hidalgo 62 A, Guadalajara* ✣ *Head east from gas station and take 2nd street to right* ☎ *376/765–5719* 🕒 *Closed Wed. No dinner.*

## Hotels

There's a nice selection of hotels in Ajijic, with prices varying from budget to somewhat pricey. All hotels are small or boutique style, with a focus on personalized service.

**Casa Blanca**

$ | **HOTEL** | Gracious gardens, tinkling fountains, bright colors, and arched windows give the traveler a sense of sleeping in a Mexican hacienda while also enjoying the comforts of home. **Pros:** full of character; manicurist and massage therapist by reservation; complimentary shoe shine. **Cons:** small rooms; pricey; useless curtains. [$] *Rooms from: $74* ✉ *Calle 16 de Septiembre 29, Centro* ☎ *376/766–4440, 800/436–0759 toll-free* 🌐 *www.casablancaajijic.com* 🛏 *8 rooms* 🍴 *Free Breakfast.*

★ **Donaire Hotel Boutique**

$$$ | **HOTEL** | This relatively new hotel offers stylish rooms with modern decor overlooking all of Ajijic and the lake. **Pros:** very clean; comfortable, spacious rooms; fantastic views. **Cons:** unpaved parking; can be noisy during festive days; pool water may not be warm enough

on cloudy days. [$] *Rooms from: $164* ✉ *Privada de Juarez 21 Entre Colón y Juarez, Ajijic* ☎ *332/338–3871* 🌐 *www.donairehotelboutique.com* 🛏 *9 rooms* 🍴 *Free Breakfast.*

**La Nueva Posadada**

**$$** | **B&B/INN** | The well-kept gardens framed in bougainvillea define this inviting inn. **Pros:** uniquely decorated, airy rooms; great restaurant; discounts given for paying with cash. **Cons:** TVs in rooms are small; pleasant rooms; Wi-Fi spotty when there's a storm. [$] *Rooms from: $72* ✉ *Calle Donato Guerra 9, Ajijic* ☎ *37/6766–1344* 🌐 *www.hotelnuevaposada.com* 🛏 *19 rooms, 4 villas* 🍴 *Free Breakfast.*

# Chapter 8

# SAN BLAS AND THE MOUNTAIN TOWNS

Updated by
Federico Arrizabalaga

8

| 👁 Sights | 🍴 Restaurants | 🛏 Hotels | 🛍 Shopping | 🍸 Nightlife |
|---|---|---|---|---|
| ★★★★★ | ★★★★☆ | ★★★☆☆ | ★★☆☆☆ | ☆☆☆☆☆ |

# WELCOME TO SAN BLAS AND THE MOUNTAIN TOWNS

## TOP REASONS TO GO

★ **Alchemic atmosphere:** San Blas's basic but charismatic attractions—beaches, markets, churches, and boat trips—combine like magic for a destination that's greater than the sum of its parts.

★ **Highland rambles:** Drop-dead-gorgeous hills and river valleys from Talpa de Allende to San Sebastián get you out into nature and away from coastal humidity.

★ **Amazing photography:** In the mountain towns like San Sebastián, Mascota, and Talpa, even amateurs can capture excellent small-town and nature photos.

★ **Local food:** The food scene here is more casual than in Puerto Vallarta, and focuses on fresh, local produce.

★ **Peace and quiet:** Find tranquillity away from the major towns.

**1 San Blas.** Change happens slowly in San Blas, which has yet to experience a tourism boom. Cruise wide dirt streets on one-speed bikes, read books in the shade, dig your toes in the sand, and just enjoy life—one lazy day at a time. Blue mountains and green hills provide a beautiful backdrop.

**2 San Sebastián.** Located about 1,500 meters above sea level, San Sebastián is a former small mining town where you can spend a day away from Puerto Vallarta's heat and beach scene. Wander its cobblestone streets, eat local pastries, and stay at its simple but charming hacienda-style hotels.

**3 Mascota.** At the bottom of the valley, is this charming town and commercial hub. Rather than palm trees and sand you'll find pines and cobblestone streets, where local villagers roam after a day of work.

**4 Talpa De Allende.** Smack in the middle of town is the church Nuestra Señora del Rosario, to which few tourists venture. Pleasant year-round temperatures and pine tree surroundings make it a popular getaway.

San Blas

*Bahía de San Blas*

Chacala
*Bahía de Jaltemba*
La Peñita
Rincón de Guayabitos
Lo de Marcos
San Francisco
Sayulita
Ixtapa
Punta Mita
*Las Islas Marietas*
Bucerías
La Cruz de Huanácaxtle
Nuevo Vallarta
*Bahía de Banderas*
Puerto Vallarta
Mismaloya
Boca de Tomatlán
El Chimo

Aquiles Serdán
El Tuito
*Bahía Tehualmixtle*
El Tequesquite

La Cruz de Loreto

La Cumbre

José María Morelos

*Bahía Chamel*

0          20 mi

0          20 km

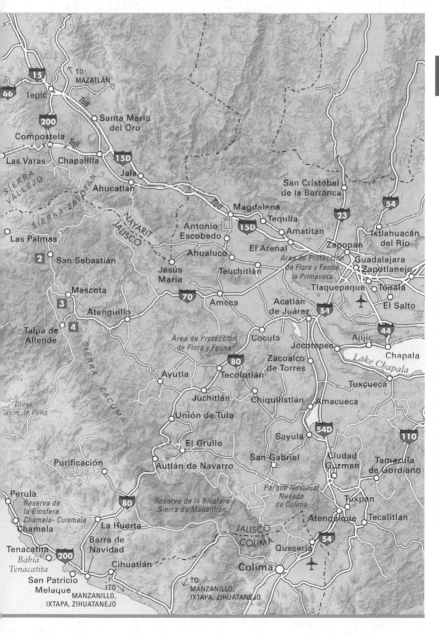

Puerto Vallarta's location means variety. You can explore little-visited beaches and miles of mangrove canals in San Blas. You can shop and absorb culture in historic Guadalajara. Or, you can head to the mountains and visit former mining towns and enjoy long walks along trails that cut through pine tree forests.

Although San Blas is the northern end of Riviera Nayarit (the stretch of coast from San Blas to the southern Nayarit State border at Nuevo Vallarta), little has changed. Things here are low-key and friendly—a nice break from bustling Vallarta and environs, where traffic sometimes snarls. There are no supermarkets; everyone shops at mom-and-pop grocery stores or the daily market for tropical fruits and vegetables, tortillas, and hot or cold snacks. Many of the restaurants around the plaza are relatively simple and inexpensive.

Founded by the Spanish but soon all but abandoned for busier ports, San Blas has several historic structures to visit, including the old customs and counting houses, and original churches. But more of a draw are its miles of sandy beaches and La Tovara, a serpentine series of mangrove-lined channels leading to a freshwater spring.

Even less sophisticated than San Blas are a handful of former silver-mining towns and supply centers in the hills behind Puerto Vallarta. Until a 21st-century road improvement, Mascota, Talpa de Allende, San Sebastián, and other villages en route to Guadalajara were accessible only by narrow, treacherous, snaky mountain roads or a small plane. Today sunny, unpolluted days and crisp nights lure people out of the fray and into a more relaxed milieu, where lingering over coffee or watching kids play in the town plaza are the activities of choice. If this sounds too tame, there's horseback riding, hiking, and fishing at Presa Coriches, among other activities.

Guadalajara—Mexico's second-largest city—makes an excellent add-on to a Vallarta beach vacation. You can shop in megamalls or in surrounding towns (consider Tonalá, where artisans were producing pottery centuries before the Spanish invasion). You can take in modern Russian ballet or Mexican folkloric dances; see a fast-paced *charrería,* with riders on well-groomed Arabian horses; listen to a 12-piece mariachi band; or visit one of a dozen museums. Although at times overwhelming, this modern city provides an excellent overview of all Mexico has to offer. For a foray outside the metropolis, head for Lago de Chapala, Mexico's largest natural lake, or to Tequila, land of the blue agave, where the country's national drink is produced and bottled.

## MAJOR REGIONS

The former mining and supply towns within the Sierra Madre—**Talpa de Allende, Mascota,** and tiny **San Sebastián,** referred to as the **Mountain Towns**—were isolated for centuries by narrow roads and dangerous drop-offs and remain postcards of the past. Soak up the small-town atmosphere and alpine air.

A trip into the Sierra Madre is an excellent way to escape the coastal heat and the hordes of vacationers. The Spanish arrived to extract ore from these mountains at the end of the 16th century; after the Mexican Revolution the mines were largely abandoned in favor of richer veins. The isolation of these tiny towns has kept them old-fashioned. The air is crisp and clean with a pine scent; the valley and mountain views are spectacular; and the highland towns are earthy, unassuming, and charming. Whitewashed adobe homes radiate from plazas where old gents remember youthful exploits. Saturday night, teens court each other alfresco while oompah bands entertain their parents from the bandstand. Although most of the hotels in the region have only basic amenities (construction of a massively improved road from PV is encouraging entrepreneurs, however), the chill mountain air and heavy blankets mean a great night's sleep.

# Planning

## When to Go

Thanks to a springlike climate, Guadalajara is pleasant at most times of year, though May and June can be uncomfortably hot for some. Book well in advance to visit during the October Festival or other holidays. Roads can be dangerous during summer rains, which start in June and last through the end of October. This is definitely not the best time to visit the mountain towns by land.

San Blas and the coast begin to heat up in May and the high temperatures last until the end of October. The rainy season usually begins late in June, providing short breaks to the summer heat, time during which the ocean is also warmest yet remains pleasant. In Guadalajara, rain tends to be limited to thunderstorms late in the afternoon and evening.

## FESTIVALS AND SPECIAL EVENTS

Guadalajara's major events include the International Mariachi Festival in September, the Tequila Festival in March, and a cultural festival in May. The entire month of October is dedicated to mariachis, *charreadas* (rodeos), soccer matches, and theater.

At the San Blas Festival (February 3), a statue of the town's patron saint gets a boat ride around the bay and the town invests in a major fireworks show. In the Sierra Madre, Talpa's equally admired icon brings the faithful en masse four times a year for street dances and mariachi serenades.

# Getting Here and Around

If you plan to visit both Puerto Vallarta and Guadalajara, consider flying into one and out of the other. Some open-jaw trips cost even less than a round-trip flight to/from PV. If you plan your trip right, travel between PV and Guadalajara by bus is $32–$37, but could increase once the highway that is being built between PV and Guadalajara is finished (it was due at the end of 2017 but is still only halfway complete). One-way drop-off charges for rental cars are steep. Access to Mascota and Talpa from Guadalajara is more direct than from PV, although the latter road is now paved, with new bridges in place. Nonetheless, this windy mountain route is occasionally impassable in rainy season. Buses take you directly from PV to San Blas, or you can get off at nearby beaches. That said, a car is handier for exploring the coast. The mostly two-lane PV–San Blas road is curvy but otherwise fine.

■ **TIP→ Most small towns that don't have official stations sell gas from a home or store. Ask around before heading out on the highway if you're low on gas.**

For an effortless excursion, go on a tour with Vallarta Adventures. It has excellent day trips for $92 to San Sebastián by bus or jeep, depending on the number of passengers.

ATM (Autotransportes Talpa–Mascota) buses depart from the bus station in PV three times a day around 9 am, 2:30 pm, and 6:30 pm, stopping at La Estancia (11 km [7 miles] from San Sebastián; 1½ hours), then Mascota (2 to 2½ hours) and Talpa (3 to 3½ hours). The cost is about $5 one-way to San Sebastián (La Estancia); $9 to Mascota; and $10 to Talpa (all prices in USD).

Buses also depart several times a day from Guadalajara's new bus station (Entronque Carretera Libre a Zapotlanejo, modules 3 and 4). Note that the bus doesn't enter San Sebastián; you'll be dropped at a small rest area, where taxis usually are available to transport you to town. The cost for the short drive is a bit steep at about $12. Share the cab with others on the bus to split the cost; or get a lift with a local and offer to pay (note that many will decline or ask just a small amount to help out with gas).

From Puerto Vallarta the road to San Sebastián is paved now, but those going to San Sebastián still have to get off the bus at La Estancia and take a taxi those last few miles. A suspension bridge was inaugurated in early 2007 to cover the last 8 km (5 miles) of the road to Mascota, which used to get washed out regularly in the rainy season. (Note that this road still may become dangerous or at least frightening during the rainy season, when landslides can occur.) Lago Juanacatlán is an hour from Mascota on a rough one-lane road of dirt and rock.

You can also get to any of these towns by car, which will make the trip more affordable and possibly fun if you're traveling in a small group. It takes about 1½ hours to San Sebastián and slightly more to Mascota from Puerto Vallarta, although the trip should only be attempted during the dry season (November to June) because of poor road conditions the rest of the year. Once you reach the mountains expect some potholes, fresh air, spectacular views, and the feeling of adventure; during the right time of year, going independently is really worth it if you don't like joining tours.

Taxis hang out near the main square in Talpa, Mascota, and San Sebastián.

# Planning Your Time

## DAY TRIPS VERSUS EXTENDED STAYS

The San Blas area is best as an overnight unless you go with an organized tour, though you could easily drive to Platanitos, south of San Blas, for a day at the beach.

If taking a bus or driving to the mountain towns, it is relatively easy to visit and return in a single day, but when possible plan to overnight. Single day trips are effortless with day tours such as those offered by Vallarta Adventures or any other PV tour company. Alternatively, you can fly on your own with **Aerotaxis de la Bahía** (*322/221–1990*) for a day trip or an overnight stay.

Guadalajara is too far to go for the day from Vallarta or San Blas; we recommend at least three nights if you're doing a round-trip.

## PLANNING YOUR TIME

If you'll be in the Sayulita, San Francisco (aka San Pancho) , and Chacala areas in Nayarit, it's easy to do an overnight jaunt up to San Blas, enjoying the myriad beaches and small towns as you travel up and back. Or make San Blas your base and explore from there.

You could also feasibly spend one night in San Blas and two in Guadalajara, about 4½ hours by rental car and 6 hours by bus. For lovers of the road less traveled, two to three nights gives you ample time to explore the mountain towns of San Sebastián, Mascota, and Talpa as well as the surrounding countryside. Or you could spend one night in the mountains and continue to Guadalajara the next day. To fully appreciate Guadalajara, plan to spend at least three nights as traveling there takes half a day.

## Tours

### Charter Club Tours

The bilingual guides of Ajijic's Charter Club Tours lead tours of Guadalajara, shopping and factory trips in Tlaquepaque and Tonalá, Tequila, the Teuchitlán archaeological site, and treks to Jalisco's lesser-known towns. Tours cost approximately $99 per person. ⊠ *Carr. Oriente, 1 Loc. Centro, Ajijic* ☎ *376/766–1777, 408/626–7479 in U.S.* ⊕ *www.charter-clubtours.com.mx.*

### Vallarta Adventures

Highly recommended Vallarta Adventures has daily, seven-hour jeep tours to San Sebastián ($92). ⊠ *Edifício Marina Golf, Loc. 13–C, Calle Mástil, Marina Vallarta* ☎ *322/297–1212, 888/526–2238 in U.S. and Canada* ⊕ *www.vallarta-adventures.com.*

### Driving Times from Puerto Vallarta

| | |
|---|---|
| San Blas | 3–3½ hours |
| San Sebastián | 1½–2 hours |
| Mascota | 2½ 3 hours |
| Talpa de Allende | 3–3½ hours |

## Restaurants

The most popular international restaurants are scattered about west Guadalajara, but some of the best Mexican food is near the main attractions in downtown Guadalajara, Tlaquepaque, and Tonalá.

If sitting down to a meal before 8 pm, you may find you don't need reservations—and you might even have the restaurant to yourself. By around 10 pm, the locals will start filling up the place, and reservations become a must. Good food tends to be very low-priced compared to comparable food in the States, even at the best restaurants in town. A main course is $6 to $15, and alcoholic beverages start at $2. Some of the best food in the city can be found at smaller taco shops and stands, where you can come away full having spent less than $5 for four tacos and a soda. It's important to be careful when eating food from street vendors, however; the best sign of a stand worth trying is a long line of locals waiting to order.

## Hotels

Choosing a place to stay is a matter of location, price, and comfort. Tourists are often drawn to the Centro, where colonial-style hotels are convenient to the historical center and other sights. But hotels in the center tend to be a bit run down and don't offer the amenities available at those farther west. Businesspeople and those looking for more modern digs head for the area around Avenida López Mateos Sur, a 16 km (10-mile) strip extending from the Minerva Fountain to the Plaza del Sol shopping center, or Avenida Americas in Providencia where they can take advantage of newer facilities and four-star comforts. Several hotels, like the polished Hilton, are near the Expo Guadalajara convention center.

## What it Costs in U.S. Dollars and Mexican Pesos

| $ | $$ | $$$ | $$$$ |
|---|---|---|---|
| **RESTAURANTS IN DOLLARS** | | | |
| under $13 | $13–$19 | $20–$25 | over $25 |
| **RESTAURANTS IN PESOS** | | | |
| under M$160 | M$160– M$250 | M$251– M$330 | over M$330 |
| **HOTELS IN DOLLARS** | | | |
| under $120 | $120–$180 | $181–$250 | over $250 |
| **HOTELS IN PESOS** | | | |
| under M$1600 | M$1600– M$2400 | M$2401– M$3300 | Over M$3300 |

*Hotel reviews have been shortened. For full information, visit Fodors.com.*

## Visitor Information

**CONTACTS Oficina de Turismo de Mascota.** ⊠ *La Presidencia [Town Hall], Calle Ayuntamiento, at Calle Constitución, facing plaza, Mascota* ☎ *388/386–1179.* **Oficina de Turismo de San Sebastián del Oeste.** ⊠ *Juárez 3, Col. Centro, San Sebastián* ☎ *322/226–7863* ⊕ *www.sansebastiandeloeste.gob.mx.* **Oficina de Turismo de Talpa.** ⊠ *La Presidencia [Town Hall], Calle Independencia 32, Talpa de Allende* ☎ *388/385–0009* ⊕ *www.talpadeallende.gob.mx.*

# San Blas

San Blas and the surrounding beaches are authentic, and cater more to locals than tourists. Sure, there's an expat community, but it's minuscule compared to that of Puerto Vallarta. Parts of San Blas itself remain ungentrified. The lively square is a nice place to polish off an ice-cream cone and watch the world go by. If you're looking for posh restaurants and tony neighborhoods, this isn't the place for you.

Most people come to the San Blas area for basic R&R, to enjoy the long empty beaches and seafood shanties. The town's sights can be seen in less than a day, but stay for a few days at least to catch up on your reading, visit the beaches, and savor the town as it deserves. A La Tovara jungle cruise through the mangroves should not be missed.

Many travelers come here looking for Old Mexico, or the "real Mexico," or the Mexico they remember from the 1960s. New Spain's first official Pacific port has experienced a long, slow slide into obscurity since losing out to better-equipped ports in the late 19th century. But there's something to be said for being a big player rather than a superstar. Industrious but not overworked, residents of this drowsy seaside city hit the beaches on weekends and celebrate their good fortune during numerous saints' days and civic festivals.

## GETTING HERE AND AROUND

If you want to head directly to San Blas from outside Mexico, fly to Mexico City and on to Tepic (69 km [43 miles] from San Blas), capital of the state of Nayarit, on Aeromar. To get to San Blas by road from Tepic, head north on Highway 15D, then west on Highway 11. Most visitors, however, make San Blas a road trip from PV.

The Puerto Vallarta bus station is less than 5 km (3 miles) north of the PV airport; there are usually four daily departures for San Blas ($12; three hours). These buses generally don't stop, and most don't have bathrooms. Departure times vary throughout the year, but at this writing, there were no departures after 4:30 pm. To get to Platanitos Beach, about an hour south of San Blas, take the Puerto Vallarta bus. ■TIP➜ Always check the return schedule with the driver when taking an out-of-town bus. A taxi to the bus station from Puerto Vallarta or from the airport costs about $8.

A car is handy for more extensive explorations of the coast between PV and around San Blas. Within San Blas, the streets are wide, traffic is almost nonexistent, and, with the exception of the streets immediately surrounding the main plaza, parking is very easy. From Puerto Vallarta, abandon Highway 200 just past Las Varas in favor of the coast road. (Follow the sign toward Zacualpan, where you must go around the main plaza to continue on the unsigned road. Ask locals "San Blas?" and they'll point you in the right direction.) The distance of about 160 km (100 miles) takes 3 to 3½ hours.

From Guadalajara, you can take 15D (the toll road, about $13) and get off at the Libramiento to San Blas. From Puerto Vallarta head North on Highway 200 until Las Varas, and then head north on the coastal route (road 16) to San Blas.

To really go native, rent a bike from Wala Wala Restaurant, a half block up from the plaza on Avenida Benito Juárez, and cruise to your heart's content. To get to the beaches south of town, to Matanchén Bay, and to the village of Santa Cruz, take a bus (they usually leave on the hour) from the bus station across the street from the church on the main plaza. To come back, just stand by the side of the road and flag down a passing bus.

## ESSENTIALS
**TOURIST BOARD Oficina de Turismo de San Blas.** ⊠ *Calle Canalizo at Calle Sinaloa in Municipal Palace, 2nd fl., on main plaza* 📞 *323/285–1180* ⊕ *ayuntamientosanblas. wordpress.com.*

### Singayta
**TOUR—SPORTS | FAMILY |** Singayta is a typical Nayarit village that is attempting to support itself through simple and ungimmicky ecotours. The basic tour includes a look around the town, where original adobe structures compete with more practical but less picturesque structures with corrugated tin roofs. Take a short guided hike through the surrounding jungle and a boat ride around the estuary ($6 per person). This is primo birding territory. The townspeople are most geared up for tours on weekends and during school holidays and vacations: Christmas, Easter, July, and August. The easiest way to book a tour is to look for English-speaking Juan Bananas, who sells banana bread from a shop called Tumba de Yako (look for the sign on the unmarked road Avenida H. Batallón between calles Comonfort and Canalizo, en route to Playa Borrego). He can set up a visit and/or guide you there. Groups of five or more can call ahead to make a reservation with Juan (*323/285–0462*, ecomanglar@yahoo.com) or with Santos (*323/100–4191*); call at least a day ahead if you want to have a meal. ⊠ *8 km (5 miles) from San Blas on road to Tepic.*

##  Sights

### Cerro de San Basilio
**VIEWPOINT | FAMILY |** For a bird's-eye view of the town and coast, hike or drive up Calle Juárez, the main drag, to Cerro de San Basilio. You can also take road 74 out of town, turn right at the fork and then right at calle del Panteon, which is the only road you'll find before reaching the river. ⊠ *San Blas.*

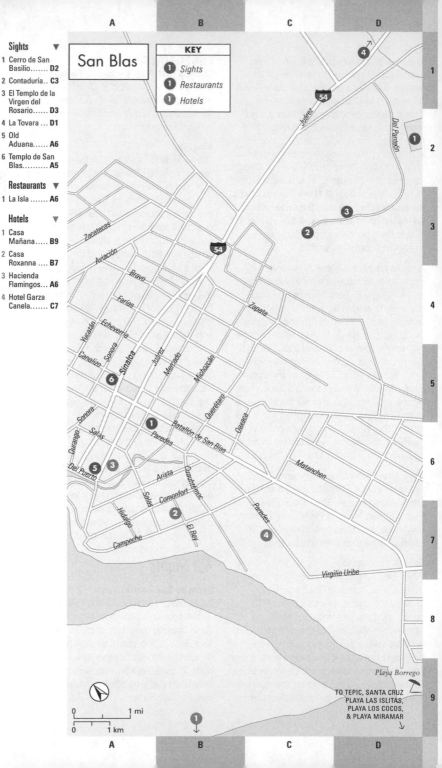

# San Blas

**KEY**

1 *Sights*

1 *Restaurants*

1 *Hotels*

Playa Borrego

TO TEPIC, SANTA CRUZ
PLAYA LAS ISLITAS,
PLAYA LOS COCOS,
& PLAYA MIRAMAR

0        1 mi

0      1 km

### Contaduría (*Counting House*)

**HISTORIC SITE | FAMILY |** Cannons protect the ruined Contaduría, built during colonial times when San Blas was New Spain's first official port. ⊠ *Cerro de San Basilio.*

### El Templo de la Virgen del Rosario

**RELIGIOUS SITE |** Continuing down the road from the Contaduría brings you to El Templo de la Virgen del Rosario. Note the new floor in the otherwise ruined structure; the governor's daughter didn't want to soil the hem of her gown when she married here in 2005. A bit farther on, San Blas's little cemetery is backed by the sea and the mountains. ⊠ *Calle Joao Ma. Mercado, at Echevarria*

### ★ La Tovara

**LOCAL INTEREST | FAMILY |** Turtles sunning themselves on logs, crocodiles masquerading as logs, water-loving birds, and exotic orchids make the maze of green-brown canals that is La Tovara—an out-of-town must for nature lovers. Launches putter along these waterways from El Conchal Bridge, at the outskirts of San Blas, about a three-hour drive from Marina Vallarta, or from the nearby village of Matanchén. After cruising along for about 45 minutes—during which you'll have taken *way* too many photos of the mangrove roots that protrude from the water and the turtles—you arrive at the spring-fed freshwater pools for which the area is named. You can hang out at the restaurant overlooking the pool or play Tarzan and Jane on the rope swing. Most folks take the optional trip to a crocodile farm on the way back, stretching a two-hour tour into three hours. ⊠ *Carr. Las Islitas s/n. Embarcadero principal, Matanchen* ☎ *323/116–9997* ⊕ *www.latovara.com* 🖃 *$8.*

### Old Aduana (*Former Customs House*)

**ARTS VENUE | FAMILY |** The old Aduana has been partially restored and is now a cultural center with sporadic art or photography shows and theatrical productions. ⊠ *Calle Juárez, near Calle del Puerto.*

## Birder's Paradise

More than 500 species of birds settle in the San Blas area; 23 are endemic. Organize a birding tour through Hotel Garza Canela *(below).*

**International Festival of Migratory Birds** In late January, you can attend the International Festival of Migratory Birds for bird-watching tours and conferences with experts and fellow enthusiasts. ⊠ *San Blas* ⊕ *www.fiamsanblas.org.*

### Templo de San Blas

**RELIGIOUS SITE |** Templo de San Blas, called *La Iglesia Vieja* ("the old church") by residents, is on the town's busy plaza. It's rarely open these days, but you can admire its diminutive beauty and look for the words to Henry Wadsworth Longfellow's poem "The Bells of San Blas," inscribed on a brass plaque outside. (The long-gone bells were actually at the church dedicated to the Virgin of the Rosary, on Cerro de San Basilio.) ⊠ *On corner between Sinaloa St. and Batallon de San Blas.*

### BEACHES

Like San Blas itself, the surrounding beaches attract mostly local people and travelers fleeing glitzier resort scenes. Beaches here are almost uniformly long, flat, and walkable, with light brown sand, moderate waves, and seriously bothersome no-see-ums, especially around sunrise and sunset (and during the waxing and waning moons). Almost as ubiquitous as these biting bugs are simple *ramadas* (open-sided, palm-thatch-roof eateries) on the beach whose owners don't mind if you hang out all day, jumping in the ocean and then back into your shaded hammock to continue devouring John Grisham or leafing through magazines. Order a cold lemonade or a beer, or have a meal of fish fillets, ceviche, or chips and guacamole. Don't expect a full

Take in the expansive landscape from San Blas Fort at Cerro de San Basilio.

menu, rather what's fresh and available. All these beaches are accessible by bus from San Blas's centrally located bus station.

### ★ Playa Borrego

**BEACH—SIGHT | FAMILY** | You can walk or ride a bike to long, lovely Playa Borrego, 1 km (½ mile) south of town. Rent a surfboard at Stoners' or Mar y Sol restaurant to attack the year-round (but sporadic) shore or jetty breaks here, or stroll down to the southern end to admire the lovely, palm-fringed estuary. ⊠ *Turistico Playa del Borrego.*

### Playa Las Islitas

**BEACH—SIGHT | FAMILY** | About 6 km (4 miles) south of Playa Borrego, at the northern edge of Bahía de Matanchén, Playa Las Islitas used to be legendary among surfers for its long wave, but this has diminished in recent years. The beach is now suitable for swimming, bodysurfing, and boogie boarding. ⊠ *San Blas.*

### Playa Los Cocos and Playa Miramar

**BEACH—SIGHT** | At the south end of the Matanchén Bay, Playa Los Cocos and Playa Miramar are both great for taking long walks and for hanging out at ramadas. ⊠ *San Blas.*

### Playa Platanitos

**BEACH—SIGHT** | Beyond Matanchén Bay the road heads inland and reemerges about 8 km (5 miles) later at Playa Platanitos, a lovely little beach in a sheltered cove that also produces a fun wave for surfers right along the cove's end. Fishermen park their skiffs here and simple shacks cook up the catch of the day. ⊠ *San Blas.*

### Santa Cruz

**TOWN** | Adjacent to Miramar Beach is the well-kept fishing village of Santa Cruz. Take a walk on the beach or around the town; buy a soft drink, find the bakery, and pick up some banana bread. Outdoor dances are occasionally held on the diminutive central plaza. ⊠ *San Blas.*

#  Restaurants

### La Isla

**$ | SEAFOOD |** Shell lamps; pictures made entirely of scallops, bivalves, and starfish; shell-drenched chandeliers—every inch of wall space is decorated in different denizens of the sea. Service isn't particularly brisk (pretty much par for the course in laid-back San Blas), but the seafood, filet mignon, and fajitas are all quite good. **Known for:** relaxed service; delicious seafood; near the main plaza. $ *Average main: $10* ✉ *Calle Paredes 33* ☎ *323/285-0407* 🚫 *No credit cards* ⊘ *Closed Mon.*

## Hotels

### Casa Mañana

**$$ | HOTEL | FAMILY |** Some of the pleasant rooms overlook the beach from a balcony or terrace, but most people stay here for easy access to the good burgers, guacamole, and seafood platter for two ($13) at the adjoining El Alebrije restaurant. **Pros:** good burgers; nice beachfront location; recently remodeled. **Cons:** unheated pool; mosquitoes in summer; unswimmable beach right in front. $ *Rooms from: $65* ✉ *South end of Playa Los Cocos, 13 km (8 miles) south of San Blas* ☎ *323/254-9070, 800/202-2079 in Mexico* ⊕ *www.casa-manana.com* ⇴ *40 rooms* ⦿ *Free Breakfast.*

### Casa Roxanna

**$ | HOTEL |** This is an attractive little enclave of cozy and clean (albeit basic) cottages with screened windows. **Pros:** personable staff; great lap pool; location. **Cons:** so-so a/c units; lackluster interior decor; 10-minute walk to beach. $ *Rooms from: $50* ✉ *Callejón El Rey 1* ☎ *323/285-0573* ⊕ *www.casaroxanna.com* 🚫 *No credit cards* ⇴ *6 cottages* ⦿ *No meals.*

### Hacienda Flamingos

**$$ | HOTEL |** Built in 1882, this beautifully restored mansion-turned-hotel was once part of a large hacienda. **Pros:** lovely decor; close to town center; breakfast included. **Cons:** sometimes eerily devoid of other guests; staff can be chilly; restaurant open two hours per day $ *Rooms from: $115* ✉ *Calle Juárez 105* ☎ *323/285-0930, 669/985-1818 for information in English* ⊕ *www.sanblas.com. mx* ⇴ *20 rooms* ⦿ *Free Breakfast.*

### Hotel Garza Canela

**$$ | HOTEL | FAMILY |** Opened decades ago by a family of dedicated bird-watchers, this meandering, three-story hotel with expansive grounds is the home base of choice for birding groups. **Pros:** very good French restaurant; suites have hot tub; quiet. **Cons:** estuary location means there are some biting bugs; not all rooms have been renovated; thin towels. $ *Rooms from: $95* ✉ *Calle Paredes 106 Sur* ☎ *323/285-0112, 01800/713-2313 toll-free in Mexico* ⊕ *www.garzacanela.com* ⇴ *50 rooms* ⦿ *No meals.*

# San Sebastián

Physically, there are only about 80 km (50 miles) between Puerto Vallarta and San Sebastián, but metaphorically they're as far apart as the Earth and the moon. Sleepy San Sebastián is the Mayberry of Mexico, but a little less lively. It's the kind of place where strangers greet one another in passing. The miners who built the town have long gone, and more recently, younger folks are drifting away in search of opportunity. Most of the 800 or so people who have stayed seem perfectly content with life as it is, although rat-race dropouts and entrepreneurs are making their way here along improved roads.

##  Sights

The most interesting thing to see in San Sebastián is the town itself. Walk the cobblestone streets and handsome brick sidewalks, admiring the white-faced

## Great Itineraries

If you're not joining an organized day tour, there is still a lot to see, and plenty of opportunities to just relax and enjoy the tranquillity, mountain- and valley-views, and quaint lifestyle.

From Puerto Vallarta, consider a two-day trip to the area beginning in San Sebastián and returning to PV (or Guadalajara) from Talpa de Allende. There are many ways to go, but avoid driving at night and try to enjoy the slow pace. Drive to San Sebastián, taking in the mountain scenery en route. After a look around the quaint old mining village and an early lunch, continue to Mascota, the area's largest town and a good base. Spend the night in Mascota. The Sierra Lodge on Lake Juanacatlán, which serves excellent food, can be added as an overnight trip, but it doesn't take day-trippers and you'll probably want a vehicle with 4WD to get there. If you prefer, make a day trip from Mascota to Talpa de Allende, whose raison d'être is the tiny, beloved Virgin statue in the town's ornate basilica.

Each of the three towns has hills to climb for excellent vistas and photos. Otherwise, activities include wandering the streets, visiting small museums and Catholic churches, tasting regional food, and drinking in the mountain air and old-fashioned ambience. Make sure you get where you're going before dark, as mountain roads are unlighted and narrow and in many cases have sheer drop-offs.

adobe structures surrounding the plaza. Take any side street and wander at will. Enjoy the enormous walnut trees lining the road into town, and diminutive peach trees peaking over garden walls. The reason to go to this cozy, lazy, beautiful town at 5,250 feet above sea level is to look inward, reflecting on life, or outward, greeting or chatting as best you can with those you meet. Look anywhere, in fact, except at a laptop or, if possible, a television screen. That's just missing the point.

San Sebastián has a few attractions, although none of them are the main reason to visit.

**Casa Museo de Doña Conchita**
**LOCAL INTEREST** | You're welcome any time at the Casa Museo de Doña Conchita. The affable owner shows visitors photos of her venerable family—which she traces back six generations. See bank notes from the mining days, bloomers, shirts made by hand by the lady for her many children, and other memorabilia. If you speak Spanish, ask Doña Conchita to tell you about the ghosts that haunt her house, which is right on the square between the basketball court and *la presidencia,* or town hall. ✉ *Pase del Norte 2* ☎ *322/297–2860* 🎟 *$1.*

**Iglesia de San Sebastián**
**RELIGIOUS SITE** | Iglesia de San Sebastián is a typically restored 1800s-era church that comes to life in the days preceding its saint's day, January 20. ✉ *San Sebastián.*

## 🍴 Restaurants

**Comedor La Lupita**
**$** | **MEXICAN** | **FAMILY** | Typical food of the countryside—enchiladas, tamales, pozole, beefsteak with beans and tortillas, and so on—is served in an equally typical family home. The house has been expanded to welcome guests. **Known for:** friendly owner; small bar behind the kitchen; serves breakfast. [$] *Average main: $6* ✉ *Calle Gral Aguirre 183* ☎ *322/297–2803* 💳 *No credit cards* 🕒 *No dinner.*

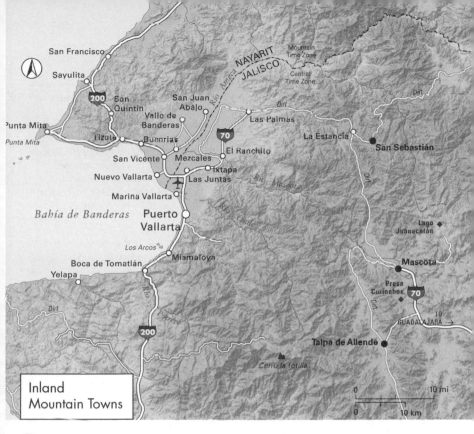

Inland
Mountain Towns

##  Hotels

### Hacienda Matel

**$$** | **HOTEL** | At this hacienda-style boutique hotel at the town limit of San Sebastián del Oeste, the inner courtyard has a small pool, spacious rooms with traditional Mexican decor, good Wi-Fi, comfortable beds, a fireplace, and high-quality toiletries. **Pros:** cozy and comfortable rooms; quiet; stylish location. **Cons:** somewhat away from downtown; steep, unpaved road that gets dark once the sun sets; no dinner service. $ *Rooms from: $130 ⊠ Sendero el Nogalito # 2 Col. Centro ☎ 322/297–2133 ➷ 8 rooms* ¶◯¶ *Free Breakfast.*

### Las Galeritas de San Sebastián

**$$** | **HOTEL** | A pair of displaced *tapatíos* (Guadalajarans) have created a cluster of pretty cabins on their property about four blocks from the plaza. **Pros:** stylish; has in-room fireplaces; lovely garden. **Cons:** pricey compared to other area digs; extra charge for each child; many stairs. $ *Rooms from: $120 ⊠ Camino a Las Galeritas 62, Barrio La Otra Banda ☎ 322/297–3040 ⊕ www.lagalerita.com. mx ➷ 3 bungalows* ¶◯¶ *Free Breakfast.*

##  Activities

### La Bufa

**HIKING/WALKING** | You can hire a driver with a truck capable of making the journey to take you to La Bufa, a half-dome visible from the town square (speak with the hotel front desk or ask at any restaurant downtown). The truck will wait while you climb—about 15 minutes to the top—and enjoy the wonderful view of the town, surrounding valleys, and, on a clear day, Puerto Vallarta. San Sebastián was founded as a silver- and gold-mining town; ask the driver to stop for a quick visit to a mine en route. The excursion takes about three hours. Alternatively you can hike both ways; it takes most folks two hours or more to reach the top. ⊠ *San Sebastián.*

# Mascota

Mascota's cool but sunny climate is perfect for growing citrus, avocados, nuts, wheat, corn, and other crops. Fed by the Mascota and Ameca rivers and many springs and year-round streams, the blue-green hills and valleys surrounding town are lusciously forested; beyond them rise indigo mountains to form a painterly tableau. This former mining town and municipal seat is home to some 13,000 people. Its banks, shops, and hospital serve surrounding villages. On its coat of arms are a pine tree, deer, and rattlesnake. The town's name derives from the Nahuatl words for "deer" and "snake."

 Sights

### Cerro de la Cruz
**TOWN** | The countryside just outside town is ideal for hikes and drives. From Mascota's plaza you can walk up Calle Morelos out of town to Cerro de la Cruz. The hike to the summit takes about a half hour and rewards with great valley views. ⊠ *Mascota.*

### Iglesia de la Virgen de los Dolores
**RELIGIOUS SITE** | On one corner of the plaza is the town's white-spire Iglesia de la Virgen de los Dolores. The Virgin of Sorrow is feted on September 15, which segues into Mexican Independence Day on the 16th. ⊠ *Calle Ponciano Arriaga 110.*

### La Iglesia de la Preciosa Sangre
**RELIGIOUS SITE** | Mascota's pride is La Iglesia de la Preciosa Sangre (Church of the Precious Blood), started in 1909 but

unfinished due to the revolution and the ensuing Cristero Revolt. Weddings, concerts, and plays are sometimes held here under the ruins of Gothic arches. Note the 3-D blood squirting from Jesus's wound in the chapel—you could hardly miss it. ⊠ *Calle Rosa Davalos s/n.*

### Lago Juanacatlán
**BODY OF WATER** | Lago Juanacatlán is a lovely lake in a volcanic crater at 7,000 feet above sea level. Nestled in the Galope River valley, the pristine lake is surrounded by alpine woods, and the trip from Mascota past fields of flowers and self-sufficient *ranchos* is bucolic. ⊠ *Mascota.*

### Museo de Mascota
**MUSEUM** | A block beyond the other end of the plaza, the Museo de Mascota is worth a look. ⊠ *Calle Morelos, near Calle Allende.*

### Palacio de Cultura y el Arte de Mascota
**MUSEUM** | Around the corner from the Mascota Museum, the Palacio de Cultura y el Arte has rotating exhibits of photography and art. It's open 10–7 pm Tuesday through Saturday, and 10 am to 1:30 pm on Sunday. ⊠ *Calle Allende 115* ☎ *388/386–1679* ⊘ *Closed Mon.*

### Plaza Principal
**PLAZA** | Walk around the plaza, where old gents share stories and kids chase balloons. Couples dance the stately *danzón* on Thursday and Saturday evening as the band plays in the wrought-iron

bandstand. The town produces ceramics, saddles, and *Raicilla,* a relative of tequilla made from the green agave plant (tequila comes from the blue one). ⊠ *Corner of Av. Hidalgo with 5 de Mayo* ✣ *In front of Basilica de la Virgen de los Dolores.*

### Presa Corinches

**DAM** | Presa Corinches, a dam about 5 km (3 miles) south of town, has bass fishing, picnic spots (for cars and RVs), and a restaurant where locals go for fish feasts on holidays and weekend afternoons. To get to the dam, head east on Calle Juárez (a block south of the plaza) and follow the signs to the reservoir. Take a walk along the shore or set up a tent near the fringe of pine-oak forest coming down to meet the cool blue water, which is fine for swimming when the weather is warm. ⊠ *Mascota.*

##  Restaurants

### Café Napolés

**$** | **CAFÉ** | Originally a coffee-and-dessert stop and fashionable hangout for Mascotans, this snug little eatery serves big breakfasts and now main dishes at lunch and dinner, too. Sit on the small street-facing patio, in the small dining room, or facing the glass case featuring fantastic-looking cakes, pies, and tarts. **Known for:** local hangout; beer and wine; Italian dishes. $ *Average main: $6* ⊠ *Calle Hidalgo 105, Centro* ☎ *388/386–0051* ▭ *No credit cards.*

### La Casa de Mi Abuelita

**$** | **MEXICAN** | Everyone loves "Grandma's House," which is conveniently open all day (and evening), every day, starting at around 8 am with breakfast. In addition to beans, rice, carne asada, and other recognizable Mexican food, there are backcountry recipes that are much less familiar to the average traveler. **Known for:** beloved eatery; authentic cuisine; open all day, every day. $ *Average main: $7* ⊠ *Calle Corona, at Calle Zaragoza* ☎ *388/386–1975.*

### Navidad

**$** | **MEXICAN** | It's named for the small town 14 km (9 miles) from Mascota, not the Christmas holiday, which is the only day this restaurant closes. The cavernous space, lined in red brick, makes the restaurant look rather generic, but it's actually family-owned and run and oh-so-personable. **Known for:** regional specialties like goat stew; rotating daily specials; family-run. $ *Average main: $4* ⊠ *Calle Juan Diaz de Sandi 28, Centro* ☎ *388/386–0469.*

##  Hotels

### Mesón de Santa Elena

**$$** | **HOTEL** | Beautiful rooms in this converted 19th-century house have lovely old tile floors, beige cotton drapes covering huge windows, rag-rolled walls, and wonderful tile floors and sinks. **Pros:** two blocks from the town square; feels like you're a guest in someone's home. **Cons:** Internet intermittent in some rooms; somewhat pricey. $ *Rooms from: $95* ⊠ *Hidalgo 155* ☎ *388/386–0313* ⊕ *santaelenahotelboutique.com* ⇆ *15 rooms* ⦿ *Free Breakfast.*

### Rancho La Esmeralda

**$** | **HOTEL** | Catering to small groups and family outings, this ranch-style lodging near the entrance to town also accepts individual travelers. **Pros:** newer construction; fireplaces and king-size beds; swimming pool. **Cons:** 10-minute drive from town center; bumpy cobblestone entry road; pool may lack maintenance. $ *Rooms from: $50* ⊠ *Calle Salvador Chavez 47* ☎ *388/386–0953* ⊕ *www.rancholaesmeralda.com.mx* ⇆ *10 rooms, 7 cabins.*

### Sierra Lago Resort & Spa

**$$$** | **HOTEL** | An hour north of Mascota, this lodge of knotty pine is a tranquil lakeside retreat. **Pros:** beautiful scenery and mountain air; activities included in all-inclusive room rate; good food. **Cons:** no phone in room; difficult driving to reach the hotel. $ *Rooms from: $230* ✉ *Domicilio Conocido, Lago Juanacatlán* ☎ *855/704–7344 in U.S. and Canada, 01800/099–0362 toll-free in Mexico* ⊕ *www.sierralago.com* ⤵ *24 suites* ❍ *All-inclusive.*

##  Shopping

Stores in town sell homemade preserves, locally grown coffee, *raicilla* (an alcoholic drink made of green agave), and sweets.

**Mercado Municipal**
**FOOD/CANDY** | A good place to shop for local products and produce is the Mercado Municipal. ✉ *Calle P. Sánchez, at Hidalgo, 1 block west of plaza.*

# Talpa de Allende

Another tranquil town surrounded by pine-oak forests, Talpa, as it's called, has just over 7,000 inhabitants but welcomes 4 million visitors a year. They come to pay homage or ask favors of the diminutive Virgen del Rosario de Talpa, one of Jalisco's most revered Virgins. Some people walk three days from Puerto Vallarta as penance or a sign of devotion; others come by car, horse, bicycle, or truck but return annually to show their faith.

## ◉ Sights

**Basilica de Talpa**
**RELIGIOUS SITE** | On the large plaza, the Basilica de Talpa is the main show in town. The twin-spire limestone temple is Gothic with neoclassic elements. After visiting the royally clad Virgin in her side chapel, stroll around the surrounding square. Shops and stalls sell sweets, miniature icons of the Virgin in every possible presentation, T-shirts, and other souvenirs. *Chicle* (gum) is harvested in the area, and you'll find small keepsakes in the shapes of shoes, flowers, and

# Holy City

During several major annual fiestas, the town swells with visitors. The Fiesta de la Candelaria culminates in Candlemass on February 2. The town's patron saint, St. Joseph, is honored on March 19. May 12, September 10, September 19, and October 7 mark rituals devoted to the Virgen del Rosario de Talpa.

animals made of the (nonsticky) raw material. ✉ *Talpa de Allende.*

## 🍴 Restaurants

**Casa Grande**
**$$** | **STEAKHOUSE** | This steak house also serves grilled chicken and seafood. Under a roof but open on all sides and with an incredible view, it's highly recommended by visitors and locals. $ *Average main: $11* ✉ *Panoramica 11* ☎ *388/385–0709* ⊘ *Closed Tues.*

**El Herradero**
**$** | **MEXICAN** | "The Blacksmith" will win no awards for cuisine or, for that matter, decoration. But it's often filled with families of pilgrims, and the locals recommend it, too. $ *Average main: $6* ✉ *Calle 23 de Junio 8* ☎ *388/385–0376* ▭ *No credit cards.*

**Renovación**
**$$** | **HOTEL** | Basic yet comfortable rooms in this three-story hotel have king-size beds with dark blue, hunting-theme spreads and desks of shiny lacquered wood. **Pros:** newer property; a couple of blocks from the main plaza; managed by owners. **Cons:** no elevator; no credit cards accepted; no restaurant. $ *Rooms from: $27* ✉ *Calle Independencia 45, Centro* ☎ *388/385–1412* ▭ *No credit cards* ⤵ *18 rooms* ❍ *No meals.*

# Index

# Photo Credits

# Notes

# Notes

# Notes

# Notes

# Notes

# Notes

# Notes

# Notes

# Notes

# Notes

# Fodor's PUERTO VALLARTA

**Publisher:** Stephen Horowitz, *General Manager*

**Editorial:** Douglas Stallings, *Editorial Director;* Jill Fergus, Jacinta O'Halloran, Amanda Sadlowski, *Senior Editors;* Kayla Becker, Alexis Kelly, Rachael Roth, *Editors*

**Design:** Tina Malaney, *Director of Design and Production;* Jessica Gonzalez, *Graphic Designer;* Mariana Tabares, *Design and Production Intern*

**Production:** Jennifer DePrima, *Editorial Production Manager;* Elyse Rozelle, *Senior Production Editor;* Monica White, *Production Editor*

**Maps:** Rebecca Baer, *Senior Map Editor;* Mark Stroud (Moon Street Cartography) *Cartographer*

**Photography:** Viviane Teles, *Senior Photo Editor;* Namrata Aggarwal, Ashok Kumar, Carl Yu, *Photo Editors;* Rebecca Rimmer, *Photo Intern*

**Business and Operations:** Chuck Hoover, *Chief Marketing Officer;* Robert Ames, *Group General Manager;* Devin Duckworth, *Director of Print Publishing;* Victor Bernal, *Business Analyst*

**Public Relations and Marketing:** Joe Ewaskiw, *Senior Director Communications and Public Relations;* Esther Su, *Senior Marketing Manager*

**Fodors.com:** Jeremy Tarr, *Editorial Director;* Rachael Levitt, *Managing Editor;* Teddy Minford, *Editor*

**Technology:** Jon Atkinson, *Director of Technology;* Rudresh Teotia, *Lead Developer;* Jacob Ashpis, *Content Operations Manager*

**Writers:** Federico Arrizabalaga, Luis Domínguez

**Editor:** Rachael Roth

**Production Editor:** Jennifer DePrima

7th Edition

ISBN 978-1-64097-264-3

ISSN 1558–8718

**SPECIAL SALES**
This book is available at special discounts for bulk purchases for sales promotions or premiums. For more information, e-mail SpecialMarkets@fodors.com.

PRINTED IN CANADA

10 9 8 7 6 5 4 3 2 1

# About Our Writers

It was surfing waves in foreign countries that initially drove **Federico Arrizabalaga** to hit the road and explore the world, at first around Europe, then overseas. Travel became a passion and his quest to visit new places and learn about different cultures has taken him to South America, Africa, the Middle East, South East Asia and the Pacific, often with his backpack, and other times in a less budget-conscious style. He landed in Puerto Vallarta over half a decade ago where he still surfs almost every week, yet he continues to travel the world, stopping in Spain to visit his family whenever possible and keeping his popular travel blog up-to-date. Federico is based in Puerto Vallarta where he lives with his wife and son.

**Luis Domínguez** is a freelance writer and independent journalist interested in travel, art, books, history, philosophy, politics, and sports. He has written for Fodor's, Yahoo!, Sports Illustrated, Telemundo, and Villa Experience, among other publications in Europe and North America.